CliffsStudySolver™

Spanish II

By Gail Stein

WILEY

Wiley Publishing, Inc.

Published by:
Wiley Publishing, Inc.
111 River St.
Hoboken, NJ 07030
www.wiley.com

Copyright © 2004 Wiley Publishing, Inc. Hoboken, New Jersey

Published by Wiley Publishing, Inc., Hoboken, NJ
Published simultaneously in Canada

ISBN: 0-7645-4112-9

Printed in the United States of America

10 9 8 7 6 5 4 3 2 1

1B/QY/QR/QU/IN

...tion

...edicated to

...mendously patient and supportive husband, Douglas

...credibly loving and understanding sons, Eric and Michael

...roud parents, Sara and Jack Bernstein

...talented sister and her family, Susan, Jay, and Zachary Opperman

...y superior consultant and advisor, Roger H. Herz

My best friend and supporter, Christina Levy

My seventh-grade buddy, who ensures that my books are highly visible, Ray Elias

Acknowledgments

The author would like to acknowledge the contributions, input, and support of the people at Wiley Publishing: Greg Tubach, Ben Nussbaum, Kelly Henthorne, Suzanne Thompson, and Wigberto Rivera.

Publisher's Acknowledgments

Editorial

Project Editor: Kelly Dobbs Henthorne

Acquisitions Editor: Greg Tubach

Technical Editor: Wigberto Rivera

Composition

Project Coordinator: Kristie Rees

Indexer: Publication Services

Proofreaders: Publication Services

Wiley Publishing, Inc. Composition Services

About the Author

Gail Stein, M.A., is a recently retired foreign language instructor who taught in New
public junior and senior high schools for more than 33 years. She has authored several
text and review books including the *French Is Fun* series, the *French Practice and Testing*
the *Spanish Practice and Testing* series, *French First Year*, *French Two Years*, *French Three*
and *English Is Fun*. She currently is working on a new, three-book series, *Le Français ess*
Her trade books include *French at a Glance*, *The Traveler's Dictionary*, *The Traveler's Phra*
The Complete Idiot's Guide to French, *The Complete Idiot's Guide to Spanish*, *The Complet*
Idiot's Guide to Spanish Verbs, *The Pocket Idiot's Guide to French*, *The Pocket Idiot's Guide*
Spanish, *Cliff's Quick Review French 1* and *French 2*, *CliffsStudySolver: Spanish 1*, *Countdown to*
Spanish, *Countdown to French*, and a book for the beauty industry, *Salon Stories: The Best Kept*
Secrets. Gail Stein has also assisted in a revision project of the French curriculum for the New
York City Board of Education and has served as an adjunct professor to St. John's University in its
Early Admission Extension Program. She has given presentations and demonstration lessons at
numerous foreign language conferences, has had her lessons videotaped by the New York City
Board of Education for national distribution, and has appeared on the Barry Farber radio show
promoting foreign language study. Mrs. Stein is a multiple-time honoree in *Who's Who Among
America's Teachers*.

Guide Checklist

ne Pretest, which will test your initial understanding of this workbook's subject
er.

the answer sections of the Pretest to guide you to the chapters and chapter sections
u need to review.

miliarize yourself with the content of the chapters you need to review.

Take the self tests provided in the chapters, including the Chapter Problems and
Supplemental Chapter Problems tests located at the end of each chapter.

5. If, upon checking your answers to the Chapter Problems and Supplemental Chapter
   Problems self tests, you find you have some errors, go back to the specific section(s) of
   the chapter and review the section(s) again.

❑ 6. Take the Full-Length Customized Exam, which tests your overall knowledge of Spanish
   grammar. The Full-Length Customized Exam presents various levels of difficulty with
   directions on which questions to answer.

❑ 7. Review chapter sections as directed in the Customized Full-Length Exam.

❑ 8. Explore the Glossary, Thematic Vocabulary, and Tasks List presented at the end of the
   book.

Table of Contents

Pretest

Questions 1–5

You are taking a bus trip. Read the ticket below and give the numbers, conventional time, and date indicated in Spanish.

```
┌─────────────────────────────────────────────────────────────────┐
│                                                                   │
│                 Autobuses                    HERRANZ               │
│                                                                   │
│                 Línea de Autobuses           Madrid-Escorial      │
│                                                                   │
│        (Por Guadarrama)                                           │
│     Coche N° 76 (1)                                               │
│                                                                   │
│                 N° asiento 18                N° 180.640 (3)       │
│                                                                   │
│                 El Escorial-Valle de los Caídos y Viceversa      │
│                                                                   │
│                 Precio total del billete 310 euros (2)           │
│                                                                   │
│     (incluido impuestos)                                          │
│                                                                   │
│     Servicio de las 15:15 horas (4)    Expedido el día 28 jul. 2003 (5) │
│                                                                   │
└─────────────────────────────────────────────────────────────────┘
```

1. _____

2. _____

3. _____

4. _____

5. _____

Questions 6–10

Express your opinion by selecting the correct missing word.

6. _____ agua me refresca.

    a. La

    b. El

    c. Lo

    d. Ese

7. El señor Marín es _____ persona muy importante.

   a. el

   b. uno

   c. una

   d. este

8. No puedes imaginar _____ rápidamente que hablan.

   a. lo

   b. la

   c. el

   d. ellos

9. Esta_____ es muy difícil.

   a. libro

   b. pasajes

   c. idioma

   d. lección

10. La hermana _____ es muy diligente.

    a. ella

    b. ésta

    c. suya

    d. aquella

Questions 11–15

Express what happens on a dreary day by giving the correct present tense form of the verb in parentheses.

11. (llover) _____ mucho.

12. (escoger) Yo _____ un buen programa para mirar en la televisión.

13. (conducir) Yo _____ al centro.

14. (hacer) Yo _____ mis quehacéres domésticos.

15. (querer) Yo _____ descansar un rato.

Questions 16–20

Form questions about cooking and food that would give you the italic answers.

16.   Usa esta olla *para preparar la sopa*.

17.   Pagó *cien dólares* por esta olla.

18.   Cocina *bastante bien*.

19.   Prefiere preparar *la sopa de cebolla*.

20.   Su plato favorito es *el pescado*.

Questions 21–25

Answer each question using an appropriate negative.

21.   ¿Buscas algo? –No busco _____.

22.   ¿Hablas con alguien? –No hablo con _____.

23.   ¿Dices mentiras de vez en cuando? –_____ digo mentiras.

24.   ¿Tienes algunos problemas? –No tengo _____ problemas.

25.   ¿Te gustan las legumbres? –No me gustan _____ zanahorias _____ espinacas.

Questions 26–30

Express what the following subjects do to clean their rooms by substituting direct and indirect object pronouns for the nouns provided.

26.   Juan devuelve (los CDs/a su amigo).

27.   María va a dar (la camisa roja/a Rosa).

28.   Roberto está dando (sus fotografías/a sus hermanos).

29.   Gisela dice a Carlota: Presta (ese libro/a mí).

30.   Julio y Ricardo dicen a Tomás: No pidas (ayuda/a nosotros).

Questions 31–35

Express each person's likes in Spanish.

31.   (I like) _____ la música clásica y la música rock.

32.   (He is interested in) _____ dibujar y pintar.

33. (We appreciate) _____ las obras teatrales.

34. (You [informal singular] adore) _____ leer.

35. (They are fascinated by) _____ los deportes.

Questions 36–40

Two friends are speaking about clothing. Complete their thoughts with the correct relative pronoun or adjective.

a quien	cuyos	las cuales
con quien	de que	los cuales
cuya	de quien	lo que
cuyas	el cual	que
cuyo	la cual	quien

36. La camisa, _____ está en el escaparate, es muy linda.

37. Es la joven _____ voy de compras.

38. La madre de Ernesto, _____ hace suéteres, se viste elegantemente.

39. Quiero ver _____ estás llevando hoy.

40. Esa mujer, _____ niños están en mi clase, trabaja en mi tienda favorita.

Questions 41–45

Compare the follow people using adjectives, adverbs, and nouns as necessary.

Examples:

1. Julia es inteligente. (–/Esteban)

   Julia es menos inteligente que Esteban.

2. Roberto juega con cuidado. (+/su amigo)

   Roberto juega más cuidadosamente que su amigo.

3. Carlos tiene problemas. (=/Juan)

   Carlos tiene tantos problemas como Juan.

41. Yo soy optimista. (=/tú)

42. Ella toca el violín con perfección. (+/él)

43. Tú esquías mal. (+/yo)

44. Nosotros compramos vestidos. (=/Uds.)

45. Uds. bailan con gracia. (–/nosotros)

Questions 46–50

Choose the preposition or conjunction that best completes each thought.

46. Este regalo es _____ ti.
    a. por
    b. para
    c. hasta
    d. hacia

47. No trabajo _____ descanso.
    a. sino
    b. pero
    c. para
    d. por

48. Juan _____ Isabel salen.
    a. u
    b. o
    c. y
    d. e

49. No tengo ganas de jugar al tenis, _____ iré al parque con Uds.
    a. por consiguiente
    b. a pesar de
    c. sin embargo
    d. porque

50. Ella siempre piensa _____ sí misma.
    a. para
    b. por
    c. de
    d. sin

Questions 51–55

Complete the subject's personal thoughts by using a preposition, if necessary.

51. Este anillo me cabe _____ el dedo.

52. Gozo _____ buena salud.

53. Sé _____ pilotar un avión.

54. Yo me conformo _____ todo.

55. Yo estoy aprendiendo _____ hablar español.

Questions 56–60

Complete the story using the correct form of the preterit or the imperfect for the verbs in parentheses.

Anoche yo (leer) _____ el periódico cuando el teléfono (sonar) _____. Mi amigo, Esteban, me (decir) _____ que él (querer) _____ hablarme de algo muy importante. (Pedir) _____ mi ayuda.

Questions 61–65

Express facts about a party. Use the correct tense of each verb, either the future or the conditional.

61. Yo _____ una fiesta.

     (will throw [make])

62. Nosotros _____ mucho.

           (will eat)

63. Mi madre _____ comida mexicana.

     (will prepare)

64. Tú _____ que ayudarme.

     (would have to)

65. ¿_____ si todo el mundo pudiera venir?

(Would you know)

Questions 66–70

Talk about the events of the day by using the correct progressive tense.

66. (were playing) Los niños _____ todo el día.

67. (are eating) Ahora ellos _____.

68. (were reading) A las tres, ellos _____ tebeos.

69. (will be studying) Ellos _____ después de la cena.

70. (wouldn't be going to sleep) Si pudieran, ellos no _____ hasta la medianoche.

Questions 71–75

Express the chores that were completed by choosing the correct compound tense.

71. (did) Yo _____ limpiado la casa.

   a. había

   b. he

   c. habría

   d. haya

72. (had) Tú _____ sacudido los muebles.

   a. habrás

   b. hayas

   c. habías

   d. hube

73. (will have) Ella _____ dado de comer al perro dos veces.

   a. ha

   b. habrá

   c. habría

   d. hube

74. (would have) Nosotros _____ hecho las camas.

   a. hemos

   b. hayamos

   c. habíamos

   d. habríamos

75. (had) Uds. _____ prometido ayudarnos.

   a. habrán

   b. harán

   c. habían

   d. habrían

Questions 76–80

Write the thoughts people express to a newlywed couple by completing each sentence with the correct form of the subjunctive or the present tense.

76. Es imperativo que Uds. siempre (pagar) _____ sus cuentas.

77. Yo aconsejo que Uds. (tener) _____ tiempo para visitar a su familia.

78. Sugiero que Uds. no (pedir) _____ ayuda a nadie.

79. Es evidente que Uds. (estar) _____ alegres.

80. Le ayudaré a Uds., a condición de que Uds. no (perder) _____ la paciencia.

Questions 81–85

Complete each thought about chores with the correct form of the verb in the subjunctive.

81. Yo no creo que él _____ la carta esta mañana.
    (escribir)

82. Yo dudo que ellos ya _____ la mesa.
    (poner)

83. Si ellos _____ al centro, ellos comprarían leche.
    (ir)

84. Si ella _____ las camas esta mañana, no tendría nada que hacer ahora.
    (hacer)

85. Si él _____las ventanas durante la tormenta, la casa se habría inundado.
    (abrir)

Questions 86–90

Express the rules and suggestions of the parents and children of the house by giving the correct command form.

86. (Uds./salir) No _____ solos de noche.

87. (tú/demostrar) _____ ser muy buen amigo.

88. (tú/conducir) No _____ rápidamente.

89. (vosotros/decir) _____ la verdad.

90. (nosotros/seguir) _____ todas las reglas.

Questions 90–95

A group is going on a ski trip. Express what different people say by giving the correct form of the reflexive verb.

91. (wake up) Es importante que nosotros _____ temprano.

92. (will become) Él _____ enfermo.

93. ([informal "you"] are you worrying) ¿_____?

94. (I want to put on) _____ un abrigo.

95. ([formal plural "you"] Have fun!) ¡_____!

Questions 96–100

Use the passive voice of the verb indicated to describe the preparations for a party.

Example: Lucinda pasará la aspiradora.

La aspiradora será pasada por Lucinda.

96. Elena escribe las invitaciones.

97. Carlos compró las bebidas.

98. Yo organizaba poco a poco todos los preparativos.

99. Minerva y Gisela arreglarán el salón.

100. Pedro y Arturo escogerían la música.

Answer Key

1. setenta y seis

2. trescientos diez

3. ciento ochenta mil seiscientos cuarenta

4. las tres y cuarto

5. el veintiocho de julio de dos mil tres

If you missed question 1, study Ordinal Numbers, p. 19.

If you missed question 2, study Ordinal Numbers, p. 19.

If you missed question 3, study Ordinal Numbers, p. 19.

If you missed question 4, study Time, p. 31.

If you missed question 5, study Dates, p. 27.

6. b

7. c

8. a

9. d

10. c

If you missed question 6, study Definite Articles, p. 41.

If you missed question 7, study Indefinite Articles, p. 45.

If you missed question 8, study The Neuter *Lo,* p. 42.

If you missed question 9, study Gender of Nouns, p. 50.

If you missed question 10, study Possessive Adjectives, p. 56.

11. Llueve

12. escojo

13. conduzco

14. hago

15. quiero

If you missed questions 11 or 12, study Present Tense Stem-Changing Verbs, p. 69.

If you missed question 13, study Present Tense Spelling-Change Verbs, p. 67.

If you missed questions 14 or 15, study Present Tense Irregular Verbs, p. 71.

16. ¿Para qué usa esta olla?

17. ¿Cuánto pagó por esta olla?

18. ¿Cómo cocina?

19. ¿Qué prefiere preparar?

20. ¿Cuál es su plato favorito?

If you missed any of the preceding questions, study Interrogatives, p. 93.

21. nada

22. nadie

23. Nunca

24. ningunos

25. ni . . . ni

If you missed any of the preceding questions, study Negatives, p. 105.

26. Juan se los devuelve.

27. María se la va a dar. María va a dársela.

28. Roberto se las está dando. Roberto está dándoselas.

29. Préstamelo.

30. No nos la pidas.

If you missed any of the preceding questions, study Double Object Pronouns, p. 139.

31. Me gustan

32. Le interesa

33. Nos sientan bien

34. Te encanta

35. Les fascinan

If you missed any of the preceding questions, study *Gustar* and Other Similar Verbs, p. 135.

36. que

37. con quien

38. la cual

39. lo que

40. cuyos

If you missed any of the preceding questions, study Relative Pronouns, p. 143.

41. Yo soy tan optimista como tú.

42. Ella toca el violín más perfectamente que él.

43. Tú esquías peor que yo.

44. Nosotros compramos tantos vestidos como Uds.

45. Uds. bailan menos graciosamente que nosotros.

If you missed questions 41 or 44, study Comparisons of Equality, p. 169.

If you missed questions 42 or 45, study Comparison of Adverbs, p. 163.

If you missed question 43, study Irregular Comparisons, p. 174.

46. b

47. a

48. d

49. c

50. b

If you missed question 46 or 50, study Prepositions, p. 183.

If you missed questions 47 or 48, study Conjunctions, p. 191.

If you missed question 49, study Subordinating Conjunctions, p. 194.

51. en

52. de

53. no preposition necessary

54. con

55. a

If you missed question 51, study Verbs Requiring *En*, p. 208.

If you missed question 52, study Verbs Requiring *De*, p. 207.

If you missed question 53, study Verbs Requiring No Preposition, p. 208.

If you missed question 54, study Verbs Requiring *Con*, p. 208.

If you missed question 55, study Verbs Requiring *A*, p. 206.

56. leía

57. sonó

58. dijo

59. quería

60. Pidió

If you missed questions 56 or 59, study The Imperfect, p. 225; Use of the Imperfect, p. 225.

If you missed question 57, study The Preterit of Regular Verbs, p. 219; Use of the Preterit, p. 222.

If you missed question 58, study The Preterit of Irregular Verbs, p. 220; Use of the Preterit, p. 222.

If you missed question 60, study The Preterit of Stem-Changing Verbs, p. 220; Use of the Preterit, p. 222.

61. haré

62. comeremos

63. preparará

64. tendrías

65. Sabrías

If you missed question 61, study The Future Tense of Irregular Verbs, p. 240.

If you missed questions 62 or 63, study The Future Tense of Most Verbs, p. 239.

If you missed questions 64 or 65, study The Conditional, p. 243.

66. estuvieron jugando

67. están comiendo

68. estaban leyendo

69. estarán estudiando

70. se estarían durmiendo

If you missed question 66, study The Past Progressive, p. 258; The Formation of Gerunds, p. 253.

If you missed question 67, study The Present Progressive, p. 255; The Formation of Gerunds, p. 253.

If you missed question 68, study The Past Progressive, p. 258; The Formation of Gerunds, p. 253.

If you missed question 69, study The Future Progressive, p. 260; The Formation of Gerunds, p. 253.

If you missed question 70, study The Conditional Progressive, p. 262; The Formation of Gerunds, p. 253.

71. b

72. c

73. b

74. d

75. c

If you missed question 71, study The Present Perfect Tense, p. 274.

If you missed question 72, study The Pluperfect Subjunctive, p. 283.

If you missed question 73, study The Future Perfect Tense, p. 279.

If you missed question 74, study The Conditional Perfect, p. 281.

If you missed question 75, study The Pluperfect Subjunctive, p. 283.

76. paguen

77. tengan

78. pidan

79. están

80. pierdan

If you missed question 76, study Spelling Changes in the Present Subjunctive, p. 299; The Subjunctive after Impersonal Expressions, p. 304.

If you missed question 77, study Irregular Verbs in the Present Subjunctive, p. 302; The Subjunctive Verbs of Wishing, Emotion, Need, and Doubt, p. 307.

If you missed question 78, study Stem Changes in the Present Subjunctive, p. 299; The Subjunctive Verbs of Wishing, Emotion, Need, and Doubt, p. 307.

If you missed question 79, study Using the Present Subjunctive, p. 302.

If you missed question 80, study Stem Changes in the Present Subjunctive, p. 299; Using the Subjunctive after Certain Conjunctions, p. 311.

81. haya escrito

82. hayan puesto

83. fueran

84. hubiera hecho

85. hubiera abierto

If you missed question 81, study Forming and Using the Present Perfect Subjunctive, p. 317; The Subjunctive after Verbs of Wishing, Emotion, Need, and Doubt, p. 307.

If you missed question 82, study Forming and Using the Present Perfect Subjunctive, p. 317; The Subjunctive after Verbs of Wishing, Emotion, Need, and Doubt, p. 307.

If you missed questions 83 or 84, study The Imperfect Subjunctive, p. 325; Conditional Sentences, p. 341.

If you missed question 85, study The Pluperfect Subjunctive, p. 335; Conditional Sentences, p. 341.

86. salgan

87. Demuestra

88. conduzcas

89. Decid

90. Sigamos

If you missed question 86, study Formal Commands of Irregular Verbs, p. 352.

If you missed question 87, study Informal Commands, p. 355.

If you missed questions 88, study Informal Commands, p. 355.

If you missed question 89, study Informal Plural Commands with Vosotros, p. 359.

If you missed question 90, study Indirect Commands p. 363.

91. nos depertemos

92. se pondrá

93. ¿Te estás preocupando? ¿Estás preocupándote?

94. Quiero ponerme

95. ¡Diviértanse!

If you missed question 91, study Reflexive Pronouns, p. 375; Reflexive Verbs in Simple Tenses, p. 383; The Subjunctive after Impersonal Expressions, p. 304.

If you missed question 92, study Reflexive Pronouns, p. 375; Reflexive Verbs in Simple Tenses, p. 383; The Future of Irregular Verbs, p. 243.

If you missed questions 93, study Reflexive Pronouns, p. 375; Reflexive Verbs in Simple Tenses, p. 383; The Present Progressive, p. 255.

If you missed question 94, study Reflexive Pronouns, p. 375; Other Uses of Reflexive Verbs, p. 388.

If you missed question 90, study Reflexive Pronouns, p. 375; Formal Commands, p. 351; Other Uses of Reflexive Verbs, p. 388.

96. Las invitaciones son escritas por Elena.

97. Las bebidas fueron compradas por Carlos.

98. Todos los preparativos eran organizados poco a poco por mí.

99. El salón será arreglado por Minerva y Gisela.

100. La música sería escogida por Pedro y Arturo.

If you missed any of the preceding questions, study The Passive Voice, p. 399.

Chapter 1
Daily Tools

Numbers

In numerals and decimals, Spanish uses commas where English uses periods, and vice versa:

English	Spanish
9,000	9.000
0.50	0,50
$13.75	$13,75

Cardinal Numbers

Cardinal numbers are the numbers used in counting: 1, 2, 3, 4, and so on.

Number	Spanish	Number	Spanish
0	cero	24	veinticuatro (veinte y cuatro)
1	uno	25	veinticinco (veinte y cinco)
2	dos	26	veintiséis (veinte y seis)
3	tres	27	veintisiete (veinte y siete)
4	cuatro	28	veintiocho (veinte y ocho)
5	cinco	29	veintinueve (veinte y nueve)
6	seis	30	treinta
7	siete	40	cuarenta
8	ocho	50	cincuenta
9	nueve	60	sesenta
10	diez	70	setenta
11	once	80	ochenta
12	doce	90	noventa
13	trece	100	ciento (cien)
14	catorce	101	ciento uno
15	quince	200	doscientos
16	dieciséis (diez y seis)	500	quinientos
17	diecisiete(diez y siete)	1000	mil
18	dieciocho (diez y ocho)	2000	dos mil
19	diecinueve (diez y nueve)	100.000	cien mil
20	veinte	1.000.000	un millón
21	veintiuno (veinte y uno)	2.000.000	dos millones
22	veintidós (veinte y dos)	1.000.000.000	mil millones
23	veintitrés(veinte y tres)	2.000.000.000	dos mil millones

Note the following about Spanish numbers:

❑ *Uno*, used only when counting, becomes *un* before a masculine noun and *una* before a feminine noun.

❑ The conjunction *y* (and) is used only for numbers between 16 and 99.

❑ The numbers 16–19 and 21–29 are generally written as one word. The numbers 16, 22, 23, and 26 have accents on the last syllable. When used before a masculine noun, *veintiún* has an accent on the last syllable:

   veintiún libros   21 books

❑ In compounds of *ciento (doscientos, trescientos)*, there must be agreement with a feminine noun.

❑ *Ciento* becomes *cien* before nouns and before the numbers *mil* and *millones*. Before all other numbers, use *ciento*.

❑ *Un*, which is not used before *cien(to)* or *mil*, is used before *millón*. When a noun follows *millón*, use *de* between *millón* and the noun.

❑ The following words are used to express common arithmetic functions:

y	plus (+)
menos	minus (−)
por	times (×)
dividido por	divided by (÷)
son	equals (=)

Example Problems

1. You are in Uruguay trying to figure out how many miles you put on your rental car. Express how to figure the cost in Spanish if you rented a car for four days at $54.95 per day.

   Answer: Cincuenta y cuatro dólares noventa y cinco por cuatro son doscientos diez y nueve dólares ochenta.

   1. Express the price of the car: *cincuenta y cuatro dólares noventa y cinco*.

   2. The word *por* is used to multiply. Multiply the price by *cuatro* (four).

   3. The total is $219.80. Use *son* to express "equals." The phrase for 219 is *doscientos diez y nueve*.

   4. Add the plural *dólares*, and then the amount of change: *ochenta* (80).

2. You are in Spain and want to travel from Sevilla to Barcelona. Express that the distance is 1,279 kilometers.

   Answer: La distancia es mil doscientos setenta y nueve kilómetros.

   1. Use *la distancia* to express "the distance" and *es* to express "is."

   2. Select *mil* for 1,000, *doscientos* for 200, and *setenta y nueve* for 79.

   3. The Spanish word for kilometers is *kilómetros*.

Work Problems

You are doing a report on El Yunque, the beautiful rain forest in Puerto Rico. Fill in the missing numbers in your notes.

1. El Yunque está (40) _____ kilómetros al este de la ciudad de San Juan.

2. Tiene más de (240) _____ especies de plantas.

3. Tiene elevaciones de más de (3,280) _____ pies.

4. Tiene un área de (28,000) _____ hectáreas.

5. Más de (1,000,000,000) _____ galones de agua caen cada año.

6. El año pasado, más de (3,167,000) _____ personas visitaron El Yunque.

Worked Solutions

1. **cuarenta**   Select *cuarenta* to express 40.

2. **doscientos cuarenta**   Select the number *doscientos* to express 200. Remember that the two numbers, *dos* and *cientos*, are joined and that *cientos* must be in the plural. The word for 40 is *cuarenta*.

3. **tres mil doscientos ochenta**   Use *tres mil* to express 3,000. Add *doscientos* to express 200 and *ochenta* to express 80.

4. **veintiocho (veinte y ocho) mil**   Use *veintiocho or veinte y ocho* to express 28. Add *mil* without making it plural.

5. **mil millones**   In Spanish, use "one thousand million" to express "one billion."

6. **tres millones ciento sesenta y siete mil**   Use *tres millones* to express "three million." Use *ciento* to express 100 before another number. Use *sesenta y siete* to express 67. Use *mil* to express 1,000.

Ordinal Numbers

Ordinal numbers allow you to express numbers in a series:

Ordinal	Spanish
1st	primero
2nd	segundo
3rd	tercero
4th	cuarto
5th	quinto
6th	sexto
7th	séptimo
8th	octavo
9th	noveno
10th	décimo

Note the following about ordinal numbers:

❏ In Spanish, ordinal numbers are used only through the 10th. After that, cardinal numbers are used.

❏ A cardinal number used in place of an ordinal number is always masculine because *número* is presumed to precede the number.

❏ Ordinal numbers must agree in gender with the nouns they modify. Ordinal numbers are made feminine by changing the final -o of the masculine form to -a.

❏ *Primero* and *tercero* drop their final -o before a masculine singular noun.

❏ The Spanish ordinal numbers are abbreviated as follows:

primero $1^{o(a)}$ primer 1er

segundo $2^{o(a)}$

tercero $3^{o(a)}$ tercer 3er

cuarto $4^{o(a)}$

❏ In dates, *primero* is the only ordinal number used. All other dates use the cardinal number.

❏ Unlike in English, where we would use an ordinal number before a cardinal number (the first two minutes), in Spanish, cardinal numbers precede ordinal numbers (los dos primeros minutos).

Example Problems

1. You are walking in the streets of Chile. Someone stops you and asks where the nearest grocery is. Express that it is fourth store on the right.

    Answer: Es la cuarta tienda a la derecha.

    The word *tienda* is feminine and singular. Select the word for *fourth* that will agree with *tienda: cuarta.* Use *a la derecha* to express "to the right."

2. You are visiting a Spanish web site to get information you need for your Spanish project. Express that you are the 4,713th person to visit this site.

    Answer: Soy la persona cuatro mil setecientos trece a visitar este sitio.

    1. Use *soy* to express "I am."

    2. Any number in a series above 10 must be expressed by a cardinal number.

    3. Select the correct cardinal number for 4,713: *cuatro mil setecientos trece.*

    4. Put the cardinal number after the noun it modifies, *persona.*

    5. Use *a visitar* to express "to visit."

    6. Use *este* to express "this" before the masculine singular noun for "site:" *sitio.*

Work Problems

Use these problems to give yourself additional practice.

Los aniversarios de bodas reciben nombres específicos:

1°	Algodón
2°	Papel
3°	Cuero
4°	Artículos de cocina
5°	Madera
6°	Dulces o azúcar
7°	Lana o cobre
8°	Bronce
9°	Loza o vajilla
10°	Lata o aluminio
15°	Cristal
20°	Porcelana
25°	Plata
50°	Oro
60°	Diamante

Different families recently celebrated their wedding anniversaries. Express the particular anniversary each celebrated by referring to the gift received.

1. Los Ricardo recibieron sábanas para su cama.

2. Los López recibieron un horno de microondas.

3. Los Herrera recibieron una caja de chocolates de Bélgica.

4. Los Muñoz recibieron vasos y copas.

5. Los Recinos recibieron relojes de oro.

Worked Solutions

1. **Es su primer aniversario de bodas.**

    The word *sábanas* refers to bedsheets, which are generally made of cotton. Use *primero* to express "first." Because *aniversario* is masculine and singular, remove the final *-o* from *primero*.

2. **Es su cuarto aniversario de bodas.**

    The phrase *un horno a microondas* refers to a microwave oven. Use *cuarto* to express "fourth."

3. **Es su sexto aniversario de bodas.**

   The phrase *una caja de chocolates de Bélgica* refers to sweets. Use *sexto* to express "sixth."

4. **Es su quince aniversario de bodas.**

   The words *vasos* and *copas* refer to glasses and wine goblets. Because Spanish ordinal numbers revert to the cardinal number after 10th, use the cardinal number for 15: *quince*.

5. **Es su cincuenta aniversario de bodas.**

   The words *relojes de oro* refer to gold watches. Because Spanish ordinal numbers revert to the cardinal number after 10th, use the cardinal number for 50: *cincuenta*.

Fractions

Except for one-half and one-third, noun fractions are formed with ordinal numbers through 10ths. Note how fractions and fractional parts of things are expressed (as illustrated in the examples that follow):

Fractions	Fractional Part (of something)
½ medio(a)	la mitad (de)
⅓ un tercio	la tercera parte (de)
¼ un cuarto	la cuarta parte (de)
⅔ dos tercios	dos terceras partes (de)
¾ tres cuartos	tres cuartas partes (de)
⅘ cuatro quintos	cuatro quintas partes (de)
⅙ un sexto	la sexta parte (de)
⅐ un séptimo	la séptima parte (de)
⅛ un octavo	la octava parte (de)
⅑ un noveno	la novena parte (de)
1/10 un décimo	la décima parte (de)

After tenths, *-avo* may be added to the cardinal number to form the fraction and to express fractional parts of something (as illustrated in the examples that follow):

Fraction	Fractional Part (of something)
1/12 un doceavo	la doceava parte (de)
1/15 un quinceavo	la quinceava parte (de)
1/20 un veinteavo	la veinteava parte (de)
1/30 un treintavo	la treintava parte (de)

Note the following about fractions:

❑ The adjective *medio* (half) becomes *media* before a feminine noun. The noun *la mitad (de)* expresses "half (of)" something.

medio día	half a day
media libra	half a pound
Dame *la mitad.*	Give me half (of something).
la mitad de mis amigos	half of my friends

❏ Fractions are masculine nouns:

2¼ teaspoons   dos y un cuarto cucharaditas

3⅔ cups   tres tazas y dos tercios

Note that native speakers place the fraction either before or after the noun, depending on where it makes logical sense and sounds best.

❏ If a thing is divided into parts, the fraction may or may not be used with the feminine noun *parte* unless a unit of measure is used:

un cuarto (una cuarta parte) de la clase   a quarter of the class

un cuarto de taza   a quarter of a cup

Example Problems

You are teaching your Spanish-speaking friend how to make your favorite cookies. Explain the ingredients that are needed in Spanish.

GALLETITAS DE ALMENDRAS

1. 1¼ cups almonds

    Answer: Una taza y un cuarto de almendras

    1. The word for "a cup" is *una taza*.

    2. Use *y* to express "and."

    3. Use *un cuarto* to express the fraction "one-fourth."

    4. The preposition *de* expresses "of."

    5. Use *almendras* to express "almonds."

2. 2⅓ cups confectioner's sugar

    Answer: Dos tazas y un tercio de azúcar glaseada

    1. Use *dos tazas* to express "two cups."

    2. Use *y* to express "and."

    3. Use *un tercio* for "one-third."

    4. The preposition *de* expresses "of."

    5. The Spanish phrase for "confectioner's sugar" is *azúcar glaseado*.

3. ½ cup egg whites

    Answer: Una media taza de claras de huevo

    1. Use *una media* to express "half" before the phrase for "a cup": *una taza*.

    2. The preposition *de* expresses "of."

    3. The Spanish phrase for "egg whites" is *claras de huevo*.

Work Problems

Use these problems to give yourself additional practice.

The Zoppolo family is preparing its budget *(presupuesto)* for the upcoming year. Rewrite their proposal in Spanish.

BUDGET

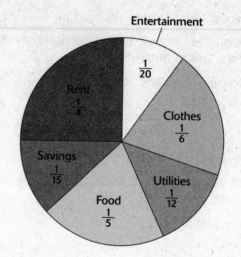

1. ¼ for rent

2. ¹⁄₂₀ for entertainment

3. ⅙ for clothes

4. ¹⁄₁₂ for utilities

5. ⅕ for food

6. ¹⁄₁₅ for savings

Worked Solutions

1. **un cuarto para el alquiler**

   1. Use *un cuarto* to express "one-fourth."

   2. Use *para* to express "for."

   3. The Spanish phrase for "rent" is *el alquiler.*

2. **un veinteavo (la veinteava parte) para diversiones**

   1. Use *un veinteavo* or *la veinteava parte* to express "one-twentieth."

   2. Use *para* to express "for."

   3. The Spanish phrase for "entertainment" is *la diversión.*

   4. Make *diversión* plural because entertainment is used in a plural sense in Spanish (meaning diversions or things to do). Because *diversión* ends in a consonant, drop the accent and add the plural -*es* ending.

3. **un sexto para ropa**

   1. Use *un sexto* to express "one-sixth."

   2. Use *para* to express "for."

   3. The Spanish phrase for "clothing" is *ropa.*

4. **un doceavo (la doceava parte) para servicios públicos**

   1. Use *un doceavo* or *la doceava parte* to express "one-twelfth."

   2. Use *para* to express "for."

   3. The Spanish phrase for "utilities" is *servicios públicos.*

5. **un quinto para comestibles**

   1. Use *un quinto* to express "one-fifth."

   2. Use *para* to express "for."

   3. The Spanish phrase for "food" is *comestibles*.

6. **un quinceavo (la quiceava parte) para ahorros**

   1. Use *un quinceavo* or *la quinceava parte* to express "one-fifteenth."

   2. Use *para* to express "for."

   3. The Spanish phrase for "savings" is *ahorros*.

Multiples

Multiple Spanish numbers are used like their English counterparts. To express the number of times of an occurrence, use the cardinal number and the feminine singular noun *vez*, which becomes *veces* in the plural.

una vez	once
dos veces	twice
tres veces	three times
Fui a España dos veces.	I went to Spain twice (two times).

Multiples such as *solo (sola)*, *doble*, *triple*, and so on may be used as adjectives, as nouns, or as adverbs.

una calle de doble sentido	a two-way street
Ahora él gana el doble.	Now he earns double (twice as much).
Ve doble.	He sees double.
Nuestra casa vale el triple de lo que pagamos.	Our house is worth three times what we paid for it.
Ni una sola persona fue a ayudarlo.	Not one person came to help him.

Example Problems

1. Express that you called your friend three times.

   Answer: Telefoneé a mi amigo tres veces.

   1. Use the verb *telefonear* to express "to call." Change this *-ar* verb to the preterit by dropping the *-ar* infinitive ending and adding the *yo* preterit *-ar* verb ending: *é*. (See Chapter 10.)

   2. Insert the personal *a* before the direct object *mi amigo* (my friend).

   3. Use *tres* to express "three." Use the plural *veces* for "times."

2. Tell your friend that today you ran three times the distance that Rogelio ran.

   Answer: Hoy corrí el triple de la distancia que Rogelio.

1. Use the word for "today": *hoy.*

2. Use the verb *correr* to express "to run." Change this *-er* verb to the preterit by dropping the *-er* infinitive ending and adding the *yo* preterit *-er* verb ending: *í.* (See Chapter 10.)

3. Select *el triple* for "triple."

4. The Spanish word for "of" *(de)* is required although there is no equivalent in the English phrase.

5. The phrase *la distancia* expresses "the distance."

6. *Que* expresses "that."

7. Use Rogelio's name.

8. It is unnecessary to repeat the word "ran" because it is implied in the meaning of the sentence.

Work Problems

Use these problems to give yourself additional practice.

Two of your friends, Rosa and Felipe, had an argument. Describe what happened in Spanish.

1. Rosa called Felipe two times.

2. She spoke three times as much as he did.

3. She cried once.

4. Sometimes her words had a double meaning.

5. Finally, Felipe gave her a single rose.

Worked Solutions

1. **Rosa telefoneó a Felipe dos veces.**

   1. Use the verb *telefonear* to express "to call."

   2. Change this *-ar* verb to the preterit by dropping the *-ar* infinitive ending and adding the third-person singular preterit *-ar* verb ending: *-ó.* (See Chapter 10.)

   3. Insert the personal *a* before the direct object *Felipe.*

   4. Use *dos* to express "two."

   5. Use the plural *veces* for "times."

2. **Ella habló el triple que él.**

   1. Use the verb *hablar* to express "to speak."

   2. Change this *-ar* verb to the preterit by dropping the *-ar* infinitive ending and adding the third-person singular preterit *-ar* verb ending: *-ó.* (See Chapter 10.)

3. Select *el triple* for "three times."

4. Use the Spanish word for "than:" *que*.

5. *Él* expresses "he."

6. It is unnecessary to translate "did" because it is implied.

3. **Ella lloró una vez.**

1. Use the verb *llorar* to express "to cry."

2. Change this *-ar* verb to the preterit by dropping the *-ar* infinitive ending and adding the third-person singular preterit *-ar* verb ending: *-ó*. (See Chapter 10.)

3. Use the singular feminine noun, *vez* for "time."

4. Use *una* to express "one" before the noun.

4. **Algunas veces, sus palabras tenían doble sentido.**

1. *Algunas veces* expresses "sometimes."

2. Use *sus palabras* to express "her words."

3. Use the third-person plural imperfect (see Chapter 10) of the verb *tener* to express that her words "had," in general, a double meaning. Drop the *-er* infinitive ending and add *-ían* as the imperfect ending.

4. Use *un sentido* to express "a meaning."

5. Place the word *doble* (double) before the noun.

5. **Finalmente, Felipe le dió una sola rosa.**

1. *Finalmente* expresses "finally."

2. Use the irregular third-person singular preterit of the verb *dar* (to give: *dió*), to show that the action was completed in the past. (See Chapter 10.)

3. Put the indirect object pronoun *le* (to her) before the conjugated verb form.

4. *Una rosa* expresses "a rose."

5. Use the adjective *sola* to express a single (only one) rose.

Dates

To enquire about the date, ask:

¿Cuál es la fecha de hoy?

¿A cuántos estamos?

What is today's date?

Dates in Spanish are expressed as follows:

Es (Estamos a) day + *(el)* +cardinal number (except for *primero*)+ *de* + month + *de* + year.

Es (Estamos a) jueves (el) veintidós de abril de dos mil cuatro.

It is Thursday, April 22, 2004.

Note the following when expressing a date:

❑ To express "it is," use *es* or *estamos a* before the date. Then add the day, (*el*), the number + *de* + the month.

❑ When "on" is expressed or implied, the definite article *el* may precede either the day of the week or the number of the day.

❑ The first of each month is expressed by *primero*. Cardinal numbers are used for all other days.

❑ Years are expressed in thousands and hundreds, not in hundreds only, as in English.

❑ Unlike in English dates, where we put the month, then the day, then the year, in Spanish, dates are expressed by using the day, then the month, then the year.

❑ To express *on* with Spanish days of the week or dates, use *el*.

Here is some date-related vocabulary:

Words/ Expressions	Spanish	Words/ Expressions	Spanish
a day	un día	yesterday	ayer
a week	una semana	today	hoy
a month	un mes	tomorrow	mañana
a year	un año	tomorrow morning	mañana por la mañana
in	en	tomorrow afternoon	mañana por la tarde
ago	hace	tomorrow night	mañana por la noche
per	por	day after tomorrow	pasado mañana
during	durante	from	desde
next	próximo(a)	a week from today	de hoy en una semana
last	pasado(a)	two weeks	de mañana en
last (in a series)	último(a)	from tomorrow	dos semanas
eve	la víspera	until	hasta
day before yesterday	anteayer		

Example Problems

Tell your friend when certain people in your family were born.

1. Your mother was born on Friday, February 21, 1947.

   Answer: Mi madre nació el viernes, veintiuno de febrero de mil novecientos cuarenta y siete.

   1. Use *mi madre* to express "my mother."

   2. Use the preterit of the verb *nacer* to express "was born." Drop the *-er* infinitive ending and add *-ió* for the third-person singular preterit form of the verb. (See Chapter 10.)

   3. Express "on" by using *el*, which may be placed either before the name of the day, or the number of the date. Use *viernes* to express "Friday."

4. Use the cardinal number *veintiuno (veinte y uno)* for the 21st of the month.

5. The cardinal number is followed by *de* (of).

6. Write the name of the month *(febrero)* remembering to begin the name of the month with a lowercase letter.

7. The month is followed by *de* (of).

8. Begin the date with the word for 1,000 *(mil)* because dates cannot be given in hundreds alone.

9. The word for 900 is irregular and must be memorized: *novecientos.*

10. Join the words for 40 *(cuarenta)* and seven *(siete)* with the word *y.*

2. Your son was born on Thursday, August 1, 2002.

Answer: Mi hijo nació el jueves, primero de agosto de dos mil dos.

1. Use *mi hijo* to express "my son."

2. Use the preterit of the verb *nacer* to express "was born."

3. Use *jueves* to express "Thursday."

4. Drop the *-er* infinitive ending and add *-ió* for the third-person singular preterit form of the verb. (See Chapter 10.)

5. Express "on" by using *el,* which may be placed either before the name of the day, or the number of the date.

6. Use the ordinal number *primero* for the first of the month. The cardinal number is followed by *de* (of).

7. Write the name of the month *(agosto)* remembering to begin with a lowercase letter. The month is followed by *de* (of).

8. Begin the date with the words for 2,000 *(dos mil),* remembering that *mil* does not change in the plural. Add the word for two: *dos.*

Work Problems

Use these problems to give yourself additional practice.

You are doing research on famous Spanish painters. Write the dates of their deaths in Spanish.

1. Murillo died on Wednesday, April 3, 1682.

2. Goya died on Wednesday, April 16, 1828.

3. Picasso died on Tuesday, April 8, 1973.

4. Miró died on Thursday, December 25, 1983.

5. Dalí died on Wednesday, January 23, 1989.

Worked Solutions

1. **Murillo murió el miércoles, treinta y uno de diciembre de mil seiscientos diecisiete (diez y siete).**

   1. Use the third-person singular form of the preterit (past tense) of the verb *morir* (to die). (See Chapter 10.)

   2. Express "on" by using *el*, which may be placed either before the name of the day, or the number of the date. Use *miércoles* to express "Wednesday," remembering to begin the name of the day in a lowercase letter.

   3. Use the cardinal number 3 for the 3rd of the month. The cardinal number is followed by *de* (of).

   4. Write the name of the month *(abril)*, remembering to begin the name of the month in a lowercase letter. The month is followed by *de* (of).

   5. Begin the date with the word for 1,000 *(mil)*, since dates cannot be given in hundreds alone.

   6. The word for 600 is *seiscientos*. Use one of the words for 82: *ochento y dos*.

2. **Goya murió el miércoles, dieciséis (diez y seis) de abril de mil ochocientos veintiocho (veinte y ocho).**

   1. Use the third-person singular form of the preterit (past tense) of the verb *morir* (to die). (See Chapter 10.)

   2. Express "on" by using *el*, which may be placed either before the name of the day, or the number of the date. Use *miércoles* to express "Wednesday," remembering to begin the name of the day in a lowercase letter.

   3. Use the cardinal number *dieciséis* or *diez y seis* for the 16th of the month. The cardinal number is followed by *de* (of).

   4. Write the name of the month *(abril)*, remembering to begin the name of the month in a lowercase letter. The month is followed by *de* (of).

   5. Begin the date with the word for 1,000 *(mil)*, since dates cannot be given in hundreds alone.

   6. The word for 800 is *ochocientos*. Use one of the words for 28: *veintiocho* or *veinte y ocho*.

3. **Picasso murió el martes, ocho de abril de mil novecientos setenta y tres.**

   1. Use the third-person singular form of the preterit (past tense) of the verb *morir* (to die). (See Chapter 10.)

   2. Express "on" by using *el*, which may be placed either before the name of the day, or the number of the date. Use *martes* to express "Tuesday," remembering to begin the name of the day in a lowercase letter.

   3. Use the cardinal number *ocho* for the 8th of the month. The cardinal number is followed by *de* (of).

   4. Write the name of the month *(abril)*, remembering to begin the name of the month in a lowercase letter. The month is followed by *de* (of).

   5. Begin the date with the word for 1,000 *(mil)*, since dates cannot be given in hundreds alone.

   6. The word for 900 is *novecientos*. Use the words for 73: *setenta y tres*.

4. **Miró murió el jueves, veinticinco (viente y cinco) de diciembre de mil ochocientos noventa y tres.**

   1. Use the third-person singular form of the preterit (past tense) of the verb *morir* (to die). (See Chapter 10.)

   2. Express "on" by using *el,* which may be placed either before the name of the day, or the number of the date. Use *jueves* to express "Thursday," remembering to begin the name of the day in a lowercase letter.

   3. Use the cardinal number *veinticinco* or *veinte y cinco* for the 25th of the month. The cardinal number is followed by *de* (of).

   4. Write the name of the month *(diciembre),* remembering to begin the name of the month in a lowercase letter. The month is followed by *de* (of).

   5. Begin the date with the word for 1,000 *(mil),* since dates cannot be given in hundreds alone.

   6. The word for 900 is *novecientos.* Use the words for 83: *ochenta y tres.*

5. **Dalí murió el miércoles, veintitrés (veinte ye tres) de enero de mil novecientos ochenta y nueve.**

   1. Use the third-person singular form of the preterit of the verb *morir* (to die). (See Chapter 10.)

   2. Express "on" by using *el,* which may be placed either before the name of the day, or the number of the date. Use *miércoles* to express "Wednesday," remembering to begin with a lowercase letter.

   3. Use the cardinal number *once* for the 23rd of the month. The cardinal number is followed by *de* (of).

   4. Write the name of the month *(enero),* remembering to begin with a lowercase letter. The month is followed by *de* (of).

   5. Begin the date with the word for 1,000 *(mil)* because dates cannot be given in hundreds alone.

   6. The word for 900 is irregular and must be memorized: *novecientos.* Use the word for 89: *ochenta y nueve.*

Time

To ask or give the time, use the following:

¿Qué hora es?   What time is it?
Es (Son) . . .   It is . . .

To ask or explain "at" what time something will occur, use the following:

¿A qué hora . . .? At what time . . .?
A la (las) . . .   At . . .

Time	Spanish
1:00	la una
2:05	las dos y cinco
3:10	las tres y diez

4:15	las cuatro y cuarto
5:20	las cinco y veinte
6:25	las seis y veinticinco
7:30	las siete y media
7:35	las ocho menos veinticinco
8:40	las nueve menos veinte
9:45	las diez menos cuarto
10:50	las once menos diez
11:55	las doce menos cinco
noon	el mediodía
midnight	la medianoche

To express time:

❑ Use *es* for "it is" when it is one o'clock. The other numbers are plural and require *son*.

❑ Use *a la* to express "at" one o'clock and *a las* to express "at" for every other hour.

❑ To express the time before half past, use the number of the current hour + *y* + the number of minutes after the hour.

❑ Use the number of the following hour + *menos* + the number of minutes left in the current hour to express time after half past.

❑ Time before the hour may also be expressed by *faltar* + the number of minutes left in the current hour + *para* + the number of the next hour.

❑ Time may also be expressed by using the number of minutes past the hour.

❑ *Media* (half) is used as an adjective, and it agrees with *hora* (hour). *Cuarto* (quarter) is used as a noun and shows no agreement.

❑ *De la madrugada* expresses "a.m." in the early morning hours, while *de la mañana* expresses "a.m." in the later morning.

Here is a list of time-related vocabulary:

Expression	Spanish	Expression	Spanish
a second	un segundo	until 1:00	hasta la una
a minute	un minuto	before 6:00	antes de las seis
a quarter of an hour	un cuarto de hora	after 11:00	después de las once
a half hour	media hora	sharp	en punto
an hour	una hora	since what time?	¿desde qué hora?
in the morning (a.m.)	por la madrugada, por la mañana	since 4:00	desde las cuatro
in the afternoon (p.m.)	por la tarde	two hours ago	hace dos horas
in the evening (p.m.)	por la noche	per hour	por hora
at what time?	¿a qué hora?	early	temprano
at exactly 8:00	a las ocho en punto	late	tarde
at about 3:00	a eso de las tres	late (in arriving)	de retraso
in an hour	en una hora	on time	a tiempo
in a while	dentro de un rato	ago	hace (*amount of time*) que
often	a menudo		

Example Problems

You are traveling throughout Spain. Right now, you are in Madrid and want to visit other cities. Using standard times, express at what times the trains depart from Madrid and arrive in the places you want to visit.

HORARIO DE TRENES

SALIDA	LLEGADA
1. Madrid 10:05	Cádiz 14:54
2. Madrid 15:45	Barcelona 22:30

1. **Sale de Madrid a las diez y cinco de la mañana y llega a Cádiz a las tres menos seis de la tarde.**

    1. Use the third-person singular of the present tense of the verb *salir* to express when the train leaves. Drop the *-er* infinitive ending and add *-e.* (See Chapter 3.)

    2. Express "from" by using *de.*

    3. Express "at" by using *a.*

    4. Use *las diez y cinco* for "five minutes after 10."

    5. Use *de la mañana* to express "in the morning."

    6. Use *y* to express "and."

    7. Use the third-person singular of the present tense of the verb *llegar* to express when the train will arrive. Drop the *-ar* infinitive ending and add *-a.* (See Chapter 3.)

    8. Express "at" by using *a.*

    9. Use *las tres menos seis* for "six minutes to three."

    10. Use *de la tarde* to express "in the afternoon."

2. **Sale de Madrid a las cuatro menos cuarto de la tarde y llega a Barcelona a las diez y media de la noche.**

    1. Use the third-person singular of the present tense of the verb *salir* to express when the train leaves. Drop the *-er* infinitive ending and add *-e.* (See Chapter 3.)

    2. Express "from" by using *de.*

    3. Express "at" by using *a.*

    4. Use *las cuatro menos cuarto* for "a quarter to four."

    5. Use *de la tarde* to express "in the afternoon."

    6. Use *y* to express "and."

    7. Use the third-person singular of the present tense of the verb *llegar* to express when the train will arrive. Drop the *-ar* infinitive ending and add *-a.* (See Chapter 3.)

    8. Express "at" by using *a.*

    9. Use *las diez y media* for "half past 10."

    10. Use *de la noche* to express "in the evening."

Work Problems

Use these problems to give yourself additional practice.

Answer the questions in Spanish.

1. Son las tres y media. Alberto llegó a casa hace dos horas y cuarto. ¿A qué hora llegó Alberto a casa?

2. Carolina mira su reloj. Falta un cuarto de hora para las cinco. Ella va a salir en tres cuartos de hora. ¿A qué hora va Carolina a salir?

3. Julia va al salón de belleza a las nueve y veinte de la mañana. Ella pasa una hora y media allá. ¿A qué hora sale Julia del salón de belleza?

4. A las tres menos cuarto Ramón juega al fútbol en el parque. Puede pasar solamente cincuenta minutos más allá. ¿A qué hora tiene que partir Ramón?

5. Susana quiere ir al cine. La película empieza a las ocho y diez y dura una hora y cuarenta minutos. ¿A qué hora termina la película?

Worked Solutions

1. **A la una y cuarto.**

   1. It is 3:30. Alberto arrived home two and a quarter hours ago. He arrived home, therefore, at 1:15.

   2. Use *a la* to express "at" before the feminine singular number *una*, which modifies the feminine singular noun, *hora*.

   3. Use *y* to express "and."

   4. Use *cuarto* to express "a quarter of an hour."

2. **A las cinco y media.**

   1. It is 4:45. Carolina is going to leave in three-quarters of an hour. She will leave, therefore, at 5:30.

   2. Use *a las* to express "at" before the feminine plural number *cinco*, which modifies the feminine singular noun, *hora*.

   3. Use *y* to express "and."

   4. Use *media* to express "half past the hour."

3. **A las once menos diez.**

   1. Julia goes to beauty parlor at 9:20. She is going to spend an hour and a half there. She will leave, therefore, at 10:50.

   2. Use *a las* to express "at" before the feminine plural number *once*, which modifies the feminine singular noun, *hora*.

   3. Use *menos* to express the time before the hour.

   4. Use *diez* to express "10 minutes."

4. **A las cuatro menos veinticinco (veinte y cinco).**

   1. Ramón is playing soccer in the park at a quarter to three. He can only spend 50 minutes there. He has to leave, therefore, at 3:35.

   2. Use *a las* to express "at" before the feminine plural number *cuatro,* which modifies the feminine singular noun, *hora.*

   3. Use *menos* to express the time before the hour.

   4. Use *veinticinco (veinte y cinco)* to express "25 minutes."

5. **A las diez menos diez.**

   1. Susana is going to see a film that starts at 8:10. The movie runs for one hour and 40 minutes. The film ends, therefore, at 9:50.

   2. Use *a las* to express "at" before the feminine plural number *diez,* which modifies the feminine singular noun, *hora.*

   3. Use *menos* to express the time before the hour.

   4. Use *diez* to express "10 minutes".

Chapter Problems and Solutions

Problems

Complete the story by filling in the blanks in Spanish.

El señor Moreno tiene (54) _____ años y su esposa, Linda, tiene (46) _____ años.

Ellos se casaron en (1978) _____ pero ellos se conocieron en (1975) _____. (A week

from today) _____, (Sunday, June 1, 2003), _____ ellos van a celebrar su (25th) _____

aniversario de bodas. Su fiesta va a tener lugar en un restaurante muy elegante, La Cava,

que está situado en la esquina de la Avenida (18th) _____ y la Calle (113th) _____.

(Ago) _____ (one) _____ mes los Moreno enviaron invitaciones a (137) _____

personas. (115) _____ personas han aceptado. (two-thirds) _____ de los invitados

son miembros de su familia y el otro (one-third) _____ son amigos. (97) _____ de los

invitados van a pasar (the eve) _____ de la fiesta en un hotel. La noche de la fiesta,

(from) _____ (7:30 p.m.) _____ (until) _____ (1:30 a.m.) _____ todo el mundo

va a celebrar. Es seguro que mucha gente les va a brindar a ellos (often) _____. El señor

Moreno va a bailar el tango con su esposa (five times) _____. (At midnight) _____

(sharp) _____ él va a regalarle a ella una pulsera de (25) _____ diamantes que cuesta
        25   26

más de ($13,500) _____ y que pesa (one-half) _____ libra. Ella va a abrazarlo (one
                    27   28

time) _____ pero va a darle (1,500) _____ besos. Todo el mundo va a aplaudir.
        29   30

Answers and Solutions

1. **Answer: cincuenta y cuatro.** The Spanish word for 50 is *cincuenta*. Join the word for "four" *(cuatro)* to *cincuenta* with the word *y*.

2. **Answer: cuarenta y seis.** The Spanish word for 40 is *cuarenta*. Join the word for "six" *(seis)* to *cuarenta* with the word *y*.

3. **Answer: mil novecientos setenta y ocho.** Use *mil* to express 1,000. The word for 900 is irregular in Spanish: *novecientos*. The Spanish word for 70 is *setenta*. Join the word for "eight" *(ocho)* to *setenta* with the word *y*.

4. **Answer: mil novecientos setenta y cinco.** Use *mil* to express 1,000. The word for 900 is irregular in Spanish: *novecientos*. The Spanish word for 70 is *setenta*. Join the word for "five" *(cinco)* to *setenta* with the word *y*.

5. **Answer: de hoy en una semana.** *De hoy en una semana* expresses "a week from today."

6. **Answer: el domingo, primero de junio de dos mil tres.** *Domingo* expresses "Sunday." Express "on" by using *el*, which may be placed either before the name of the day, or the number of the date. In dates, "the first" is expressed by *el primero*. *Junio* expresses "June." Use *de* before the number of the year. Use *dos mil* to express 2,000. Note that *mil* is not changed to the plural. Use *tres* to express "three."

7. **Answer: veinticinco (veinte y cinco).** The Spanish word for 20 is *veinte*. Join the word for "five" *(cinco)* to *veinte* with the word *y* or, alternatively, use the more common *veinticinco*.

8. **Answer: dieciocho (diez y ocho).** Cardinal numbers are used to express ordinal numbers above 10. Use *diez y ocho* to express "18th."

9. **Answer: ciento trece.** The Spanish word for 100 is *ciento*. The Spanish word for 13 is *trece*.

10. **Answer: Hace.** *Hace* expresses "ago."

11. **Answer: un.** Use the shortened form *un* before the noun *mes*.

12. **Answer: ciento treinta y siete.** The Spanish word for 100 is *ciento*. The Spanish word for 30 is *treinta*. Join the word for "seven" *(siete)* to *treinta* with the word *y*.

13. **Answer: ciento quince.**   The Spanish word for 100 is *ciento*. The Spanish word for 15 is *quince*.

14. **Answer: Dos tercios.**   The fraction "two-thirds" is expressed by *dos tercios*.

15. **Answer: tercio.**   The fraction "one-third" is expressed by *tercio*. *Un* is not required because *otro* (another) is used.

16. **Answer: noventa y siete.**   The Spanish word for 90 is *noventa*. Join the word for "seven" *(siete)* to *noventa* with the word *y*.

17. **Answer: la víspera.**   *La víspera* expresses "the eve."

18. **Answer: desde.**   *Desde* expresses "from."

19. **Answer: las siete y media de la noche.**   *Las siete* expresses "seven o'clock." Use *media* to express "half past the hour." Because this time is at night, use the expression *de la noche* for "p.m."

20. **Answer: hasta.**   *Hasta* expresses "until."

21. **Answer: la una y media de la madrugada.**   *La una* expresses "one o'clock." Use *media* to express "half past the hour." Because this time is in the very early morning hours, use the expression *de la madrugada* for "a.m."

22. **Answer: a menudo.**   *A menudo* expresses "often."

23. **Answer: cinco veces.**   *Cinco veces* expresses "five times." Note that the singular *vez* becomes *veces* in the plural (*z* changes to *c*).

24. **Answer: A la medianoche.**   *A la medianoche* expresses "at midnight."

25. **Answer: en punto.**   *En punto* expresses "sharp."

26. **Answer: veinticinco (veinte y cinco).**   The Spanish word for 20 is *veinte*. Join the word for "five" *(cinco)* to *veinte* with the word *y* or, alternatively, use the more common *veinticinco*.

27. **Answer: trece mil quinientos dólares.**   *Trece* expresses 13. Use *mil* to express 1,000. The Spanish word for 500 is irregular: *quinientos*.

28. **Answer: media.**   *Una media* expresses "one-half" before the feminine singular noun *libra*.

29. **Answer: una vez.**   *Una vez* expresses "one time."

30. **Answer: mil quinientos.**   Use *mil* to express 1,000. The Spanish word for 500 is irregular: *quinientos*.

Supplemental Chapter Problems

Problems

Complete the story by filling in the blanks in Spanish.

(Last year) _____ (on Sunday, February 16, 2003) _____, mis amigos Bárbara y Roberto y
$\quad$ 1

mi esposo y yo fuimos a Las Vegas por (the first time) _____. Llegamos al aeropuerto
$\quad$ 3

muy (early) _____, (at 6:30 a.m.)_____, en la puerta de embarque (27) _____.
$\quad$ 4 $\qquad$ 5 $\qquad$ 6

Desafortunadamente, nuestro vuelo, que costó ($295.50) _____ por persona, tuvo
$\quad$ 7

(three-quarters) _____ de hora (late) _____. Pasamos (a while) _____ leyendo el
$\quad$ 8 $\qquad$ 9 $\qquad$ 10

periódico y hablando de nuestro viaje. Finalmente el vuelo número (546) _____
$\quad$ 11

despegó (at 7:50 a.m.) _____. Aterrizó en al aeropuerto de Las Vegas (two hours and
$\quad$ 12

43 minutes) _____ (later) _____ (at 10:33 a.m.) _____. Fuimos inmediatamente al
$\quad$ 13 $\qquad$ 14 $\qquad$ 15

hotel. Mi esposo y yo tuvimos la habitación (1891) _____ en el (19th) _____ piso.
$\quad$ 16 $\qquad$ 17

Bárbara y Roberto tuvieron la habitación (767) _____ en el (seventh) _____ piso. Las
$\quad$ 18 $\qquad$ 19

habitaciones eran magníficas y pagamos solamente ($152) _____ al día. Mi esposo y yo
$\quad$ 20

no jugamos ni (one time) _____ pero a Bárbara y a Roberto les gusta jugar. ¡Qué sorpresa!
$\quad$ 21

En (three) _____ horas ellos ganaron ($3,262) _____. Nosotros nos divertimos
$\quad$ 22 $\qquad$ 23

muchísimo. Regresamos a Nueva York (Tuesday, February 25) _____ en el vuelo
$\quad$ 24

(379) _____ . Otra vez tuvimos que esperar el despegue del avión (from) _____
$\quad$ 25 $\qquad$ 26

(noon) _____ (until) _____ (2 p.m.) _____. Por fin llegamos a Nueva York (at
$\quad$ 27 $\qquad$ 28 $\qquad$ 29

9:52 p.m.) _____. ¡Qué vacaciones tan maravillosas!
$\quad$ 30

Answers

1. El año pasado (dates, p. 27)

2. el domingo, dieciséis (diez y seis) (domingo, el dieciséis [diez y seis]de febrero de dos mil
   tres (dates, p. 27)

3. la primera vez (multiples, p. 25)

4. temprano (time, p. 31)

5. a las seis y media de la mañana (time, p. 31)

6. veintisiete (veinte y siete) (cardinal numbers, p. 17)

7. doscientos noventa y cinco dólares cincuenta (cardinal numbers, p. 17)

8. tres cuartos (fractions, p. 22)

9. de retraso (time, p. 31)

10. un rato (time, p. 31)

11. quinientos cuarenta y seis (cardinal numbers, p. 17)

12. a las ocho menos diez de la mañana (time, p. 31)

13. dos horas y cuarenta y tres mintuos (time, p. 31)

14. más tarde (time, p. 31)

15. a las once menos veintisiete (veinte y siete) de la mañana (time, p. 31)

16. mil ochocientos noventa y uno (cardinal numbers, p. 17)

17. diecinueve (diez y nueve) (ordinal numbers, p. 19)

18. setecientos sesenta y siete (cardinal numbers, p. 17)

19. séptimo (ordinal numbers, p. 19)

20. ciento cincuenta y dos dólares (cardinal numbers, p. 17)

21. una vez (multiples, p. 25)

22. tres (cardinal numbers, p. 17)

23. tres mil doscientos sesenta y dos dólares (cardinal numbers, p. 17)

24. martes, el veinticinco (veinte y cinco) de febrero (dates, p. 27)

25. trescientos setenta y nueve (cardinal numbers, p. 17)

26. desde (time, p. 31)

27. el mediodía (time, p. 31)

28. hasta (time, p. 31)

29. las dos de la tarde (time, p. 31)

30. a las diez menos ocho de la noche (time, p. 31)

Chapter 2
Articles, Nouns, and Possession

Definite and Indefinite Articles

The **definite** article, which expresses the English word "the," indicates a specific person or thing, such as the pen or the pencil, for example. The **indefinite** article, which expresses the English words "a," "an," or "some," refers to persons and objects not specifically identified. Both definite and indefinite articles precede the nouns they modify and agree with those nouns in number and gender.

The Definite Article

There are four Spanish definite articles that correspond to the English "the":

	Masculine	*Feminine*	
Singular	el	la	
Plural	los	las	

The definite article is used:

❑ With nouns in a general or abstract sense.

❑ With nouns in a specific sense.

❑ With names of languages, except after the verb *hablar* and after the prepositions *de* and *en*.

❑ With parts of the body (when the possessor is clear) in place of the possessive adjective.

❑ With titles and ranks when the person is not being addressed.

❑ With last names.

❑ With days of the week, except after the verb *ser*.

❑ With seasons, except after *en*, in which case it may be omitted.

❑ With dates

❑ With the hour of the day and time expressions.

❑ With the names of certain cities and countries and with the names of the continents (although there is a tendency to omit the article in current usage).

❑ With rivers, seas, and other geographical locations.

❑ With the names of boats or ships.

❑ With adverbs and infinitives used as nouns (although it is optional when the infinitive serves as the subject of the sentence).

❑ With weights and measures to express "a," "an," and "per."

❑ With clothing used in a general sense.

The definite article is omitted:

❑ Before nouns in apposition, unless they are modified or refer to a family or business relationship.

❑ Before numerals expressing the title of rulers.

Contractions with the definite article *el* occur with the preposition *a* (to become *al*) and *de* (to become *del*) except when the definite article is part of the title or name:

Voy a El Salvador.   Vamos al Perú.
Soy de El Salvador.   Soy del Perú.

The Neuter Lo

The neuter *lo*, which is used only in the singular and has no gender, is used as follows:

❑ Before an adjective used as a noun to express an abstract idea or a quality

❑ *Lo* + adjective (or adverb) + *que* = how

Note: Lo preceded by *a* means "in the manner of" or "like":

Él gasta a lo loco. He spends like crazy.

Example Problems

Complete the opinions below by using the correct form of the definite article, if needed:

1. ___ polución del aire es un problema serio.

    Answer: La

    Use the definite article *la* before the feminine noun *polución,* which is used in a general sense.

2. ___ Argentina es un país en ___ América del Sur.

    Answer: La (optional); la

    The definite article is part of the names of continents. The definite article may be used with the names of continents but may be omitted.

3.   ___ mentir es un pecado.

Answer: El (optional)

Using the masculine singular definite article with an infinitive serving as a noun is optional.

4.   ___ bellas flores cuestan mucho.

Answer: Las

Use the feminine plural definite article *las* before the feminine plural adjective *bellas* that modifies the feminine plural noun *flores,* which is used in a general sense.

5.   Cuando ando demasiado, me duele ___ espalda.

Answer: la

Use the definite article with parts of the body *(espalda)* when the possessor *(yo)* is clear.

6.   ___ importante es siempre decir la verdad.

Answer: Lo

Use the neuter definite article before an adjective that is being used as a noun to express an abstract idea.

Work Problems

Use these problems to give yourself additional practice.

Complete the story by using the correct form of the definite article, if needed.

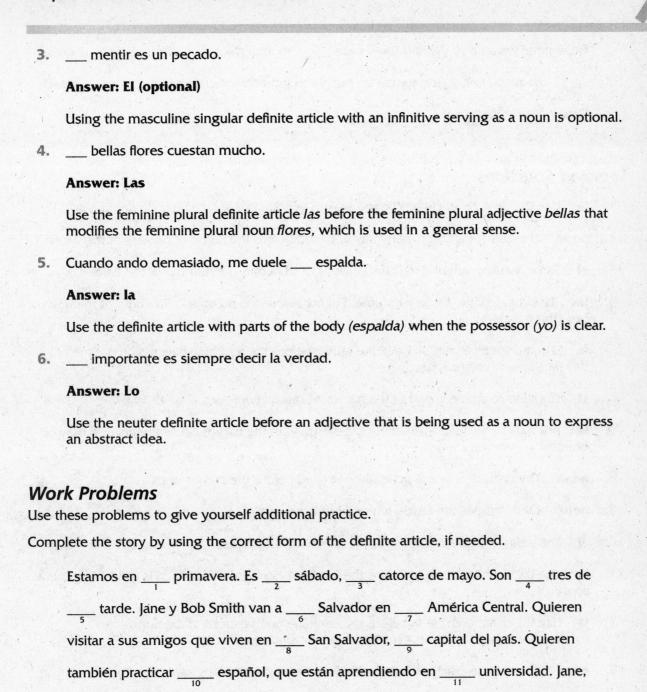

Estamos en ___ primavera. Es ___ sábado, ___ catorce de mayo. Son ___ tres de
    1   2   3   4

___ tarde. Jane y Bob Smith van a ___ Salvador en ___ América Central. Quieren
  5   6   7

visitar a sus amigos que viven en ___ San Salvador, ___ capital del país. Quieren
                                    8   9

también practicar ___ español, que están aprendiendo en ___ universidad. Jane,
                   10   11

___ esposa de Bob, habla ___ español bastante bien. Ella comprende ___
  12   13   14

importante que es hablar una lengua extranjera. ___ hablar otras lenguas es una ventaja.
                                                  15

Jane y Bob viajan en un barco que se llama ___ Santa Anita. Cuesta mil dólares ___
                                             16   17

billete. Cuando llegan al barco, todos ___ miembros de ___ tripulación les dicen, "
                                        18   19

Buenos días, ___ señores Smith."
              20

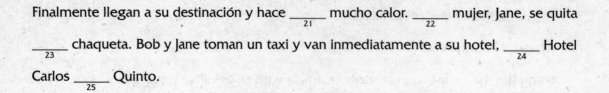

Finalmente llegan a su destinación y hace ＿＿＿ mucho calor. ＿＿＿ mujer, Jane, se quita

                                                                      21   22

＿＿＿ chaqueta. Bob y Jane toman un taxi y van inmediatamente a su hotel, ＿＿＿ Hotel

   23   24

Carlos ＿＿＿ Quinto.

           25

Worked Solutions

1.   **la**   Use the definite article before the season feminine singular season *la primavera*.

2.   **none**   The definite article is generally not used before the name of the day of the week.

3.   **el**   The masculine singular definite article is used before the number of the date.

4.   **las**   Use the definite article with time. Put *las* before the number of the hour of the day: *tres* (three o'clock).

5.   **la**   Use the feminine singular definite article before the feminine expression of time of day *(la tarde)* to express "the."

6.   **El**   The definite article is part of the names of certain countries.

7.   **la (optional)**   The definite article may be used with the names of continents or it may be omitted.

8.   **none**   The definite article is generally not used before the names of cities.

9.   **none**   Omit the definite article when there is a noun in apposition.

10.   **el**   The definite article is used with the names of languages.

11.   **la**   Use the definite article *la* before the feminine noun *escuela*, which is used in a general sense.

12.   **la**   Use the definite article *la* before the feminine noun *esposa*. If the apposition expresses a family or business relationship, the article is needed.

13.   **none**   The definite article is not used before the name of a language after the verb *hablar*.

14.   **lo**   Use the neuter definite article before an adjective that is being used as a noun to express an abstract idea.

15.   **(El)**   Using the masculine singular definite article with an infinitive serving as a noun is optional.

16.   **la**   The feminine definite article is used before the feminine name of a boat.

17.   **el**   The definite article is used with measures to express "per."

18.   **los**   Use the masculine plural definite article *los* before the masculine plural noun *miembros* to express "the."

19. **la**   Use the feminine singular definite article *la* before the feminine noun *tripulación* to express "the."

20. **none**   The definite article is omitted before a title when addressing the person.

21. **none**   The definite article is not used with weather expressions.

22. **La**   Use the definite article *la* before the feminine noun *mujer,* which is used in a general sense.

23. **la**   Use the definite article to express possession when the possessor is clear.

24. **el**   Use the definite article *el* before the masculine noun *hotel*. If the apposition expresses a family or business relationship. the article is needed.

25. **none**   The definite article is omitted before numerals expressing the titles of rulers.

Indefinite Articles

There are four Spanish indefinite articles that correspond to the English "a," "an," and "one":

	Masculine	*Feminine*
Singular	un	una
Plural	unos	unas

Omit the indefinite article:

❑ Before unmodified nouns expressing nationality, profession, or religious or political affiliation.

❑ Before unmodified nouns in apposition, unless referring to a family or business relationship.

❑ Before or after certain words that use an indefinite article in English:

cien (one hundred)	cien hombres (one hundred men)
cierto (certain)	ciertos problemas (certain problems)
mil (one thousand)	mil personas (one thousand people)
otro (other)	otro día (another day)
semejante (similar)	cosa semejante (a similar thing)
qué (what a)	qué lástima (what a pity)
tal (such a)	tal idea (such an idea)

Example Problems

Complete the news headlines by using an indefinite article, if necessary.

1. El doctor Padilla, ___ filósofo bien conocido, tiene ___ otra conferencia en ___ país extranjero.

   Answer: none, none, un

The indefinite article is not used with unmodified nouns or nouns in apposition showing a family or business relationship. The indefinite article is not used with *otra*. Use the masculine singular definite article before the noun *país* to express "a."

2. ___ cien hombres y ___ mujeres van a la luna en ___ nave espacial.

   Answer: none, none, una

   The indefinite article is omitted before the number *cien*. Because *cien* refers to the grouping of men and women *(hombres y mujeres)*, no indefinite article is needed before *mujeres*. Use the masculine singular definite article before the noun *nave* to express "a."

3. ___ mil habitantes de ___ pueblo sudamericano quieren aprender ___ lengua africana.

   Answer: none, un, una

   The indefinite article is omitted before the number *mil*. Use the masculine singular definite article before the noun *pueblo* to express "a." Use the feminine singular indefinite article before the noun *lengua* to express "a."

Work Problems

Use these problems to give yourself additional practice.

Describe the festival by using an indefinite article, if necessary.

1. Nunca ví ___ fiesta semejante.

2. ¡Qué ___ alegría!

3. Había ___ desfile.

4. Mi profesor de español, ___ persona muy importante en la comunidad, fue ___ líder del desfile.

5. El señor Rojas, fue ___ participante entusiasta.

6. Había ___ mil personas en la calle.

7. ___ ciertas personas bailaban y ___ otras cantaban.

8. ___ muchachos gritaban.

Worked Solutions

1. **una**   Use the feminine singular indefinite article before *fiesta* to express "a."

2. **none**   The indefinite article is omitted after the word *qué*.

3. **un**   Use the masculine singular indefinite article before *desfile* to express "a."

4. **una, un**   Use the indefinite article *una* before the feminine noun *persona.* If the apposition expresses a family or business relationship, the article is needed. Use the masculine singular indefinite article before *líder* to express "a."

5. **un**   Use the masculine singular indefinite article before the modified noun *participante* to express "a."

6. **none**   The indefinite article is omitted before the word *mil.*

7. **none, none**   The indefinite article is omitted before the word *ciertas.* The indefinite article is omitted before the word *otras.*

8. **Unos**   Use the masculine plural indefinite article before *muchachos* to express "some."

Demonstrative Adjectives and Pronouns

Demonstrative Adjectives

Demonstrative adjectives indicate or point out the person, place, or thing that is being referred to. They precede and agree in number and gender with the nouns they modify.

In Spanish, the demonstrative adjective is selected according to the distance of the noun from the speaker.

	Masculine	*Feminine*	*Meaning*	*Distance*
Singular	este	esta	this	near to or directly concerned
Plural	estos	estas	these	with speaker
Singular	ese	esa	that	not particularly near to or
Plural	esos	esas	those	directly concerned with speaker
Singular	aquel	aquella	that	far from and not directly
Plural	aquellos	aquellas	those	concerned with speaker

Note the following about demonstrative adjectives:

❑ They are used before each noun:

   esta profesora y ese alumno (this teacher and that student)

❑ Adverbs may be used to reinforce location:

   este coche aquí (this car here)

   esos coches ahí (those cars there)

   aquel coche allá (that car over there)

❑ When placed after the noun, the adjective is used in a pejorative sense:

   Los alumnos esos no comprenden nada de nada. (Those students understand nothing about anything.)

Demonstrative Pronouns

Demonstrative pronouns are differentiated from demonstrative adjectives by the addition of an accent.

	Masculine	*Feminine*	*Neuter*	*Meaning*	*Distance*
Singular	éste	ésta	esto	this (one)	near to or directly
Plural	éstos	éstas		these (ones)	concerned with speaker
Singular	ése	ésa	eso	that (one)	not particularly near to or
Plural	ésos	ésas		those (ones)	directly concerned with speaker
Singular	aquél	aquélla	aquello	that (one)	far from and not directly
Plural	aquéllos	aquéllas		those (ones)	concerned with speaker

Note the following about demonstrative pronouns:

❏ They agree in number and gender with the nouns they replace:

Voy a comprar esta camisa y aquéllas. (I'm going to buy this shirt and those.)

❏ Use a form of *aquél* to express "the former" and a form of *éste* to express "the latter:"

María sale con Paco; éste es grande y aquélla es pequeña.

❏ The neuter pronouns *esto, eso,* and *aquello* do not refer to specific nouns, but rather to statements, ideas, concepts, understood nouns, and the like. They have no accent marks because there is no corresponding neuter demonstrative adjective.

¿Qué es esto? Es una tarjeta postal. (What is that? It's a postcard.)

Mi hijo no me telefonea a menudo y eso me entristece. (My son doesn't call me often, and that makes me sad.)

Aquello les sorprendió mucho. (That surprised them a lot.)

❏ The special demonstrative pronouns *el, los, la, las,* and *lo* are used instead of the demonstrative pronouns noted above when they are preceded by *de* or *que* in relative clauses:

Yo tomo el tren de la mañana; ella toma el de la tarde. (I take the morning train, and she takes the one in the afternoon.)

Tú prefieres las galletitas que Ana prepara, y José prefiere las que yo preparo. (You prefer the cookies that Ana makes, and José prefers the ones that I make.)

Lo que él me dijo no es verdad. (What he told me isn't true.)

Example Problems

Tell the person in the bakery what you would like to buy by using the correct demonstrative adjective and pronoun.

1. Deme _____ panecillos y _____.

   A. esta, ésta   **B.** aquel, aquél   **C.** esos, ésos

   Answer: C

   Use *esos and ésos* because *panecillos* is a masculine plural noun.

2. Deme _____ pastel y _____.

   A. este, éstos   **B.** aquellos, aquéllas   **C.** esa, ésas

   Answer: A

   Use *este and éstos* because *pastel* is a masculine singular noun.

3. Deme _____ tortas y _____.

   A. estos, éstos   **B.** aquellas, aquéllas   **C.** ese, ése

   Answer: B

   Use *aquellas and aquéllas* because *tortas* is a feminine singular noun.

Work Problems

Use these problems to give yourself additional practice.

Describe clothing you see in a store by using the correct demonstrative adjective and pronoun.

1. _____ camisa aquí es larga y _____ lo es también.

2. _____ corbatas ahí son estrechas y _____ lo son también.

3. _____ pantalones allá son bellos y _____ lo son también.

4. _____ vestido ahí es confortable y _____. lo es también.

5. _____ blusa ahí es magnífica y _____ lo es también.

6. _____ abrigo allá es perfecto y _____ lo es también.

7. _____ guantes aquí son pequeños y _____ lo son también.

8. _____ camisetas allá son bonitas y _____ lo son también.

9. _____ impermeable aquí es práctico y _____ lo es también.

10. _____ falda allá es elegante y _____ lo es también.

11. _____ zapatos ahí son de última moda y _____ lo son también.

12. _____ chaquetas aquí son grandes y _____ lo son también.

Worked Solutions

1. **Esta, ésta**   Use the feminine singular demonstrative adjective and pronoun indicated by the adverb *aquí*.

2. **Esas, ésas**   Use the feminine plural demonstrative adjective and pronoun indicated by the adverb *ahí*.

3. **Aquellos, aquéllos**   Use the masculine plural demonstrative adjective and pronoun indicated by the adverb *allá*.

4. **Ese, ése**   Use the masculine singular demonstrative adjective and pronoun indicated by the adverb *ahí*.

5. **Esa**, **ésa**   Use the feminine singular demonstrative adjective and pronoun indicated by the adverb *ahí*.

6. **Aquel, aquél**   Use the masculine singular demonstrative adjective and pronoun indicated by the adverb *allá*.

7. **Estos, éstos**   Use the masculine plural demonstrative adjective and pronoun indicated by the adverb *aquí*

8. **Aquellas, aquéllas**   Use the feminine plural demonstrative adjective and pronoun indicated by the adverb *allá*.

9. **Este, éste**   Use the masculine singular demonstrative adjective and pronoun indicated by the adverb *aquí*.

10. **Aquella, aquélla**   Use the feminine singular demonstrative adjective and pronoun indicated by the adverb *allá*.

11. **Esos, ésos**   Use the masculine plural demonstrative adjective and pronoun indicated by the adverb *ahí*.

12. **Estas, éstas**   Use the feminine plural demonstrative adjective and pronoun indicated by the adverb *aquí*.

Gender and Number of Nouns

The gender of nouns refers to whether a noun is masculine or feminine. In Spanish, certain endings are generally a good indication as to the gender of the noun. The number of nouns refers to whether the noun is singular (the speaker is referring to only one person, place, thing, or idea) or plural (the speaker is referring to more than one).

Gender of Nouns

Spanish nouns are either masculine or feminine. Nouns that refer to males are masculine, while those that refer to females are feminine, no matter what ending they may have.

Here are more specifics about gender in Spanish:

❑ Nouns that end in *-o* (except *la mano* [the hand] and *la radio* [the radio]) and in *-aje* are masculine.

❑ Nouns belonging to certain thematic groups are masculine, including numbers (*el siete, el millón*); days of the week (*el lunes, el martes*); compass points (*el norte, el sur*); names of trees (*el manzano* [apple tree], *el pera* [pear tree]); compound nouns (*el paraguas* [umbrella], *el rascacielos* [skyscraper]); names of rivers, lakes, mountains, straits, and seas (*el Amazonas, el Canal de Panamá*); and musical notes (*el do, el mi*).

❑ Nouns that end in *-a*, as well as those ending in *-ad, -ie, -ción, -sión, -ud*, and *-umbre* are generally feminine.

❑ Nouns belonging to certain thematic groups are feminine, including many illnesses (*la fiebre, la diabetes, la bronquitis,* but *el asma*), islands and provinces *(la Tierra del Fuego, las Islas Baleares),* and letters of the alphabet *(la hache [h], la uve [v]).*

❑ Some nouns ending in *-ma* and *-eta* (those that are derived from the Greek) are masculine, as are the words *el día* (the day) and *el mapa* (the map):

-ma	*-eta*
el clima (the climate)	el atleta (the athlete)
el drama (the drama)	el planeta (the planet)
el idioma (the language)	el poeta (the poet)
el poema (the poem)	
el problema (the problem)	
el programa (the program)	
el sistema (the system)	
el telegrama (the telegram)	
el tema (the theme)	

❑ Some nouns are the same for both genders and use the appropriate article to indicate masculinity or femininity:

el artista	la artista	the artist
el ciclista	la ciclista	the cyclist
el dentista	la dentista	the dentist
el mártir	la mártir	the martyr
el astronauta	la astronauta	the astronaut
el periodista	la periodista	the journalist
el testigo	la testigo	the witness
el telefonista	la telefonista	the operator
el violinista	la violinista	the violinist
el modelo	la modelo	the model
el joven	la joven	the youth
el estudiante	la estudiante	the student

❑ Some nouns are always masculine or feminine regardless of the gender of person being described:

la persona	the person
la víctima	the victim

❑ Some nouns change meaning according to their gender:

Masculine	Meaning	Feminine	Meaning
el capital	the capital (money)	la capital	the capital (country)
el cura	the priest	la cura	the cure
el frente	the front	la frente	the forehead
el guía	the male guide	la guía	the female guide, the guidebook

el orden	the order (succession)	la orden	the order (command)
el Papa	the Pope	la papa	the potato
el policía	the police officer	la policía	the police force, the police woman

❑ Masculine nouns that refer to people and end in -or, -és, or -n require the addition of a final -a to get the female equivalent. If the masculine noun has an accented final syllable, that accent is dropped in the feminine form:

el profesor	la profesora	the teacher
el inglés	la inglesa	the English person
el alemán	la alemana	the German person

Two exceptions are:

el actor	the actor	la actriz	the actress
el emperador	the emperor	la emperatriz	the empress

❑ Some nouns have distinct masculine and feminine forms:

Masculine	Meaning	Feminine	Meaning
el duque	the duke	la duquesa	the duchess
el héroe	the hero	la heroína	the heroine
el hombre	the man	la mujer	the woman
el marido	the husband	la esposa	the wife
el poeta	the poet	la poetisa	the poet
el príncipe	the prince	la princesa	the princess
el rey	the king	la reina	the queen
el yerno	the son-in-law	la nuera	the daughter-in-law

Note: The masculine singular article *el* is used with feminine singular nouns beginning with a stressed *a* sound (*a-* or *ha-*) to prevent the clash of sounds. In the plural, *las* is used for these nouns.

el agua: the water   las aguas: the waters

The masculine singular indefinite article *un* is used with feminine singular nouns beginning with a stressed *a* (*a* or *ha*) sound to prevent the clash of sounds. In the plural, *unas* is used for these nouns.

un ave: a bird   unas aves: some birds

Noun Plurals

Noun plurals are used when the speaker is referring to more than one person, place, thing, or idea. Like in English, the letters –s and –es are used to form these plurals.

❑ The plural of nouns ending in a vowel is formed by adding an -s.

❑ Add *-es* to form the plural of nouns ending in a consonant, an accented vowel, or *-y*. Exceptions are:

el café	los cafés	the cafes
la mamá	las mamás	the mothers
el papá	los papás	the fathers
el sofá	los sofás	the sofas

❑ Some nouns ending in *-n* or *-s* add or delete an accent mark to maintain the original stress:

el joven	los jóvenes	the youths
el examen	los exámenes	the tests
la canción	las canciones	the songs
el francés	los franceses	the Frenchmen
el inglés	los ingleses	the Englishmen
el limón	los limones	the lemons
el melón	los melones	the melons
el melocotón	los melocotones	the peaches

❑ Nouns ending in *-z* change *-z* to *-ce* before adding *-es*.

❑ Nouns ending in *-es* or *-is* do not change in the plural except for *el mes → los meses* (the months).

❑ Compound nouns don't change in the plural:

el portamonedas	los portamonedas	the purses

❑ The plural of nouns of different genders is expressed by the masculine plural.

❑ Some nouns are always plural:

las gafas/los espejuelos	eyeglasses
las matemáticas	mathematics
las vacaciones	vacation

Example Problems

Express what takes place by supplying either the male or female counterpart of the noun or its plural. Look at the verb to determine what is needed.

> Examples: *La mujer* trabaja. *El hombre* trabaja también.
>
>   *La mujer* trabaja. *Las mujeres* trabajan.

1. El coquí vive en Puerto Rico. _____ viven en Puerto Rico.

   Answer: Los coquíes

   The verb *viven* is plural. Add *-es* to form the plural of nouns ending in an accented vowel.

2. La luz brilla. _____ brillan.

Answer: Las luces

The verb *brillan* is plural. Use the feminine plural definite article *las* to show that you are speaking about more than one feminine thing. Change the *-z* of *luz* to a *-c*. Then add *-es* to form the plural because *luz* ends in a consonant.

3. La atleta es fuerte. _____ es fuerte también.

Answer: El atleta

The verb *es* is singular. Use the masculine singular definite article *el* to show that you are speaking about a single masculine person.

4. El yerno llega temprano. _____ llega temprano también.

Answer: La nuera

The verb *llega* is singular. The female counterpart for *el yerno* (son-in-law) is *la nuera*.

5. El marido va al centro. _____ va al centro también.

Answer: La esposa

The verb *va* is singular. The female counterpart for *el marido* (husband) is *la esposa*.

6. El rey es estricto. _____ son estrictos.

Answer: Los reyes

The verb *son* is plural. Use the masculine plural definite article *los* to show that you are speaking about more than one masculine thing. Add *-es* to form the plural of nouns ending in *-y*.

7. El mártir muere. _____ muere también.

Answer: La mártir

The verb *muere* is singular. The female counterpart for *el mártir* (martyr) is *la mártir*.

8. La alemana viaja. _____ viaja también.

Answer: El alemán

The verb *viaja* is singular. The male counterpart for *la alemana* (German woman) is *el alemán*.

Work Problems

Use these problems to give yourself additional practice.

Complete the chart with the Spanish equivalents preceded by the corresponding definite article.

	Masculine Singular +	Feminine Singular =	Plural
1. duke			
2. poet			
3. youth			
4. French person			
5. hero			
6. emperor			
7. king			
8. doctor			
9. phone operator			
10. baby			

Worked Solutions

1. **el duque + la duquesa = los duques**   The female counterpart for *el duque* is *la duquesa*. Use the masculine plural to speak about a male and female grouping. Add *-s* to *duque* because it ends in a vowel.

2. **el poeta + la poetisa = los poetas**   The female counterpart for *el poeta* is *la poetisa*. Use the masculine plural to speak about a male and female grouping. Add *-s* to *poeta* because it ends in a vowel.

3. **el joven + la joven = los jóvenes**   The female counterpart for *el joven* is *la joven*. Use the masculine plural to speak about a male and female grouping. Add *-es* to *joven* because it ends in a consonant. Add an accent on the *o* to preserve the proper stress.

4. **el francés + la francesa = los franceses**   The female counterpart for *el francés* is *la francesa*. Remove the accent on the *e* to preserve the proper stress. Use the masculine plural to speak about a male and female grouping. Add *-es* to *francés* because it ends in a consonant. Remove the accent on the *e* to preserve the proper stress.

5. **el héroe + la heroína = los héroes**   The female counterpart for *el héroe* is *la heroína*. Use the masculine plural to speak about a male and female grouping. Add *-s* to *héroe* because it ends in a vowel.

6. **el emperador + la emperatriz = los emperadores**   The female counterpart for *el emperador* is *la emperatriz*. Use the masculine plural to speak about a male and female grouping. Add *-es* to *emperador* because it ends in a consonant.

7. **el rey + la reina = los reyes**   The female counterpart for *el rey* is *la reina*. Use the masculine plural to speak about a male and female grouping. Add *-es* to *rey* because it ends in *-y*.

8. **el médico + la médica = los médicos**   The female counterpart for *el médico* is *la médica*. Use the masculine plural to speak about a male and female grouping. Add *-s* to *médico* because it ends in a vowel.

9. **el telefonista + la telefonista = los telefonistas**   The female counterpart for *el telefonista* is *la telefonista*. Use the masculine plural to speak about a male and female grouping. Add *-s* to *telefonista* because it ends in a vowel.

10. **el bebé + la bebé = los bebés**   The female counterpart for *el bebé* is *la bebé*. Use the masculine plural to speak about a male and female grouping. Add *-s* to *bebé* because it ends in a vowel.

Expressing Possession

Using *De*

The preposition *de* (of) is used to express relationship and possession. If the sentence contains more than one noun, it is unnecessary to repeat *de* before each noun. *De* contracts with the definite article *el* to form *del* (of the) before a masculine singular noun.

A construction that is the reverse of English is used:

Son los libros de Jaime y del primo de Jaime.   They are Jaime's and his cousin's books.

To avoid repetition in a sentence, the noun being possessed may be replaced by its definite article + *de:*

Me gustan sus ideas y las de esa muchacha.   I like your ideas and that girl's.

¿De quién es (de quiénes son)? expresses "whose?":

¿De quién es ese sombrero?   Whose hat is that?

Possessive Adjectives

Possessive adjectives agree with the object possessed, never with the possessor. Short forms of the adjectives are used before the nouns they modify, while the long forms are used after the nouns they modify and are always preceded by an article or demonstrative adjective.

	Short Forms				Long Forms			
	Masculine Singular	Masculine Plural	Feminine Singular	Feminine Plural	Masculine Singular	Masculine Plural	Feminine Singular	Feminine Plural
my	mi	mis	mi	mis	mío	míos	mía	mías
your	tu	tus	tu	tus	tuyo	tuyos	tuya	tuyas
his/her/ your	su	sus	su	sus	suyo	suyos	suya	suyas
our	nuestro	nuestros	nuestra	nuestras	nuestro	nuestros	nuestra	nuestras
your	vuestro	vuestros	vuestra	vuestras	vuestro	vuestros	vuestra	vuestras
their/your	su	sus	su	sus	suyo	suyos	suya	suyas

Tu bicicleta y la bicicleta mía están en el garaje. Your bicycle and my bicycle are in the garage.

To avoid ambiguity with *su or suyo*, which can mean "his," "her," or "their," the possessive adjective may be replaced by the corresponding definite article + *de* + *Ud. (Uds., él, ellos, ella, ellas):*

> I want to borrow her (his) sweater.
> Quiero tomar prestado su suéter.
> Quiero tomar prestado el suéter de ella (él).

> Her (His) car is red.
> El coche suyo es rojo.
> El coche de ella (él) es rojo.

With parts of the body or clothing, when the possessor is clear, the possessive adjective is replaced with the definite article:

Ella se lavó las manos.	She washed her hands.
Abrí los ojos.	I opened my eyes.

Possessive Pronouns

The possessive pronoun replaces the noun in the sentence. To form a possessive pronoun, select the definite article corresponding in number and gender to the noun being possessed, and then add the long form of the corresponding possessive adjective, shown in the preceding table.

> Tu bicicleta y la mía están en el garaje.   Your bicycle and mine are in the garage.

Note the contraction with *a* and *de:*

> A tu hermano le gustan los deportes; **al** mío también.   You brother likes sports; mine, too.
> El coche de tu padre es viejo; el **del** mío es nuevo.   You father's car is old; mine's is new.

After the verb *ser* (to be), the definite article is generally omitted:

> Este bolígrafo es tuyo, no mío.   This pen is yours, not mine.

Example Problems

Express possession by supplying the correct possessive adjective or pronoun.

1. (our) _____ tíos son médicos.

   Answer: Nuestros

   The item possessed ends in *-os* and is, therefore, masculine plural. Use the masculine plural possessive adjective short form *nuestros* before the noun *tíos*.

2. (your [informal]) Las hermanas _____ son hermosas.

   Answer: tuyas

   The item possessed ends in *-as* and is, therefore, feminine plural. Use the feminine plural possessive adjective long form *tuyas* after the noun *hermanas*.

3. (mine) Su padre es importante. _____ lo es también.

Answer: El mío

The item possessed is masculine singular. Use the masculine singular possessive pronoun *el mío* to replace the masculine singular noun *padre* from the previous sentence.

Work Problems

Describe people's possessions by supplying the correct possessive adjective or pronoun.

1. (My) ___ coche es grande, (your [informal]) el coche _____ es pequeño y (his) _____ es deportivo.

2. (Our) ___ casa es moderna, (your [formal]) la casa _____ es lujosa y (theirs) ___ es magnífica.

3. (Your [formal]) ___ hijos son inteligentes, (her) los hijos ___ son amables y (mine) _____ son simpáticos.

4. (Their) ___ bicicletas son rojas, (our) las bicicletas _____ son blancas y (yours [formal]) _____ son negras.

5. (Your [informal]) ___ profesión es interesante, (my) la profesión _____ es importante, (hers) _____ es rodeada de glamour.

6. (His) ___ vacaciones son largas, (their) las vacaciones _____ son cortas y (ours) _____ son necesarias.

Worked Solutions

1. **Mi, tuyo, el suyo** The item possessed is masculine singular. Use the masculine singular possessive adjective short form *mi* before the noun *coche*. Use the masculine singular possessive adjective long form *tuyo* after the noun *coche*. Use the masculine singular possessive pronoun *el suyo* to replace the masculine singular noun *coche* from the previous statements in the sentence.

2. **Nuestra, suya, la suya** The item possessed is feminine singular. Use the feminine singular possessive adjective short form *nuestra* before the noun *casa*. Use the feminine singular possessive adjective long form *suya* after the noun *casa*. Use the feminine singular possessive pronoun *la suya* to replace the feminine singular noun *casa* from the previous statements in the sentence.

3. **Sus, suyos, los míos** The item possessed is masculine plural. Use the masculine plural possessive adjective short form *sus* before the noun *hijos*. Use the masculine plural possessive adjective long form *suyos* after the noun *hijos*. Use the masculine plural possessive pronoun *los míos* to replace the masculine plural noun *hijos* from the previous statements in the sentence.

4. **Sus, nuestras, las suyas** The item possessed is feminine plural. Use the feminine plural possessive adjective short form *sus* before the noun *bicicletas*. Use the feminine plural possessive adjective long form *nuestras* after the noun *bicicletas*. Use the feminine plural possessive pronoun *las suyas* to replace the feminine plural noun *biciletas* from the previous statements in the sentence.

5. **Tu, mía, la suya**   The item possessed is feminine singular. Use the feminine singular possessive adjective short form *tu* before the noun *profesión*. Use the feminine plural possessive adjective long form *mía* after the noun *profesión*. Use the feminine singular possessive pronoun *la suya* to replace the feminine singular noun *profesión* from the previous statements in the sentence.

6. **Sus, suyas, las nuestras**   The item possessed is feminine plural. Use the feminine plural possessive adjective short form *sus* before the noun *vacaciones*. Use the feminine plural possessive adjective long form *suyas* after the noun *vacaciones*. Use the feminine plural possessive pronoun *las nuestras* to replace the feminine plural noun *vacaciones* from the previous statements in the sentence.

Chapter Problems and Solutions

Problems

Give your opinions by filling in the missing word.

1. (sports) Me gustan ___.

2. (That [far away]) _____ país es importante.

3. (Maria's sister) _____ es chiquita.

4. (a victim) Ricardo fue _____ del crimen.

5. (The rubies) _____ son hermosos.

6. (This) _____ jardín es exótico.

7. (Tests) _____ son difíciles.

8. (like crazy) Ella practica a _____.

9. (Cooking) _____ es un pasatiempo divertido.

10. (This) _____ es imposible.

11. (The melons) _____ son deliciosos.

12. (The water) _____ está fría.

13. (Those [not very far]) _____ mujeres son amables.

14. (Our) _____ hermanos son inteligentes.

15. (The athlete) _____ italiano juega bien.

16. (Yours [formal]) A mi primo le gusta la literatura. _____ también.

17. (This) _____ tienda es muy grande.

18. (Dr. Rueda) _____ es muy simpático.

19. (Math) _____ son fáciles.

20. (Those [far away]) _____ castillos son famosos.

21. (Courage) ____ es una virtud.

22. (Mine) Su libro es interesante. _____ es aburrido.

23. (Friday) ____ es el mejor día de la semana.

24. (their) La clase ____ es grande.

25. (These) ____ edificios son grandes.

Answers and Solutions

1. **Answer: los deportes.**   Use the masculine plural definite article *los* before the noun for "sports" *(deportes)*, which is used in a general sense.

2. **Answer: Aquel.**   The word *país* is masculine singular. Use the masculine singular demonstrative adjective for things that are far from the speaker to express "that": *aquel*.

3. **Answer: La hermana de María.**   Use the definite article *la* to express "the" before the feminine singular noun *hermana*. Use the preposition *de* to express "of" before the name of the possessor, *María*.

4. **Answer: una víctima.**   The noun expressing "victim" is always feminine, regardless of the gender of the person being described. Use the feminine singular indefinite article to express "a" before the noun *víctima*.

5. **Answer: Los rubíes.**   Use the masculine plural definite article *los* before the noun for "rubies," *rubíes*, to express "the." Add *-es* to form the plural of nouns ending in an accented vowel.

6. **Answer: Este.**   The word *jardín* is masculine singular. Use the masculine singular demonstrative adjective for things that are near the speaker to express "this": *este*.

7. **Answer: Los exámenes.**   Use the masculine plural definite article *los* before the noun for "tests" *(exámenes)*, which is used in a general sense. After adding *-es* to the singular form, add an accent to maintain the proper stress.

8. **Answer: lo loco.**   Use the neuter definite article before an adjective that is being used as a noun to express an abstract idea.

9. **Answer: (El) cocinar.**   Using the masculine singular definite article with an infinitive serving as a noun is optional.

10. **Answer: Esto.**   Use the neuter pronoun *esto* to refer to a concept.

11. **Answer: Los melones.** Use the masculine plural definite article *los* before the noun for "melons" *(melones)*, which is used in a general sense. Remove the accent used in the singular *melón* to maintain the proper stress.

12. **Answer: El agua.** The noun *agua* is feminine. The masculine singular article *el* is used with feminine singular nouns beginning with a stressed *a* sound to prevent the clash of sounds.

13. **Answer: Esas.** The word *mujeres* is feminine plural. Use the feminine plural demonstrative adjective for things that are not very far from the speaker to express "that": *esas*.

14. **Answer: Nuestros.** The item possessed ends in *-os* and is, therefore, masculine plural. Use the masculine plural possessive form: *nuestros*.

15. **Answer: El atleta.** Use the masculine word for "athlete" because the masculine singular adjective *italiano* reveals the gender of the person. The noun *atleta* always ends in *-a* regardless of the gender of the person being described.

16. **Answer: Al suyo.** Use the masculine singular possessive pronoun *el suyo* to replace the masculine singular noun *primo* from the previous sentence. Include the preposition *a* (used with the verb *gustar*) in your answer. *A* contracts with the definite article *el* to become *al*.

17. **Answer: Esta.** The word *tienda* is feminine singular. Use the feminine singular demonstrative adjective for things that are near the speaker to express "this": *esta*.

18. **Answer: El doctor Rueda.** Use the masculine singular definite article *el* before the profession (in this case, *doctor*) when referring to the person.

19. **Answer: Las matemáticas.** Use the feminine plural definite article *las* before the noun for "math" *(matemáticas)*, which is used in the plural in a general sense.

20. **Answer: Aquellos.** The word *castillos* is masculine plural. Use the masculine singular demonstrative adjective for things that are far from the speaker to express "that": *aquellos*.

21. **Answer: El coraje** Nouns that end in *-aje* are generally masculine. Use the masculine singular definite article *el* before the noun for "courage" *(coraje)*, which is used in a general sense.

22. **Answer: El mío.** Use the masculine singular possessive pronoun *el mío* to replace the masculine singular noun *libro* from the previous sentence.

23. **Answer: El viernes.** Use the masculine singular definite article *el* with the name of the day of the week.

24. **Answer: suya.** Use the feminine singular possessive adjective long form *suya* after the noun *clase*.

25. **Answer: Estos.** The word *edificios* is masculine plural. Use the masculine plural demonstrative adjective for things that are near the speaker to express "this": *estos*.

Supplemental Chapter Problems

Problems

Give more opinions by filling in the missing words.

1. (Spanish) _____ es fácil.

2. (Peaches) _____ son deliciosas.

3. (This) _____ película es buena.

4. (Vacation) _____ son divertidas.

5. (like an optimista) Él piensa _____.

6. (Monday) _____ es el peor día de la semana.

7. (her) Los amigos _____ son fieles.

8. (That) _____ no es importante.

9. (Mrs. López) _____ es simpática.

10. (mine) Tu comedor es pequeño; _____ es enorme.

11. (That [not very far]) _____ libro es interesante.

12. (Our) _____ problema no es serio.

13. (Those [far away]) _____ coches son muy deportivos.

14. (Julio's brother) _____ es guapo.

15. (Dawn) _____ es bonita.

16. (Health) _____ es importante.

17. (The skyscrapers) _____ son gigantes.

18. (These) _____ vestidos están de moda.

19. (The) _____ programa es divertido.

20. (the capital) Washington D.C., _____ de los Estados Unidos, es una ciudad importante.

21. (The poem) _____ es bello.

22. (Those [not very far]) _____ casas son magníficas.

23. (a person) El señor Cruz es _____ importante.

24. (That [far away]) _____ ciudad es grande.

25. (Yours [informal]) Mi pelo es rubio. _____ es castaño.

Solutions

1. El español (definite and indefinite articles, p. 41)

2. Los melocotones (noun plurals, p. 52)

3. Esta (demonstrative adjectives, p. 47)

4. Las vacaciones (noun plurals, p. 52)

5. a lo optimista (the neuter *lo*, p. 42)

6. El lunes (definite and indefinite articles, p. 41)

7. suyos (possessive adjectives, p. 56)

8. Eso (demonstrative pronouns, p. 48)

9. La señora López (definite and indefinite articles, p. 41)

10. el mío (possessive pronouns, p. 57)

11. Ese (demonstrative adjectives, p. 47)

12. Nuestro (possessive adjectives, p. 56)

13. Aquellos (demonstrative adjectives, p. 47)

14. El hermano de Julio (using *de*, p. 56)

15. El alba (gender of nouns, p. 50)

16. La salud (definite and indefinite articles, p. 41)

17. Los rascacielos (noun plurals, p. 52)

18. Estos (demonstrative adjectives, p. 47)

19. El (gender of nouns, p. 50)

20. capital (definite and indefinite articles, p.41)

21. El poema (gender of nouns, p. 50)

22. Esas (demonstrative adjectives, p. 47)

23. una persona (gender of nouns, p. 50)

24. Aquella (demonstrative adjectives, p. 47)

25. El tuyo (possessive pronouns, p. 57)

Chapter 3
Present Tense and Verbal Distinctions

Regular Verbs

The present tense of regular verbs expresses what the subject does now. The three main families of regular verbs are conjugated as follows:

Subject	-ar Verbs	-er Verbs	-ir Verbs
	cantar (to sing)	*vender* (to sell)	*recibir* (to live)
yo	-o→canto	-o→vendo	-o→recibo
tú	-as→cantas	-es→vendes	-es→recibes
él, ella, Ud.	-a→canta	-e→vende	-e→recibe
nosotros	-amos→cantamos	-emos→vendemos	-imos→recibimos
vosotros	-áis→cantáis	-éis→vendéis	-ís→recibís
ellos, ellas, Uds.	-an→cantan	-en→venden	-en→reciben

Example Problems

Give the correct form of the verb in parentheses to express what people do when they receive an invitation to a party.

1. (leer) Yo _____ la invitación.

    Answer: leo

    To conjugate regular *-er* verbs, drop the *-er* ending and add *-o* as the ending for *yo*.

2. (decidir) Uds. _____ ir a la fiesta.

    Answer: deciden

    To conjugate regular *-ir* verbs, drop the *-ir* ending and add *-en* as the ending for *Uds.*

3. (comprar) Tú le _____ a Silvia un reloj.

Answer: compras

To conjugate regular -ar verbs, drop the -ar ending and add -as the ending for tú.

Work Problems

Use these problems to give yourself additional practice.

Give the correct form of the verb in parentheses to express what takes place at a birthday party.

1. (recibir) Silvia _____ muchos regalos.

2. (leer) Tú _____ las cartas.

3. (insistir) Esteban y yo _____ en ayudar.

4. (tocar) Uds. _____ la guitarra.

5. (abrir) Tú _____ la puerta para los invitados.

6. (comer) Nosotros _____ comida mexicana.

7. (beber) Ernesto _____ un licuado.

8. (bailar) Julia y yo _____.

Worked Solutions

1. **recibe** To conjugate regular -ir verbs, drop the -ir ending and add -e as the ending for Sylvia (ella).

2. **lees** To conjugate regular -er verbs, drop the -er ending and add -es as the ending for tú.

3. **insistimos** To conjugate regular -ir verbs, drop the -ir ending and add -imos as the ending for Esteban y yo (nosotros).

4. **tocan** To conjugate regular -ar verbs, drop the -ar ending and add -an as the ending for Uds.

5. **abres** To conjugate regular -ir verbs, drop the -ir ending and add -en as the ending for tú.

6. **comemos** To conjugate regular -er verbs, drop the -er ending and add -emos as the ending for nosotros.

7. **bebe** To conjugate regular -er verbs, drop the -er ending and add -e as the ending for Ernesto (él).

8. **bailamos** To conjugate regular -ar verbs, drop the -ar ending and add -amos as the ending for Julia y yo (nosotros).

Spelling-Change Verbs

In order to preserve the original sound of certain verbs, a spelling change occurs in the *yo* form of the present tense (and in other tenses in which the final consonant is followed by an *-o* or an *-a*) of the following verbs:

Ending	Change	Verb	Present
vowel + *cer*	c→zc	recono**cer** (to recognize)	yo recono**zc**o
vowel + *cir*	c→zc	tradu**cir** (to translate)	yo tradu**zc**o
consonant + *cer*	c→z	ven**cer** (to conquer)	yo ven**z**o
consonant + *cir*	c→z	espar**cir** (to scatter)	yo espar**z**o
-ger	g→j	prote**ger** (to protect)	yo prote**j**o
-gir	g→j	exi**gir** (to demand)	yo exi**j**o
-guir	gu→g	distin**guir** (to distinguish)	yo distin**g**o

Example Problems

Supply the correct form of the verb in parentheses to complete the personal questions a friend asks you. Then answer each question in the affirmative.

1. (conducir) ¿Tú _____ bien? _____

    Answer: conduces; Yo conduzco bien.

    To conjugate *-cir* verbs, drop the *-ir* ending and do the following: For *tú*, add *-es* as the ending; for *yo*, change the *c* to *zc* and add *-o* as the ending.

2. (proteger) ¿Tú _____ a tus amigos? _____

    Answer: proteges; Yo protejo a mis amigos.

    To conjugate *-ger* verbs, drop the *-er* ending and do the following: For *tú*, add *-es* as the ending; for *yo*, change the *g* to *j* and add *-o* as the ending.

3. (distinguir) ¿Tú _____ entre lo bueno y lo malo? _____

    Answer: distingues; Yo distingo entre lo bueno y lo malo.

    To conjugate *-guir* verbs, drop the *-ir* ending and do the following: For *tú*, add *-es* as the ending; for *yo*, change the *gu* to *g* and add *-o* as the ending.

Work Problems

Use these problems to give yourself additional practice.

Give the correct form of the verb in parentheses to complete the questions and answers a person might hear or give at a job interview.

1. (conocer)

   ¿Ud. _____ bien el trabajo?

   Yo lo _____ bien.

2. (coger)

   ¿Ud. _____ apuntes rápidamente?

   Yo los _____ rápidamente.

3. (merecer)

   ¿Ud. _____ este salario?

   Yo lo _____.

4. (esparcir)

   ¿Ud. _____ sus papeles?

   Yo no los _____.

5. (traducir)

   ¿Ud. _____ con fluidez el español?

   Yo lo _____ con fluidez.

6. (exigir)

   ¿Ud. _____ mucho de Ud. mismo?

   Yo _____ mucho de mí mismo.

Worked Solutions

1. **conoce; conozco**   To conjugate -cer verbs, drop the -er ending. For Ud., add -e as the ending; for yo, change the c to zc (because -cer is preceded by a vowel) and add -o as the ending.

2. **coge; cojo**   To conjugate -ger verbs, drop the -er ending. For Ud., add -e as the ending; for yo, change the g to j and add -o as the ending.

3. **merece; merezco**   To conjugate -cer verbs, drop the -er ending. For Ud., add -e as the ending; for yo, change the c to zc (because -cer is preceded by a vowel) and add -o as the ending.

4. **esparce; esparzo**   To conjugate -cir verbs, drop the -ir ending. For Ud., add -e as the ending; for yo, change the c to z (because -cer is preceded by a consonant) and add -o as the ending.

5. **traduce; traduzco**   To conjugate -cir verbs, drop the -ir ending. For Ud., add -e as the ending; for yo, change the c to zc (because -cir is preceded by a vowel) and add -o as the ending.

6. **exige; exijo** To conjugate *-gir* verbs, drop the *-ir* ending. For *Ud.*, add *-e* as the ending; for *yo*, change the *g* to *j* and add *-o* as the ending.

Stem-Changing Verbs

Certain verbs require an internal change in the *yo, tú, él (ella, Ud.)*, and *ellos (ellas, Uds.)* forms. The *nosotros* and *vosotros* forms are conjugated regularly.

Ending	Stem Change	Verb	Present
-ar	e→ie	comenzar (to begin)	yo comienzo; nosotros comenzamos
-ar	o→ue	mostrar (to show)	yo muestro; nosotros mostramos
	u→ue	jugar (to play)	yo juego; nosotros jugamos
-er	e→ie	entender (to understand)	yo entiendo; nosotros entendemos
-er	o→ue	poder (to be able)	yo puedo; nosotros podemos
-ir	e→ie	preferir (to prefer)	yo prefiero; nosotros preferimos
-ir	o→ue	dormir (to sleep)	yo duermo; nosotros dormimos
-ir	e→i	repetir (to repeat)	yo repito; nosotros repetimos
some -iar	i→í	guiar (to guide)	yo guío; nosotros guiamos
some -uar	u→ú	continuar (to continue)	yo continúo; nosotros continuamos
-uir (not -guir)	add y after u	incluir (to include)	yo incluyo; nosotros incluimos

Note that some verbs (and any compounds of these verbs, such as *conseguir* [to get]) have both spelling and stem changes in the present tense.

Verb	Meaning	Yo	Tú	Él	Nosotros	Vosotros	Ellos
cocer	to cook	cuezo	cueces	cuece	cocemos	cocéis	cuecen
torcer	to twist	tuerzo	tuerces	tuerce	torcemos	torcéis	tuercen
colegir	to collect	colijo	coliges	colige	colegimos	colegís	coligen
corregir	to correct	corrijo	corriges	corrige	corregimos	corregís	corrigen
elegir	to elect	elijo	eliges	elige	elegimos	elegís	eligen
regir	to rule	rijo	riges	rige	regimos	regís	rigen
seguir	to follow	sigo	sigues	sigue	seguimos	seguís	siguen

Example Problems

Give the correct form of the verb in parentheses to express what people do after dinner.

1. (comenzar) Tú _____ tus tareas.

   Answer: comienzas

   Comenzar is conjugated like a regular *-ar* verb. The *e* of *comenzar*, however, changes to *ie* in all forms except *nosotros* and *vosotros*.

2. (preferir) Mi padre _____ escuchar música.

Answer: prefiere

Preferir is conjugated like a regular *-ir* verb. The second *e* of *preferir,* however, changes to *ie* in all forms except *nosotros* and *vosotros.*

3. (querer) Los niños _____ mirar la televisión.

Answer: quieren

Querer is conjugated like a regular *-er* verb. The *e* of *querer,* however, changes to *ie* in all forms except *nosotros* and *vosotros.*

Work Problems

Use these problems to give yourself additional practice.

Give the correct form of the verb in parentheses to express what people do and do not do when a storm breaks out.

1. (poder) Yo no _____ ir de compras.

2. (dormir) Los muchachos _____.

3. (cerrar) La madre _____ todas las ventanas.

4. (advertir) Ella _____ a su amiga que no va a salir.

5. (jugar) Los niños _____ a los naipes.

6. (gemir) Jorge _____.

7. (seguir) María _____ leyendo.

8. (elegir) Nosotros _____ quedarnos en casa.

9. (encontrar) Yo no _____ a mis amigos en el centro.

10. (distribuir) Tú no _____ tus folletos.

11. (continuar) Ellas _____ a trabajar.

12. (enviar) Nosotros _____ mensajes por correo electrónico.

13. (corregir) Yo _____ mis tareas.

14. (querer) Mi padre _____ quedarse en casa.

Worked Solutions

1. **puedo** *Poder* is conjugated like a regular *-er* verb. The *o* of *poder,* however, changes to *ue* in all forms except *nosotros* and *vosotros.*

2. **duermen**   *Dormir* is conjugated like a regular *-ir* verb. The *o* of *dormir*, however, changes to *ue* in all forms except *nosotros* and *vosotros*.

3. **cierra**   *Cerrar* is conjugated like a regular *-ar* verb. The *e* of *cerrar*, however, changes to *ie* in all forms except *nosotros* and *vosotros*.

4. **advierte**   *Advertir* is conjugated like a regular *-ir* verb. The *e* of *advertir*, however, changes to *ie* in all forms except *nosotros* and *vosotros*.

5. **juegan**   *Jugar* is conjugated like a regular *-ar* verb. The *u* of *jugar*, however, changes to *ue* in all forms except *nosotros* and *vosotros*.

6. **gime**   *Gemir* is conjugated like a regular *-ir* verb. The *e* of *gemir*, however, changes to *i* in all forms except *nosotros* and *vosotros*.

7. **sigue**   *Seguir* is conjugated like a *-guir* verb. The *e* of *seguir* changes to *i* in all forms except *nosotros* and *vosotros*.

8. **elegimos**   *Elegir* is conjugated like a regular *-ir* verb in the *nosotros* form.

9. **encuentro**   *Encontrar* is conjugated like a regular *-ar* verb. The *o* of *encontrar*, however, changes to *ue* in all forms except *nosotros* and *vosotros*.

10. **distribuyes**   *Distribuir* is conjugated like a regular *-ir* verb. A *y* is added betweeen the *u* and the ending in all forms except *nosotros* and *vosotros*.

11. **continúan**   *Continuar* is conjugated like a regular *-ar* verb. The *u* of *continuar*, however, changes to *ú* in all forms except *nosotros* and *vosotros*.

12. **enviamos**   *Enviar* is conjugated like a regular *-ar* verb in the *nosotros* form.

13. **corrijo**   *Corregir* is conjugated like a regular *-ir* verb. The *e* of *corregir*, however, changes to *i* in all forms except *nosotros* and *vosotros*. Additionally, *corregir* is a *-gir* spelling-change verb. To conjugate *-gir* verbs, drop the *-ir* ending. For *yo*, change the *g* to *j* and add *-o* as the ending.

14. **quiere**   *Querer* is conjugated like a regular *-er* verb. The *e* of *querer*, however, changes to *ie* in all forms except *nosotros* and *vosotros*.

Irregular Verbs

Some verbs are irregular only in the *yo* form of the present tense:

caber	to fit	quepo
caer	to fall	caigo
dar	to give	doy
hacer	to make, to do	hago
poner	to put	pongo
saber	to know a fact, to know how to	sé
salir	to go out	salgo
traer	to bring	traigo
valer	to be worth	valgo
ver	to see	veo

Some verbs are irregular in all forms except *nosotros* and *vosotros*:

Verb	Meaning	Yo	Tú	Él	Nosotros	Vosotros	Ellos
decir	to tell	digo	dices	dice	decimos	decís	dicen
estar	to be	estoy	estás	está	estamos	estáis	están
oler	to smell	huelo	hueles	huele	olemos	oléis	huelen
tener	to have	tengo	tienes	tiene	tenemos	tenéis	tienen
venir	to come	vengo	vienes	viene	venimos	venís	vienen

Some verbs are irregular in many or all forms:

Verb	Meaning	Yo	Tú	Él	Nosotros	Vosotros	Ellos
haber	to have	he	has	ha	hemos	habéis	han
ir	to go	voy	vas	va	vamos	vais	van
oír	to hear	oigo	oyes	oye	oímos	oís	oyen
reír	to laugh	río	ríes	ríe	reímos	reís	rien
ser	to be	soy	eres	es	somos	sois	son

Some irregular verbs are used impersonally in the third person singular form only:

llover (o→ue; to rain):	llueve
nevar (e→ie; to snow):	nieva
helar (e→ie; to freeze):	hiela
tronar (o→ue; to thunder):	truena
relampaguear (to flash):	relampaguea
granizar (to hail):	graniza

For example:

Llueve mucho en la primavera.   It rains a lot in the spring.

Example Problems

Express what you do in each situation by selecting the appropriate reaction and conjugating the verb.

decir "buenos días" a mi familia   reír   hacer la cama

1. Tengo que arreglar mi cuarto.

   Answer: Hago la cama.

   When you have to straighten your room, you make the bed: *hacer la cama*. The verb *hacer* (to make, to do) is irregular only in the *yo* form and has a *-go* ending: *hago*. All other forms use the *e* from the infinitive ending.

2. Regreso a casa.

Answer: Digo "buenos días" a mi familia.

When you return home, you say hello to your family: *decir buenos días a mi familia*. The verb *decir* (to tell, to say) is irregular only in the *yo* form and has a -*go* ending: *digo*.

3. Yo miro un programa cómico.

Answer: Río.

When you watch a funny show, you laugh: *reír*. The verb *reír* (to laugh) drops the *e* from the stem in all forms except *nosotros* and *vosotros*. The *i* is accented in all forms: *í*. The ending for *yo* is -*o*.

Work Problems

Use these problems to give yourself additional practice.

Select the appropriate reaction from the following list and conjugate the verb to express what you do or what happens in each situation.

> no caber en el coche
> dar de comer al perro
> ir al banco
> oír el pronóstico
> poner la mesa
> salir aprisa de la casa
> tener que ir al supermercado
> traer un postre
> venir a su ayuda
> no ver bien

1. Necesito dinero.

2. Mi perro tiene hambre.

3. Pienso ir al mar mañana.

4. Necesito huevos.

5. Mi padre prepara la cena y tengo que ayudarlo.

6. Voy a cenar en casa de mi amigo.

7. Mi amigo tiene un problema.

8. Quiero leer el horario de trenes pero no tengo mis espejuelos.

9. No quiero faltar a mi cita con Gloria.

10. Prefiero ir a la escuela en coche y ya hay seis personas en él.

Worked Solutions

1. **Voy al banco.**   When you need money, you go to the bank. The verb *ir* (to go) is irregular in all forms and must be memorized. The *yo* form ends in *-oy*.

2. **Doy de comer al perro.**   When your dog is hungry, you feed him. The verb *dar* (to give) is irregular in the *yo* form and ends in *-oy*.

3. **Oigo el pronóstico.**   When you want to go to the sea, you listen to the weather. The verb *oír* (to hear) is irregular in all forms and must be memorized. The *yo* form has a *-go* ending: *oigo* (with an unaccented *i*).

4. **Tengo que ir al supermercado.**   When you need eggs, you go to the supermarket. The verb *tener* (to have) is irregular in the *yo* form and has a *-go* ending: *tengo*.

5. **Pongo la mesa.**   When your father is preparing dinner and you have to help him, you set the table. The verb *poner* (to put) is irregular in the *yo* form and has a *-go* ending: *pongo*.

6. **Traigo un postre.**   When you go to eat at a friend's house, you bring a dessert. The verb *traer* (to bring) is irregular in the *yo* form and has a *-go* ending: *traigo*.

7. **Vengo a su ayuda.**   When you your friend has a problem you come to his aid. The verb *venir* (to come) is irregular in the *yo* form and has a *-go* ending: *vengo*.

8. **No veo bien.**   When you want to read the train schedule but you don't have your glasses, you don't see well. The verb *ver* (to see) is irregular only in the *yo* form. The *e* from the infinitive is retained: *veo*.

9. **Salgo aprisa de la casa.**   When you don't want to miss your appointment with Gloria, you leave your house quickly. The verb *salir* (to go out) is irregular only in the *yo* form and has a *-go* ending: *salgo*.

10. **No quepo en el coche.**   When you prefer to go to school by car and there are already six people inside it, you don't fit into the car. The verb *caber* (to fit) is irregular only in the *yo* form: *quepo*.

Using the Present Tense

Use the present tense to indicate an action in progress:

> Ellos van al cine.   They are going to the movies.

Use the present tense to show a habit or custom:

> Elena lee mucho.   Elena reads a lot.

Use the present tense to ask for instructions or to discuss an action that will take place in the immediate future:

> ¿Lo hago ahora?   Shall I do it now?
> Vienen pronto.   They are coming soon.

The present tense is used idiomatically:

❏ With the verb *soler* (*o*→*ue*) to show what the subject is accustomed to doing:

Ella suele dormir hasta muy tarde. She is accustomed to sleeping until very late.

❏ With the verb *hacer* to indicate that an action started in the past and is continuing into the present:

Hace un año que aprendo el español. I've been learning Spanish for a year.

❏ With the verb *haber* to express "there is," "there are," "is there?," and "are there?":

¿Cuántos alumnos hay en la clase? How many students are in the class?

Hay solamente veinte. There are only 20.

❏ With the verb *haber* + *que* in impersonal expressions and with *haber* + *de* to show obligation:

Hay que estudiar para salir bien. You have to study to succeed.

He de ir al supermercardo. I have to go to the supermarket.

Example Problems

Express your thoughts in Spanish.

1. I am accustomed to eating early.

    Answer: Suelo comer temprano.

    Use the verb *soler* to express that you are accustomed to doing something. *Soler* is a stem-changing -*er* verb. Change the internal *o* to *ue*. Drop the -*er* ending and add -*o* for *yo*. Because *soler* is conjugated, it is followed by the infinitive expressing "to eat" *(comer)*. *Temprano* expresses "early."

2. I've been reading for an hour.

    Answer: Hace una hora que leo.

    Use the expression *hacer* to indicate that an action started in the past and is continuing into the present. Conjugate *hacer* in the third person singular: *hace*. *Una hora* expresses "an hour." Use *que* to express "that." Use the verb *leer* to express "to read." *Leer* is a regular -*er* verb. Drop the -*er* ending and add -*o* for *yo*.

3. You have to play well to win.

    Answer: Hay que jugar bien para ganar.

    Use the form of *haber* + *que* to express that you "have to" do something: *hay que*. Use an infinitive after the conjugated verb form. *Jugar* expresses "to play." *Bien* expresses "well." *Para* expresses "in order to." *Ganar* expresses "to win."

Work Problems

Use these problems to give yourself additional practice.

Express your thoughts about work.

1. There are three people who arrive late.

2. Elena has been working for six hours.

3. Those men have to travel to Spain.

4. Roberto is accustomed to speaking on the phone.

5. You have to work hard to earn a lot of money.

6. How many Spanish-speaking people are there?

Worked Solutions

1. **Hay tres personas que llegan tarde.**　　Use *hay* to express "there are." *Tres personas* expresses "three people." *Que* expresses "that." Use the *ellos* form of the verb *llegar* (to arrive) by dropping the *-ar* ending and adding *-an. Tarde* expresses "late."

2. **Hace seis horas que Elena trabaja.**　　Use the expression *hacer* to indicate that an action started in the past and is continuing into the present. Conjugate *hacer* in the third person singular: *hace. Seis horas* expresses "six hours." Use *que* to express "that." Use the verb *trabajar* to express "to work." *Trabajar* is a regular *-ar* verb. Drop the *-ar* ending and add *-a* for *Elena*.

3. **Esos hombres han de ir a España.**　　Use *esos* to express "those" before the masculine plural noun for men: *hombres.* Use the expression *haber de* to indicate an obligation. *Haber* is an irregular verb and must be memorized. Use the third person plural form: *han.* Use an infinitive after the conjugated verb form. *Ir* expresses "to go." *A España* expresses "to Spain."

4. **Roberto suele hablar por teléfono.**　　Use the verb *soler* to express that Robert is accustomed to doing something. *Soler* is a stem-changing *-er* verb. Change the internal *o* to *ue.* Drop the *-er* ending and add *-e* for *Roberto.* Because *soler* is conjugated, it is followed by the infinitive expressing "to speak" *(hablar). Por teléfono* expresses "on the phone."

5. **Hay que trabajar duro para ganar mucho dinero.**　　Use the expression *haber que* to indicate that you "have to" do something: *hay que.* Use an infinitive after the conjugated verb form. *Trabajar* expresses "to work." *Duro* expresses "hard." *Para* expresses "in order to." *Ganar la vida* expresses "to earn." *Mucho* expresses "a lot of." *Dinero* expresses "money."

6. **¿Cuántas personas de habla española hay?**　　The feminine plural interrogative adjective *¿cuántas?* asks "how many?" before the feminine plural noun for people: *personas. De habla española* expresses "Spanish-speaking." Use *hay* to ask "are there?"

Verbal Distinctions

Some English verbs with different meanings and/or connotations are expressed by only one verb infinitive. In Spanish, however, these very same verbs are expressed by more than one infinitive, depending upon the intended meaning of the speaker. It is essential, therefore, to understand how to correctly select the Spanish verb that best conveys the meaning you are trying to impart.

Ser and Estar and Other Distinctions

Both *ser* and *estar* mean "to be." Use the following rules to help distinguish between these two verbs.

Use *ser:*

- To express origin and nationality.
- To express ownership.
- To describe or identify the subject.
- To express the time and date.
- To express destination.

- To show material.
- In impersonal expressions.
- In general with the adjectives *pobre* (poor), *rico* (rich), *joven* (young), *viejo* (old), and *feliz* (happy).
- In passive constructions.

Use *estar:*

- To express health.
- To show a temporary condition.
- To indicate location.

- When something is the result of a past action.
- In progressive tenses.

Conocer means "to know" in the sense of being acquainted with a person, place, or thing. *Saber* means "to know a fact" or, when followed by an infinitive, "to know how to do something":

Yo sé que Enrique conoce a su hermana.   I know that Enrique knows your sister.

Deber generally expresses a moral obligation, and *tener que* is used to express something that the subject has to do:

Tengo que telefonear a mis padres porque debo pedirles permiso antes de salir.
I have to call my parents because I must ask their permission before going out.

Dejar means "to leave something behind," and *salir* means "to leave a place":

Cuando él sale de su casa siempre deja algo importante en la mesa.
When he leaves his house, he always leaves something important on the table.

Use *gastar* when you are spending money and *pasar* when you are spending time:

Gasto mucho dinero cuando paso mucho tiempo en mi tienda favorita.
I spend a lot of money when I spend a lot of time in my favorite store.

Use *jugar* + *a* to express that the subject is playing a sport or game and *tocar* when the subject is playing a musical instrument:

Ella juega al tenis después de tocar el piano.   She plays tennis after playing the piano.

Llevar (to take) is used when the item or person can be carried or transported in one's hands or when someone is being led to a place. *Tomar* (to take) is used when something is picked up and can be held in one's hands:

Tomo el libro y lo llevo a mi clase.   I take the book and I bring it to my class.

Pedir (to ask) means "to request" or "to ask for something" and *preguntar* (to ask) means "to ask a question" or "to inquire about something or someone":

Ella me pregunta por qué yo pido la cuenta.   She asks me why I ask for the bill.

Poder (can) shows that the subject possesses the ability to perform an action, and *saber* (can) shows that the subject actually knows how to perform the action:

Yo sé bailar la rumba y yo puedo hacerlo ahora si tú quieres.
I can dance the rumba and I can do it now if you want.

Volver means "to return" or "to come back." *Devolver* means "to return" or "to give something back to its owner":

Siempre te devuelvo tu dinero cuando vuelvo a casa.
I always return your money when I return home.

Example Problems

Complete each sentence to talk about people. Make sure to use the correct verb according to its connotation.

1. (estar/ser) _____ evidente que él _____ ahora en Chile.

    Answer: Es; está

    Ser is used in impersonal expressions, while *estar* expresses a location. The third person singular of *ser* is irregular and must be memorized. The third person singular form of *estar* is also irregular and must be memorized.

2. (poder/saber) Nosotros _____ cocinar pero no _____ preparar la comida ahora.

    Answer: sabemos; podemos

    Saber expresses what the subject knows or doesn't know how to do. Use the *nosotros* form of *saber*, which is regular. *Poder* expresses what the subject is able to (can) do and is also regular in the *nosotros* form.

3. (dejar/salir) Siempre _____ la llave de contacto puesta cuando yo _____ de mi coche.

    Answer: dejo; salgo

    Dejar means "to leave something behind" while *salir* means "to leave a place." *Dejar* is a regular -*ar* verb. Drop the -*ar* ending and add the -*o* ending for *yo*. The *yo* form of *salir* is irregular and must be memorized.

Work Problems

Use these problems to give yourself additional practice.

Complete each sentence, making sure to use the correct verb according to its connotation.

1. (estar/ser)

   _____ claro que ellos _____ ausentes hoy.

2. (devolver/volver)

   Cuando tú _____, nosotros te _____ tu libro.

3. (llevar/tomar)

   Ella _____ las llaves y ella las _____ a la oficina.

4. (pedir/preguntar)

   Yo le _____ por qué él siempre _____ permiso para salir.

5. (conocer/saber)

   Yo _____ que ella _____ a mi hermano.

6. (jugar/tocar)

   Él _____ al fútbol y él _____ el piano también.

Worked Solutions

1. **Es; están**   *Ser* is used in impersonal expressions, while *estar* expresses a temporary condition. The third person singular of *ser* is irregular and must be memorized. The third person plural form of *estar* is also irregular and must be memorized.

2. **vuelves; devolvemos**   *Volver* means "to come back," while *devolver* means "to give something back to its owner." The *tú* form changes the internal *o* to *ue*. Drop the *-er* ending and add the *-es* ending for *tú*. There is no internal change for the *nosotros* form of *devolver*. Drop the *-er* ending and add *-emos*.

3. **toma; lleva**   *Tomar* is used when something is picked up and held, while *llevar* is used when the item can be carried.. Both are regular *-ar* verbs. Drop the *-ar* ending and add the *-a* ending for *ella*.

4. **pregunto; pide**   *Preguntar* means "to inquire about something," while *pedir* means "to request something." *Preguntar* is a regular *-ar* verb. Drop the *-ar* ending and add the *-o* ending for *yo*. *Pedir* changes the internal *e* to *i* in all forms except *nosotros* and *vosotros*. Add *-e* for the third person singular ending.

5. **sé; conoce**   *Saber* means "to know a fact," while *conocer* means "to be acquainted with." The *yo* form of *saber* verbs is irregular and must be memorized. The third person singular form of *conocer* is regular. Drop the *-er* ending and add *-e*.

6. **juega; toca**   *Jugar* means "to play a game or sport," while *tocar* means "to play an instrument." The *él* form of *jugar* has a stem change: The internal *u* changes to *ue*. Drop the *-ar* ending and add the *-a* ending for *él*. *Tocar* is a regular *-ar* verb. Drop the *-ar* ending and add the *-a* ending for *él*.

Ser and Estar—Exceptions to the Rule

Ser is generally used to express permanent or inherent qualities of the subject, while *estar* expresses temporary conditions or states. Note the exceptions to the rule, which depend on the meaning of the speaker:

La muchacha es alta. The girl is tall. (Her height is an inherent characteristic.)
La muchacha está alta. The girl is tall. (She is tall for her age.)

La nieve es blanca. Snow is white. (Its color is an inherent characteristic.)
La nieve ya está sucia. The snow is already dirty. (Because it snowed yesterday, the snow has become dirty.)

Las manzanas son rojas. The apples are red. (That is their color.)
La fruta está verde todavía. The fruit is still green. (That's not its normal color; it just hasn't ripened yet.)

Some adjectives change their meaning depending on whether they are used with *ser* or *estar*. For example:

La carne está fresca.		The meat is fresh.
Juan está fresco con su traje nuevo.		Juan looks dapper in his new suit.
El hermano de Juan es fresco.		Juan's brother is fresh (rude).

Ser	Meaning	Estar	Meaning
borracho	to be an alcoholic	borracho	to be drunk
fresco	to be fresh (nasty, forward)	fresco	to be fresh (new), to be cool
listo	to be intelligent	listo	to be ready
loco	to be insane	loco	to be crazy for the moment
malo	to be a bad person	malo	to be a sick (ill) person
nervioso	to be a nervous individual	nervioso	to be nervous for the moment
verde	to be green	verde	to be unripe
vivo	to be astute	vivo	to be alive

Example Problems

Give your opinions by using the correct form of *ser* or *estar*.

1. Ese señor no murió en el accidente. _____ vivo.

    Answer: Está

If the man didn't die in the accident, he is still alive. Use the third person singular of the verb *estar*.

2. Ellas _____ locas de alegría.

   Answer: están

   If they are crazy with happiness, this is a momentary state. Use the third person plural of the verb *estar*.

3. Esos hombres _____ malos individuos.

   Answer: son

   The men are bad individuals. Use the third person plural of the verb *ser*.

Work Problems

Use these problems to give yourself additional practice.

Express facts by using the correct form of *ser* or *estar*.

1. Tengo un resfriado. _____ malo.

2. La Tierra _____ redondo.

3. Él bebe doce botellas de vino cada día. Él _____ borracho.

4. Alma tiene un examen hoy. Por eso ella _____ nerviosa.

5. Quiero salir. ¿_____ Uds. listos?

6. El tiempo es muy agradable. _____ fresco.

Worked Solutions

1. **Estoy**   If you have a cold, you are sick. Use the first person singular of the verb *estar*.

2. **es**   The earth is round. Use the third person singular of the verb *ser*.

3. **es**   If he drinks 12 bottles of wine every day, he is an alcoholic. Use the third person singular of the verb *ser*.

4. **está**   She is temporarily nervous because she has an exam. Use the third person singular of the verb *estar*.

5. **Están**   The person wants to leave and asks the others if they are ready. Use the third person plural of the verb *estar*.

6. **Está**   You are speaking about the weather and saying that it is cool. Use the third person singular of the verb *estar*.

Common Verbal Expressions

The irregular verbs *dar* (to give), *hacer* (to make, to do) and *tener* (to have), as well as a few other irregular verbs are commonly used in everyday Spanish expressions. Verbs ending in -*se* are reflexive and will be discussed in Chapter 17.

High-frequency verbal expressions with *dar* include the following:

Expression	Meaning	Expression	Meaning
dar un abrazo (a)	to hug, to embrace	dar recuerdos (a)	to give regards (to)
dar celos a	to make jealous	dar una vuelta	to take a stroll
dar las gracias (a)	to thank	darse cuenta de	to realize
dar gritos	to shout	darse prisa	to hurry
dar un paseo	to take a walk		

For example:

Dame un abrazo.	Give me a hug.
¿Por qué das gritos?	Why are you shouting?

High-frequency verbal expressions with *hacer* include the following:

Expression	Meaning	Expression	Meaning
hacer mucho (poco)	a long (short) while ago	hacer una pregunta	to ask a question
hacer buen (mal) tiempo	to be nice (bad) weather	hacer una visita	to pay a visit
hacer frío (calor)	to be cold (hot) weather	hacer un viaje	to take a trip
hacerse como si	to act as if	hacer viento	to be windy
hacer el tonto	to act foolishly	hacer pedazos	to break into pieces

For example:

Su hermano siempre se hace el tonto.	Your brother always acts foolishly.
Quisiera hacerle una pregunta.	I'd like to ask you a question.

High-frequency verbal expressions with *tener* include the following:

Expression	Meaning	Expression	Meaning
tener calor (frío)	to be warm (cold)	tener lugar	to take place
tener celos de	to be jealous of	tener miedo de	to be afraid of
tener cuidado	to be careful	tener prisa	to be in a hurry
tener dolor de . . .	to have a . . . ache	tener razón	to be right
tener éxito	to succeed	tener sueño	to be sleepy
tener ganas de	to feel like	tener suerte	to be lucky
tener hambre (sed)	to be hungry (thirsty)	tener vergüenza (de) + infinitive	to be ashamed (of)
tener la culpa (de)	to be to blame (for something)		

For example:

Tengo ganas de ir al cine.	I feel like going to the movies.
La fiesta va a tener lugar el sábado.	The party is going to take place Saturday.

Other common expressions include the following:

Expression	Meaning	Expression	Meaning
dejar caer	to drop	pensar + infinitive	to intend
echar al correo	to mail	perder de vista	to lose sight of
guardar cama	to stay in bed	prestar atención	to pay attention
llegar a ser	to become	querer decir	to mean
oír decir que	to hear that	valer la pena	to be worth the effort
oír hablar de	to hear about	volverse + adjective	to become

For example:

Vale la pena trabajar duro.	It's worth the effort to work hard.
¿Qué quiere decir esta palabra?	What does this word mean?

Example Problems

Express your thoughts in Spanish.

1. I stroll in the park.

   Answer: Doy un paseo por el parque.

   The expression *dar un paseo* means "to take a stroll." The verb *dar* (to give) is irregular only in the *yo* form. As with a few other irregular verbs, the *yo* form ends in *-oy*.

2. It's windy.

   Answer: Hace viento.

   The expression *hacer viento* means "to be windy." Use the third person singular form of the verb to express "it is."

3. I have a headache.

   Answer: Tengo un dolor de cabeza.

   The expression *tener un dolor de . . .* means "to have a . . . ache." The word *cabeza* expresses "head." The verb *tener* (to have) is irregular in the *yo* form and has a *-go* ending: *tengo*.

Work Problems

Use these problems to give yourself additional practice.

Express your thoughts in Spanish.

1. I'm afraid of dogs.

2. They intend to learn Spanish.

3. She hugs her friend.

4. I'm taking a trip to Buenos Aires.

5. He pays attention in class.

6. It's worth the effort to work hard.

Worked Solutions

1. **Tengo miedo de los perros.**   The expression *tener miedo de* means "to be afraid of." The verb *tener* (to have) is irregular in the *yo* form and has a *-go* ending: *tengo*. The word *los perros* expresses "dogs." To speak about dogs in a general sense, use the masculine plural definite article *los*.

2. **Piensan aprender el español.**   The expression *pensar* + infinitive means "to intend to." The verb *aprender* expresses "to learn." The word *el español* expresses "Spanish."

3. **Ella da un abrazo a su amigo(-a).**   The expression *dar un abrazo a* means "to hug." The possessive adjective *su* expresses "her" before the masculine or feminine singular noun, *amigo (-a)*.

4. **Hago un viaje a Buenos Aires.**   The expression *hacer un viaje* means "to take a trip." The verb *hacer* (to make) is irregular only in the *yo* form and has a *-go* ending: *hago*. Use the preposition *a* to express "to."

5. **Presta atención en clase.**   The expression *prestar atención* means "to pay attention." The verb *prestar* is regular. Drop the *-ar* ending and add the third person singular ending: *-a*.

6. **Vale la pena trabajar duro.**   The expression *valer la pena* means "to be worth the effort." Conjugate *valer* in the third person singular form to express "it is." *Valer la pena* is followed by the infinitive of the verb expressing "to work" (*trabajar*).

Verbal Idioms

Idioms are words or expressions whose meaning cannot be readily understood through translation or a grammatical explanation. Some common Spanish idioms include the following:

Idiom	Meaning
aburrirse como una ostra	to be bored stiff
acostarse con las gallinas	to go to bed early
ahogarse en un vaso de agua	to make a mountain out of a molehill
amargar la vida a (alguien)	to make someone's life miserable
andarse con chiquitas	to beat around the bush
buscarle cinco patas al gato	to complicate matters
cantar las cuarenta a (alguien)	to give someone a piece of one's mind
coger el toro por los cuernos	to take the bull by the horns

comer como un cerdo	to eat like a pig
crecer como la espuma	to mushroom
crispar los nervios a (alguien)	to get on someone's nerves
decir . . . con la boca chica	to say something without really meaning it
decir cuatro cosas a (alguien)	to give someone a piece of one's mind
distinguir lo blanco de lo negro	to distinguish right from wrong
echar un cable (capote) a (alguien)	to give someone a helping hand
empezar de cero	to start from scratch
enseñar el cobre	to show one's true colors
estar bobo (-a) con . . . (alguien)	to be crazy about something/someone
estar colado (-a) por (alguien)	to be madly in love with
estar como pez en el agua	to feel completely at home
estar en el ajo	to be in on the secret
estar hasta el gorro	to be fed up
estar verde de envidia	to be green with envy
examinar . . . con lupa	to go over something with a fine-toothed comb
hacer algo en las barbas de alguien	to do something right under someone's nose
ir al grano	to get to the point
leer entre líneas	to read between the lines
leer la cartilla a (alguien)	to tell someone off
llorar a moco tendido	to cry one's eyes out
llover a cántaros	to rain cats and dogs
matar dos pájaros de un tiro	to kill two birds with one stone
pagar a (alguien) con la misma moneda	to give someone a taste of his own medicine
partir el corazón a (alguien)	to break someone's heart
pasar la noche en blanco	to have a sleepless night
perder los estribos	to lose one's temper
poner las cartas sobre la mesa	to put one's cards on the table
saber . . . a ciencia cierta	to know something for sure
sacar a (alguien) de quicio	to drive someone up the wall
soltarse la melena	to let one's hair down
tener carta blanca	to have a free hand
tener un hambre de lobo	to be extremely hungry
tirar la toalla	to throw in the towel
tocar fondo	to hit rock bottom
trabajar como un burro	to work like a dog
valer su peso en oro	to be worth one's weight in gold
vivir a todo tren	to live in style

For example:

Tengo que empezar de cero.	I have to start from scratch.
Ellos viven a todo tren.	They live in style.

Example Problems

Express your feelings by using the correct idiomatic expression from the following list.

estar verde de envidia

perder los estribos

vivir a todo tren

1. Yo gasto todo el dinero que gano. Es decir, yo _____.

   Answer: vivo a todo tren

   If you spend all the money you earn, you live in the fast lane. *Vivir* is a regular *-ir* verb. Drop the *-ir* ending and add *-o* for the *yo* form.

2. Yo estoy muy furioso. Es decir, yo _____.

   Answer: pierdo los estribos

   If you are very angry, you lose your temper. *Perder* is conjugated like a regular *-er* verb. The *e* of *perder*, however, changes to *ie* in all forms except *nosotros* and *vosotros*.

3. Yo tengo celos de mi amigo. Es decir, yo _____.

   Answer: estoy verde de envidia

   If you are jealous of your friend, you are green with envy. The verb *estar* (to be) is irregular in all forms except *nosotros* and *vosotros*. The *yo* form ends in *-oy*.

Work Problems

Use these problems to give yourself additional practice.

Express your feelings by using the correct idiomatic expression from the list below.

comer como un cerdo   pasar la noche en blanco

estar colada por él   tener un hambre de lobo

matar dos pájaros de un tiro   tirar la toalla

1. No puedo hacer más y estoy muy agotado. Es decir, yo _____.

2. Tengo mucha hambre. Es decir, yo _____.

3. No puedo dormir. Es decir, yo _____.

4. Quiero muchísimo a mi novio. Es decir, yo _____.

5. Yo como demasiado. Es decir, yo _____.

6. Trabajo y hablo por teléfono al mismo tiempo. Es decir, yo _____.

Worked Solutions

1. **tiro la toalla**   If you can't continue and are exhausted, you throw in the towel. *Tirar* is a regular *-ar* verb. Drop the *-ar* ending and add *-o* for the *yo* form.

2. **tengo un hambre de lobo**   If you are very hungry, you are as hungry as as a wolf. The verb *tener* (to have) is irregular in the *yo* form and has a *-go* ending: *tengo*.

3. **paso la noche en blanco**   If you can't sleep, you have a sleepless night. *Pasar* is a regular *-ar* verb. Drop the *-ar* ending and add *-o* for the *yo* form.

4. **estoy colada por él**   If you love your boyfriend very much, you are madly in love with him. The verb *estar* (to be) is irregular in all forms except *nosotros* and *vosotros*. The *yo* form ends in *-oy*.

5. **como como un cerdo**   If you eat too much, you eat like a pig. *Comer* is a regular *-er* verb. Drop the *-er* ending and add *-o* for the *yo* form.

6. **mato dos pájaros de un tiro**   If you can work and speak on the phone at the same time, you can kill two birds with one stone. *Matar* is a regular *-ar* verb. Drop the *-ar* ending and add *-o* for the *yo* form.

Chapter Problems

Problems

Complete the story about this person's favorite restaurant by supplying the correct form of the verb in parentheses.

Cuando yo (tener) _____ mucha hambre siempre (ir) _____ a mi restaurante favorito:
             1   2

Los Mariscos. Yo (elegir) _____ este restaurante porque el cocinero, Jaime, (cocer) _____
                        3   4

muy bien. Ud. no (poder) _____ comer en un lugar mejor. Yo (saber) _____ que Jaime
                       5   6

(seguir) _____ las recetas más famosas del mundo. Él nunca (sustituir) _____
        7   8

ingredientes inferiores. Yo (poner) _____ a Jaime contento porque yo siempre le (decir)
                                   9

_____ que todo (oler) _____ bien y que todos sus platos (ser) _____ deliciosos.
   10   11   12

Algunas veces yo le (dar) _____ un abrazo. Cada día Jaime (servir) _____ especialidades
                        13   14

diferentes. Yo siempre (querer) _____ comer pescado porque yo lo (preferir) _____ a la
                               15   16

carne. Yo (soler) _____ comer pescado o mariscos por lo menos cuatro veces a la
                 17

semana. Yo (pensar) _____ que ellos (ser) _____ buenos para la salud. Después de
                   18   19

comer, cuando yo (pedir) _____ la cuenta, yo siempre (sonreír) _____ porque los platos
                        20   21

no (costar) _____ mucho. Cuando yo (salir) _____ del restaurante yo (estar) _____ muy
           22   23   24

contento. Es seguro que yo (volver) _____ a Los Mariscos mañana.
                                   25

Answers and Solutions

1. **tengo**   *Tener* is irregular in all forms except *nosotros* and *vosotros*. The *yo* form retains the *-e* from the stem and ends in *-go*.

2. **voy**   *Ir* is irregular in all forms (which begin with a *v-*) and must be memorized.

3. **elijo**   *Elegir* is conjugated like a regular *-ir* verb. The *e* of *elegir*, however, changes to *i* in all forms except *nosotros* and *vosotros*. Additionally, *elegir* is a *-gir* spelling-change verb. To conjugate *-gir* verbs, drop the *-ir* ending. For *yo*, change the *g* to *j* and add *-o* as the ending

4. **cuece**   *Cocer* is spelling-change and stem-changing verb. Change the internal *o* to *ue* in all forms except *nosotros* and *vosotros*.

5. **puede**   *Poder* is conjugated like a regular *-er* verb. The *o* of *poder*, however, changes to *ue* in all forms except *nosotros* and *vosotros*. Drop the *-er* ending and add *-e* for the third person singular.

6. **sé**   *Saber* has an irregular *yo* form that must be memorized.

7. **sigue**   *Seguir* is conjugated like a *-guir* verb. The *e* of *seguir* changes to *i* in all forms except *nosotros* and *vosotros*. Drop the *-ir* ending and add *-e* for the third person singular.

8. **sustituye**   *Sustituir* is conjugated like a regular *-ir* verb. A *y* is added after the *u* before the ending in all forms except *nosotros* and *vosotros*. Drop the *-ir* ending and add *-e* for the third person singular.

9. **pongo**   The verb *poner* (to put) is irregular in the *yo* form and has a *-go* ending: *pongo*.

10. **digo**   The verb *decir* (to tell, to say) is irregular only in the *yo* from and has a *-go* ending: *digo*.

11. **huele**   *Oler* is irregular in all forms except *nosotros* and *vosotros*. An *h* is added to the beginning of all other forms, and the *o* changes to *ue*. The third person singular form ends in *-e*.

12. **son**   *Ser* is irregular in all forms and must be memorized.

13. **doy**   The verb *dar* (to give) is irregular in the *yo* form and ends in *-oy*.

14. **sirve**   *Servir* is conjugated like a regular *-ir* verb. The *e* of *servir*, however, changes to *i* in all forms except *nosotros* and *vosotros*. The third person singular ending is *-e*.

15. **quiero**   *Querer* has an internal stem change: The *e* changes to *ie* in all forms except *nosotros* and *vosotros*. Drop the *-er* ending and add *-o* for the *yo* form.

16. **prefiero**   *Preferir* has an internal stem change: The *e* changes to *ie* in all forms except *nosotros* and *vosotros*. Drop the *-ir* ending and add *-o* for the *yo* form.

17. **suelo**   Use the verb *soler* to express that you are accustomed to doing something. *Soler* is a stem-changing *-er* verb. Change the internal *o* to *ue*. Drop the *-er* ending and add *-o* for *yo*.

18. **pienso**   *Pensar* has an internal stem change. The *e* changes to *ie* in all forms except *nosotros* and *vosotros*. Drop the *-ar* ending and add *-o* for the *yo* form.

19. **son**   *Ser* is irregular in all forms and must be memorized.

20. **pido**   *Pedir* changes the internal *e* to *i* in all forms except *nosotros* and *vosotros*. Drop the *-ir* ending and add *-o* for the *yo* form.

21. **sonrío**   The verb *sonreír* (to smile) drops the *e* from the stem in all forms except *nosotros* and *vosotros*. The *i* is accented in all forms: *í*. The ending for *yo* is *-o*.

22. **cuestan**   *Costar* has an internal stem change. The *o* changes to *ue* in all forms except *nosotros* and *vosotros*. Drop the *-ar* ending and add *-an* for the third person plural form.

23. **salgo**   *Salir* has an irregular *yo* form: Drop the *-ir* ending and add *-go*.

24. **estoy**   *Estar* is irregular in all forms and must be memorized. Like several other irregular verbs, the *yo* form ends in *-oy*.

25. **vuelvo**   *Volver* has an internal change from *o* to *ue* in all forms except *nosotros* and *vosotros*. Drop the *-er* ending and add *-o* for the *yo* form.

Supplemental Chapter Problems

Problems
Express what a candidate says about himself by giving the correct form of the verb in parentheses.

1. (escoger) Yo no _____ a mis amigos para posiciones importantes.

2. (saber) Yo _____ dirigir el gobierno.

3. (tener) Yo _____ experiencia.

4. (ser) Yo _____ responsible.

5. (corregir) Yo _____ los errores del pasado.

6. (exigir) Yo _____ mucho de mis empleados.

7. (dar) Yo _____ buenos consejos a todo el mundo.

8. (oír) Yo _____ las quejas de los ciudadanos.

9. (torcer) Yo no _____ la verdad.

10. (ejercer) Yo _____ la profesión de abogado.

11. (perseguir) Yo _____ la verdad.

12. (hacer) Yo _____ lo mejor para todos.

13. (venir) Yo _____ a la ayuda de todos.

14. (distinguir) Yo _____ entre lo bueno y lo malo.

15. (entender) Yo _____ los pensamientos de la gente.

16. (poder) Yo _____ ayudar a todos.

17. (soler) Yo _____ trabajar duro.

18. (servir) Yo _____ al público.

19. (contribuir) Yo _____ a la sociedad.

20. (demostrar) Yo _____ la sensibilidad.

21. (estar) Yo _____ estudiando los problemas sociales.

22. (proteger) Yo _____ a la gente.

23. (querer) Yo _____ ser alcalde otra vez.

24. (pensar) Yo _____ ser el mejor candidato.

25. (contar) Yo _____ con Uds.

Choose the best expression to complete each phrase.

dar un paseo	qué quiere decir
guardar cama	tener celos de
hacer frío	

26. Cuando estoy enfermo yo _____.

27. No comprendo esta frase. ¿_____ esta palabra?

28. Lola es más bonita que su hermana, Gloria. Por eso, Gloria _____ Lola.

29. Hace mucho viento hoy. _____ en la cuidad.

30. Cuando hay sol, yo _____ por el parque.

Complete each sentence with the correct form of the correct verb.

31. (dejar/salir) Yo no _____ mi tarjeta de crédito _____ a casa cuando yo salgo.

32. (estar/ser) _____ la chaqueta de Julio que _____ en la silla.

33. (conocer/saber) Yo no _____ si yo _____ a tu hermana.

34. (llevar/tomar) Nosotros _____ los libros y los _____ a la biblioteca.

35. (jugar/tocar) Elena _____ al golf y _____ la guitarra.

Express what happens during this particular day by completing each sentence with the appropriate phrase.

estar como un pez en el agua
ir al grano
llorar a moco tendido
llover a cántaros
trabajar como un burro

36. Voy a la oficina a las ocho de la mañana y no regreso a casa hasta las ocho de la noche. Yo _____

37. Hay un huracán. Ahora _____

38. Carlos habla mucho pero no dice nada importante. Él nunca _____

39. Marisol es muy triste. Ella _____

40. Voy a casa de mi amigo y me recibe con los brazos abiertos. En su casa, yo _____

Solutions

1. escojo (spelling-change verbs, p. 67)
2. sé (irregular verbs, p. 71)
3. tengo (irregular verbs, p. 71)
4. soy (irregular verbs, p. 71)
5. corrijo (spelling-change verbs, p. 67; stem-changing verbs, p. 69)
6. exijo (spelling-change verbs, p. 67)
7. doy (irregular verbs, p. 71)
8. oigo (irregular verbs, p. 71)
9. tuerzo (spelling-change verbs, p. 67)
10. ejerzo (spelling-change verbs, p. 67)
11. persigo (spelling-change verbs, p. 67; stem-changing verbs, p. 69)
12. hago (irregular verbs, p. 71)
13. vengo (irregular verbs, p. 71)
14. distingo (irregular verbs, p. 71)
15. entiendo (stem-changing verbs, p. 69)
16. puedo (stem-changing verbs, p. 69)
17. suelo (stem-changing verbs, p. 69)

18. sirvo (stem-changing verbs, p. 69)

19. contribuyo (stem-changing verbs, p. 69)

20. demuestro (stem-changing verbs, p. 69)

21. estoy (irregular verbs, p. 71)

22. protejo (spelling-change verbs, p. 67)

23. quiero (stem-changing verbs, p. 69)

24. pienso (stem-changing verbs, p. 69)

25. cuento (stem-changing verbs, p. 69)

26. guardo cama (regular verbs, p. 65; common verbal expression, p. 82)

27. qué quiere decir (common verbal expressions, p. 82)

28. tiene celos de (irregular verbs, p. 71; common verbal expressions, p. 82)

29. hace frío (irregular verbs, p. 71; common verbal expressions, p. 82)

30. doy un paseo (irregular verbs, p. 71; common verbal expressions, p. 82)

31. dejo/salgo (regular verbs, p. 65; irregular verbs, p. 71; ser and estar and other distinctions, p. 80)

32. es/está (irregular verbs, p. 71; ser and estar and other distinctions, p. 80)

33. sé/conozco (irregular verbs, p. 71; ser and estar and other distinctions, p. 80)

34. tomamos/llevamos (regular verbs, p. 65; ser and estar and other distinctions, p. 80)

35. juega/toca (stem-changing verbs, p. 69; regular verbs, p. 65; ser and estar and other distinctions. p. 80)

36. trabajo como un burro (regular verbs, p. 65; verbal idioms, p. 84)

37. llueve a cántaros (stem-changing verbs, p. 69; verbal idioms, p. 84)

38. va al grano (irregular verbs, p. 71; verbal idioms, p. 84)

39. llora a moco tendido (regular verbs, p. 65; verbal idioms, p. 84)

40. estoy como un pez en el agua (irregular verbs, P. 71; verbal idioms, p. 84)

Chapter 4

Interrogation and Exclamations

Yes/No Questions

There are four ways to ask questions that demand a simple yes or no answer:

❏ Use intonation:

¿Ud. quiere ir al parque? Do you want to go to the park?

❏ Use the tag ¿(No es) verdad? (Isn't that so?):

Ud. quiere ir al parque, ¿no es verdad? You want to go to the park, isn't that so?

❏ Use the phrase ¿Está bien? (All right?):

Nosotros queremos ir al parque, ¿está bien? We want to go the park, all right?

❏ Use inversion:

¿Quiere Ud. ir al parque? Do you want to go to the park?

Example Problems

Using all four methods described previously, ask whether your friend, Miguel, is going to the movies.

1. Use intonation.

Answer: ¿Miguel va al cine?

1. Select *ir* to express "to go." Use the irregular third person singular "he" *(él)* form.

2. The preposition *a* express "to."

3. Use the word *cine* to express "movies." Words ending in -*e* tend to be masculine. The masculine singular definite article *el* contracts with *a* to become *al* and expresses "to the."

4. Place an upside-down question mark at the beginning of the sentence and a regular question mark at the end.

2. Use the tag ¿*(no es) verdad?*

   Answer: Miguel va al cine, ¿(no es) verdad?

   1. Follow the steps in Answer 1.

   2. Add the tag ¿*no es verdad?* to the end of the phrase.

3. Use the phrase ¿*Está bien?*

   Answer: Miguel va al cine. ¿Está bien?

   1. Follow the steps in Answer 1.

   2. Add the phrase ¿*Está bien?* after the sentence.

4. Use inversion.

   Answer: ¿Va Miguel al cine?

   1. Conjugate the verb *ir* as stated in Answer 1.

   2. Invert the conjugated form of *ir* and the subject *Miguel*.

   3. Complete the rest of the sentence and add the appropriate punctuation.

Work Problems

Use these problems to give yourself additional practice.

Using all four methods described previously, ask whether your mother can lend some money to your friend.

1. Use intonation.

2. Use the tag ¿*(no es) verdad?*

3. Use the phrase ¿*Está bien?*

4. Use inversion.

Worked Solutions

1. ¿Tú puedes prestar dinero a mi amigo?

   1. Select *poder* to express "to be able to." Because you are speaking to your mother, use the familiar "you" *(tú)* form.

   2. *Poder* is a stem-changing verb. Change the internal *o* to *ue*, then drop the *-er* ending and add the ending for *Ud. (-e)*.

   3. The verb *prestar* expresses "to lend." Because there is only one subject but two verbs, the second verb remains in the infinitive.

4. The preposition *a* expresses "to."

5. Use the possessive adjective *mi* to express "my" before the masculine singular noun *amigo* (friend).

6. Place an upside-down question mark at the beginning of the sentence and a regular question mark at the end.

2. Tú puedes prestar dinero a mi amigo, ¿verdad?

    1. Follow the steps in Answer 1.

    2. Add the tag *¿no es verdad?* to the end of the phrase.

3. Tú puedes prestar dinero a mi amigo. ¿Está bien?

    1. Follow the steps in Answer 1.

    2. Add the phrase *¿Está bien?* after the sentence.

4. ¿Puedes tú prestar dinero a mi amigo?

    1. Conjugate the verb *poder* as stated in Answer 1.

    2. Invert the conjugated form of *poder* and the subject *Tú.*

    3. Complete the rest of the sentence and add the appropriate punctuation.

Information Questions Using Interrogative Adjectives

The invariable interrogative adjective *¿qué?* (what? which?) usually refers to a noun that cannot be counted:

    ¿Qué planes tienes para mañana?   What plans do you have for tomorrow?

¿Cuánto(a)? (how much?) and *¿cuántos (as)?* (how many?) agree in number and gender with the noun that is being modified:

¿Cuánto dinero has tomado prestado?	How much money did you borrow?
¿Cuántos dólares perdiste?	How many dollars did you lose?
¿Cuánta ayuda necesitas?	How much help do you need?
¿Cuántas muchachas has invitado?	How many girls have you invited?

Interrogative adjectives may be preceded by a preposition:

¿De qué profesora hablas?	Which teacher are you talking about?
¿A cuántos estamos?	What is today's date?
¿Para cuántas personas trabajas?	For how many people do you work?

Example Problems

Ask about a friend's trip by completing the question with the correct interrogative adjective.

1. ¿En _____ hotel pasaste tus vacaciones?

   Answer: qué

   The invariable interrogative adjective *¿qué?* (what? which?) refers to a noun that cannot be counted.

2. ¿_____ moneda te quedó?

   Answer: Cuánta

   Words that end in *-a* tend to be feminine. *Moneda,* which means "money" (in coins), is singular. Select the feminine singular interrogative adjective that expresses an amount or quantity.

3. ¿_____ países has visitado?

   Answer: Cuántos

   The word *país* is masculine. *Países,* which has the plural *-es* ending, means "countries." Select the masculine plural interrogative adjective that expresses an amount or quantity.

Work Problems

Ask questions about a person's job by completing the question with the correct interrogative adjective.

¿cuánta?	¿cuántas?	¿cuánto?	¿cuántos?	¿qué?

1. ¿Para _____ sociedad trabaja?

2. ¿_____ empleados hay?

3. ¿_____ experiencia tiene Ud.?

4. ¿_____ tiempo tiene Ud. que trabajar cada día?

5. ¿_____ personas están contratando?

6. ¿_____ responsabilidades tiene Ud.?

Worked Solutions

1. **qué**   Because no amount or quantity is being measured, use the invariable *¿qué?* to express "which?" or "what?"

2. **Cuántos**   Words that end in *-o* end to be masculine. *Empleados,* which has the plural *-s* ending, means "employees." Select the masculine plural interrogative adjective that expresses an amount or quantity.

3. **Cuánta** Words that end in -*a* tend to be feminine. *Experiencia,* which means "experience," is singular. Select the feminine singular interrogative adjective that expresses an amount or quantity.

4. **Cuánto** Words that end in -*o* tend to be masculine. *Tiempo,* which means "time," is singular. Select the masculine singular interrogative adjective that expresses an amount or quantity.

5. **Cuántas** Words that end in -*a* tend to be feminine. *Personas,* which has the plural -*s* ending, means "people." Select the feminine plural interrogative adjective that expresses an amount or quantity.

6. **Cuántas** Words that end in -*dad* tend to be feminine. *Responsabilidades,* which has the plural -*es* ending, means "responsibilities." Select the feminine plural interrogative adjective that expresses an amount or quantity.

Information Questions Using Interrogative Adverbs

Interrogative adverbs are most often used with inversion to form questions:

❑ *¿Cómo?* (how?)

¿Cómo está Ud.? How are you?

❑ *¿Cuándo?* (when?)

¿Cuándo llegó el vuelo? When did the flight arrive?

❑ *¿Dónde?* (where?)

¿Dónde vive Ud.? Where do you live?

❑ *¿Por qué?* (why [for what reason or cause]?)

¿Por qué no vino Ana a la fiesta? Why didn't Ana come to the party?

❑ *¿Para qué? (*why [for what purpose, goal, or aim]?)

¿Para qué usas ese cuchillo? Why are you using that knife?

Some interrogative adverbs can be preceded by prepositions:

¿ Adónde (A dónde) vas?	Where are you going?
¿De dónde es Ud.?	Where are you from?
¿Para cuándo necesitas este papel?	By when do you need this paper?

Example Problems

Complete the questions with interrogative adverb that would give you the answer that is provided.

1. ¿_____ usan Uds. este libro? Para aprender.

   Answer: Para qué

   Use the interrogative adverb ¿qué? to express "what?" Use the preposition *para* to express "for." *Para* is generally used to express purpose.

2. ¿_____ estudian Uds. el español? Porque queremos hablarlo más fluidamente.

   Answer: Por qué

   Use the interrogative adverb ¿por qué? to express "why?"

3. ¿_____ hacen Uds. sus tareas? Con cuidado.

   Answer: Cómo

   Use the interrogative adverb ¿cómo? to express "how?"

Work Problems

Ask about a person's trip using the Ud. form. Substitute the italic phrase with an interrogative adverb to form the question that the problem sentence answers.

1. Va a España *en avión*.

2. Viaja *porque quiere aprender*.

3. Va *a Madrid* a pasar cinco días.

4. Va a regresar *al fin del mes*.

5. Va a pasar un rato *en un hotel lujoso*.

6. Su diccionario sirve *para darle palabras de vocabulario*.

Worked Solutions

1. **¿Cómo va (Ud.) a España?**

   1. The answer tells "how" the person is going to Spain.

   2. Use the interrogative adverb ¿cómo? to express "how?"

   3. Because you are speaking to someone you don't know well, use the formal singular (*Ud.*) form to express "you."

   4. Use the irregular verb *ir* to express "to go." The irregular *Ud.* form is *va*.

   5. Invert the pronoun and verb after the interrogative adverb.

   6. Use *a* to express "to" before the feminine singular word for "Spain" *(España)*.

2. **¿Por qué viaja (Ud.)?**

    1. The answer expresses "because" and tells "why" the person is going to Spain.

    2. Use the interrogative adverb *¿por qué?* to express "why?"

    3. Because you are speaking to someone you don't know well, use the formal singular *(Ud.)* form to express "you."

    4. *Viajar* is a regular verb. Drop the *-ar* ending and add *-a* for the subject *(Ud.)*.

    5. Invert the pronoun and verb after the interrogative adverb.

3. **¿Adónde va (Ud.) a pasar cinco días?**

    1. The answer tells "where" the person is going.

    2. Use the interrogative adverb *¿adónde?* to express "to where?"

    3. Because you are speaking to someone you don't know well, use the formal singular *(Ud.)* form to express "you."

    4. Use the irregular verb *ir* followed by the preposition *a* to express "going to." The irregular *Ud.* form is *va*.

    5. Use the infinitive *pasar* "to spend (time)" after the conjugated form of *ir + a*.

    6. Invert the pronoun and verb after the interrogative adverb.

    7. Use the number *cinco* to express "five" before the word for "days" *(días)*.

4. **¿Cuándo va (Ud.) a regresar?**

    1. The answer tells "when" the person is returning from Spain.

    2. Use the interrogative adverb *¿cuándo?* to express "when."

    3. Because you are speaking to someone you don't know well, use the formal singular form, *Ud.,* to express "you."

    4. Use the irregular verb *ir* followed by the preposition *a* to express "going to." The irregular *Ud.* form is *va*.

    5. Invert the pronoun and verb after the interrogative adverb.

    6. Use the infinitive *regresar* "return" after the conjugated form of *ir + a*.

5. **¿Dónde va (Ud.) a pasar un rato?**

    1. The answer tells "where" the person is going to spend a short time.

    2. Use the interrogative adverb *¿dónde?* to express "where?"

    3. Because you are speaking to someone you don't know well, use the formal singular *(Ud.)* form to express "you."

4. Use the irregular verb *ir* followed by the preposition *a* to express "going to." The irregular *Ud.* form is *va*.

5. Invert the pronoun and verb after the interrogative adverb.

6. Use the infinitive *pasar* "to spend (time)" after the conjugated form of *ir* + *a*.

7. Use the masculine singular definite article *un* to express "a" before the word for "a short time" *(rato)*.

6. **¿Para qué sirve su diccionario?**

1. The answer tells "for what purpose" the person uses his dictionary.

2. Use the interrogative adverb *¿qué?* to express "what?"

3. Use the preposition *para* to express "for." *Para* is generally used to express purpose.

4. *Servir* is a spelling-change *-ir* verb that changes the internal *e* to *i* in all forms except *nosotros* and *vosotros*. Drop the *-ir* ending and add *-e* for the third person singular subject.

5. Use the third person singular possessive adjective *su* to express "your" before the word for "dictionary" *(diccionario)*.

Information Questions Using Interrogative Pronouns

¿Quién(es)? (who? whom?) refers to people and agrees in number only with the noun being replaced:

¿Quiénes te han ayudado?	Who helped you?
¿A quién ayudaste?	Whom did you help?

¿Qué? (what?) refers to things and asks about a definition, description, or explanation. *¿Qué?* is invariable (note that in modern Spanish qué may be used instead of cuál, but cuál may not always be used instead of qué):

¿Qué prefieres hacer?	What do you prefer to do?
¿A qué hora llegaron?	At what time did they arrive?
¿Qué color prefieres?	What color do you prefer?

¿Cuál(es)? (what? which one(s)?) asks about a choice or a selection and is used to distinguish one person or thing from another. *¿Cuál?* agrees in number only with the noun being replaced:

¿Cuáles de ellos deseas?	Which (of them) do you want?
¿Cuál es la fecha?	What is the date?
¿Cuál es su dirección?	What is your address?

¿Cuánto? (how much?) is invariable:

¿Cuánto cuesta esta camisa?	How much does that shirt cost?

¿Cuántos(as)? (how many?) is plural and agrees in gender with the noun being replaced:

¿Cuántos vienen a jugar?   How many are coming to play?

Example Problems

Complete the questions about the concert by selecting the correct interrogative pronoun:

¿cuál?	¿cuáles?	¿cuántas?
¿cuántos?	¿qué?	¿quién?

1. ¿_____ es su cantante favorito?

    Answer: Quién

    A *cantante* is a singer. Use the interrogative pronoun *¿quién?* to ask "who?"

2. ¿_____ personas bailan? ¿Diez?

    Answer: Cuántas

    Diez refers to the number 10. Use the feminine plural interrogative pronoun *¿cuántas?* to ask "how many?" before the feminine plural noun *personas.*

3. ¿_____ tipo de música prefieres?

    Answer: Cuál

    Tipo de música refers to a selection (from many styles of music, select one). Use the interrogative pronoun *¿cuál?* to ask "which?"

Work Problems

You are in a store. Complete the questions with the correct interrogative pronoun:

1. ¿_____ de estos pantalones me van?
    a. Cuáles
    b. Qué
    c. Quiénes
    d. Cuántas

2. ¿_____ estilo es tu favorito?
    a. Cuál
    b. Qué
    c. Quién
    d. Cuánto

3. ¿_____ tengo que pagar por los dos pares?

   a. Cuáles

   b. Qué

   c. Quiénes

   d. Cuánto

4. ¿_____ tengo que pedir ayuda?

   a. Quién

   b. A quién

   c. Qué

   d. Cuánta

5. ¿_____ puede contestar una pregunta?

   a. Quién

   b. De quién

   c. Cuáles

   d. Cuánto

6. ¿_____ camisas necesito?

   a. Cuál

   b. Quiénes

   c. Cuántas

   d. Qué

Worked Solutions

1. **a** Use the plural interrogative pronoun *¿cuáles?* to ask "which ones?" before the masculine plural noun *pantalones*. The question asks: "Which of these pants fit me?"

2. **b** Use the interrogative pronoun *¿qué?* to ask "which" before the word *estilo*, which refers to a thing: "style." The questions asks: "Which (What) is your favorite style?"

3. **d** Use the interrogative pronoun *¿cuánto?* to ask "how much?" The question asks: "How much do I have to pay for the two pairs (of pants)?"

4. **b** Use the interrogative pronoun *¿a quién?* to ask "whom?" The question asks: "Whom do I have to ask for help?" The verb *pedir* (to ask) is followed by the preposition *a* (to) and *a* must, therefore, remain part of the question.

5. **a** Use the interrogative pronoun *¿quién?* to ask "who?" The question asks: "Who can answer a question?"

6. **c** Use the interrogative pronoun *¿cuántas?* to ask "how many?" The question asks: "How many shirts do I need?"

Exclamations

Exclamations are used to express feelings and sentiments.

¡Qué! (what a! how!) is used to express a quality:

  ¡Qué misterioso es! How mysterious it is!
  ¡Qué idea! What an idea!

To make this exclamation more emphatic, use *más* or *tan* after the noun and before the adjective:

  ¡Qué idea tan (más) interesante! What an interesting idea!

¡Qué! can also be followed by *de* to express a number and is the equivalent of *¡cuánto!:*

  ¡Qué de gente camina en el parque! How many people are walking in the park!

¡Cuánto (a)! (how much!) may be used in the masculine or feminine singular form:

  ¡Cuánto dinero ganas! How much money you earn!
  ¡Cuánta gracia tiene! How much grace she has!

¡Cuántos (as)! (how many!) may be used in the masculine or feminine plural form:

  ¡Cuántos libros leyó! How many books he read!
  ¡Cuántas oportunidades perdiste! How many opportunities you missed!

¡Cómo! (how!) expresses means or manner:

  ¡Cómo canta ese hombre! How that man sings!

¡Cuán! (how!) is invariable and is used primarily in a literary sense with adjectives and adverbs:

  ¡Cuán pronto pasa la vida! How quickly life passes!
  ¡Cuán magnífico es el amor! How magnificent love is!

Example Problems

You are visiting an ancient castle. Express the following.

1. What an ancient castle!

  Answer: ¡Qué castillo tan antiguo!

  Use the exclamation *¡qué!* (what a! how!) to express the ancient quality of the castle. The word *castillo* expresses "castle." To make this exclamation more emphatic, use *tan* after the noun and before the adjective. Use the masculine singular adjective *anciano* to express "ancient" before the noun.

2. How many floors it has!

  Answer: ¡Cuántos pisos tiene!

  Use the exclamation *¡cuántos!* to express "how many!" The word *pisos* expresses "floors." Use the third person singular form of the irregular verb *tener* to express "has." *Tener* has an internal stem change from *e* to *ie* in all forms except *nosotros* and *vosotros*.

3. How charming it is!

   Answer: ¡Cómo es encantador!

   Use the exclamation *¡cómo!* (how!) to express means or manner. The word *encantador* expresses "charming." Use the third person singular form of the irregular verb *ser* to express "is."

Work Problems

You are at the ballet. Express the following.

1. ¡(How many) _____ mujeres hay aquí!

2. ¡(How) _____ bailan esas mujeres!

3. ¡(How many) _____ errores hace esa bailarina!

4. ¡(What a) _____ ballet tan bello!

5. ¡(How much) _____ entusiasmo demuestran esos bailarines!

6. ¡(What a) _____ espectáculo!

Worked Solutions

1. **Cuántas** Use the feminine plural exclamation *¡cuántas!* to express "how many!" before the feminine plural noun *mujeres*.

2. **Cómo** Use the exclamation *¡cómo!* (how!) to express means or manner.

3. **Cuántos** Use the exclamation *¡cuántos!* to express "how many!" before the masculine plural noun *errores*.

4. **Qué** Use the exclamation *¡qué!* (what a! how!) to express quality.

5. **Cuánto** Use *¡cuánto!* to express "how much!" before the masculine or feminine singular noun *entusiasmo*.

6. **Qué** Use the exclamation *¡qué!* to express "what a!"

Chapter Problems

Problems

A friend of yours seems to be going out. Ask the following questions.

1. Are you going out?

2. Where are you going?

3. How are you going downtown?

4. At what time are you leaving?

5. What is your cellphone number?

6. When are you returning?

7. What are you looking for?

8. How much money are you going to spend?

9. Do you want to buy something special?

10. With whom are you going?

A friend just bought a new car. Express your opinions.

11. How sporty it is!

12. How many airbags it has!

13. What a fabulous car!

14. How much speed it picks up!

15. How it runs!

Answers and Solutions

1. **Answer: ¿Sales?** Use the verb *salir* to express "to go out." To ask a yes/no question, conjugate the verb. Because you are speaking to a friend, use the informal *tú* form of the verb. Drop the *-ir* ending and add *-es*. Using the subject pronoun is optional.

2. **Answer: ¿Adónde vas?** Use the interrogative adverb *¿adónde?* to express "to where?" Because you are speaking to someone you know well, use the informal singular *(tú)* form to express "you." Use the irregular verb *ir* followed by the preposition *a* to express "going to." The irregular *tú* form is *vas*.

3. **Answer: ¿Cómo vas al centro?** Use the interrogative adverb *¿cómo?* to express "how?" Because you are speaking to someone you know well, use the informal singular *(tú)* form to express "you." Use the irregular verb *ir* to express "to go." The irregular *tú* form is *vas*. The preposition *a* that normally follows *ir* contracts with the masculine singular definite article *el* to become *al* (to the).

4. **Answer: ¿A qué hora sales?** Use the preposition *a* to express "at." Use the interrogative pronoun *¿qué?* (what?) to ask for an explanation. Use the word *hora* to express "hour." The verb *salir* expresses "to leave." Because you are speaking to a friend, use the informal *tú* form of the verb. Drop the *-ir* ending and add *-es*.

5. **Answer: ¿Cuál es el número de tu teléfono celular?** Use the singular interrogative pronoun *¿cuál?* (what?) to distinguish which phone number is needed. Use the third person singular form of the irregular verb *ser* to express "is." The English possessive phrase "cellphone number" has an opposite construction in Spanish: "the number of your cellphone." *El número* expresses "the number." Use the informal singular possessive adjective *tu* to express "your." *Teléfono celular* expresses "cellphone."

6. **Answer: ¿Cuándo regresas?**   Use the interrogative adverb *¿cuándo?* to express "when." Because you are speaking to someone you know well, use the informal singular *(tú)* form to express "you." *Regresar* is a regular *-ar* verb that means "to return." Drop the *-ar* ending and add the *-as* ending for *tú.*

7. **Answer: ¿Qué estás buscando?**   Use the interrogative pronoun *¿qué?* (what?) to ask for an explanation. Because the action is in progress, the present progressive tense is needed. Use the informal form of the irregular verb *estar.* Drop the *-ar* ending and add *-as* for *tú.* Use the verb *buscar* to express "to look for." To form the present participle, drop the *-ar* ending and add *-ando.*

8. **Answer: ¿Cuánto dinero vas a gastar?**   Use the masculine singular interrogative adjective *¿cuánto(a)?* to express "how much?" Use the irregular verb *ir* followed by the preposition *a* to express "going to." The irregular *tú* form is *vas.* Use the infinitive *gastar* (to spend [money]) after the conjugated form of *ir + a.*

9. **Answer: ¿Quieres comprar algo especial?**   Use the verb *querer* to express "to want." The internal *e* of *querer* changes to *ie* in all forms except *nosotros* and *vosotros.* Drop the *-er* ending and add the *-es* ending for *tú.* Because there is only one subject but two verbs, the second verb remains in the infinitive. Use *comprar* to express "to buy." Use the phrase *algo especial* to express "something special."

10. **Answer: ¿Con quién vas?**   Use the preposition *con* to express "with." Use the interrogative pronoun *¿quién?* to refer to one person. Use the irregular verb *ir* to express "to go." The irregular *tú* form is *vas.*

11. **Answer: ¡Qué deportivo es!**   Use the exclamation *¡qué!* (how!) to express quality. The word for car, *coche,* is masculine singular. Use the adjective *deportivo* to express "sporty." Use the third person singular form of the irregular verb *ser* to express "it is."

12. **Answer: ¡Cuántas bolsas de aire tiene!**   Use the feminine plural exclamation *¡cuántas!* to express "how many!" before the feminine plural noun *bolsas de aire* (air bags). The internal *e* of *tener* changes to *ie* in all forms except *nosotros* and *vosotros.* Drop the *-er* ending and add the *-e* ending for the third person singular form to express "it has."

13. **Answer: ¡Qué coche tan fabuloso!**   Use the exclamation *¡qué!* (what a!) to express a quality. To make this exclamation more emphatic, use *tan* after the noun and before the adjective. Use the masculine singular adjective *fabuloso* to express "fabulous" before the noun.

14. **Answer: ¡Cuánta velocidad cobra!**   Use the feminine singular exclamation *¡cuánta!* to express "how much!" before the feminine singular noun *velocidad* (speed). The regular verb *cobrar* expresses "to pick up." Drop the *-ar* ending and add the third person singular *-a* ending to express "it runs."

15. **Answer: ¡Cómo corre!**   Use the exclamation *¡cómo!* (how!) to express means or manner. The regular verb *correr* expresses "to run." Drop the *-er* ending and add the third person singular *-e* ending to express "it runs."

Supplemental Chapter Problems

Problems
Your friend is preparing dinner for guests. Ask the following questions.

1. Whom are you going to invite for dinner?

2. At what time are they coming?

3. Whose birthday is it?

4. What are you serving?

5. What is your favorite appetizer?

6. How will you prepare the meat?

7. Why are you also serving fish?

8. Do you need help?

9. For what do you need that dish?

10. How many desserts are you going to prepare?

Your friend has a young baby. Express your opinions.

11. What a beautiful baby!

12. How many teeth she has!

13. How much hair she has!

14. How she smiles!

15. How adorable she is!

Solutions

1. A quién(es) vas a invitar a cenar? (interrogative pronouns, p. 100)

2. ¿A qué hora vienen? (interrogative pronouns, p. 100)

3. ¿De quién es el cumpleaños? (interrogative pronouns, p. 100)

4. ¿Qué sirves? (interrogative pronouns, p. 100)

5. ¿Cuál es su aperitivo favorito? (interrogative pronouns, p. 100)

6. ¿Cómo vas a preparar la carne? (interrogative adverbs, p. 97)

7. ¿Por qué sirves pescado también? (interrogative pronouns, p. 100)

8. ¿Necesitas ayuda? (yes/no questions, p. 93)

9. ¿Para qué necesitas ese plato? (interrogative adverbs, p. 97)

10 ¿Cuántos postres vas a preparar? (interrogative adjectives, p. 95)

11.   ¡Qué bebé tan (más) hermosa! (exclamations, p. 103)

12.   ¡Cuántos dientes tiene! (exclamations, p. 103)

13.   ¡Cuánto pelo tiene! (exclamations, p. 103)

14.   ¡Cómo sonríe! (exclamations, p. 103)

15.   ¡Qué adorable es! (exclamations, p. 103)

Chapter 5
Negatives and Indefinites

Negatives

Besides the word *no,* several words in Spanish express a negative thought or feeling. Unlike in English, Spanish sentences may contain a double negative.

Negative Words

Common negatives in Spanish include:

no	no, not
tampoco	neither, not either
jamás, nunca	never, (not) ever
nadie	no one, nobody
ninguno (-a, -os, -as)	none, (not) any
nada	nothing

Use of Negatives

To use negatives properly, remember the following:

❑ Put the adverb *no* before the conjugated verb:

  No tengo hambre. I'm not hungry.

❑ When there are two verbs, place *no* before the conjugated verb and another negative word after the second verb:

  No quiero hacer nada. I don't want to do anything.

❑ If the conjugated verb is preceded by a pronoun, put *no* before the pronoun:

  No lo ví. I didn't see it.

❑ *No* may be repeated for emphasis:

  No, no quiero salir. No, I don't want to go out.

❑ A double or triple negative is acceptable in Spanish:

  No hablé con nadie. I didn't speak with anyone.

  Él no explica nada nunca. He never explains anything.

❑ If *no* is one of the negatives, it precedes the conjugated verb. When *no* is omitted, another negative precedes the verb:

> No voy nunca a la playa en febrero. I never go to the beach in February.

> Nunca voy a la playa en febrero. I never go to the beach in February.

❑ Negatives may be used alone (without *no*):

> ¿Qué quieres comer? What do you want to eat?

> Nada. Nothing.

> ¿Fuma Ud.? Do you smoke?

> Jamás. Never

❑ A negative preceded by a preposition retains that preposition when placed before the verb:

> No tiene celos de nadie. He isn't jealous of anyone.

> De nadie tiene celos. He isn't jealous of anyone.

❑ An infinitive may be negated:

> Es importante no decir nada. It's important not to say anything.

❑ The negatives *nadie, nada, ninguno, nunca,* and *jamás* are used after comparisons and in phrases beginning with *sin* (without) or *antes de* or *antes que* (before):

> Él juega mejor que nadie. He plays better than anyone.

> Ella habla español mejor que nunca. She speaks Spanish better than ever.

> Ellos llegaron sin traer nada. They arrived without bringing anything.

> Ellas salieron antes que nadie. They left before anyone else.

> Te llamo antes de llamar a nadie. I'll call you before calling anyone else.

Example Problems

You are making plans. Answer questions about yourself in the negative.

1. ¿Quieres ir al museo?

   Answer: No, no quiero ir al museo.

   Use *no* to answer the question. Put *no* before the conjugated verb. Answer the question about yourself using the *yo* form of the verb *querer*, which undergoes a stem change from *e* to *ie* in all forms except *nosotros* and *vosotros*. Complete the rest of the sentence.

2. ¿Vas a hacer algo interesante esta tarde?

   Answer: No, no voy a hacer nada interesante esta tarde.

   Use *no* to answer the question. Put *no* before the conjugated verb. Answer the question about yourself using the *yo* form of the verb *ir*, which is irregular *(voy)*. *Nada* (nothing) answers the question *algo* (something). The negative word *nada* comes after the conjugated verb. Complete the rest of the sentence.

3. ¿A quién esperas?

    Answer: No espero a nadie.

    Use *no* to answer the question. Put *no* before the conjugated verb. Answer the question about yourself using the *yo* form of the verb *esperar*. Drop the *-ar* ending and add *-o*. *Nadie* (no one) answers the question *alguien* (someone). The negative word *nadie* comes after the conjugated verb. Because the personal *a* (see Chapter 7) is included in the question, it must also be included in the answer.

Work Problems

Use these problems to give yourself additional practice.

A friend wants to get to know you better. Answer questions about yourself in the negative.

1. ¿Te gusta bailar?

2. ¿Estás pensando en algo?

3. ¿ Haces algunos errores cuando trabajas?

4. ¿Cuando eras joven, decías mentiras algunas veces?

5. A tu hermano no le gusta viajar. ¿Y a tí?

6. ¿Tienes miedo de alguien?

Worked Solutions

1. **No, no me gusta bailar.**   Use *no* to answer the question. Put *no* before the conjugated verb. Answer the question about yourself using *me* (to me) to respond to the question *te* (to you). Complete the rest of the sentence.

2. **No, no estoy pensando en nada.**   Use *no* to answer the question. Put *no* before the conjugated verb. Answer the question about yourself using the present progressive. Use the *yo* form of the verb *estar*, which is irregular *(estoy)*. Form the gerund of the regular *-ar* verb *pensar* by dropping the *-ar* ending and adding *-ando*. The verb *pensar* is followed by the preposition *en* to express "to think about." *Nada* (nothing) answers the question *algo* (something).

3. **No, no hago ningunos errores cuando trabajo.**   Use *no* to answer the question. Put *no* before the conjugated verb. Answer the question about yourself using the *yo* form of the verb *hacer*, which is irregular *(hago)*. *Ningunos* (not any) answers the question *algunos* (any), which refers to a masculine plural noun *(errores)*. Use the *yo* form of the verb *trabajar*. Drop the *-ar* ending and add *-o*.

4. **Cuando yo era joven nunca decía mentiras.**   Answer the question about yourself using the imperfect *yo* form of the verb *ser*. *Nunca* (never) answers the question *algunas veces* (sometimes) and is placed before the conjugated verb that follows. Continue using the imperfect *yo* form of the verb *decir*. Drop the *-ir* ending and add *-ía* and complete with the word *mentiras*.

5. **A mí tampoco me gusta viajar.**   Use the expression *a mí tampoco* to express "me neither." Answer the question about yourself using *me* (to me) to respond to the question *te* (to you). Complete the rest of the sentence.

6. **No tengo miedo de nadie.**   Put *no* before the conjugated verb. Use the *yo* form of the verb *tener*, which is irregular *(tengo)*. The entire expression is *tener miedo de* (to be afraid of). *Nadie* (no one) answers the question *alguien* (someone).

Negative Expressions

Negative expressions include:

ahora no	not now
creo que no	I don't believe so
de nada	you're welcome
de ningún modo	by no means
de ninguna manera	by no means
más que nunca	more than ever
más que nada	more than anything
ni + subject pronoun + tampoco	neither do(es) + subject
ni siquiera	not even
no cabe duda	there's no doubt
no es así	it's not so
no es para tanto	it's not such a big deal
no hay remedio	it can't be helped
no importa	it doesn't matter
no obstante	however
no puede ser	it (that) can't be
¿no te parece?	don't you think so?
no . . . más que	no more than
¿por qué no?	why not?
sin novedad	nothing new
todavía no	not yet
ya no	no longer

Here are some examples of these negative expressions in sentences:

Ud. tiene que trabajar mañana. Lo siento pero no hay remedio.

You have to work tomorrow. I'm sorry but it can't be helped.

Example Problems

Pick the best response to each statement or question a friend makes.

1.   ¿Está lloviendo?

   a. No hay remedio.

   b. No obstante.

   c. Creo que no.

   d. Sin novedad.

Answer: c

The best negative response to "Is it raining?" is *Creo que no* (I don't believe so).

2. ¿Quiere acompañarme a la fiesta?

    a. ¿Por qué no?

    b. No importa.

    c. Ya no.

    d. Ni siquiera.

Answer: a

The best negative response to "Do you want to accompany me to the party?" is *¿Por qué no?* (Why not?).

3. Muchas gracias.

    a. No es así.

    b. De ningún modo.

    c. No puede ser.

    d. De nada.

Answer: d

The best response to "Thank you" is *De nada* (You're welcome).

Work Problems

Use these problems to give yourself additional practice.

Complete each dialogue with the best appropriate answer from the list below.

    ¿por qué no?

    ni siquiera

    no cabe duda

    no es para tanto

    no hay remedio

    no obstante

    no puede ser

    todavía no

1. —¿Ella no tiene dinero?

    —¡No! ¡_____ un dólar!

2. —La hermana de Gloria gana cien mil dólares al año.

    —_____.

3. —El vuelo tiene tres horas de retraso a causa de un problema mecánico.

   —_____.

4. —¡Ay, ay, ay! ¡Tenemos que limpiar la casa otra vez!

   —_____.

5. —No quiero ir al cine con Uds.

   —_____.

6. —¿Has visitado España?

   —_____.

7. —Ella estudia muchísimo.

   —_____ que va a salir bien en sus exámenes.

8. —A Marco no le gustan los deportes.

   —Es verdad. _____ él juega al fútbol todos los días.

Worked Solutions

1. **Ni siquiera**   The best negative response to "Doesn't she have any money?" is "No, not even a dollar!"

2. **No puede ser**   The best negative response to "Gloria's sister earns $100,000 a year" is "That can't be."

3. **No hay remedio**   The best negative response to "The flight is three hours late due to mechanical problems " is "It can't be helped."

4. **No es para tanto**   The best negative response to "We have to clean the house again!" is "It's not such a big deal."

5. **¿Por qué no?**   The best negative response to "I don't want to go to the movies with you" is "Why not?"

6. **Todavía no**   The best negative response to "Have you visited Spain?" is "Not yet."

7. **No cabe duda**   The best negative response to "She studies a lot" is "There is no doubt that she will do well on her tests."

8. **No obstante**   The best negative response to "Marco doesn't like sports" is "However, he plays soccer every day."

Indefinite Pronouns and Their Negatives

The following indefinite pronouns have negative counterparts:

Indefinite	Meaning	Negative	Meaning
alguien	someone, somebody	nadie	no one, anyone, nobody, anybody
algo	something	nada	nothing, anything
alguno (-a, -os, -as)	some	ninguno (-a, -os, -as)	not any
cualquiera quien(es)quiera	anyone, anybody, anything whoever, anybody	ninguno nadie	none, not any, no one, anyone, nobody, anybody no one, anyone, nobody, anybody
todo	all	nada	nothing
todo el mundo	everyone, everybody	nadie ninguno	no one, anyone, nobody, anybody not any (person)

¿Él habló de alguien?	Did he speak about someone?
No, no habló de nadie.	No, he didn't speak about anybody.
¿Tu aprendiste algo?	Did you learn anything?
No, no aprendí nada.	No, I didn't learn anything.
¿Algunos van al cine?	Are some (of them) going to the movies?
Ninguno (de ellos) va al cine.	None (of them) is going to the movies.
Puedes escoger cualquiera.	You can choose any one (you like).
Yo no quiero ninguno.	I don't want any of them.
Quienquiera sea culpable . . .	Whoever is guilty . . .
Nadie es culpable . . .	Nobody is guilty . . .
Cualquiera puede hacerlo.	Anybody can do it.
No, nadie puede hacerlo.	No, nobody can do it.
Todo va bien.	Everything is going all right.
Nada va bien.	Nothing is going right.
Todo el mundo participa.	Everybody is participating.
Nadie participa.	Nobody is participating.

Example Problems

You want to help out a friend, but your offer is being refused. Write the negative response you receive to each of your questions.

1. ¿Las tareas? ¿Puedo hacer cualquiera?

   Answer: No, no puedes hacer ninguna.

   You are asking whether you can do any of the chores. The negative response begins with *no*. Your friend answers using the irregular verb *poder* in the *tú* form. The internal *o* of *poder* changes to *ue* in all forms except *nosotros* and *vosotros*. Drop the *-er* ending and add *-es* for *tú*. Your friend uses the feminine-singular indefinite *ninguna* to express that you can't do even one of the chores.

2. ¿Puedo ayudar a alguien?

Answer: No, no puedes ayudar a nadie.

You are asking whether you can help anyone. The negative response begins with *no*. Your friend answers using the irregular verb *poder* in the *tú* form. The internal *o* of *poder* changes to *ue* in all forms except *nosotros* and *vosotros*. Drop the *-er* ending and add *-es* for *tú*. Add the infinitive *ayudar* followed by the preposition *a*. Your friend uses the indefinite *nadie* to express that you can't help anyone.

3. ¿ Puedo hacer algo?

Answer: No, no puedes hacer nada.

You are asking if you can do anything. The negative response begins with *no*. Your friend answers using the irregular verb *poder* in the *tú* form. The internal *o* of *poder* changes to *ue* in all forms except *nosotros* and *vosotros*. Drop the *-er* ending and add *-es* for *tú*. Add the infinitive *hacer*. Your friend uses the indefinite *nada* to express that you can't do anything.

Work Problems

Use these problems to give yourself additional practice.

A friend witnessed an accident and is shaken up. You are being asked questions about him; give negative answers to these questions.

1. ¿Quiere hablar con alguien?

2. ¿Busca algo?

3. ¿Alguien lo espera?

4. ¿Vio a algunas víctimas?

5. ¿Conoce a quienquiera sea responsable?

6. ¿Dijo algo?

7. ¿Alguien le habló?

8. ¿Alguien puede ayudarlo?

Worked Solutions

1. **No, no quiere hablar con nadie.**   The negative response begins with *no*. Because you are being asked a question about a third person, the verb does not change. *Alguien* refers to "someone." Use *nadie* in a negative answer to refer to "no one."

2. **No, no busca nada.**   The negative response begins with *no*. Because you are being asked a question about a third person, the verb does not change. *Algo* refers to "something." Use *nada* in a negative answer to refer to "nothing."

3. **Nadie lo espera.**   The question asks whether "someone is waiting for him." Use *nadie* to respond that "no one is waiting for him." Because the subject is singular, give the third

person singular form of the verb *esperar* (to wait). Drop the *-ar* ending and add *-a*. The negative *no* is not required before the negative subject.

4. **No, no vio a nadie.**   The negative response begins with *no*. Because you are being asked a question about a third person, the verb does not change. The question asks whether he saw some victims. Use *ninguno* to respond that he saw "none."

5. **No, no conoce a quienquiera sea responsable.**   The negative response begins with *no*. Because you are being asked a question about a third person, the verb does not change. *Quienquiera* refers to the indefinite "whoever." Complete the rest of the sentence.

6. **No, no dijo nada.**   The negative response begins with *no*. Because you are being asked a question about a third person, the verb does not change. *Algo* refers to "something." An appropriate negative response is *nada* (nothing).

7. **No, nadie le habló.**   *Alguien* refers to "somebody." An appropriate negative response is *nadie* (nobody). The negative *no* is not required before the verb. Because you are being asked a question about a third person, the verb does not change.

8. **No, nadie puede ayudarlo.**   *Alguien* refers to "someone." An appropriate negative response is *nadie* (no one). The negative *no* is not required before the verb. Because you are being asked a question about a third person, the verb does not change.

Indefinite Adjectives and Their Negatives

The following indefinite adjectives have negative counterparts:

Indefinite	Meaning	Negative	Meaning
alguno (algún) (-a, -os, -as) *	some, any	ninguno (ningún) (-a, -os, -as) *	not any
cierto (-a, -os, -as)	certain	ninguno (ningún) (-a, -os, -as) *	not any
uno (un) (-a, -os, -as) *	one, some	ninguno (ningún) (-a, -os, -as) *	not any
mucho (-a, -os, -as)	many, much	ninguno (ningún) (-a, -os, -as) *	not any
tal (-es)	such	ninguno (ningún) (-a, -os, -as) *	not any
cada	each, every	ninguno (ningún) (-a, -os, -as) *	not any
cualquier (-a)	any, some	ninguno (ningún) (-a, -os, -as) *	not any
todo (-a, -os, -as)	all, every	ninguno (ningún) (-a, -os, -as) *	not any
otro (-a, -os, -as)	other, another	ninguno (ningún) (-a, -os, -as) *	not any

Note that alguno, ninguno, and uno become algún, ningún, and un (respectively) before a masculine singular noun.

¿Has asistido a alguna clase del señor Jacinto?

Have you attended any class of Mr. Jacinto?

¿No has asistido a ninguna clase del señor Jacinto?

Haven't you attended any class of Mr. Jacinto?

Algunos alumnos recibieron becas.

Some students received scholarships.

Ningún alumno de nuestra escuela recibió una.

No student from our school received one.

Un hombre puede defenderse.

A man can defend himself.

Ningún hombre puede defenderse contra esos terroristas.

No man can defend himself against those terrorists.

Cuando van a la escuela, cada una lleva su mochila.

When they go to school, each one brings her backpack.

Cuando van a la escuela, ninguna lleva su mochila.

When they go to school, none of them brings her backpack.

Algún día será doctor.

One day, he will be a doctor.

Note the use of *ningunos (-as)* in the plural:

¿Me das esos libros?	Will you give me those books?
No tengo ningunos libros.	I don't have any books.
¿Tienes ganas de ir al centro?	Do you feel like going downtown?
No tengo ningunas ganas de ir al centro.	I don't feel at all like going downtown.

Example Problems

Your friend is very negative. Change his negative thoughts to positive ones by selecting the appropriate word.

1. *No* prefiero *ninguna* comida extranjera.

    a. otros

    b. tales

    c. cualquier

    d. cierto

    Answer: c

    No . . . ninguna refers to the feminine singular noun *comida* (meal). The opposite of *no . . . ninguna* (not any) is *cualquier* (any).

2. *No* viajo a *ninguna parte.*

    a. otras partes

    b. tales partes

    c. cualquier parte

    d. todas partes

    Answer: d

    No . . . ninguna parte refers to *nowhere.* The opposite of *no . . . ninguna parte* is *todas partes* (everywhere).

3. *No* quiero visitar *ningún* país de habla española.

   a. algún

   b. ciertos

   c. todos

   d. una

   Answer: a

   No . . . ningún refers to the masculine singular noun *país* (country). The opposite of *no . . . ningún* (any) is *algún* (some).

Work Problems

Use these problems to give yourself additional practice.

Change the negative thoughts to positive ones by selecting the appropriate word.

1. *Nunca* será un muchacho responsable.

   a. Cualquiera

   b. Cierta

   c. Algún día

   d. Tal

2. *Ningún* niño puede aprender todo.

   a. Un

   b. Cierto

   c. Muchos

   d. Cualquier

3. *Ninguna* muchacha quiere salir con él.

   a. Otras

   b. Alguna

   c. Cualquier

   d. Cada

4. *No* ha participado en *ningún* partido deportivo.

   a. tal

   b. muchos

   c. todos

   d. algún

5. *No* le interesa *ninguna* materia.

   a. tales

   b. cada

   c. ciertas

   d. muchos

6. *No* le molesta *ninguna* cosa.

   a. cada

   b. otros

   c. cierta

   d. alguna

Worked Solutions

1. **c** The best word to replace *nunca* (never) is *algún día* (some).

2. **d** *Ningún* refers to the masculine singular noun *niño* (child). The best word to replace *ningún* (no) is *cualquier* (any).

3. **c** *Ninguna* refers to the feminine singular noun *muchacha* (girl). The best word to replace *ninguna* (not one) is *cualquier* (any).

4. **d** *Ningún* refers to the masculine singular noun *partido* (match). The best word to replace *ningún* (not any) is *algún* (some).

5. **b** *Ninguna* refers to the feminine singular noun *materia* (subject). The best word to replace *ninguna* (not any) is *cada* (each).

6. **a** *Ninguna* refers to the feminine singular noun *cosa* (thing). The best word to replace *ninguna* (not one) is *cada* (each).

Indefinite Adverbs and Their Negatives

The following indefinite adverbs have negative counterparts:

Indefinite	Meaning	Negative	Meaning
ya	already	todavía no	not yet, still
todavía, aún	still	ya no	no longer, anymore
siempre	always	nunca, jamás	never
también	also, too	tampoco ni . . . (tampoco)	not either, neither
más de + *numeral*	more than	no más de + *numeral*	not more than

Here are some examples of these indefinite adverbs in sentences:

¿Ya ha visto esa película?	Have you seen that film already?
Todavía no la he visto.	I haven't seen it yet.
Todavía tengo que practicar.	I still have to practice.
Ya no tengo que practicar.	I don't have to practice anymore.
Siempre mira ese programa.	She always watches that program.
Nunca mira ese programa.	She never watches that program.
Como legumbres y también frutas.	I eat vegetables and also fruits.
No como legumbres ni frutas tampoco.	I eat neither vegetables nor fruits.
Son más de treinta en su clase.	There are more than 30 in her class.
No son más de treinta en su clase.	There aren't more than 30 in her class.

Example Problems

Match the question you ask an acquaintance with the appropriate answer.

1. ¿Ya ha terminado sus estudios?

   Answer: Todavía no.

   The question asks whether the acquaintance has already finished his studies. The best answer is *todavía no* (not yet).

2. ¿Siempre estudia en la biblioteca?

   Answer: No, nunca.

   The question asks whether the acquaintance always studies in the library. The best answer is *no, nunca* (not ever).

3. ¿Aún asiste a la universidad?

   Answer: Ya no.

   The question asks whether the acquaintance still attends college. The best answer is *ya no* (no longer).

Work Problems

Use these problems to give yourself additional practice.

You meet a friend that you haven't seen in a long time. Write an appropriate negative response to the questions your friend asks you.

1. ¿Fumas todavía?

2. ¿Siempre sales con Julio?

3. ¿Ya has viajado por Europa?

4. ¿Tienes más de tres niños?

5. ¿Hablas español y francés también?

Worked Solutions

1. **Ya no.**   The question asks whether you still smoke. A correct negative answer is *ya no* (no longer).

2. **Nunca salgo con Julio.**   The question asks whether you always go out with Julio. The correct negative answer is *nunca* (never). To speak about yourself, give the irregular *yo* form for the verb *salir: salgo.*

3. **Todavía no.**   The question asks whether you have already traveled through Spain. The correct negative answer is *todavía no* (not yet).

4. **No más de tres.**   The question asks whether you have more than three children. The correct negative answer is *no más de tres* (no more than three).

5. **No hablo español ni francés (tampoco).**   The question asks whether you speak Spanish and French, too. The correct negative answer uses *ni . . . tampoco* (neither . . . nor). Begin the answer with *no*. To speak about yourself, give the *yo* form for the regular verb *hablar: hablo.* Replace *y* (and) with *ni* (nor) and add the word *francés*. The negative *tampoco* (neither) is optional.

Negative Conjunctions

The following conjunctions have negative counterparts:

Conjunction	Meaning	Negative	Meaning
o . . . o	either . . . or	ni . . . ni	neither . . . nor
pero	but	sino	but

Note that each part of the *o . . . o* and *ni . . . ni* construction precedes the word or words stressed and the use of the first *o* or *ni* is optional.

Bebo (o) té o café.	I drink either tea or coffee.
No bebo (ni) vino ni cerveza.	I drink neither wine nor beer.
No le gusta (ni) trabajar ni estudiar.	He doesn't like to work nor study.
El postre no es (ni) bueno ni malo.	The dessert is neither good nor bad.

Pero and *sino* both express "but." *Pero* is used in a more general sense and may also mean *however*:

No sé bailar, pero quiero ir a la fiesta.	I don't know how to dance, but I want to go to the party.

Sino is used only after a negative statement to express a contrast and to make an affirmation (on the contrary):

Ella no quiere trabajar, sino jugar.	She doesn't want to work, but to play.

Negative Prefixes

The following prefixes can be added to words to give a negative meaning or connotation:

> anti
>
> contra
>
> des
>
> dis
>
> in (which changes to *im* before the letters *b* or *p*)

Affirmative	Meaning	Negative	Meaning
comunista	communist	anticomunista	anticommunist
héroe	hero	antihéroe	antihero
decir	to say	contradecir	to contradict
revolución	revolution	contrarevolución	counterrevolution
aparecer	to appear	desaparecer	to disappear
hacer	to do	deshacer	to undo
culpa	fault, blame	disculpa	excuse, apology
conformidad	agreement	disconformidad	disagreement
perfecto	perfect	imperfecto	imperfect
posible	possible	imposible	impossible
capaz	capable	incapaz	incapable
creíble	credible	increíble	incredible

Example Problems

Express the following negatives about yourself in Spanish.

1. I don't want to rest but to work.

   Answer: No quiero descansar, sino trabajar.

   Express "don't" by beginning the sentence with *no*. *Querer* is a stem-changing verb whose internal *e* changes to *ie* in all forms except *nosotros* and *vosotros*. Drop the *-er* ending and add *-o* for the *yo* form. The conjugated form of *querer* is followed by the infinitive *descansar* (to rest). *Sino* is used to express "but" in a negative sentence. *Sino* is followed by the infinitive *trabajar* (to work).

2. I prefer either water or juice.

   Answer: Prefiero (o) agua o jugo.

   Preferir is a stem-changing verb whose internal *e* changes to *ie* in all forms except *nosotros* and *vosotros*. Drop the *-ir* ending and add *-o* for the *yo* form. Use *o . . . o* to express "either . . . or." The first *o,* which is optional, is followed by *agua* to express "water." The second *o* is followed by *jugo* to express "juice."

3. Sometimes I'm indiscreet.

   Answer: Algunas veces soy indiscreto (-a).

   Use the phrase *algunas veces* to express "sometimes." Use the *yo* form of the irregular verb *ser* (to be) to show a personality trait. Change the adjective *discreto (-a)* (discreet) to the opposite by adding the prefix *in-*.

Work Problems

Express the following things about yourself in Spanish.

1. Sometimes I want to go out, but I am tired.

2. I play neither golf nor tennis.

3. I don't like to watch television but to listen to music.

4. I wear either black or red.

5. I am never insensitive.

6. I don't like to contradict others.

Worked Solutions

1. **Algunas veces quiero salir, pero estoy cansado (-a).** Use the phrase *algunas veces* to express "sometimes." *Querer* is a stem-changing verb whose internal *e* changes to *ie* in all forms except *nosotros* and *vosotros*. Drop the *-er* ending and add *-o* for the *yo* form. The conjugated form of *querer* is followed by the infinitive *salir* (to go out). *Pero* is used to express "but" in an affirmative sentence. Use the *yo* form of the irregular verb *estar* (to be) to show a temporary state. Use *cansado (cansada)* to express "tired."

2. **No juego (ni) al golf ni al tenis.** Begin the sentence with *no*. *Jugar* is a stem-changing verb whose internal *u* changes to *ue* in all forms except *nosotros* and *vosotros*. Drop the *-ar* ending and add *-o* for the *yo* form. To play a sport is expressed by the expression *jugar* + *a* + definite article. *A* contracts with *el* before *golf* and *tenis*, both masculine singular nouns. Use *ni...ni* to express "neither...nor." The first *ni*, which is optional, is followed by *al golf* to express "golf." The second *ni* is followed by *al tenis* to express "tennis."

3. **No me gusta mirar la televisión, sino escuchar música.** Begin the sentence with *no*. Use the indirect object *me* to express that watching television isn't pleasing to you. The verb *gustar* is used in its singular form *(gusta)* before an infinitive. Because *gustar* is conjugated, the only verb form that may follow it is the infinitive. Use *mirar la televisión* to express "to watch television." *Sino* is used to express "but" in a negative sentence. *Sino* is followed by the infinitive expression *escuchar la música* (to listen to music).

4. **Llevo (o) el negro o el rojo.** Use the regular verb *llevar* to express "to wear." Drop the *-ar* ending and add *-o* for the *yo* form. Use *o . . . o* to express "either . . . or." The first *o*, which is optional, is followed by *el negro* to express "black." The second *o* is followed by *el rojo* to express "red." The definite article must be used with nouns used in a general sense.

5. **Nunca soy insensible.** Use *nunca* to express "never." Use the *yo* form of the irregular verb *ser* (to be) to show a personality trait. Change the adjective *sensible* (sensitive) to the opposite by adding the prefix *in-*.

6. **No me gusta contradecir a los demás.** Begin the sentence with *no*. Use the indirect object *me* to express that contradicting isn't pleasing to you. The verb *gustar* is used in its singular form *(gusta)* before an infinitive. Because *gustar* is conjugated, the only verb form that may follow it is the infinitive. Use the prefix *contra-* to give the opposite of *decir*: *contradecir* (to contradict). Use the personal *a* before the pronoun *los demás* (the others).

Chapter Problems

Problems

Complete the story about a negative person by filling in the missing words.

A mi amigo Roberto no le gusta (neither) _____ (anything) _____ (nor)
1   2

_____ (anybody) _____. Es increíble su actitud antipática. (Either) _____
3   4   5

se queja (or) _____ maldice a los demás. (Still) _____ no sabe entenderse con
6   7

(any) _____ otra persona y siempre (contradicts) _____ las ideas de sus
8   9

amigos. Siempre insiste en que sabe todo, (but) _____ (no) _____ sabe
10   11

(anything) _____. Él (not) _____ quiere escuchar a (others) _____, (but)
12   13   14

_____ discutir con ellos. Si (someone) _____ lo invita a hacer (something)
15   16

_____ siempre contesta, "(by no means) _____." (Never) _____ dice
17   18   19

"sí" y no tiene (any) _____ intención de cambiar su comportamiento. (There is no
20

doubt) _____ que (never) _____ será un hombre simpático. (It can't be helped)
21   22

_____. (no longer) _____ salgo con él porque (neither) _____ yo (nor)
23   24   25

_____ mis amigos podemos tolerar su negatividad. (No more than) _____ una
26   27

o dos personas quieren hablarle, (not even) _____ yo. (No one) _____ quiere
28   29

acompañarlo a (any) _____ parte. Es muy triste.
30

Answers and Solutions

1. **Answer: ni**   Use *ni* to express "neither."

2. **Answer: nada**   Use *nada* to express "anything."

3. **Answer: ni**   Use *ni* to express "nor."

4. **Answer: nadie**   Use *nadie* to express "anybody."

5.   **Answer: O**   Use *o* to express "either."

6.   **Answer: o**   Use *o* to express "or."

7.   **Answer: Todavía**   Use *todavía* to express "still."

8.   **Answer: ninguna**   Use *ninguna* to express "(not) any" before the feminine singular noun *persona*.

9.   **Answer: contradice**   Use the prefix *contra-* to give the opposite of *decir: contradecir* (to contradict). Use the third person singular form of the irregular verb *contradecir: contradice*.

10.   **Answer: pero**   Use *pero* to express "but" in an affirmative sentence.

11.   **Answer: no**   Use *no* to express "no."

12.   **Answer: nada**   Use *nada* to express "anything."

13.   **Answer: no**   Use *no* to express "no."

14.   **Answer: los demás**   Use *los demás* to express "the others."

15.   **Answer: sino**   Use *sino* to express a contrast.

16.   **Answer: alguien**   Use *alguien* to express "someone."

17.   **Answer: algo**   Use *algo* to express "something."

18.   **Answer: De ninguna manera/De ningún modo**   Use *de ninguna manera* or *de ningún modo* to express "by no means."

19.   **Answer: Nunca**   Use *nunca* to express "never."

20.   **Answer: ninguna**   Use *ninguna* to express "any" before the feminine singular noun *intención*.

21.   **Answer: No cabe duda**   Use *no cabe duda* to express "there is no doubt."

22.   **Answer: nunca**   Use *nunca* to express "never."

23.   **Answer: No hay remedio**   Use *no hay remedio* to express "it can't be helped."

24.   **Answer: Ya no**   Use *ya no* to express "no longer."

25.   **Answer: ni**   Use *ni* to express "neither."

26.   **Answer: ni**   Use *ni* to express "nor."

27.   **Answer: No más de**   Use *no más de* to express "no more than."

28.   **Answer: ni siquiera**   Use *ni siquiera* to express "not even."

29.   **Answer: Nadie**   Use *nadie* to express "no one."

30.   **Answer: ninguna**   Use *ninguna* before the feminine singular noun *parte* to express "anywhere."

Supplemental Chapter Problems

Problems

Express this person's ideas about cooking by filling in the blanks with the appropriate words or expressions.

Cocinar. (Anybody) _____ puede hacerlo. (Not) _____ es una tarea imposible,
     1   2

(by no means) _____. (It's not such a big deal) _____. (However) _____,
              3   4   5

a (some) _____ de mis amigos, (not) _____ les gusta cocinar. Mi amiga Bárbara
         6   7

(not) _____ quiere cocinar, (but) _____ comprar comida rápida. Ella (not)
      8   9

_____ prepara (neither) _____ el desayuno (nor) _____ el almuerzo (nor)
     10   11   12

_____ la cena. Cuando ella quiere comer (something) _____, come (either)
     13   14

_____ hamburguesas (or) _____ pizza. (Some) _____ veces telefonea a
     15   16   17

(someone) _____ y espera una invitación. (Each) _____ vez que la invito a mi
          18   19

casa para una comida, (never) _____ rehusa mi invitación. (Unfortunately)
                              20

_____, (not) _____ come pescado (nor . . . either) _____ pollo. Ella (not)
     21   22   23

_____ hace (anything) _____ para ayudarme, (not even) _____ poner la
     24   25   26

mesa, (but) _____ no me importa. A mí me gusta cocinar (more than anything)
            27

_____ y (some) _____ día quiero ser jefe en un restaurante.
     28   29

Solutions

1. Cualquiera (indefinite pronouns, p. 115)

2. No (using negatives, p. 109)

3. de ninguna manera/de ningún modo (negative expressions, p. 112)

4. No es para tanto (negative expressions, p. 112)

5. No obstante (negative expressions, p. 112)

6. algunos (indefinite adjectives, p. 117)

7. no (using negatives, p. 109)

8. no (using negatives, p. 109)

9. sino (negative conjunctions, p. 122)

10. no (using negatives, p. 109)

11. ni (negative conjunctions, p. 122)

12. ni (negative conjunctions, p. 122)

13. ni (negative conjunctions, p. 122)

14. algo (indefinite pronouns, p. 122)

15. o (negative conjunctions, p. 122)

16. o (negative conjunctions, p. 122)

17. Algunas (indefinite adjectives, p. 117)

18. alguien (indefinite pronouns, p. 114)

19. Cada (indefinite adjectives, p. 117)

20. nunca (indefinite adverbs, p. 120)

21. Desafortunadamente (negative prefixes, p. 123)

22. no (using negatives, p. 109)

23. ni (tampoco) (indefinite adverbs, p. 120)

24. no (using negatives, p. 109)

25. nada (indefinite pronouns, p. 115)

26. ni siquiera (negative expressions, p. 112)

27. pero (negative conjunctions, p. 122)

28. no me importa (negative expressions, p. 112)

29. algún (indefinite adjectives, p. 117)

Chapter 6
Object and Relative Pronouns

Direct and Indirect Object Pronouns

A direct object answers the question "whom?" (*¿a quién?*) or "what?" (*¿qué?*) the subject is acting upon and may refer to people, places, things, or ideas. A direct object pronoun replaces a direct object noun and, unlike in English, is usually placed before the conjugated verb.

Note that the personal *a* conveys no meaning and is used before a direct object noun indicating a person or persons, a pet, a pronoun referring to a person, or an unmodified geographic name (although modern usage tends to omit the latter). The personal *a* is not used with *tener*.

Conozco a Ana.	I know Ana.
Está buscando a su perro.	He is looking for his dog.
No veo a nadie.	I don't see anyone.
¿Piensas visitar a España?	Do you intend to visit Spain?
Tengo dos hijos.	I have two sons.

An indirect object refers only to people (and pets) and answers the question "to whom?" or "for whom?" (*¿a quién?*) is the subject doing something. An indirect object pronoun replaces an indirect object noun but is also used in Spanish when the noun is mentioned. To avoid ambiguity, use *a él, a ella,* or *a Ud.* to clarify to whom you are referring.

The Spanish object pronouns are as follows:

Direct		Indirect	
Singular Pronoun	**Meaning**	**Singular Pronoun**	**Meaning**
me	me	me	(to) me
te	you (informal)	te	(to) you (informal)
le *	you (formal), him	le	(to) you (formal), him, her, it
lo	you, him, it (masculine)		
la	you, her, it (feminine		

Plural Pronoun		Plural Pronoun	
nos	us	nos	(to) us
os	you (informal)	os	(to) you (informal)
los	you (formal), them (masculine)	les	(to) you (formal), them
las	you (formal), them (feminine)		

* Note that le is the direct object pronoun used in certain parts of Spain to refer to people. In Latin America, however, lo is preferred.

Verbs Requiring Direct and Indirect Objects

Verbs requiring a direct object in English do not necessarily require a direct object in Spanish. These verbs take an indirect object in Spanish either because "to" or "for" is implied or because the verb is followed by *a* and refers to a person:

aconsejar	to advise
contar	to relate, to tell
contestar	to answer
dar	to give
decir	to tell, to say
devolver	to return
enviar	to send
escribir	to write
explicar	to explain
mandar	to send
ofrecer	to offer
pagar	to pay ([to] someone)
pedir	to ask
perdonar *	to forgive
preguntar	to ask
prestar	to lend
prohibir	to forbid
prometer	to promise
recordar *	to remind
regalar	to give a gift
telefonear	to call

For example:

Él perdona a su amigo.	He forgives his friend.
Él lo perdona a él.	He forgives him.

Verbs with an asterisk (*) take an indirect object only when a direct object is also present in the sentence:

La recuerdo.	I remember her.
Le recuerdo la hora.	I remind him of the time.

Lo perdono.	I forgive him.
Le perdono su error.	I forgive him/her for his/her mistake.

Verbs requiring an indirect object in English do not necessarily require an indirect object in Spanish because "to" or "for" is included in the meaning of the infinitive:

buscar	to look for
escuchar	to listen to
esperar	to hope for (to)
llamar	to call, to name
pagar	to pay for (something)
mirar	to look at

For example:

Escuchamos la música.	We listen to the music.
La escuchamos.	We listen to it.

Example Problems

Speak about your friends by completing each sentence with the appropriate object pronoun.

1. ¿Hernando? Yo _____ contesto.

    Answer: le

    In this case, the verb *contestar* requires an indirect object. Use the indirect object pronoun *le* to refer to *Hernando* and to express "(to) him."

2. ¿Isabel y Carmen? Yo _____ pido un consejo.

    Answer: les

    The verb *pedir* requires an indirect object because it requires the preposition *a* to express "to." Use the indirect object pronoun *les* to refer to *Isabel y Carmen* and to express "them."

3. ¿Enrique y Miguel? Yo _____ miro.

    Answer: los

    The verb *mirar* requires a direct object. Use the direct object pronoun *los* to refer to *Enrique y Miguel* and to express "them."

Work Problems

Speak about more friends by completing each sentence with the appropriate object pronoun.

1. ¿Julia? Yo _____ llamo.

2. ¿Luisa y Marta? Yo ____ espero.

3. ¿Carlos y Ramón? Yo ___ escribo mensajes electrónicos.

4. ¿Rogelio? Yo _____ perdono.

5. ¿Pablo? Yo _____ telefoneo.

6. ¿Patricia? Yo ____ escucho.

7. ¿Ernesto? Yo _____ busco.

8. ¿Luz y Beatriz? Yo _____ aconsejo.

Worked Solutions

1. **la** The verb *llamar* requires a direct object. Use the direct object pronoun *la* to refer to *Julia* and to express "her."

2. **las** The verb *esperar* requires a direct object. Use the direct object pronoun *las* to refer to *Luisa y Marta* and to express "them."

3. **les** The verb *escribir* requires an indirect object because it requires the preposition *a* to express "to." Use the indirect object pronoun *les* to refer to *Carlos y Ramón* and to express "to them."

4. **lo** The verb *perdonar* requires a direct object. Use the direct object pronoun *lo* to refer to *Rogelio* and to express "him."

5. **le** The verb *telefonear* requires an indirect object because it requires the preposition *a* to express "to." Use the indirect object pronoun *le* to refer to *Carlos* and to express "to him."

6. **la** The verb *escuchar* requires a direct object. Use the direct object pronoun *la* to refer to *Patricia* and to express "her."

7. **lo** The verb *buscar* requires a direct object. Use the direct object pronoun *lo* to refer to *Rogelio* and to express "him."

8. **les** The verb *aconsejar* requires an indirect object because it requires the preposition *a* to express "to." Use the indirect object pronoun *les* to refer to *Luz y Beatriz* and to express "to them."

The Position of Object Pronouns

Note the following about the placement of object pronouns:

❏ Object pronouns are generally placed before the conjugated verb:

¿Esa película? Yo no **la** ví.   That film? I didn't see it.

Yo **le** telefoneo a menudo **a él.**   I call him often.

❏ Object pronouns may be placed after an infinitive (see Chapter 9) or a gerund (see Chapter 12) forming one word or may be placed before the conjugated verb:

Tengo que ver**lo.**	**Lo** tengo que ver.	I have to see him.
Estoy hablándo**le.**	**Le** estoy hablando.	I'm speaking to him.

❑ Object pronouns are placed before negative commands but after affirmative commands (see Chapter 16):

¡No digas mentiras!	Don't tell lies.
¡No **las** digas!	Don't tell them.
¡Diga la verdad!	Tell the truth!
¡Díga**la!**	Tell it!

Example Problems

Place the object pronoun in its proper location to express what people do.

1. (you, informal) él está mirando

Answer: Él está mirándote./Él te está mirando.

Use the informal direct object pronoun *te* to express "you." Attach *te* to the end of the gerund. Count back three vowels from the end and add an accent. Alternatively, *te* may be placed before the conjugated verb.

2. (me) ella puede hablar

Answer: Ella puede hablarme./Ella me puede hablar.

Use the indirect object pronoun *me* to express "to me." Attach *me* to the end of the infinitive. Alternatively, *me* may be placed before the conjugated verb.

3. (us) ¡compre estos libros!

Answer: ¡Cómprenos estos libros!

Use the indirect object pronoun *nos* to express "for us." In an affirmative command, attach *nos* to the end of the command form. Count back three vowels and add an accent.

4. (him) ¡no envíe esta carta!

Answer: ¡No le envíe esta carta!

Use the indirect object pronoun *le* to express "to him." In a negative command, place *le* before the conjugated verb.

Work Problems

Place the object pronoun in its proper location to express what people do.

1. (me) Enrique está pidiendo un favor

2. (you, informal) Elena quiere decir sus planes

3.   (us) ¡ayude!

4.   (you, formal plural) nosotros estamos escuchando

5.   (them, feminine) tú vas a buscar

6.   (her) ¡no telefonee!

7.   (them, masculine) ella escribe una carta

8.   (him) yo estoy esperando

9.   (her) ¡mire Ud.!

10.   (him) ¡no diga nada!

Worked Solutions

1.   **Enrique está pidiéndome un favor./Enrique me está pidiendo un favor.**   The verb *pedir* requires an indirect object because it requires the preposition *a* to express "to." Use the indirect object pronoun *me* to express "to me." Attach *me* to the end of the gerund. Count back three vowels from the end and add an accent. Alternatively, *me* may be placed before the conjugated verb.

2.   **Ella quiere decirte sus planes./Elena te quiere decir sus planes.**   The verb *decir* requires an indirect object because it requires the preposition *a* to express "to." Use the indirect object pronoun *te* to express "to you." Attach *te* to the end of the infinitive. Alternatively, *te* may be placed before the conjugated verb.

3.   **¡Ayúdenos!**   The verb *ayudar* requires a direct object. Use the direct object pronoun *nos* to express "us." In an affirmative command, attach *nos* to the end of the command form. Count back three vowels and add an accent.

4.   **Nosotros estamos escuchándolos./Nosotros los estamos escuchando.**   The verb *escuchar* requires a direct object. Use the direct object pronoun *los* to express "you." Attach *los* to the end of the gerund. Count back three vowels from the end and add an accent. Alternatively, *los* may be placed before the conjugated verb.

5.   **Tú vas a buscarlas./Tú las vas a buscar.**   The verb *buscar* requires a direct object. Use the direct object pronoun *las* to express "them." Attach *las* to the end of the infinitive. Alternatively, *las* may be placed before the conjugated verb.

6.   **¡No le telefonee!**   The verb *telefonear* requires an indirect object because it requires the preposition *a* to express "to." Use the indirect object pronoun *le* to express "to her." In a negative command, place *le* before the conjugated verb.

7.   **Ella les escribe una carta.**   The verb *escribir* requires an indirect object because it requires the preposition *a* to express "to." Use the indirect object pronoun *les* to express "to them." Place the indirect object before the conjugated verb.

8.   **Yo estoy esperándolo./Yo lo estoy esperando.**   The verb *esperar* requires a direct object. Use the direct object pronoun *lo* to express "him." Attach *lo* to the end of the

gerund. Count back three vowels from the end and add an accent. Alternatively, *lo* may be placed before the conjugated verb.

9. **¡Mírela Ud.!**   The verb *mirar* requires a direct object. Use the direct object pronoun *la* to express "her." In an affirmative command, attach *nos* to the end of the command form. Count back three vowels and add an accent.

10. **¡No le diga nada!**   The verb *decir* requires an indirect object because it requires the preposition *a* to express "to." Use the indirect object pronoun *le* to express "to him." In a negative command, place *le* before the conjugated verb.

Gustar and Other Similar Verbs

Gustar (to please, to like) and a few other Spanish verbs use indirect objects to express the subject of their English counterparts. These verbs include:

Verb	Meaning
aburrir	to bore
agradar	to please, to be pleased with
bastar	to be enough
caer bien	to like
convenir	to be suitable, to be convenient
disgustar	to upset, to displease
doler	to be painful
encantar	to adore
entusiasmar	to enthuse, to love
faltar	to lack, to need
fascinar	to fascinate
fastidiar	to annoy, to bother
hacer daño	to harm
importar	to be important
interesar	to interest
molestar	to bother
parecer	to seem
quedar	to remain to someone, to have left
resultar	to result
sentar bien	to appreciate
sentar mal	to upset
sobrar	to be left over
sorprender	to surprise
tocar	to be one's turn

The Spanish indirect object is the subject of the English sentence:

Me gustan los deportes.	I like sports. (Sports are pleasing to me.)
Les queda un dólar.	They have a dollar left. (One dollar is left to them.)

Note that the subject of the Spanish sentence may not be replaced by a direct-object pronoun:

Me interesan las películas.	I like films. (Sports interest me.)
Me interesan.	They interest me.

The third person singular form is used with one or more verb infinitives:

Nos interesa comer y beber.	We are interested in eating and drinking.

The indirect object pronoun may be preceded by the preposition *a* + the corresponding prepositional pronoun (*mí, ti, él, ella, Ud, nosotros, vosotros, ellos, ellas,* or *Uds.*) for stress or clarification:

A ti te sorprenden sus respuestas.	His answers surprise you.
A ellas les entusiasma la ópera.	They love the opera.

The indirect object pronoun may be preceded by the preposition *a* + the indirect object noun:

A Jorge no le sienta esa música.	Jorge doesn't appreciate that music.
A las mujeres les molesta ese hombre.	That man bothers the women.

Example Problems

Combine the elements to speak about people's dislikes or discomforts.

> Example: a ti/molestar los insectos
> A ti te molestan los insectos.

1. a Uds./aburrir los viajes en avión

   Answer: A Uds. les aburren los viajes en avión.

   Use *a Uds.* to express "to you" at the beginning of the sentence for emphasis or clarity. Use the indirect object pronoun *le* to express "to you." The verb *aburrir* must agree with the subject, *los viajes*. Drop the *-ir* ending and add the third person plural ending *(-en)*.

2. a mí/doler la cabeza

   Answer: A mí me duele la cabeza.

   Use *a mí* to express "to me" at the beginning of the sentence for emphasis or clarity. Use the indirect object pronoun *me* to express "to me." The verb *doler* must agree with the subject, *la cabeza. Doler* undergoes a stem change from *o* to *ue*. Drop the *-er* ending and add the third person singular ending *(-e)*.

3. a ella/disgustar limpiar la casa y lavar el coche

   Answer: A ella le disgusta limpiar la casa y lavar el coche.

   Use *a ella* to express "to her" at the beginning of the sentence for emphasis or clarity. Use the indirect object pronoun *le* to express "to her." The verb *disgustar* must be used in the singular with verb infinitives. Drop the *-ar* ending and add the third person singular ending *(-a)*.

Work Problems

Combine the elements to speak about people's.

1. a ti/fascinar el ballet y la ópera

2. a él/entusiasmar hacer ejercicios

3. a mí/agradar los deportes

4. a vosotros/interesar escribir y leer

5. a ellas/importar tocar el piano

6. a nosotros/encantar los espectáculos

Worked Solutions

1. **A tí te fascinan el ballet y la ópera.**   Use *a tí* to express "to you" at the beginning of the sentence for emphasis or clarity. Use the indirect object pronoun *te* to express "to you." The verb *fascinar* must agree with the subject: *el ballet y la ópera*. Drop the *-ar* ending and add the third person plural ending *(-an)*.

2. **A él le entusiasma hacer ejercicios.**   Use *a él* to express "to him" at the beginning of the sentence for emphasis or clarity. Use the indirect object pronoun *le* to express "to him." The verb *entusiasmar* must be used in the singular with verb infinitives. Drop the *-ar* ending and add the third person singular ending *(-a)*.

3. **A mí me agradan los deportes.**   Use *a mí* to express "to me" at the beginning of the sentence for emphasis or clarity. Use the indirect object pronoun *me* to express "to me." The verb *agradar* must agree with the subject: *los deportes*. Drop the *-ar* ending and add the third person plural ending *(-an)*.

4. **A vosotros os interesa escribir y leer.**   Use *a vosotros* to express "to you" at the beginning of the sentence for emphasis or clarity. Use the indirect object pronoun *os* to express "to you." The verb *interesar* must be used in the singular with verb infinitives. Drop the *-ar* ending and add the third person singular ending *(-a)*.

5. **A ellas les importa tocar el piano.**   Use *a ellas* to express "to them" at the beginning of the sentence for emphasis or clarity. Use the indirect object pronoun *les* to express "to them." The verb *importar* must be used in the singular with verb infinitives. Drop the *-ar* ending and add the third person singular ending *(-a)*.

6. **A nosotros nos encantan los espectáculos.**   Use *a nosotros* to express "to us" at the beginning of the sentence for emphasis or clarity. Use the indirect object pronoun *nos* to express "to us." The verb *encantar* must agree with the subject: *los espectáculos*. Drop the *-ar* ending and add the third person plural ending *(-an)*.

The Neuter *Lo*

The neuter pronoun *lo* refers to an idea or concept and can substitute for an adjective (or adjectival phrase), a prepositional phrase, or a subordinate clause:

Él es un buen profesor, ¿no?	He's a good teacher, right?
Sí, lo es.	Yes, he is.
¿Estamos de acuerdo?	Are we agreed?
Sí, lo estamos.	Yes, we are.
¿Sabe Ud. que ella no viene?	Do you know that she isn't coming?
Sí, lo sé.	Yes, I do.

Example Problems

You give an opinion about a friend and another friend agrees with you. Express what your friend says.

Example: Él prefiere quedarse en casa.
Sí, él lo prefiere.

1. Él es pobre.

   Answer: Sí, él lo es.

   Use the neuter pronoun *lo* to substitute for the adjective *pobre*.

2. Él está sin fondos.

   Answer: Sí, él lo está.

   Use the neuter pronoun *lo* to substitute for the prepositional phrase *sin fondos*.

3. Él sabe que tiene que trabajar.

   Answer: Sí, él lo sabe.

   Use the neuter pronoun *lo* to substitute for the subordinate clause *que tiene que trabajar*.

Work Problems

You talk about a friend and another friend agrees with you. Express what your friend says.

1. Ella es una buena amiga.

2. Ella es simpática.

3. Ella está de buen humor hoy.

4. Ella aprende que su amiga viene.

5. Ella comprende que su amiga va a llegar a la una.

6. Ella está contenta.

Worked Solutions

1. **Ella lo es.** Use the neuter pronoun *lo* to substitute for the adjectival phrase *una buena amiga*.

2. **Ella lo es.** Use the neuter pronoun *lo* to substitute for the adjective *simpática*.

3. **Ella lo está.** Use the neuter pronoun *lo* to substitute for the prepositional phrase *de buen humor hoy*.

4. **Ella lo aprende.** Use the neuter pronoun *lo* to substitute for the subordinate clause *que su amiga viene*.

5. **Ella lo comprende.** Use the neuter pronoun *lo* to substitute for the subordinate clause *que su amiga va a llegar a la una*.

6. **Ella lo está.** Use the neuter pronoun *lo* to substitute for the adjective *contenta*.

Double-Object Pronouns

In Spanish, unlike in English, the indirect object pronoun precedes the direct object pronoun:

Ella me la explica.	She explains it to me.
Yo te los muestro.	I show them to you.

Note the following:

❑ When there are two third person object pronouns, the indirect object pronouns *le* and *les* change to *se* before the direct object pronouns *lo, la, los,* and *las*:

Yo se la presto.	I lend it to you (him, her).

❑ The phrases *a Ud. (a Uds.), a él (a ellos)* and *a ella (a ellas)* may be used to clarify the meaning of *se*:

Él se lo compra a ella. He buys it for her.

❑ The same rules for the position of single-object pronouns apply for double-object pronouns (see rules for single-object pronouns above):

Infinitive: Te las quiero enviar.	I want to send them to you.
Quiero enviártelas.	
Gerund: Me lo está escribiendo.	She's writing it to me.
Está escribiéndomelo.	
Negative command: No me lo digas.	Don't tell it to me.
Affirmative command: Dímelo.	Tell it to me.

Using Accents

When using two pronouns with an infinitive, the general rule of thumb is to count back three vowels and add an accent:

> Quiero mostrárselo.   I want to show it to you
> 　　　　3　21

When using two pronouns with an affirmative command, the general rule of thumb is to count back four vowels and add an accent:

> Muéstremelo.   Show it to me.
> 　4　3　21

If, however, the command itself has only one syllable, count back three vowels and add the accent:

> Démelo.   Give it to me.
> 　3　21

No accent is added for the negative command:

> No me lo muestre.   Don't show it to me.

When using two pronouns in a progressive tense, count back 4 vowels:

> Ella está mostrándomelo.   She is showing it to me.
> 　　　　　4　3　21

If, however, only one pronoun is used, count back 3 vowels:

> Él estaba preparándolo.   He was preparing it.
> 　　　　　3　21

Example Problems

Use double-object pronouns to express what people in different professions do.

> Example: el profesor enseña (la lección/a los alumnos)
> El profesor se la enseña.

1. un arquitecto muestra (los diseños/a mí)

   Answer: El arquitecto me los muestra.

   Replace the indirect object *a mí* with *me*. Replace the masculine plural direct object noun *los diseños* with the masculine plural direct object pronoun *los,* which expresses "them." The indirect object pronoun precedes the direct object pronoun. Place both pronouns before the conjugated verb.

2. un árbito va a explicar (las reglas/a los jugadores)

   Answer: Un árbitro va a explicárselas./Un árbitro se las va a explicar.

   Replace the feminine plural direct object noun *las reglas* with the feminine singular direct object pronoun *las*, which expresses "them." Replace the masculine plural indirect object noun phrase *a los jugadores* with the masculine plural indirect object pronoun *les*, which expresses "to them." When a third person direct object pronoun (*lo, los, la,* or *las*) and a third person indirect object pronoun (*le* or *les*) are used together, *les* becomes *se*. The indirect object pronoun precedes the direct object pronoun. Because there are two verbs but only one subject, the pronouns may be attached to the end of the infinitive. Count back three vowels and add an accent. Alternatively, place both pronouns before the conjugated verb.

3. un agricultor está vendiendo (sus productos/al público)

   Answer: Un agricultor está vendiéndoselos./Un agricultor se los está vendiendo.

   Replace the masculine plural direct object noun *sus productos* with the masculine plural direct object pronoun *los*, which expresses "them." Replace the masculine singular indirect object noun phrase *al público* with the masculine singular indirect object pronoun *le*, which expresses "to them." When a third person direct object pronoun (*lo, los, la,* or *las*) and a third person indirect object pronoun (*le* or *les*) are used together, *le* becomes *se*. The indirect object pronoun precedes the direct object pronoun. In the progressive tenses, the pronouns may be attached to the end of the gerund. When two pronouns are attached, count back four vowels and add an accent. Alternatively, place both pronouns before the conjugated form of *estar*.

Work Problems

Use double object pronouns to express what people in different professions do.

1. un dependiente dice (los precios/a los compradores)

2. una profesora está enseñando (las reglas/a las alumnas)

3. un abogado quiere dar (consejos legales/a un cliente)

4. ¡preste! (dinero/a mí)

5. ¡no prepare! (carne/a nosotros)

6. un fotógrafo va a sacar (fotografías/a ti)

7. un peluquero corta (el pelo/a vosotros)

8. un médico da (pastillas/a los enfermos)

Worked Solutions

1. **Un dependiente se los dice.**   Replace the masculine plural direct object noun *los precios* with the masculine plural direct object pronoun *los*, which expresses "them." Replace the masculine plural indirect object noun *a los compradores* with the masculine plural indirect object pronoun *les*, which expresses "them." When a third person direct object pronoun (*lo, los, la,* or *las*) and a third person indirect object pronoun (*le* or *les*) are used together, *les* becomes *se*. The indirect object pronoun precedes the direct object pronoun. Place both pronouns before the conjugated verb.

2. **Una profesora está enseñándoselas./Una profesora se las está enseñando.**   Replace the feminine plural direct object noun *las reglas* with the feminine plural direct object pronoun *las*, which expresses "them." Replace the feminine plural indirect object noun *a las alumnas* with the feminine plural indirect object pronoun *les*, which expresses "them." When a third person direct object pronoun (*lo, los, la,* or *las*) and a third person indirect object pronoun (*le* or *les*) are used together, *les* becomes *se*. The indirect object pronoun precedes the direct object pronoun. Because there are two verb forms in the progressive tense, the pronouns may be attached to the end of the gerund. Count back four vowels and add an accent. Alternatively, place both pronouns before the conjugated verb.

3. **Un abogado quiere dárselos./Un abogado se los quiere dar.**   Replace the masculine plural direct object noun *consejos legales* with the masculine plural direct object pronoun *los*, which expresses "them." Replace the masculine singular indirect object noun phrase *a su cliente* with the masculine plural object pronoun *les*, which expresses "to them." When a third person direct object pronoun (*lo, los, la,* or *las*) and a third person indirect object pronoun (*le* or *les*) are used together, *les* becomes *se*. The indirect object pronoun precedes the direct object pronoun. Because there are two verbs and only one subject, the pronouns may be attached to the end of the infinitive. Count back three vowels and add an accent. Alternatively, place both pronouns before the conjugated verb.

4. **¡Préstemelo!**   Replace the masculine singular direct object noun *dinero* with the masculine singular direct object pronoun *lo*, which expresses "it." Replace the indirect object *a mí* with *me*. The indirect object pronoun precedes the direct object pronoun. With an affirmative command, attach the pronouns to the end of the command form. Count back four vowels and add an accent.

5. **¡No nos la prepare!**   Replace the feminine singular direct object noun *carne* with the feminine singular direct object pronoun *la*, which expresses "it." Use the indirect object pronoun *nos* rather than *a nosotros* to express "to us." With a negative command, place the pronouns before the conjugated verb.

6. **Un fotógrafo va a sacártelas./Un fotógrafo te las va a sacar.**   Replace the feminine plural direct object noun *fotografías* with the feminine plural direct object pronoun *las*, which expresses "them." Replace the indirect object *a ti* with *te*. The indirect object pronoun precedes the direct object pronoun. Because there are two verbs and only one subject, the pronouns may be attached to the end of the infinitive. Count back three vowels and add an accent. Alternatively, place both pronouns before the conjugated verb.

7. **Un peluquero os lo corta.**   Replace the masculine singular direct object noun *el pelo* with the masculine singular direct object pronoun *lo*, which expresses "it." Use the indirect object pronoun *os* rather than *a vosotros* to express "to you." The indirect object pronoun precedes the direct object pronoun. Place both pronouns before the conjugated verb.

8. **Un médico se las da.**   Replace the feminine plural direct object noun *pastillas* with the feminine plural direct object pronoun *las*, which expresses "them." Replace the masculine plural indirect object noun phrase *a los enfermos* with the masculine plural indirect object pronoun *les*, which expresses "them." When a third person direct object pronoun (*lo, los, la,* or *las*) and a third person indirect object pronoun (*le* or *les*) are used together, *les* becomes *se*. The indirect object pronoun precedes the direct object pronoun. Place both pronouns before the conjugated verb.

Relative Pronouns

Relative pronouns (who, which, that) join a main clause to a dependent clause. A relative pronoun introduces the dependent clause that describes someone or something mentioned in the main clause. The person or thing to which the pronoun refers is the antecedent. A relative clause may serve as a subject, a direct object, or an object of a preposition.

The following relative pronouns are used in Spanish:

If the Antecedent Is:	Use:	Which Means:
a person (subject) a thing (object) an object of the prepositions *a, en, con,* or *de* (refers only to things)	que	who(m) that which
a person (subject or direct/indirect object an object of the prepositions *a, en, con,* or *de*	quien/quienes	who(m)
a person or a thing	el (la, los, las) cual(es) el (la, los, las) que	who which
used after a preposition (except *a, en, con,* and *de*)	el (la, los, las) cual(es) el (la, los, las) que	which
implied but not mentioned	el (la, los, las) que quien/quienes	those
neuter (an object or an idea)	lo que	which
neuter (and previously mentioned)	lo cual	which

Que

Que (who, whom, which, that), is the subject or object of a relative clause or the object of the prepositions *a, en, con,* or *de. Que* is the most frequently used relative pronoun and may refer to people or things:

> He's the man who I'm looking at.
> Es *el hombre* que estoy mirando.
> (antecedent = person = subject of relative clause)
> It's the program that I'm looking at.
> Es *el programa* que estoy mirando.
> (antecedent = thing = subject of relative clause)

She's a woman I respect.

Es *una mujer* que yo respeto.

(antecedent = person = object of relative clause)

It's an idea I respect.

Es *una idea* que yo respeto.

(antecedent = thing = object of relative clause)

Que (which, whom) is an object of a preposition that refers to things. Note that the preposition precedes the relative pronoun *que:*

Es la película de que hablamos.   That's the film we're speaking about.

The relative pronoun is always expressed in Spanish, although it is frequently omitted in English:

Es una lengua que yo utilizo frecuentemente.   It's a language (that) I use often.

Quien

Quien (who) can refer to the subject or to a direct or indirect object:

El hombre que está hablando es mi esposo.   The man who is talking is my husband.
La muchacha a quien él mira es su novia.   The girl he is looking at is his girlfriend.
El muchacho a quien escribió una carta es su   The boy to whom she wrote a letter is
amigo por correspondencia.   her pen pal.

Quien (whom) is used as the object of a preposition referring to people:

Julio es el muchacho con quien ella estudia.   Julio is the boy with whom she is studying.

Quien may be used:

❑ Instead of *que* to introduce a clause that is unnecessary to the meaning of the sentence:

La mujer, que (quien) me llamó, quiere encontrarme.

The woman, who called to me, wants to meet me.

❑ As a direct object. The personal *a* is required in *a quien* (whom), which may replace *que* as the direct object in more formal style:

That is the boy the principal spoke to this afternoon.

Es el muchacho (que) a quien el director vio esta tarde.

❑ As a subject (when no antecedent is mentioned) to express "he (she, those, the one, the ones) who":

Quien estudia mucho, aprende mucho.   He who studies a lot, learns a lot.

El (la, los, las) que may be used in place of *quien* as a subject:

La que estudia mucho, aprende mucho.   She who studies a lot, learns a lot.

El Cual and El Que

The longer forms of the relative pronouns—*el cual (la cual, los cuales, las cuales)* and *el que (la que, los que, las que)*—are used:

❑ When no antecedent is mentioned:

Los que siguen un régimen, bajan de peso.   Those who are on a diet lose weight.

❑ When there are two antecedents for clarity and emphasis, *el (la, los, las) cual(es)* or *el (la, los, las) que* refer to the more distant antecedent (the former), especially when the first of two antecedents are of the same gender:

La hermana de la señora Martín, la cual (la que) es mi profesora, la lleva a la escuela en su coche.

Mrs. Martín's sister, who is my teacher, drives her to work.

(The sister is my teacher.)

Note: Que or *quien(es)* refers to the nearer of the two (the latter):

La hermana de la señora Martín, que (quien) es mi profesora, la lleva a la escuela en su coche.

The sister of Mrs. Martín, who is my teacher, drives her to work.

(La señora Martín is my teacher.)

❑ After prepositions other than *a, con, de,* and *en* (which are used with *que* and *quien*) to refer to things:

Es la empresa para la cual (la que) yo trabajo. It's the firm for which I work.

Note that *de + el = del* before *que* and *cual:*

Es el rascacielos delante del que (del cual) hay una estatua.

It's the skyscraper in front of which there is a statue.

Lo Que

Lo que is the neuter form of *el que* and is used when there is no antecedent. *Lo que* means:

❑ "What" (that which) and is the subject of a verb:

No comprendo lo que pasó. I don't understand what happened.

❑ "What" (that which) and is the object of a verb:

Comprendo lo que Ud. está diciendo. I understand what you are saying.

Lo que is used after the pronoun *todo* to express "everything that" or "all that":

I like everything that is Spanish.   Me gusta todo lo que es español.

I didn't understand everything he wrote.   No comprendí todo lo que él escribió.

Cuyo

Cuyo (-a,-os,-as) (whose) is a relative adjective that agrees in gender and number with the people or things possessed, not with the possessor:

Las camisas, cuyas mangas son cortas, son bellas.

The shirts, whose sleeves are short, are beautiful.

Example Problems

Select the correct relative pronoun or adjective to express what one friend says to another.

1. Ese muchacho, _____ camisetas yo tomé por prestado, es mi mejor amigo.

    a. el cual

    b. lo que

    c. cuyas

    d. que

    Answer: c

    The relative adjective *cuyas* (whose) agrees in gender and number with the thing possessed *camisetas*.

2. Yo no comprendo _____ me estás explicando.

    a. la cual

    b. cuyo

    c. lo que

    d. quien

    Answer: c

    Lo que means "what" (that which) and is the object of a verb.

3. La señora _____ trabaja en esta tienda es mi madre.

    a. que

    b. cuya

    c. la cual

    d. a quien

    Answer: a

    Que is the subject of a relative clause, refers to people, and means "who."

Work Problems

Select the correct relative pronoun or adjective to express what one friend says to another.

1. Tengo un libro en _____ anoto mis pensamientos íntimos.

    a. lo cual

    b. que

    c. quien

    d. lo que

2. La madre de Tomás, _____ está ocupada, no puede ayudarnos con nuestras tareas.

   a. de quien

   b. lo que

   c. cuya

   d. la cual

3. Carlota es la amiga con _____ hice un viaje.

   a. que

   b. quien

   c. lo que

   d. la que

4. _____ practican mucho, hablan bien el español.

   a. Los que

   b. Cuyos

   c. Que

   d. Lo que

5. Subí una vez al tejado, desde _____ podía ver toda la ciudad.

   a. lo que

   b. el cual

   c. que

   d. quien

6. Este hombre es el doctor a _____ yo llamé.

   a. que

   b. cuyo

   c. quien

   d. cual

Worked Solutions

1. **b**   *Que* is the object of the preposition *en* and refers to things.

2. **d**   *La cual* refers to the more distant antecedent, *la madre,* when two antecedents are mentioned.

3. **b**   *Quien* is the object of the preposition *con* and refers to people.

4. **a**   *Los que* can be used as a subject when no antecedent is mentioned.

5. **b** *El cual* is used after prepositions other than *a, con, de,* and *en* to refer to things. *El cual* refers to the masculine singular antecedent *el tejado*.

6. **c** *Quien* is the object of the preposition *a* and refers to people.

Chapter Problems

Problems

Answer questions about yourself by replacing the noun objects with object pronouns.

Examples: ¿Lavas el coche?
             Lo lavas.
             ¿Envías cartas a tus amigos?
             Se las envío.

1. ¿Limpias tu casa?

2. ¿Vas a preparar las comidas para la familia?

3. ¿Estás estudiando el español?

4. ¿Quieres ayudar a tus primos?

5. ¿Te gustan los deportes?

6. ¿Escribes cartas a tus parientes?

7. ¿Das consejos a tus amigas?

8. ¿Ofreces regalos a tus padres?

9. ¿Muestras tu casa a tu amigo?

10. ¿Compras chocolate a tu novio (-a)?

You are on vacation. Express what you say to a person you meet.

11. The church? (You, formal singular) Show it to me.

12. Her friend? He is going out but she doesn't know it.

13. The museums? They don't visit them.

14. Our room? The maid is going to clean it for us.

15. That T-shirt? (You, formal singular) Don't buy it for her.

16. His brothers? He doesn't want to introduce them to you (formal singular).

17. The problem? (You, formal singular) Don't tell it to them.

18. The tickets? I am buying them for us.

19. Your (formal singular) suitcase? The porter is looking for it for you (formal singular).

20. The information? My friends are going to send it to us.

Complete each sentence about what is happening in the park by using a relative pronoun and any appropriate preposition.

21. Los padres de Ana, _____ están hablando, no prestan atención a su hija.

22. Yo sé _____ necesitan esos niños.

23. El hombre, _____ Rogelio escucha, es su padre.

24. Mira al muchacho _____ ellos se burlan.

25. Esa mujer, _____ niñas se están riendo, es mi tía.

26. Carlota lanza una pelota sin prestar atención, _____ no les gusta a sus padres.

27. Los muchachos _____ juegan mis nietos son muy amables.

28. El deporte _____ les gusta más es el béisbol.

29. _____ es sincero siempre gana.

30. La muchacha _____ vende helados es simpática.

Answers and Solutions

1. **Answer: La limpio.**   Answer with the *yo* form of the verb. To conjugate *limpiar*, drop the -*ar* ending and add -*o* as the ending. Replace the feminine singular direct object noun *tu casa* with the feminine singular direct object pronoun *la*, which expresses "it." Place the direct object noun before the conjugated verb.

2. **Answer: Voy a prepararlas para la familia./Las voy a preparar para la familia.** Answer with the *yo* form of the verb. The verb *ir* (to go) is irregular in all forms and must be memorized. The *yo* form, like that of a few irregular verbs, ends in -*oy*. All forms start with a *v-*. Replace the feminine plural direct object noun *las comidas* with the feminine plural direct object pronoun *las*, which expresses "them." Because there are two verbs and only one subject, the pronoun may be attached to the end of the infinitive. Count back three vowels and add an accent. Alternatively, place the pronoun before the conjugated verb.

3. **Answer: Estoy estudiándolo./Lo estoy estudiando.**   Answer with the *yo* form of the verb. The verb *estar* (to go) is irregular in all forms and must be memorized. The *yo* form, like that of a few irregular verbs, ends in -*oy*. Replace the masculine singular direct object noun *el español* with the masculine singular direct object pronoun *lo*, which expresses "it." Because there are two verb forms in the progressive tense, the pronoun may be attached to the end of the gerund. Count back three vowels and add an accent. Alternatively, place both pronouns before the conjugated verb.

4. **Answer: Quiero ayudarlos./Los quiero ayudar.**   Answer with the *yo* form of the verb. *Querer* is conjugated like a regular *-er* verb. The internal *e* of *querer*, however, changes to *ie* in all forms except *nosotros* and *vosotros*. *Ayudar* is followed by the personal *a* and, therefore, requires a direct object. Replace the masculine plural direct object noun phrase *a tus primos* with the masculine plural direct object pronoun *los*, which expresses "them." Because there are two verbs and only one subject, the pronoun may be attached to the end of the infinitive. Count back three vowels and add an accent. Alternatively, place the pronoun before the conjugated verb.

5. **Answer: Me gustan.**   Use the indirect object pronoun *me* to express "to me" to respond to the question containing *te* (to you). The verb *gustar* must be used in the third person plural to agree with the subject, *los deportes*. Drop the *-ar* ending and add the third person plural ending *(-an)*.

6. **Answer: Se las escribo.**   Answer with the *yo* form of the verb. To conjugate *escribir*, drop the *-ir* ending and add *-o* as the ending. Replace the feminine plural direct object noun *cartas* with the feminine plural direct object pronoun *las*, which expresses "them." Replace the masculine plural indirect object noun phrase *a tus parientes* with the masculine plural indirect object pronoun *les*, which expresses "them." When a third person direct object pronoun (*lo, los, la,* or *las*) and a third person indirect object pronoun (*le* or *les*) are used together, *les* becomes *se*. The indirect object pronoun precedes the direct object pronoun. Place both pronouns before the conjugated verb.

7. **Answer: Se las doy.**   Answer with the *yo* form of the verb. The verb *dar* (to give) is irregular in the *yo* form only. The *yo* form, like that of a few irregular verbs, ends in *-oy*. Replace the masculine plural direct object noun *consejos* with the masculine plural direct object pronoun *los*, which expresses "them." Replace the feminine plural indirect-object noun phrase *a tus amigas* with the feminine plural indirect object pronoun *les*, which expresses "them." When a third person direct object pronoun (*lo, los, la,* or *las*) and a third person indirect object pronoun (*le* or *les*) are used together, *les* becomes *se*. The indirect object pronoun precedes the direct object pronoun. Place both pronouns before the conjugated verb.

8. **Answer: Se los ofrezco.**   Answer with the *yo* form of the verb. Because *ofrecer* ends in a vowel + *cer*, the *yo* form requires that the final *c* be changed to *zc* before adding *-o*. Replace the masculine plural direct object noun *regalos* with the masculine plural direct object pronoun *los*, which expresses "them." Replace the masculine plural indirect object noun phrase *a tus padres* with the masculine plural indirect object pronoun *les*, which expresses "them." When a third person direct object pronoun (*lo, los, la,* or *las*) and a third person indirect object pronoun (*le* or *les*) are used together, *les* becomes *se*. The indirect object pronoun precedes the direct object pronoun. Place both pronouns before the conjugated verb.

9. **Answer: Se la muestro.**   Answer with the *yo* form of the verb. *Mostrar* undergoes an internal stem change of *o* to *ue* in all forms except *nosotros* and *vosotros*. Drop the *-ar* ending and add *-o* for the first person singular. Replace the feminine singular direct object noun *casa* with the feminine singular direct object pronoun *la*, which expresses "it." Replace the masculine singular indirect object noun phrase *a tu amigo* with the masculine plural indirect object pronoun *le*, which expresses "to him." When a third person direct object pronoun (*lo, los, la,* or *las*) and a third person indirect object pronoun (*le* or *les*) are used together, *le* becomes *se*. The indirect object pronoun precedes the direct object pronoun. Place both pronouns before the conjugated verb.

10. **Answer: Se lo compro.** Answer with the *yo* form of the verb. To conjugate *comprar*, drop the *-ar* ending and add *-o* as the ending. Replace the masculine singular direct object noun *chocolate* with the masculine singular direct object pronoun *lo*, which expresses "it." Replace the masculine or feminine singular indirect object noun phrase *a tu novio (-a)* with the masculine or feminine singular indirect object pronoun *le*, which expresses "to him/to her." When a third person direct object pronoun (*lo, los, la,* or *las*) and third person indirect object pronoun (*le* or *les*) are used together, *le* becomes *se*. The indirect object pronoun precedes the direct object pronoun. Place both pronouns before the conjugated verb.

11. **Answer: ¿La iglesia? Muéstremela.** Use *la iglesia* to express "the church." Use the formal command form of *mostrar*. *Mostrar* undergoes an internal stem change from *o* to *ue* in all forms except *nosotros* and *vosotros*. For the formal command, use the *Ud.* form and change *-a* to *-e*. Use the indirect object pronoun *me* to express "to me." Use the feminine singular direct object pronoun *la* to substitute for the feminine singular direct object noun *iglesia*. The indirect object pronoun precedes the direct object pronoun. With an affirmative command, attach the pronouns to the end of the command form. Count back four vowels and add an accent.

12. **Answer: ¿Su amigo? Él sale pero ella no lo sabe.** Use *su amigo* to express "her friend." *Salir* is regular in the third person singular form. Drop the *-ir* ending and add *-e*. Use *pero* to express "but." *Saber* is regular in the third person singular form. Drop the *-er* ending and add *-e*. Use the masculine singular direct object pronoun *lo* to substitute for the masculine singular direct object noun phrase *su amigo* and place it before the conjugated verb. Use *no* to make the sentence negative and place it before the direct object pronoun *lo*.

13. **Answer: ¿Los museos? Ellos no los visitan.** Use *los museos* to express "the museums." Conjugate the *visitar* in the third person plural by dropping the *-ar* ending and adding *-an*. Use the masculine plural direct object pronoun *los* to substitute for the masculine singular direct object noun phrase *los museos* and place it before the conjugated verb. Use *no* to make the sentence negative and place it before the direct object pronoun *los*.

14. **Answer: ¿Nuestra habitación? La criada va a limpiárnosla./La criada nos la va a limpiar.** Use *nuestra habitación* to express "our room." Use *la criada* to express "the maid." Use *ir + a +* infinitive to express what the maid is going to do. Use the verb *limpiar* to express "to clean." Use the irregular third person singular form of *ir: va*. Use the feminine singular direct object pronoun *la* to substitute for the feminine singular direct object noun phrase *nuestra habitación*. Use the indirect object pronoun *nos* to express "for us." The indirect object pronoun precedes the direct object pronoun. Because there are two verbs and only one subject, the pronouns may be attached to the end of the infinitive. Count back three vowels and add an accent. Alternatively, place both pronouns before the conjugated verb.

15. **Answer: ¿Esa camiseta? No se la compre.** Use *esa camiseta* to express "that T-shirt." Use the formal command form of *comprar*. For the formal command, use the *Ud.* form and change *-a* to *-e*. Use the feminine singular direct object pronoun *la* to substitute for the feminine singular direct object noun phrase *esa camiseta*. Use the indirect object pronoun *le* to express "to her." When a third person direct object pronoun (*lo, los, la,* or *las*) and a third person indirect object pronoun (*le* or *les*) are used together, *le* becomes *se*. The indirect object pronoun precedes the direct object pronoun. In a negative command, place both pronouns before the conjugated verb.

16. **Answer: ¿Sus hermanos? Él no quiere presentárselos./Él no se los quiere presentar.**
Use *sus hermanos* to express "his brothers." *Querer* is conjugated like a regular -*er* verb. The internal *e* of *querer*, however, changes to *ie* in all forms except *nosotros* and *vosotros*. Because there is only one subject and *querer* is conjugated, a verb infinitive must follow. Use *presentar* to express "to introduce." Use the masculine plural direct object pronoun *los* to substitute for the masculine plural direct object noun phrase *sus hermanos*. Use the indirect object pronoun *le* to express "to you" in the formal form. When a third person direct object pronoun (*lo, los, la,* or *las*) and a third person indirect object pronoun (*le* or *les*) are used together, *le* becomes *se*. The indirect object pronoun precedes the direct object pronoun. Because there are two verbs and only one subject, the pronouns may be attached to the end of the infinitive. Count back three vowels and add an accent. Alternatively, place both pronouns before the conjugated verb.

17. **Answer: ¿El problema? No se lo diga.** Use *el problema* to express "the problem." To form the command of the irregular verb *decir*, use the *yo* form of the present: *digo*. Drop the -*o* ending and add -*a*. Use the masculine singular direct object pronoun *lo* to substitute for the masculine singular direct object noun *el problema* and place it before the conjugated verb. Use the indirect object pronoun *les* to express "to them." The indirect object pronoun precedes the direct object pronoun. When a third person direct object pronoun (*lo, los, la,* or *las*) and a third person indirect object pronoun (*le* or *les*) are used together, *les* becomes *se*. In a negative command, place both pronouns before the conjugated verb.

18. **Answer: ¿Los billetes? Yo estoy comprándonoslos./Yo nos los estoy comprando.**
Use *los billetes* to express "the tickets." The verb *estar* (to go) is irregular in all forms and must be memorized. The *yo* form, like that of a few irregular verbs, ends in -*oy*. Form the gerund of *comprar* by dropping the -*ar* ending and adding -*ando*. Replace the masculine plural direct object noun *los billetes* with the masculine plural direct object pronoun *los*, which expresses "them." Use the indirect object pronoun *nos* to express "for us." The indirect object pronoun precedes the direct object pronoun. Because there are two verb forms in the progressive tense, the pronouns may be attached to the end of the gerund. Count back four vowels and add an accent. Alternatively, place both pronouns before the conjugated verb.

19. **Answer: ¿Su maleta? El portero está buscándosela./El portero se la está buscando.**
Use *su maleta* to express "your suitcase." Use *el portero* to express "the porter." The verb *estar* (to go) is irregular in all forms and must be memorized. Use the third person singular form: *está*. Form the gerund of *buscar* by dropping the -*ar* ending and adding -*ando*. Replace the feminine singular direct object noun phrase *su maleta* with the feminine singular direct object pronoun *la*, which expresses "it." Use the indirect object pronoun *le* to express "for you." The indirect object pronoun precedes the direct object pronoun. Because there are two verb forms in the progressive tense, the pronouns may be attached to the end of the gerund. Count back four vowels and add an accent. Alternatively, place both pronouns before the conjugated verb.

20. **Answer: ¿La información? Mis amigos van a enviárnosla./Mis amigos nos la van a enviar.** Use *la información* to express "the information." Use *mis amigos* to express "my friends." Use *ir* + *a* + infinitive to express what the friends are going to do. Use the irregular third person plural form of *ir: vas*. Use the verb *enviar* to express "to send." Use the feminine singular direct object pronoun *la* to substitute for the feminine singular direct object noun *la información*. Use the indirect object pronoun *nos* to express "for us." The indirect object pronoun precedes the direct object pronoun. Because there are two verbs and only one subject, the pronouns may be attached to the end of the infinitive. Count back three vowels and add an accent. Alternatively, place both pronouns before the conjugated verb. The indirect object pronoun precedes the direct object pronoun.

21. **Answer: los cuales**   *Los cuales* refers to the more distant antecedent, *los padres,* when two antecedents are mentioned.

22. **Answer: lo que**   *Lo que* means "what" (that which) and is the object of a verb.

23. **Answer: que/a quien**   *Que* is the subject of a relative clause, refers to people, and means "who." The personal *a* is required in *a quien* (whom), which may replace *que* as the direct object in more formal style.

24. **Answer: de quien**   The preposition *de* (of) must be used in this context with the verb *burlarse* (to make fun of). *Quien* is the object of the preposition *con* and refers to people.

25. **Answer: cuyas**   The relative adjective *cuyas* (whose) agrees in gender and number with the thing possessed: *niñas.*

26. **Answer: lo que**   *Lo que* means "what" (that which) and is the object of a verb.

27. **Answer: con quienes**   The preposition *con* (with) must be used in this context with the verb *jugar* (to play).*Quienes* is the object of the preposition *con* and refers to people.

28. **Answer: que**   *Que* is the subject of a relative clause, refers to things, and means "that."

29. **Answer: El que**   *El que* can be used as a subject when no antecedent is mentioned.

30. **Answer: que**   *Que* is the subject of a relative clause, refers to people, and means "who."

Supplemental Chapter Problems

Problems
Answer questions about yourself by replacing the noun objects with object pronouns.

1.   ¿Hablas a tus primos a menudo?

2.   ¿Estás escribiendo a tus amigos?

3.   ¿Puedes tocar el piano?

4.   ¿Sabes nadar?

5.   ¿Te falta dinero?

6.   ¿Te duelen los ojos?

7.   ¿Prestas dinero a tus amigos?

8.   ¿Envías cartas a tu amigo por correspondencia?

9.   ¿Vas a traer flores a tu madre?

10.   ¿Mandas fotografías a tu familia?

Express what you say to someone at a garage sale.

11. That chair? Bring it to me.

12. Those boots? They will sell them to you (informal singular)

13. The cups? They are cleaning them for you (formal plural).

14. The bicycle? Don't give it to him.

15. The dolls? He is going to buy them for us.

16. Those lamps? They want to show them to him.

17. That poster? Don't bring it to them.

18. The price? She doesn't want to tell it to you (formal singular).

19. The toys? I am buying them for them.

20. That radio? He offers it to me.

Complete each sentence about what is happening in the office by using a relative pronoun and any appropriate preposition.

21. _____ tienen paciencia, salen bien.

22. Sarita llega tarde a la oficina, _____ no le gusta al jefe.

23. Esos hombres, _____ trabajo es difícil, son nuestros mejores empleados.

24. Los empleados, _____ ellos hablan, son muy buenos.

25. El documento, _____ yo acabo de recibir, es ilegible.

26. Le envié todo_____ me pidió.

27. El jefe de Ricardo y Ernesto, _____ habla por teléfono, es simpático.

28. La mujer _____ él sale es muy importante.

29. El procesador de textos _____ utilizan es muy anticuado.

30. El muchacho, _____ yo busco, me ayudará.

Solutions

1. Les hablo a menudo. (direct and indirect object pronouns, p. 129; position of object pronouns, p. 132)

2. Estoy escribiéndoles./Les estoy escribiendo. (direct and indirect object pronouns, p. 129; position of object pronouns, p. 132)

3. Puedo tocarlo./Lo puedo tocar. (direct and indirect object pronouns, p. 129; position of object pronouns, p. 132)

4. Lo sé. (direct and indirect object pronouns, p. 129; position of object pronouns, p. 132)

5. Me falta. (double-object pronouns, p. 139; position of object pronouns, p. 132; verbs like *gustar,* p. 135)

6. Me duelen. (double-object pronouns, p. 139; position of object pronouns, p. 132; verbs like *gustar* and other similar verbs, p.135)

7. Se lo presto. (double-object pronouns, p. 139; position of object pronouns, p. 132)

8. Se las envío. (double-object pronouns, p. 139; position of object pronouns, p. 132)

9. Voy a traérselas./Se las voy a traer. (double-object pronouns, p. 139; position of object pronouns, p. 132)

10. Se las mando. (double-object pronouns, p. 139; position of object pronouns, p. 132)

11. ¿Esa silla? Traígamela. (position of object pronouns, p. 132; double-object pronouns, p. 139)

12. ¿Esas botas? Van a vendértelas./Te las van a vender. (position of object pronouns, p. 132; double-object pronouns, p. 139)

13. ¿Las tazas? Están lavándoselas./Se las están lavando. (position of object pronouns, p. 132; double-object pronouns, p. 139)

14. ¿La bicicleta? No se la dé. (position of object pronouns, p. 132; double-object pronouns, p. 139)

15. ¿Las muñecas? Va a comprárnoslas./Nos las va a comprar. (position of object pronouns, p. 132; double-object pronouns, p. 139)

16. ¿Esas lámparas? Quieren mostrárselas./Se las quieren mostrar. (position of object pronouns, p. 132; double-object pronouns, p. 139)

17. ¿Ese póster? No se lo traiga. (position of object pronouns, p. 132; double-object pronouns, p. 139)

18. ¿El precio? No quiere decírselo./No se lo quiere decir. (position of object pronouns, p. 132; double-object pronouns, p. 139)

19. ¿Los juguetes? Estoy comprándoselos./Se los estoy comprando. (position of object pronouns, p. 132; double-object pronouns, p. 139)

20. ¿La radio? Él me la ofrece. (position of object pronouns, p. 132; double-object pronouns, p. 139)

21. Los que/Quienes (relative pronouns, p. 143)

22. lo que (relative pronouns, p. 143)

23. cuyo (relative pronouns, p. 143)

24. a (de) quienes (relative pronouns, p. 143)

25. que (relative pronouns, p. 143)

26. lo que (relative pronouns, p. 143)

27. el cual (relative pronouns, p. 143)

28. con quien (relative pronouns, p. 143)

29. que (relative pronouns, p. 143)

30. a quien (relative pronouns, p. 143)

Chapter 7
Adjectives, Adverbs, and Comparisons

Adjectives

Spanish adjectives agree in number (singular or plural) and gender (masculine or feminine) with the nouns they describe.

The Gender of Adjectives

Note how to form the feminine of Spanish adjectives:

❑ Masculine singular adjectives ending in -o form the feminine by changing -o to -a:

un hombre afortunado	a fortunate man
una mujer afortunada	a fortunate woman

❑ Masculine singular adjectives ending in -a, -e, or a consonant require no change to get the feminine form:

un alumno optimista	an optimistic male student
una alumna optimista	an optimistic female student
un abogado importante	an important male lawyer
una abogada importante	an important female lawyer
un amigo fiel	a faithful male friend
una amiga fiel	a faithful female friend

❑ Adjectives ending in -or, -ón, -án, or -ín drop the accent (if one is present) and add -a to form the feminine:

un profesor hablador	a talkative male teacher
una profesora habladora	a talkative female teacher
un muchacho picarón	a naughty (roguish) boy
una muchacha picarona	a naughty (roguish) girl
un chico holgazán	a lazy boy
una chica holgazana	a lazy girl

un niño chiquitín	a tiny boy
una niña chiquitina	a tiny girl

❑ Adjectives of nationality whose masculine form ends in a consonant drop the accent on the final vowel and add -a to form the feminine:

Él es japonés.	He is Japanese.
Ella es japonesa.	She is Japanese.
Él es alemán.	He is German.
Ella es alemana.	She is German.

The Plural of Adjectives

All Spanish adjectives must agree in number (singular or plural) with the nouns they describe. Plurals are formed as follows:

❑ Add -s to form the plural of adjectives ending in a vowel:

Él es bajo.	He is short.	Ella es rubia.	She is blond.
Ellos son bajos.	They are short.	Ellas son rubias.	They are blond.

❑ Add -es to form the plural of adjectives ending in a consonant:

Él es popular.	He is popular.	Ellos son populares.	They are popular.

❑ Singular adjectives ending in -z change z to c in the plural:

Ella es feliz.	She is happy.	Ellas son felices.	They are happy.

❑ Some adjectives add or drop an accent mark to maintain original stress:

Él es joven.	He is young.	Ellos son jóvenes.	They are young.
Él es cortés.	He is courteous.	Ellos son corteses.	They are courteous.

❑ When an adjective modifies two or more nouns of different genders, the masculine plural form of the adjective is used:

El niño y la niña son españoles.	The boy and the girl are Spanish.

Example Problems

Describe people by giving the appropriate form of the adjective.

1. Jorge es sincero. Luisa es _____ también.

   Answer: sincera

   To describe Luisa, you must change *sincero* to the feminine singular form by changing the -o to -a.

2. Marco es feliz. Alma y Luz son _____ también.

   Answer: felices

   To form the plural of an adjective ending in a -z, change z to c and add -es.

3.   Manuela es alerta. Arturo es _____ también.

  Answer: alerta

  Alerta remains unchanged in the masculine form because certain adjectives always end in *-a*.

Work Problems

Describe more people by giving the appropriate form of the adjective.

1.   Graciela es popular. Ricardo y Miguel son _____ también.

2.   Tomás y Ana son sagaces. Felipe es _____ también.

3.   Sarita es española. Claudio es _____ también.

4.   Pedro es joven. Marta y Susana son _____ también.

5.   Clara es pesimista. Francisco es _____ también.

6.   Javier y Paco son alegres. María y Josefina son _____ también.

7.   Alejandra es chiquitina. Alfonso es _____ también.

8.   Alberto es inglés. Roberto y Luis son _____ también.

Worked Solutions

1.   **populares**   To form the plural of an adjective ending in a consonant, add *-es*.

2.   **sagaz**   To change a plural adjective ending in *-ces* to the singular, drop *-ces* and add *-z*.

3.   **español**   To change this irregular feminine adjective of nationality ending in *-a* to the masculine, drop the final *-a*.

4.   **jóvenes**   To form the plural of an adjective ending in a consonant, add *-es*. The *o* of *jóvenes* requires an accent to maintain the proper stress.

5.   **pesimista**   *Pesimista* remains unchanged in the masculine form because certain adjectives always end in *-a*.

6.   **alegres**   *Alegres* remains unchanged in the feminine plural form because adjectives ending in *-e* are invariable in the singular.

7.   **chiquitín**   To change this irregular masculine adjective ending in *-a* to the masculine, drop the final *-a* and put an accent over the final *i* to maintain proper stress.

8.   **ingleses**   To form the plural of an adjective ending in a consonant, add *-es*. The *é* of *inglés* drops its accent to maintain the proper stress.

Position of Adjectives

Descriptive adjectives normally follow the nouns they describe, unless they refer to an inherent quality of the noun or are being used stylistically in literature:

La casa blanca es grande.
The white house is big.
La tierra está cubierta de un manto de blanca nieve.
The earth is covered with a blanket of white snow.

Adjectives that impose limits (numbers, possessive adjectives, demonstrative adjectives, and adjectives of quantity) usually precede the noun:

Hay mucho ruido.	There's a lot of noise.
El lunes es el peor día de la semana.	Monday is the worst day of the week.

The meaning of some adjectives changes depending on whether they are positioned before or after the nouns they modify. Adjectives before the noun tend to have a more literal meaning, while those following the noun are more figurative in nature.

Before the Noun		*After the Noun*	
una antigua costumbre	a former custom	una costumbre antigua	an ancient custom
una cierta cosa	a certain thing	una cosa cierta	a true thing
las diferentes ideas	various ideas	las ideas diferentes	different ideas
una gran catedral	a great cathedral	una catedral grande	a big cathedral
el mismo hombre	the same man	el hombre mismo	the man himself
una nueva casa	a new (different) house	una casa nueva	a brand-new house
una pobre mujer	an unfortunate woman	una mujer pobre	a poor woman
una simple idea	a simple idea	una idea simple	a foolish idea
una sola muchacha	only one girl	una muchacha sola	a solitary girl
un triste niño	a sorry boy	un niño triste	an unhappy boy
un viejo colega	a long-time colleague	un colega viejo	an elderly colleague

When a noun is modified by more than one adjective, each adjective is positioned according to the previously mentioned rules. An adjective with more emphasis generally precedes the noun. Two adjectives in the same position are joined by *y* (and) or are separated by a comma:

unos libros importantes	some important books
una sola simple idea	only one big idea
un edificio grande y moderno	a big, modern building
un castillo antiguo, majestuoso	an ancient, majestic castle

Shortened Forms of Adjectives

Some Spanish adjectives take on shortened forms in the following situations:

❏ Some adjectives (generally used before the nouns they modify) drop the final -o directly before a masculine singular noun:

uno	un hombre	one man
bueno	un buen día	a good day
malo	un mal momento	a bad moment
primero	el primer beso	the first kiss
tercero	el tercer mes	the third month
alguno	algún elemento	some element
ninguno	ningún problema	no problem

If a preposition separates the adjective from its noun, however, the original adjective is used:

uno de mis amigos   one of my friends

❏ *Grande* becomes *gran* (important, famous) **before** (but not after) a singular masculine or feminine noun:

una gran persona	a great person
una casa grande	a big house

❏ *Ciento* becomes *cien* before nouns and before the numbers *mil* and *millones:*

cien libros	100 books
cien mil dólares	100,000 dollars
cien millones de dólares	100 million dollars

❏ The masculine *Santo* becomes *San* before the name of a saint whose name does not begin with *To-* or *Do-:*

San Antonio	Saint Anthony
Santo Domingo	Saint Dominick
Santo Tomás	Saint Thomas

Example Problems

Express in Spanish what each person is looking for.

Example: Pedro/a new shirt

Pedro busca una camisa nueva.

1. los Hidalgo/a big house

   Answer: Los Hidalgo buscan una casa grande.

   Use the third person plural ending of the regular -ar verb *buscar (-an).* Use *una casa* to express "a house." Use *grande* to express "big." Adjectives that end in -e are invariable in the singular. *Grandes* is a descriptive adjective that follows the noun it modifies.

2. Alberto/a good restaurant

   Answer: Alberto busca un buen restaurante.

   Use the third person singular ending of the regular -ar verb *buscar (-a)*. Use *un restaurante* to express "a restaurant." Use *bueno* to express "good." *Bueno* is an adjective that generally precedes the noun it modifies. *Bueno* drops the final -o directly before a masculine singular noun.

3. Diego y Vicente/certain sports cars

   Answer: Diego y Vicente buscan ciertos coches deportivos.

   Use the third person plural ending of the regular -ar verb *buscar (-an)*. Use *coches* to express "cars." Use *cierto* to express "certain." Add -s to the singular form of the adjective to form the plural. *Ciertos* is an adjective that generally precedes the noun it modifies. Use *deportivo* to express "sports." Add -s to the singular form of the adjective to form the plural. *Deportivos* is a descriptive adjective that follows the noun it modifies.

Work Problems

Express in Spanish what each person is looking for.

1. Blanca/a red dress

2. Domingo/a good job

3. los López/famous museums

4. la señora Rodolfo/100 dollars

5. Benjamín y Miguel/a simple solution

6. el señor Rivera/some important documents

7. Carlota/several longtime (female) friends

8. Alicia/a poor faithful dog

Worked Solutions

1. **Answer: Blanca busca un vestido rojo.** Use the third person singular ending of the regular -ar verb *buscar (-a)*. Use *un vestido* to express "a dress." *Rojo* is a descriptive adjective that follows the noun it modifies.

2. **Answer: Domingo busca un buen puesto.** Use the third person singular ending of the regular -ar verb *buscar (-a)*. Use *un puesto* to express "a job." *Bueno* is an adjective that generally precedes the noun it modifies. *Bueno* drops the final -o directly before a masculine singular noun.

3. **Answer: Los López buscan museos famosos.** Use the third person plural ending of the regular -ar verb *buscar (-an)*. Use *museos* to express "museums." *Famoso* is a descriptive adjective that follows the noun it modifies. Add -s to the singular form of the adjective to form the plural.

4. **Answer: La señora Rodolfo busca cien dólares.** Use the third person singular ending of the regular -ar verb *buscar* (-a). Use *dólares* to express "dollars." Use *ciento* to express "dollars." *Ciento* becomes *cien* before a noun.

5. **Answer: Benjamín y Miguel buscan una simple solución.** Use the third person plural ending of the regular -ar verb *buscar* (-an). Use *una solución* to express "a solution." Use *simple* to express "simple." *Simple* has the connotation of "easy" and, therefore, precedes the noun it modifies.

6. **Answer: El señor Rivera busca algunos documentos importantes.** Use the third person singular ending of the regular -ar verb *buscar* (-a). Use *documentos* to express "documents." *Alguno* expresses "some." Add -s to the singular form of the adjective to form the plural. *Algunos* is an adjective that generally precedes the noun it modifies. *Importante* is a descriptive adjective that follows the noun it modifies. Add -s to the singular form of the adjective to form the plural.

7. **Answer: Carlota busca a varias viejas amigas.** Use the third person singular ending of the regular -ar verb *buscar* (-a). The personal *a* is needed because Carlota is looking for people. Use *amigos* to express "friends." Change *o* to *a* to form the feminine plural noun. *Varios* is an adjective that generally precedes the noun it modifies. Change *o* to *a* to form the feminine plural adjective. Use *viejo* to express "old." Add -s to the singular form of the adjective to form the plural. Change *o* to *a* to form the feminine plural adjective. *Viejas* has the connotation of "longtime" and, therefore, precedes the noun it modifies.

8. **Answer: Alicia busca un pobre perro fiel.** Use the third person singular ending of the regular -ar verb *buscar* (-a). Use *un perro* to express "a dog." Use *pobre* to express "poor." *Pobre* has the connotation of "unfortunate" and, therefore, precedes the noun it modifies. Use *fiel* to express "faithful."

Adverbs

Formation of Adverbs

Adverbs are formed by adding -*mente* to the **feminine singular** form of an adjective:

Masculine Adjective	Feminine Adjective	Adverb	Meaning
perfecto	perfecta	perfectamente	perfectly
paciente	paciente	pacientemente	patiently
fiel	fiel	fielmente	faithfully
feroz	feroz	ferozmente	ferociously

Note that the adverb *recientemente* (recently) becomes *recién* before a past participle:

recién nacido   recently born (newborn)

When more than one adverb ending in -*mente* is used, only the last adverb in the series uses the -*mente* ending; the other adverbs use the feminine form of the adjective:

Él habla paciente, lenta y claramente.

He speaks patiently, slowly, and clearly.

Adverbial Phrases

The prepositions *con* (with), *en* (in), and *por* (by) + noun, and the expressions *de manera* + adjective or *de modo* + adjective may be used to form an adverbial phrase:

Phrase	Adverb	Meaning
con franqueza	francamente	frankly
en silencio	silenciosamente	silently
por instinto	instintivamente	instinctively

For example:

>   Los alumnos escuchan en silencio.
>
>   Los alumnos escuchan silenciosamente.
>
>   Los alumnos escuchan de manera silenciosa (de modo silencioso).
>
>   The students listen silently.

Position of Adverbs

In simple tenses, adverbs are generally placed directly after the verbs they modify. Sometimes, however, the position of the adverb is variable and is placed where you would logically put an English adverb. Note that adverbs expressing doubt are placed before the verb:

>   Como mucho en mi restaurante favorito.   I eat a lot in my favorite restaurant.
>
>   Generalmente, no trabajo los domingos.   I generally don't work on Sunday.
>
>   Quizá(s) venga el lunes.   Perhaps he will come on Monday.

Example Problems

Express what people do by replacing the adverbial phrase with an adverb.

1. Ella corre *con rapidez*.

    Answer: Ella corre rápidamente.

    To form the adverb, drop the preposition *con*. Adverbs are formed by adding *-mente* to the feminine singular form of an adjective. Select the adjective expressing "quick": *rápido*. Change *rápido* to its feminine singular form by changing the final *-o* to *-a*. Add *-mente*.

2. Yo salgo *con frecuencia*.

    Answer: Yo salgo frecuentemente.

    To form the adverb, drop the preposition *con*. Adverbs are formed by adding *-mente* to the feminine singular form of an adjective. Select the adjective expressing "frecuent": *frecuente*. Adjectives ending in *-e* are invariable in the singular. Add *-mente*.

3. Nosotros jugamos *con cuidado*.

   Answer: Nosotros jugamos cuidadosamente.

   To form the adverb, drop the preposition *con*. Adverbs are formed by adding *-mente* to the feminine singular form of an adjective. Select the adjective expressing "careful": *cuidadoso*. Change *cuidadoso* to its feminine singular form by changing the final *-o* to *-a*. Add *-mente*.

Worked Problems

Replace the adverbial phrase with an adverb to express how people do things.

1. Él trabaja con habilidad.

2. Ellas escuchan con atención.

3. Nosotros nos explicamos con claridad.

4. Tú contestas con franqueza.

5. Yo hablo con cariño.

6. Vosotros lloráis con tristeza.

Worked Solutions

1. **Answer: Él trabaja hábilmente.**   To form the adverb, drop the preposition *con*. Adverbs are formed by adding *-mente* to the feminine singular form of an adjective. Select the adjective expressing "skilled": *hábil*. Adjectives ending in a consonant are generally invariable in the singular. Add *-mente*.

2. **Answer: Ellas escuchan atentamente.**   To form the adverb, drop the preposition *con*. Adverbs are formed by adding *-mente* to the feminine singular form of an adjective. Select the adjective expressing "attentive": *atento*. Change *atento* to its feminine singular form by changing the final *-o* to *-a*. Add *-mente*.

3. **Answer: Nosotros nos explicamos claramente.**   To form the adverb, drop the preposition *con*. Adverbs are formed by adding *-mente* to the feminine singular form of an adjective. Select the adjective expressing "clear": *claro*. Change *claro* to its feminine singular form by changing the final *-o* to *-a*. Add *-mente*.

4. **Answer: Tú contestas francamente.**   To form the adverb, drop the preposition *con*. Adverbs are formed by adding *-mente* to the feminine singular form of an adjective. Select the adjective expressing "frank": *franco*. Change *franco* to its feminine singular form by changing the final *-o* to *-a*. Add *-mente*.

5. **Answer: Yo hablo cariñosamente.**   To form the adverb, drop the preposition *con*. Adverbs are formed by adding *-mente* to the feminine singular form of an adjective. Select the adjective expressing "affectionate": *cariñoso*. Change *cariñoso* to its feminine singular form by changing the final *-o* to *-a*. Add *-mente*.

6. **Answer: Vosotros lloráis tristemente.** To form the adverb, drop the preposition *con*. Adverbs are formed by adding *-mente* to the feminine singular form of an adjective. Select the adjective expressing "sad": *triste*. Adjectives ending in *-e* are invariable in the singular. Add *-mente*.

Words That Are Both

The following Spanish words may be used as adjectives or adverbs:

más	more
menos	fewer (adj.), less (adv.)
poco	few (adj.), a little (adv.)
mucho	many (adj.), a lot (adv.)
mejor	better
peor	worse
demasiado	too many (adj.), too much (adv.)

As adjectives:

❑ *Mucho, poco,* and *demasiado* agree in number and gender with the nouns they modify.

❑ *Mejor* and *peor* agree with the plural of the nouns they modify only by adding *-es*.

❑ *Más* and *menos* do not change.

As adverbs, all of these words remain invariable.

Note the use of the word *mucho* as an adjective to describe the noun *notas* and as an adverb to describe the verb *estudia*:

Susana tiene muchas buenas notas porque ella estudia mucho.
Susana has many good grades because she studies a lot.

Note the following words that have distinct forms as an adjective or as an adverb:

Adjective	*Adverb*
bueno (good)	bien (well)
malo (bad)	mal (badly)

La señora López enseña bien. Es una buena profesora.
Mrs. Lopez teaches well. She is a good teacher.

Example Problems

Complete each sentence with the correct form of the adjective or adverb indicated.

1. (mucho) Ella tiene _____ energía y por eso corre _____.

   Answer: Ella tiene mucha energía y por eso corre mucho.

   In the first blank, use the feminine singular adjective to describe the feminine sinuglar noun, *energía*. In the second blank, use the adverb *mucho* to modify the verb *correr* (to run).

2. (demasiado) Él trabaja _____ porque tiene _____ responsabilidades.

Answer: Él trabaja demasiado porque tiene demasiadas responsabilidades.

In the first blank, use the adverb *demasiado* to modify the verb *trabajar* (to work). In the second blank, use the feminine plural adjective to describe the feminine plural noun, *responsabilidades*.

Worked Problems

Describe your classmates by completing each sentence with the correct form of the adjective or the adverb indicated.

1. (peor) Enrique sale _____ porque tiene _____ ideas.

2. (bien/bueno) Isabela prepara _____ comidas porque cocina _____.

3. (menos) Clara recibe _____ buenas notas porque estudia _____.

4. (poco) Ricardo lee _____ porque tiene _____libros.

5. (mal/malo) Julio tiene _____ accidentes porque conduce _____.

6. (más) Elena estudia _____ porque tiene _____ tareas.

Worked Solutions

1. **Answer: Enrique sale peor porque tiene peores ideas.** In the first blank, use the adverb *peor* to modify the verb *ganar* (to earn). In the second blank, use the plural adjective to describe the plural noun, *ideas*.

2. **Answer: Isabela prepara buenas comidas porque cocina bien.** In the first blank, use the feminine plural adjective to describe the feminine plural noun, *comidas*. In the second blank, use the adverb *bien* to modify the verb *cocinar* (to cook).

3. **Answer: Clara recibe menos buenas notas porque estudia menos.** In the first blank, use the invariable adjective to describe the plural noun, *notas*. In the second blank, use the adverb *menos* to modify the verb *cocinar* (to cook).

4. **Answer: Ricardo lee poco porque tiene pocos libros.** In the first blank, use the adverb *poco* to modify the verb *leer* (to read). In the second blank, use the masculine plural adjective to describe the masculine plural noun, *libros*.

5. **Answer: Julio tiene malos accidentes porque conduce mal.** In the first blank, use the masculine plural adjective to describe the masculine plural noun, *accidentes*. In the second blank, use the adverb *mal* to modify the verb *conducir* (to drive).

6. **Answer: Elena estudia más porque tiene más tareas.** In the first blank, use the adverb *más* to modify the verb *estudiar* (to study). In the second blank, use the adjective *más* to describe the feminine plural noun, *tareas*.

Comparisons of Inequality

Comparisons of inequality showing superiority follow this pattern:

> noun
> *más* + adjective + *que* + name, noun, or subject pronoun
> adverb

Hay más días en julio que en junio.	There are more days in July than in June.
Soy más joven que tú.	I'm younger than you.
Corre más rápidamente que su amigo.	He runs faster than his friend.

Comparisons of inequality showing inferiority follow this pattern:

> noun
> *menos* + adjective + *que*
> adverb

Hay menos alumnos que alumnas en esta escuela.	There are fewer male students in this school than female students.
La riqueza es menos importante que la salud.	Wealth is less important than health.
La plata vale menos que el oro.	Silver is worth less than gold.

Example Problems

Combine the elements to make comparisons.

> Example: escribo/+/elocuentemente/él
> Escribo más elocuentemente que él.

1. siento/+/alegría/pena

   Answer: Siento más alegría que pena.

   Use *más* to express "more" and place it before the noun it modifies. Use *que* to express "than" when comparing two things.

2. la música es/−/interesante/el arte

   Answer: La música es menos interesante que el arte.

   Use *menos* to express "less" and place it before the adjective it modifies. Use *que* to express "than" when comparing two things.

3. generalmente un viejo anda/+/lentamente/un joven

   Answer: Un viejo anda más lentamente que un joven.

   Use *más* to express "more" and place it before the adverb it modifies. Use *que* to express "than" when comparing two people.

Work Problems

Combine the elements to make comparisons.

1. la carne es/–/saludable/las legumbres

2. un tigre corre/+/rápidamente/un gato

3. necesito/+/energía/paciencia

4. un deportista piensa/–/profundamente/un filósofo

5. el español es/+/fácil/el francés

6. el poder es/–/importante/la inteligencia

Worked Solutions

1. **Answer: La carne es menos saludable que las legumbres.** Use *menos* to express "less" and place it before the adjective it modifies. Use *que* to express "than" when comparing two things.

2. **Answer: Un tigre corre más rápidamente que un gato.** Use *más* to express "more" and place it before the adverb it modifies. Use *que* to express "than" when comparing two things.

3. **Answer: Necesito más energía que paciencia.** Use *más* to express "more" and place it before the noun it modifies. Use *que* to express "than" when comparing two things.

4. **Answer: Un deportista piensa menos profundamente que un filósofo.** Use *menos* to express "less" and place it before the adverb it modifies. Use *que* to express "than" when comparing two things.

5. **Answer: El español es más fácil que el francés.** Use *más* to express "more" and place it before the adjective it modifies. Use *que* to express "than" when comparing two things.

6. **Answer: El poder es menos importante que la inteligencia.** Use *menos* to express "less" and place it before the noun it modifies. Use *que* to express "than" when comparing two things.

Comparisons of Equality

Comparisons of equality follow this pattern (*tanto* agrees in number and gender with the noun it modifies):

$$
tan + \begin{array}{l} \text{+ adjective} \\ \text{adverb} \end{array} + como
$$
$$
tanto\ (os, a, as) + \text{noun}
$$

Ella es tan bonita como su hermana.	She is as pretty as her sister.
Él habla tan elocuentemente como Ud.	He speaks as eloquently as you.
Mi casa tiene tantas habitaciones como la suya.	My house has as many rooms as yours.

Tanto como is used after a verb to express an indefinite quantity:

Yo estudio tanto como ella.   I study as much as she does.

Example Problems

Make comparisons of equality about the following people.

Example: yo soy/=/grande/él
Yo soy tan grande como él.

1. ella habla español/=/fluidamente/su amiga

Answer: Ella habla español tan fluidamente como su amiga.

Use *tan* to express "as" and place it before the adverb it modifies. Use *como* to express "as" when comparing two people.

2. yo tengo/=/problemas/tú

Answer: Yo tengo tantos problemas como tú.

Use *tanto* to express "as much" and place it before the noun it modifies. Because the noun is masculine plural, add *-s* to the adjective *tanto* to form its plural. Use *como* to express "as" when comparing two things.

3. Ud. es/=/paciente/ellos

Answer: Ud. es tan paciente como ellos.

Use *tan* to express "as" and place it before the adjective it modifies. Use *como* to express "as" when comparing two people.

Work Problems

Make comparisons of equality about the following people or things.

1. tú eres/=/simpático/tu hermano

2. mi tío tiene/=/años/mi padre

3. nuestro coche es/=/nuevo/el suyo

4. yo trabajo/=/duro/tú

5. ella recibe/=/buenas notas/él

6. nosotros hablamos/=/respetuosamente/Uds.

Worked Solutions

1. **Answer: Tú eres tan simpático como tu hermano.**   Use *tan* to express "as" and place it before the adjective it modifies. Use *como* to express "as" when comparing two people.

2. **Answer: Mi tío tiene tantos años como mi padre.**   Use *tanto* to express "as many" and place it before the noun it modifies. Because the noun is masculine plural, add *-s* to the adjective *tanto* to form its plural. Use *como* to express "as" when comparing two things.

3. **Answer: Nuestro coche es tan nuevo como el suyo.**   Use *tan* to express "as" and place it before the adverb it modifies. Use *como* to express "as" when comparing two things.

4. **Answer: Yo trabajo tan duro como tú.**   Use *tan* to express "as" and place it before the adverb it modifies. Use *como* to express "as" when comparing two people.

5. **Answer: Ella recibe tantas buenas notas como él.**   Use *tanto* to express "as many" and place it before the noun it modifies. Because the noun is feminine plural, add *-as* to the adjective *tanto* for its feminine plural form. Use *como* to express "as" when comparing two things.

6. **Answer: Nosotros hablamos tan respetuosamente como Uds.**   Use *tan* to express "as" and place it before the adverb it modifies. Use *como* to express "as" when comparing two people.

The Superlative

Whereas the comparative compares different people or things, the superlative indicates who or which is the best among the group or the lot. In English, the comparative form usually ends in *–er*: John is taller than Mike. The superlative form usually ends in *–est*: Randy is the tallest.

The Relative Superlative

The relative superlative expresses the superiority of someone or something with relation to other people or things and is formed as follows:

> noun or verb + *el, los, la, las* (noun) + *más* or *menos* + (adjective or adverb) *de*

Mi madre es la más bella de todas sus hermanas.
My mother is the most beautiful of all of her sisters.

California es el estado más poblado de los Estados Unidos.
California is the most populous state in the United States.

The Absolute Superlative

The absolute superlative expresses the highest grade. Add *-ísimo, -ísima, ísimos,* or *ísimas* to the adjective according to the gender (masculine or feminine) and number (singular or plural) of the noun being described. Note that adjectives or adverbs ending in a vowel drop the final vowel before adding the absolute superlative ending. The meaning is the same as *muy* + adjective. Use *muchísimo* to express "very much."

Ella es malísima.	She is the very worst.
Esos hombres son guapísimos.	Those men are very handsome.
Lo siento muchísimo.	I regret it very much.

Adjectives ending in *-co (-ca)*, *-go (-ga)*, *-ble*, or *-z* change *c* to *qu*, *g* to *gu*, *ble* to *bil*, and *z* to *c*, respectively, before adding *-ísimo:*

Ese postre es riquísimo.	That dessert is very delicious.
Las avenidas son larguísimas.	The avenues are very long.
Es una mujer amabilísima.	She is a very polite woman.
Esos tigres son ferocísimos.	Those tigers are very ferocious.

The adverbial superlative formed with the neuter article *lo* may be used as an absolute superlative, not a superlative of comparison. It is usually followed by a word or phrase expressing possibility:

Él conduce lo más prudentemente posible.	He drives the most prudently possible.

Example Problems

Express what is said at a wedding by using the superlative.

1. He eats the fastest possible.

    Answer: Él come lo más rápidamente posible.

    Use the verb *comer* to express "to eat." Drop the *-er* ending and add the third person singular ending *-e*. To express the superlative, use *más* to express "most." Use the neuter article *lo* before *más* to express "the." Form the adverb *rápidamente* by adding *-mente* to the feminine form of the adjective *rápido (rápida)*, which means "fast." Use *posible* to express "possible."

2. She is the least popular in the family.

    Answer: Ella es la menos popular de la familia.

    Use the third person singular of the irregular verb *ser* (to be): *es*. To express the superlative, use *menos* to express "least." Use the definite article *la* before *menos* to express "the." Use the adjective *popular* to express "popular." Use *de* to express "of." Use *la familia* to express "the family."

3. You (informal singular, feminine) are very, very beautiful.

    Answer: Tú eres bellísima.

    Use the second person singular of the irregular verb *ser* (to be): *eres*. Use the adjective *bello* to express "beautiful." Drop the final *-o* from *bello* and add *-ísima* to describe the feminine subject.

Work Problems

Use the superlative to express what is said at a wedding.

1. You (informal singular) are the most handsome of all of your brothers.

2. Los Gringos is the most popular musical group in Mexico.

3. He speaks the least eloquently possible.

4. I love you very much.

5. Your (familiar singular) grandparents are very wise.

6. Your (familiar singular) cousins are very funny.

Worked Solutions

1. **Answer: Tú eres el más guapo de todos sus hermanos.**   Use the second person singular of the irregular verb *ser* (to be): *eres*. To express the superlative, use *más* to express "most." Use the definite article *el* before *más* to express "the." Use the adjective *guapo* to express "handsome." Use *de* to express "of." Use *todos* to express "all." Use *tus* to express "your" before the plural noun. Use *hermanos* to express "brothers."

2. **Answer: Los Gringos es el grupo musical más popular de México.**   Use the third person singular of the irregular verb *ser* (to be): *es*. Use *grupo* to express "group." Use the definite article *el* before the noun *grupo* to express "the." To express the superlative, use *más* to express "most." Use the adjective *popular* to express "popular." Use *de* to express "of." Use *México* to express "Mexico."

3. **Answer: Él habla lo menos elocuentemente posible.**   Use the verb *hablar* to express "to speak." Drop the *-er* ending and add the third person singular ending *-a*. To express the superlative, use *menos* to express "least." Use the neuter article *lo* before *más* to express "the." Form the adverb *elocuentement* by adding *-mente* to the adjective *elocuente*, which means "eloquent." Use *posible* to express "possible."

4. **Answer: Te quiero muchísimo.**   Use the verb *querer* to express "to love." *Querer* undergoes an internal stem change from *e* to *ie* in all forms except *nosotros* and *vosotros*. Drop the *-er* ending and add the first person singular ending *(-o)*. Use the indirect object pronoun *te* to express "you." Drop the final *-o* from *mucho* and use *muchísimo* to express "very much."

5. **Answer: Tus abuelos son sagacísimos.**   Use *tus* to express "your" before the plural noun. Use *abuelos* to express "grandparents." Use the third person singular of the irregular verb *ser* (to be): *son*. Change the final *-z* from *sagaz* to *c* and add *-ísimos* to describe the plural noun.

6. **Answer: Tus primos son comiquísimos.**   Use *tus* to express "your" before the plural noun. Use *primos* to express "cousins." Use the third person singular of the irregular verb *ser* (to be): *son*. Change the final *-co* from *cómico* to *-qu* and add *-ísimos* to describe the plural noun. Drop the accent from the *o* to maintain proper stress.

Irregular Comparatives and Superlatives

A few adjectives and adverbs have irregular forms in the comparative and superlative:

Positive	Comparative	Superlative
bueno (buena, buenos, buenas) good (adjective)	mejor(es) better	el (la) mejor, los (las) mejores the best
bien well (adverb)	mejor better	el mejor the best
malo (mala, malos, malas) bad	peor(es) worse	el (la) peor, los (las) peores the worst
mal badly (adverb)	peor worse	el peor the worst
viejo (vieja, viejos, viejas) old	mayor(es) greater, older	el (la) mayor, los (las) mayores the greatest, the oldest
grande(s) great, big	más grande(s) larger	el (la) más grande, los (las) más grandes the largest
	menos grande(s) less large	el (la) menos grande, los (las) menos grandes the least large
joven (jóvenes) young	menor(es) minor, lesser, younger	el (la) menor, los (las) menores the least, the youngest
pequeño (pequeña, pequeños, pequeñas) small	más pequeño (-a, -os, -as) smaller	el (la) más pequeño(-a), los (las) más pequeños(-as) the smallest
	menos pequeño (-a, -os, -as) less small	el (la) menos pequeño(-a), los (las) menos pequeños(-as) the least small

Mis notas son buenas pero las tuyas (las de Rosa) son mejores.

My grades are good, but yours (Rosa's) are better.

(El) mentir es malo pero (el) copiar es peor.

Lying is bad but cheating is worse.

Mejor and *peor* generally precede the noun, while *mayor* and *menor* generally follow the noun:

Es mi mejor amigo.   He is my best friend.

No conozco a su hermana mayor.   I don't know your older sister.

Note that the regular and irregular comparative forms of *grande* and *pequeño* have different connotations. *Más grande* and *más pequeño* are used in a physical sense to compare differences in size and height, whereas *mayor* and *menor* are used figuratively to compare differences in age or status:

mi hermana más grande	my bigger (biggest) sister
mi hermana mayor	my older (oldest) sister
de mayor importancia	of greater importance

Example Problems

Make comparisons by selecting the correct completion to each sentence.

1. Mi (bien, buena) _____ amiga baila (mal, malo) _____.

    Answer: buena, mal

    Use the adjective *buena* before the feminine singular noun *amiga*. Use the adverb *mal* after the verb *baila*.

2. Mi tío tiene ochenta años. Es (grande, viejo) _____.

    Answer: viejo

    Use the adjective *viejo* to describe age. *Grande* describes physical stature.

3. Te presento a mi hermano (menor, pequeño) _____.

    Answer: menor

    Use the adjective *menor* to express "younger." *Pequeño* describes physical stature.

Work Problems

Make comparisons by selecting the correct completion to each sentence.

1. Tú tienes (mal, malas) _____ ideas pero las mías son (peor, peores) _____.

2. Ella tiene solamente quince años. Ella es (joven, pequeña) _____. Su hermana tiene trece años. Ella es (menor, más pequeña) _____.

3. Mi hermano mide seis pies. Él es (grande, viejo) _____. Yo mido seis pies cinco. Yo soy (más grande, mayor) _____.

4. Yo canto (bien, bueno) _____ y mi amiga canta (mal, mala) _____.

Worked Solutions

1. **Answer: malas/peores**   Use the adjective *malas* before the feminine plural noun *ideas*. Use *peores* to describe *las mías* (mine), which refers back to the plural noun *ideas*. *Mal* is an adverb. *Peor* can be used as a singular adverb or adjective.

2. **Answer: joven/menor**   Use *joven* to descibe someone who is "young." Use *menor* to express that her sister is "younger." *Pequeña* and *más pequeña* refer to physical stature.

3. **Answer: grande/más grande**   Use *grande* to refer to the fact that he is tall. Use *más grande* to express that you are taller. *Viejo* and *mayor* refer to age.

4. **Answer: bien/mal**   Use the adverb *bien* after the verb *canto*. Use the adverb *mal* after the verb *canta*. *Bueno* and *malo* are adjectives.

Chapter Problems

Problems

Describe the people by giving the correct forms of the adjectives and putting them in their correct places.

1. (alerta, bueno, uno) alumno aprende mucho

2. (francés, grande, uno) mujer enseña el curso

3. (comprensible, interesante, tal) las muchachas hablan de asuntos

4. (ciento, dedicado, fiel) hay chicos en la escuela

5. (hablador, holgazán, ninguno) muchacha recibe buenas notas

Describe each person by substituting an adverb for the adverbial phrase or the adjective.

6. Ella llora con amargura.

7. Ellos bailan. Es fácil.

8. Nosotros hablamos. Es correcto.

9. Ud. escucha en silencio.

10. Tú sales con frecuencia.

Complete the comparisons.

> Example: Los muchachos grandes. Las muchachas son pequeñas. Los muchachos son__.
> Los muchachos son más grandes que las muchachas.

11. Julio juega bien al fútbol. Juan juega mal al fútbol. Juan juega _____.

12. Los médicos ganan mucho dinero. Los dentistas también ganan mucho dinero. Los dentistas ganan _____.

13. Enrique es deportivo. Ricardo no es deportivo. Ricardo es _____

14. Yo tengo diez dólares. Elena tiene veinte dólares. Elena tiene _____

15. Gloria es responsable. Cristina es responsable también. Gloria es _____

Express the superlative using *más* and also give the absolute superlative. Make sure that all adjectives agree with the nouns they modify.

Examples: muchachos/inteligente/clase
             Son los muchachos más inteligentes de la clase.
             Son muchachos inteligentísimos.

             español/curso/fácil/escuela
             El español es el curso mas fácil de la escuela.
             El español es un curso facilísimo.

16. muchacha/bello/familia

17. película/aburrido/serie

18. enero/mes/frío/todos

19. primavera/estación/bueno/año

20. béisbol/deporte/popular/Estados Unidos

Answers and Solutions

1. **Answer: Un buen alumno alerta aprende mucho.**   *Uno* is an adjective that generally precedes the noun it modifies. *Uno* drops the final *-o* directly before a masculine singular noun. *Bueno* is an adjective that generally precedes the noun it modifies. *Bueno* drops the final *-o* directly before a masculine singular noun. *Alerta* is a descriptive adjective that ends in *-a* and that follows the noun it modifies.

2. **Answer: Una gran mujer francesa enseña el curso.**   Change the masculine singular adjective *un* to *una* before the feminine singular noun *mujer*. *Una* is an adjective that generally precedes the noun it modifies. *Grande* has the connotation of "great" and, therefore, precedes the noun it modifies. *Grande* becomes *gran* directly before a singular noun. *Francés* is a descriptive adjective that follows the noun it modifies. To form the feminine and to maintain proper stress, drop the accent from the *e* and add *-a*.

3. **Answer: Las muchachas hablan de tales asuntos comprensibles e interesantes.**   *Tal* is an adjective that generally precedes the noun it modifies. To form the plural of an adjective ending in a consonant, add *-es*. *Comprensible* is a descriptive adjective that follows the noun it modifies. To form the plural of an adjective ending in a vowel, add *-s*. *Interesante* is a descriptive adjective that follows the noun it modifies. To form the plural of an adjective ending in a vowel, add *-s*. Two adjectives in the same position are joined by *y* (and). *Y* becomes *e* before the letter *i*.

4. **Answer: Hay cien chicos dedicados y fieles en la escuela.**   *Ciento* is an adjective that generally precedes the noun it modifies. *Ciento* becomes *cien* directly before a noun. *Dedicado* is a descriptive adjective that follows the noun it modifies. To form the plural of

an adjective ending in a vowel, add -s. *Fiel* is a descriptive adjective that follows the noun it modifies. To form the plural of an adjective ending in a consonant, add -es. Two adjectives in the same position are joined by *y* (and).

5. **Answer: Ninguna muchacha holgazana y habladora recibe buenas notas.**   *Ninguno* is an adjective that generally precedes the noun it modifies. To form the feminine, change -o to -a. *Holgazán* is a descriptive adjective that follows the noun it modifies. To form the feminine and to maintain proper stress, drop the accent from the *a* and add -a. *Hablador* is a descriptive adjective that follows the noun it modifies. To form the feminine of an adjective ending in -or, add -a.

6. **Answer: Ella llora amargamente.**   To form the adverb, drop the preposition *con*. Select the adjective expressing "bitter": *amargo*. Change *amargo* to its feminine singular form by changing the final -o to -a. Add -mente.

7. **Answer: Ellos bailan fácilmente.**   To form the adverb, drop the preposition *con*. Select the adjective expressing "easy": *fácil*. Adjectives ending in a consonant are generally invariable in the singular. Add -mente.

8. **Answer: Nosotros hablamos correctamente.**   To form the adverb, drop the preposition *con*. Select the adjective expressing "correct": *correcto*. Change *correcto* to its feminine singular form by changing the final -o to -a. Add -mente.

9. **Answer: Ud. escucha silenciosamente.**   To form the adverb, drop the preposition *con*. Select the adjective expressing "silent": *silencioso*. Change *silencioso* to its feminine singular form by changing the final -o to -a. Add -mente.

10. **Answer: Tú sales frecuentemente.**   To form the adverb, drop the preposition *con*. Select the adjective expressing "frequent": *frecuente*. Adjectives ending in -e are invariable in the singular. Add -mente.

11. **Answer: Juan juega peor que Julio.**   Use the irregular comparative *peor* to express "worse" and place it after the verb it modifies. Use *que* to express "than" when comparing two people.

12. **Answer: Los dentistas ganan tanto dinero como los médicos.**   Use *tanto* to express "as much" and place it before the noun it modifies. Use *como* to express "as" when comparing two things.

13. **Answer: Ricardo es menos deportivo que Enrique.**   Use *menos* to express "less" and place it before the adjective it modifies. Use *que* to express "than" when comparing two people.

14. **Answer: Elena tiene más dólares que yo.**   Use *más* to express "more" and place it before the noun it modifies. Use *que* to express "than" when comparing two people.

15. **Answer: Cristina es tan responsable como Gloria.**   Use *tan* to express "as" and place it before the adjective it modifies. Use *como* to express "as" when comparing two people.

16. **Answer: Es la muchacha más bella de la familia./Es una muchacha bellísima.**   Use the third person singular of the irregular verb *ser* (to be): *es*. Use the definite article *la* before the noun *muchacha* to express "the." To express the superlative, use *más* to express "most." Change the masculine adjective *bello* to its feminine form *bella* to express "beautiful." Use *de* to express "of" before *la familia*. For the absolute superlative,

use the indefinite article *una* to express "a" before the feminine singular noun *muchacha*. Drop the final *-o* from *bello* and add the feminine singular ending *-ísima*.

17. **Answer: Es la película más aburrida de la serie./Es una película aburridísima.** Use the third person singular of the irregular verb *ser* (to be): *es*. Use the definite article *la* before the noun *película* to express "the." To express the superlative, use *más* to express "most." Change the masculine adjective *aburrido* to its feminine form *aburrida* to express "boring." Use *de* to express "of" before the noun *la serie*. For the absolute superlative, use the indefinite article *una* to express "a" before the feminine singular noun *película*. Drop the final *-o* from *aburrido* and add the feminine singular ending *-ísima*.

18. **Answer: Enero es el mes más frío de todos./Es un mes friísimo.** Begin the comparison with *enero*, which expresses "January." Use the third person singular of the irregular verb *ser* (to be): *es*. Use the definite article *el* before the noun *mes* to express "the." To express the superlative, use *más* to express "most." Use the masculine adjective *frío* to express "cold." Use *de* to express "of" before *todos*. For the absolute superlative, use the indefinite article *un* to express "a" before the masculine singular noun *mes*. Drop the final *-o* from *frío* and add the masculine singular ending *-ísimo*.

19. **Answer: La primavera es la mejor estación del año./Es una estación buenísima.** Begin the comparison with *la primavera*, which expresses "the spring." Use the third person singular of the irregular verb *ser* (to be): *es*. To express the superlative, use the definite article *la* to express "the" before the irregular adjective *mejor* (best), which precedes the noun *estación* (season). Use *de* to express "of." *De* combines with the masculine singular definite article *el* before the noun *año*. For the absolute superlative, use the indefinite article *una* to express "a" before the masculine singular noun *mes*. Drop the final *-o* from *bueno* and add the feminine singular ending *-ísima*.

20. **Answer: El béisbol es el deporte más popular de los Estados Unidos./Es un deporte popularísimo.** Begin the comparison with *el béisbol*, which expresses "baseball." The definite article is needed before a noun used in a general sense. Use the third person singular of the irregular verb *ser* (to be): *es*. Use the definite article *el* before the noun *deporte* to express "the." To express the superlative, use *más* to express "most." Use the masculine adjective *popular* to express "popular." Use *de* to express "of" before *los Estados Unidos*. For the absolute superlative, use the indefinite article *un* to express "a" before the masculine singular noun *deporte*. Add the masculine singular ending *-ísimo*.

Supplemental Chapter Problems

Problems

Describe what happens at a conference by giving the correct form of the adjectives and putting them in their correct places.

1. (ciento, complicado, importante) los gerentes leen páginas

2. (hipócrita, mal, un) hombre sale

3. (dedicado, fiel, mil) miembros hablan

4. (grande, moderno, uno) ellos se reúnen en una universidad

5. (conservador, sencillo, varios) las mujeres escuchan ideas

Describe each person by substituting an adverb for the adverbial phrase or the adjective.

6. Ellas trabajan con cuidado.

7. Nosotros obramos por instinto.

8. Ud. se viste. Es elegante.

9. Él grita. Es feroz.

10. Tú hablas. Eres abierto.

Complete the comparisons.

11. Juanita baila bien. Yolanda baila mal. Juanita baila _____.

12. Yo soy alto. Mi hermano es alto también. Mi hermano es _____.

13. Mis abuelos no trabajan mucho. Mis padres trabajan mucho. Mis abuelos trabajan _____.

14. Gregorio come mucho. Guillermo come mucho también. Gregorio come _____.

15. Carlos es inteligente. Diego no es inteligente. Carlos es _____.

Express the superlative using *más* and also give the absolute superlative. Make sure that all adjectives agree with the nouns they modify.

16. muchacho/talentoso/grupo

17. la Nochevieja/fiesta/importante/año

18. viernes/día/bueno/semana

19. ese hombre/político/famoso/país

20. cuento/interesante/libro

Solutions

1. Los gerentes leen cien páginas importantes y complicadas. (gender of adjectives, p. 157; plural of adjectives, p. 158; position of adjectives, p. 160)

2. Un mal hombre hipócrita sale. (gender of adjectives, p. 157; position of adjectives, p. 160)

3. Mil miembros dedicados y fieles hablan. (gender of adjectives, p. 157; plural of adjectives, p. 158; position of adjectives, p. 160)

4. Ellos se reúnen en una gran universidad moderna. (gender of adjectives, p. 157; position of adjectives, p. 160)

5. Las mujeres escuchan varias ideas sencillas y conservadoras. (gender of adjectives, p. 157; plural of adjectives, p. 158; position of adjectives, p. 160)

6. Ellas trabajan cuidadosamente. (formation of adverbs, p. 163)

7. Nosotros obramos instintivamente. (formation of adverbs, p. 163)

8. Ud. se viste elegantemente. (formation of adverbs, p. 163)

9. Él grita ferozmente. (formation of adverbs, p. 163)

10. Tú hablas abiertamente. (formation of adverbs, p. 163)

11. Juanita baila mejor que Yolanda. (comparisons of inequality, p. 168)

12. Mi hermano es tan alto como yo. (comparisons of equality, p. 169)

13. Mis abuelos trabajan menos que mis padres. (comparisons of inequality, p. 168)

14. Guillermo come tanto como Gregorio. (comparisons of equality, p. 169)

15. Carlos es más inteligente que Diego. (comparisons of inequality, p. 168)

16. Es el muchacho más talentoso del grupo. (relative superlative, p. 171)

    Él es un muchacho talentosísimo. (absolute superlative, p. 171)

17. La Nochevieja es la fiesta más importante del año. (relative superlative, p. 171)

    Es una fiesta importantísima. (absolute superlative, p. 171)

18. El viernes es el mejor día de la semana. (irregular comparatives and superlatives, p. 174; relative superlative, p. 171)

    Es un día buenísimo. (absolute superlative, p. 171)

19. Ese hombre es el político más famoso del país. (relative superlative, p. 171)

    Es un hombre famosísimo. (absolute superlative, p. 171)

20. Es el cuento más interesante del libro. (relative superlative, p. 171)

    Es un cuento interesantísimo. (absolute superlative, p. 171)

Chapter 8
Prepositions and Conjunctions

Prepositions

A preposition is an invariable word that joins words and establishes a relationship between them. Prepositions are followed by the infinitive of a verb:

Él trabaja mucho para salir bien.　　　　He works a lot to succeed.

Common Prepositions and Prepositional Expressions

The most frequently used prepositions in Spanish are:

a	to, at	hacia	toward
ante	before	hasta	until
bajo	under	para	for
con	with	por	for
contra	against	según	according to
de	of, from, about	sin	without
desde	since, from	sobre	on, upon
en	at, in, by, on	tras	behind, after
entre	between, among		

For example:

Su bicicleta está contra la pared.　　　　His bicycle is against the wall.

Prepositional Expressions of Location

The most commonly used expressions of location include:

a la izquierda de	to the left of	encima de	above
a la derecha de	to the right of	debajo de	beneath
cerca de	near	hasta, a	to
lejos de	far	desde, de	from
delante de	in front of	sobre	on

detrás de	in back of	bajo	under
dentro de	inside	al final de	at the end of
fuera de	outside	al lado de	at the side of
en	in	alrededor de	around
en el interior de	on the interior of	en el centro de	in the middle of
en el exterior de	on the exterior of	en el fondo de	at the bottom of
en la cima de	on the peak of	en el medio de	in the middle of
al pie de	at the foot of	en la esquina de	on the corner of
en lo alto de	at the top of	enfrente de	opposite, in front of
en lo bajo de	at the bottom of		

For example:

| Su oficina está lejos de su casa. | His office is far from his house. |
| Espérenme enfrente del teatro. | Wait for me in front of the theater. |

Example Problems
You are talking about school. Give the opposite of the underlined preposition.

1. Me siento *detrás de* la clase.

   Answer: delante de

   Detrás de expresses "behind." The expression for "in front of" is *delante de*.

2. Vivo *lejos de* la escuela.

   Answer: cerca de

   Lejos de expresses "far." The expression for "near" is *cerca de*.

3. Mi sala de clase está *a la derecha*.

   Answer: a la izquierda

   A la derecha expresses "to the right." The expression for "to the left" is *a la izquierda*.

Work Problems
You continue talking about school. Complete each sentence with the appropriate preposition:

| bajo | desde | hasta | sin |
| contra | entre | según | |

1. Tengo que trabajar _____ las ocho _____ las cuatro.

2. _____ mi profesora, hay mucho que hacer.

3. No puedo escribir este ejercicio de gramática _____ obtener más información.

4. Siempre llevo mis libros importantes _____ el brazo.

5. Mi escritorio está _____ la puerta y las ventanas.

6. En el patio de la escuela siempre apoyo mi bicicleta _____ la pared.

Worked Solutions

1. **Answers: desde, hasta**   You have to work **from** eight o'clock **until** 4 o'clock. The preposition *desde* expresses "from," and the preposition *hasta* expresses "until" when referring to time.

2. **Answers: Según**   **According to** your teacher there is a lot to do. The preposition *según* expresses "according to."

3. **Answers: sin**   You can't write that grammar exercise **without** getting more information. The preposition *sin* expresses "without."

4. **Answers: bajo**   You always carry your important books **under** your arm. The preposition *bajo* expresses "under."

5. **Answers: entre**   Your desk is **between** the door and the windows. The preposition *entre* expresses "between."

6. **Answers: contra**   In the schoolyard, you always lean your bicicyle **against** the wall. The preposition *contra* expresses "against."

Prepositional Distinctions

Note the use of the following prepositions:

The preposition *a* (which contracts with the definite article *el* to become *al*) shows:

- ❏ Time:

  Te veré a las cinco.   I'll see you at five o'clock.

- ❏ Movement:

  Voy al cine.   I'm going to the movies.

- ❏ Location:

  Él espera a la salida.   He's waiting at the exit.

- ❏ Means or manner:

  Va a pie.   She going on foot.

  Es una camisa a cuadros.   It's a checked shirt.

- ❏ Quantity, price, or speed:

  Lo compré a 200 pesos el kilo.   I bought it for 200 pesos a kilo.

  Iba a 120 kilómetros por hora.   He was going 120 kilometers per hour.

❏ that the subject is referring to a direct object that is a person:

No veo a Carlos.	I don't see Carlos.

The preposition *de*, which contracts with the definite article *el* to become *del*, shows:

❏ Possession:

La madre de Juan es profesora.	Juan's mother is a teacher.

❏ Origin:

Somos de los Estados Unidos.	We are from the United States.

❏ Time:

Trabaja de noche.	He works at night.

❏ Cause:

Sufro del frío.	I suffer from the cold.

❏ Material, characteristics, or contents:

Tiene un collar de diamantes.	She has a diamond necklace.
Compré un billete de primera clase.	I bought a first-class ticket.
Me dio una caja de bombones.	He gave me a box of candy.

❏ Relationship:

Es el primero de febrero.	It's the first of February.

❏ Means:

Se puso de mi lado en un salto.	He jumped to my side.

The preposition *en* shows:

❏ Time:

Estamos en la primavera.	We are in spring.

❏ Location:

No está en su apartamento.	He isn't in his apartment.

❏ Means or manner:

El poema está escrito en inglés.	The poem is written in English.

❏ Movement:

Entré en la tienda.	I entered the store.

The preposition *hasta* shows:

❏ Place or location:

La falda me llega hasta los tobillos.	The skirt comes down to my ankles.

❏ Time:

Hasta mañana.	See you tomorrow.

The preposition *para* shows:

❏ Destination (a place) or direction:

Salieron para la Argentina.   They left for Argentina.

❏ Destination (a recipient):

Este regalo es para ti.   This gift is for you.

❏ A time limit in the future:

La tarea es para el jueves.   The homework is due Thursday.

❏ A purpose or goal:

Estudio para aprender.   I study to learn.

❏ The use or function of an object:

Necesito un cepillo para los dientes.   I need a toothbrush.

❏ Comparisons by expressing "for" or "considering that":

Para un niño de cinco años, sabe mucho.   For a five-year-old boy, he knows a lot.

❏ Point of view:

Para mí, sus ideas son buenas.   For me, his ideas are good.

The preposition *por* shows:

❏ Motion:

Camina por el parque.   He walks through the park.

❏ Means or manner:

Hablamos por teléfono.   We spoke on the phone.

When speaking about a means of transportation for a passenger, use *en* rather than *por* to express "by":

Viajamos mucho en avión.   We travel a lot by plane.

Envió el cheque por correo.   He sent the check by mail.

❏ "In exchange for" or substitution:

Trabajé por mi amigo.   I worked for my friend.

❏ The duration of an action:

Estudió por una hora.   He studied for an hour.

❏ An indefinite period of time:

Vendremos por la tarde.   We will come in the afternoon.

❏ "For the sake of" or "on behalf of":

Lo haré por Ud.   I will do it for your sake (on your behalf).

❑ A reason or motive:

Por no estudiar, no pasé el examen.   For not studying, I didn't pass the test.

❑ "Per" or "by the";

Gano mucho por día.   I earn a lot per day.

Cuestan muy poco por docena.   They cost very little by the dozen.

❑ Opinion or estimation (equivalent to "for" or "as"):

Lo tomé por abogado.   I took him for a lawyer.

Se le conoce por Jorge.   He is known as Jorge.

❑ An incomplete action:

Me queda un capítulo por terminar.   I have one chapter left to finish.

❑ The agent (doer) in a passive construction:

Fue escrito por Luz.   It was written by Luz.

❑ "For" after the verbs *enviar* (to send), *ir* (to go), *mandar* (to order, to send), *preguntar* (to ask) *regresar* (to return), *venir* (to come), and *volver* (to return):

Fui (envié, pregunté) por el doctor.   I went for (sent for, asked for) the doctor.

Vino (regresó, volvió) por su libro.   She came (returned, came back) for her book.

Example Problems

Tell what the subject did by completing the sentences with the appropriate preposition.

1. Pasé por su casa ayer _____ hablarle a Ud.

   Answer: para

   To express "in order to," select the preposition *para*, which is used to show a purpose.

2. Ud. no estaba _____ casa y yo lo esperé _____ las tres.

   Answer: en/hasta

   To express "in," select the preposition *en*. To express "until," select the preposition *hasta*.

3. Entonces yo fui al museo _____ arte moderno.

   Answer: de

   To express "of," select the preposition *de*.

Work Problems

Complete each sentence about the subject's vacation by supplying the appropriate preposition.

1. Estamos _____ Mallorca.

2. Vamos _____ la playa todos los días.

3. _____ no broncearme, me quedo ____ la sombra.

4. Se venden helados ____ cinco dólares.

5. Después de nadar en el mar necesito gotas _____ los ojos.

6. Pagué cien dólares ____ mi traje de baño nuevo.

7. Cada noche salimos _____ las ocho _____ las diez _____ la noche.

8. Vamos a quedarnos aquí _____ el martes.

Worked Solutions

1. **Answer: en**   To express "in," select the preposition *en*.

2. **Answer: a**   To express "to," select the preposition *a*.

3. **Answer: para, a**   To express "in order to," select the preposition *para*, which is used to show a purpose. To express "in," select the preposition *en*, which shows location.

4. **Answer: por**   To express "for," select the preposition *por*, which shows that something was done in exchange for something else.

5. **Answer: para**   To express "for," select the preposition *para*, which is used to show the use or function of an object.

6. **Answer: por**   To express "for," select the preposition *por*, which is used to show that something was done in exchange for something else.

7. **Answer: desde, hasta, de**   To express "from," select the preposition *desde* when referring to time. To express "until," select the preposition *hasta* when referring to time. To express "of," select the preposition *de*.

8. **Answer: hasta**   To express "until," select the preposition *hasta* when referring to time.

Prepositional Pronouns

The following pronouns are used after prepositions.

Subject	Prepositional Pronoun	Meaning
yo	mí	I, me
tú	ti	you (informal)
él	él	he, him
ella	ella	she, her
Ud.	Ud.	you (formal)
nosotros	nosotros	we, us

(continued)

Subject	Prepositional Pronoun	Meaning
vosotros	vosotros	you (informal)
ellos	ellos	they, them
ellas	ellas	they, them
Uds.	Uds.	you (formal)

For example:

Nosotros vivimos cerca de él.	We live near him.
No quiero partir sin ti.	I don't want to leave without you.

Note that the prepositional pronoun *sí* is used reflexively both in the singular and in the plural to express "yourself," "himself," "herself," "itself," "themselves," or "yourselves":

No puede hacerlo por sí mismo.	He can't do it by himself.
Uds. siempre piensan en sí mismos.	You always think of yourselves

The prepositional pronouns *mí*, *ti*, and *sí* combine with the preposition *con* as follows:

conmigo	with me
contigo	with you
consigo	with him/her/yourself or them/yourselves

For example:

Quiero salir contigo.	I want to go out with you.

Ello is a neuter pronoun that refers to a general idea:

Estoy pensando en ello.	I am thinking about it (an event that took place).

Example Problems

Complete each sentence with the appropriate prepositional pronoun.

1. Ellas trabajan para su padre. Trabajan para___.

   Answer: él

   Use the pronoun *él* to replace *su padre*, which is the noun object of the preposition *para*.

2. Voy al centro y Mariana quiere acompañarme. Ella va al centro _____.

   Answer: conmigo

   Use *mí* to express "me." *Mí* combines with the preposition *con* to become *conmigo*.

3. Ud. tiene sus propias ideas. Ud. piensa por _____

    Answer: sí mismo

    Use *sí mismo* to express "you think for yourself."

Work Problems
Complete each sentence with the appropriate prepositional pronoun.

1. No puedo ir al concierto _____, Federico.

2. Ella está reflexionando sobre los sucesos. Está reflexionando sobre _____.

3. Celebro mi cumpleaños hoy. ¿Tienes un regalo para _____?

4. Él no se viste elegantemente para los demás, se viste para _____.

5. ¿Conoces a Carlos? ¿Qué piensas _____ él?

6. Ella está fascinada con su idea. Está fascinada con _____.

Worked Solutions

1. **Answer: contigo** - Because you are going with a friend to the concert, use *ti* to express "you." *Ti* combines with the preposition *con* to become *contigo*.

2. **Answer: ellos** 　Use the pronoun *ellos* to replace *los sucesos*, which is the noun object of the preposition *sobre*.

3. **Answer: mí** 　Use *mí* to express "me."

4. **Answer: sí mismo** 　Use *sí mismo* to express "he dresses for himself."

5. **Answer: de** 　Use *de* to express "of."

6. **Answer: ella** 　Use *ella* to replace *su idea*, which is the noun object of the preposition *con*.

Conjunctions
A conjunction is an invariable word that links sentences or parts of sentences. Coordinating conjunctions connect two like elements in a sentence: subjects, verbs, or objects:

Y/E (And)
Note that *e* is substituted for *y* when the next word begins with *i-* or *hi-*:

Clarita y yo vamos al parque.	Clarita and I are going to the park.
Gloria e Isabel están invitadas.	Gloria and Isabel are invited.

O/U (Or)

Note that *u* is substituted for *o* when the next word begins with *o-* or *ho-*:

Lo comprendo más o menos.	I understand it more or less.
Uno u otro lo hará.	One or the other will do it.

Ni (Neither)

No tengo ni bolígrafo ni papel.	I have neither pen nor paper.

Pero (But)

Me gusta la carne pero prefiero el pescado.	I like meat, but I prefer fish.

Sino (But)

No lo hizo él, sino ella.	He didn't do it, but she did.

Que (That)

Dijo que vendría.	He said that he would come.

Pero versus Sino

Pero and *sino* both express "but." *Pero* is used in a more general sense and may also mean "however." *Sino* is used only after a negative statement to express a contrast (on the contrary):

No puedo hablarte ahora pero voy a llamarte mañana.	I can't speak to you now, but I'll call you tomorrow.
No le gusta el rojo, sino el amarillo.	She doesn't like the red one but (rather) the yellow one.

Example Problems

Complete the sentences about a party by choosing the correct conjunction.

1. Carlota ____ Hernán van a la fiesta.

   a. y
   b. e
   c. u
   d. ni

   Answer: a

   Use *y* to express "and"; however, *e* is substituted for *y* when the next word begins with *i-*.

2. No toman el autobús _____ el tren.

    a. pero

    b. y

    c. sino

    d. u

    Answer: c

    Use *sino* to express "but" in a negative sentence.

3. Se dice ___ la fiesta será magnífica.

    a. que

    b. sino

    c. o

    d. y

    Answer: a

    Use *que* to express "that."

Work Problems

Complete more sentences about the party by selecting the correct conjunction:

e	o	que	u
ni	pero	sino	y

1. Siete _____ ocho muchachos vienen.

2. A Marcos le gustan todas las chicas _____ prefiere a Mercedes.

3. Los invitados no beben leche _____ refrescos.

4. Miguel _____ Enrique van a tocar la guitarra.

5. A Diego no le gusta _____ bailar _____ cantar.

6. Todos piensan _____ la comida es deliciosa.

Worked Solutions

1. **Answer: u**   Use *o* to express "or"; however, *u* is substituted for *o* when the next word begins with *o-*.

2. **Answer: pero**   Use *pero* to express "but" in an affirmative sentence.

3. **Answer: sino**   Use *sino* to express "but" in a negative sentence.

4. **Answer: y**   Use *y* to express "and."

5. **Answer: ni . . . ni**   Use *ni . . . ni* to express "neither . . . nor."

6. **Answer: que**   Use *que* to express "that."

Subordinating Conjunctions

Subordinating conjunctions connect dependent clauses with main clauses. Some conjunctions require the subjunctive if uncertainty, doubt, anticipation, or indefiniteness is implied (see Chapter 14). Subordinating conjunctions include:

❑ *Apenas* (as soon as):

Apenas salí, empezó a nevar.	As soon as I went out, it started to snow.

❑ *Así que, de modo que, de manera que* (so [that]):

Mintió, así que ahora paga las consecuencias.	He lied, so now he is paying the consequences.

❑ *Aunque* (although):

Vivo en España aunque soy americana.	I live in Spain although I am American.

❑ *Como* (like, as, since):

Como no llegaba, nos fuimos.	Since you didn't arrive, we left.

❑ *Conque* (so, so then):

¿Conque te han visto?	So they saw you then?

❑ *Cuando* (when):

Cuando él lo hace, será necesario.	When he does it, it must be necessary.

❑ *Luego* (therefore):

Pienso, luego existo.	I think, therefore I am.

❑ *Mientras* (while):

Sonreía mientras hablaba.	He was smiling while he was speaking.

❑ *Porque* (because):

No respondió porque estaba ocupado.	He didn't respond because he was busy.

❑ *Pues* (then):

¿No le gusta? Pues no lo coma.	You don't like it? Then don't eat it.

❑ *Puesto que* (since, as):

Cómprelo, puesto que lo necesita.	Buy it since you need it.

❑ *Si* (if):

Compraremos una casa nueva si bajan los precios.	We will buy a new house if the prices go down.

❑ *Ya que* (since):

Ya que él no viene, ayúdeme por favor.   Since he isn't coming, help me please.

A conjunctive expression is a group of words that serve in the sentence as a conjunction:

❑ *A pesar de* (in spite of):

Salieron a pesar del mal tiempo.   They went out in spite of the bad weather.

❑ *No obstante* (however, nonetheless):

Está enferma; no obstante, está trabajando.   She is sick; however, she is working.

❑ *Por consiguiente* (consequently, therefore):

Tenía mucha hambre; por consiguiente, comió mucho.   He was very hungry; therefore, he ate a lot.

❑ *Sin embargo* (however, nevertheless):

No me gusta la ópera; sin embargo, iré contigo.   I don't like the opera; however, I'll go with you.

Example Problems

This person doesn't feel well. Select the best completion to each sentence about him.

1. No durmió anoche, _____ hoy no se siente bien.

    a. aunque
    b. apenas
    c. a pesar de
    d. así que

    Answer: d

    Use *así que* to express "so that."

2. Tiene un resfriado; _____, toma aspirinas.

    a. puesto que
    b. ya que
    c. por consiguiente
    d. porque

    Answer: c

    Use *por consiguiente* to express "consequently."

3. Iré al médico, _____ no me siento mejor.

    a. si
    b. aunque
    c. mientras
    d. sin embargo

    Answer: a

    Use *si* to express "if."

Worked Problems

Discuss what happens at work by completing the sentence with the appropriate conjunction:

apenas   porque
mientras   sin embargo
no obstante   ya que

1. _____ Daniel llega a la oficina, empieza a trabajar.

2. Tiene un resfriado; _____, hace su trabajo entusiastamente.

3. Necesita dinero; _____, no trabaja horas extras.

4. _____ no viene su cliente, él sale de la oficina.

5. Habla con su jefe _____ necesita información.

6. Él puede trabajar _____ escucha la radio.

Worked Solutions

1. **Answer: Apenas**   Use *apenas* to express "hardly."

2. **Answer: sin embargo**   Use *sin embargo* to express "however."

3. **Answer: no obstante**   Use *no obstante* to express "however."

4. **Answer: Ya que**   Use *ya que* to express "since" (meaning "seeing as").

5. **Answer: porque**   Use *porque* to express "because."

6. **Answer: mientras**   Use *mientras* to express "while."

Chapter Problems

Problems

Complete the story by supplying the correct preposition or conjunction.

El mes pasado trabajé (for) _____ mi amigo Arturo porque él salió (for) _____

1
2

Bolivia. (Although) _____ él vive (in) _____ los Estados Unidos, es boliviano.

3
4

Él tiene familia (in) _____ este país (and) _____ sus parientes necesitaban

5
6

su ayuda. (Consequently) _____ yo trabajaba (from) _____ las siete (of)

7
8

_____ la noche (until) _____ las tres (of) _____ la madrugada.

9
10
11

(Since) _____ Arturo es mi mejor amigo, lo ayudé (with) _____ gusto.

12
13

Arturo es camarero (in) _____ un restaurante célebre. (According to) _____ todos los

14
15

críticos, es el mejor restaurante (of) _____ la ciudad (and) _____ se dice (that)

16
17

_____ los precios son muy razonables. Está situado (on the corner) _____ (of)

18
19

_____ la Sexta Avenida (and) _____ la Calle Cólon, (near) _____ cine.

20
21
22

No sirven comida rápida, (but) _____ platos exquisitos. Cada noche hay siete (or)

23

_____ ocho especialidades excelentes. ¿Por qué no van comer allá, tú (and)

24

_____ Hilda?

25

Answers and Solutions

1. **Answer: por**   To express "for," select the preposition *por,* which expresses "on behalf of."

2. **Answer: para**   To express "for," select the preposition *para,* which expresses a destination.

3. **Answer: Aunque**   To express "although," select the conjunction *aunque.*

4. **Answer: en**   To express "in," select the preposition *en.*

5. **Answer: en**   To express "in," select the preposition *en.*

6. **Answer: y**   To express "and," select the conjunction *y.*

7. **Answer: Por consiguiente**   To express "consequently," select the conjunctive expression *por consiguiente.*

8. **Answer: desde**   To express "from," when referring to time, select the preposition *desde.*

9. **Answer: de**   To express "of," select the preposition *de.*

10. **Answer: hasta**   To express "until," when referring to time, select the preposition *hasta.*

11. **Answer: de**   To express "of," select the preposition *por.*

12. **Answer: Puesto que/Ya que**   To express "since," select the conjunction *puesto que* or *ya que.*

13. **Answer: con**   To express "with," select the preposition *con*.

14. **Answer: en**   To express "in," select the preposition *en*.

15. **Answer: Según**   To express "according to," select the preposition *según*.

16. **Answer: de**   To express "of," select the preposition *de*.

17. **Answer: y**   To express "and," select the conjunction *y*.

18. **Answer: que**   To express "that," select the conjunction *que*.

19. **Answer: en la esquina**   To express "on the corner," select the prepositional phrase *en la esquina*.

20. **Answer: de**   To express "of," select the preposition *de*.

21. **Answer: y**   To express "and," select the conjunction *y*.

22. **Answer: cerca del**   To express "near," select the prepositional phrase *cerca del*.

23. **Answer: sino**   To express "but" in a negative sentence, select the conjunction *sino*.

24. **Answer: u**   To express "or," select the conjunction *o*; however, *u* is substituted for *o* when the next word begins with *o-*.

25. **Answer: e**   To express "and," select the conjunction *y*; however, *e* is substituted for *y* when the next word begins with h*i-*.

Supplemental Chapter Problems

Problems

Complete the story by supplying the correct preposition or conjunction.

(Hardly) _____₁ salí de mi casa, sonó el teléfono. Entré (However) _____₂ entré de

nuevo (in) _____₃ mi casa (and) _____₄ respondí (because) _____₅ pensaba (that)

_____₆ era importante. Mi prima Inés habló (with me) _____₇. Ella se fue (to the)

_____₈ centro (in order to) _____₉ comprar unos regalos. Estacionó su

coche (in front of) _____₁₀ supermercado (in) _____₁₁ la Calle Victoria (for)

_____₁₂ una hora. (When) _____₁₃ llegó (in front of) _____₁₄ supermercado,

se dió cuenta de (that) _____₁₅ no tenía sus llaves. (Consequently) _____₁₆

no podía entrar (in) _____₁₇ su coche. Buscó sus llaves (everywhere) _____₁₈ todas

partes (but) _____₁₉ no las encontró. No había otro remedio (but) _____₂₀

telefonearme (because)_____ yo tenía otro juego (in) _____ mi casa. Fui (to)
                        21   22

_____ su ayuda. Abrí la puerta (and) _____ Inés se rió inmediatamente.
    23   24

¿Por qué? Sus llaves estaban (inside) _____ (of the) _____ coche.
                                            25   26

Solutions

1. Apenas (conjunctions, p. 191)

2. No obstante (conjunctions, p. 191)

3. en (common prepositions and prepositional expressions, p. 183, prepositional distinctions, p. 185)

4. y (conjunctions, p. 191)

5. porque (conjunctions, p. 191)

6. que (conjunctions, p. 191)

7. conmigo (common prepositions and prepositional expressions, p. 183, prepositional pronouns, p. 189)

8. al (common prepositions and prepositional expressions, p. 183)

9. para (prepositional distinctions, p. 185)

10. enfrente del (prepositional expressions of location, p. 183)

11. en (common prepositions and prepositional expressions, p. 183, prepositional distinctions, p. 185)

12. por (common prepositions and prepositional expressions, p. 183, prepositional distinctions, p. 185)

13. Cuando (conjunctions, p. 191)

14. cerca del (prepositional expressions of location, p. 183)

15. que (conjunctions, p. 191)

16. Por consiguiente (conjunctions, p. 191)

17. en (common prepositions and prepositional expressions, p. 183, prepositional distinctions, p. 185)

18. por (common prepositions and prepositional expressions, p. 183, prepositional distinctions, p. 185)

19. pero (conjunctions, p. 191)

20. sino (conjunctions, p. 191)

21. porque (conjunctions, p. 191)

22. en (common prepositions and prepositional phrases, p. 183, prepositional distinctions, p. 185)

23. a (common prepositions and prepositional expressions, p. 183)

24. e (conjunctions, p. 191)

25. dentro (prepositional expressions of location, p. 183)

26. del (common prepositions and prepositional expressions, p. 183)

Chapter 9
The Infinitive

The infinitive is the "to" form of the verb—the form of the verb before it is conjugated.

Using an Infinitive as a Noun

The infinitive preceded by the definite article *el* functions as a masculine singular noun. The definite article is often omitted when the infinitive acts as the subject of the sentence:

(El) Beber es necesario para vivir.

Drinking is necessary in order to live.

(El) Engañar es un vicio.

Deceit is a vice.

Negating an Infinitive

An infinitive may be negated by placing *no* before the infinitive and any other negative words after the infinitive:

Más vale no hablar.   It is better not to speak.

Es preferible no decir nada a nadie.   It is preferable not to say anything to anybody.

Example Problems

Use an infinitive to complete each thought about what is good.

1. _____ una lengua extranjera es un logro.

   Answer: Hablar

   "Speaking a language is an accomplishment." Use the infinitive *hablar* to express "to speak."

2. _____ honesto es una virtud.

   Answer: Ser

   "Being honest is a virtue." Use the infinitive *ser* to express "to be."

3.   _____ ejercicios es bueno para la salud.

   Answer: Hacer

   "Doing exercises is good for your health." Use the infinitive *hacer* to express "to do."

Work Problems

Use these problems to give yourself additional practice.

Match the English saying with its Spanish equivalent.

1. Seeing is believing.		a. Mira antes de saltar.
2. To err is human; to forgive is divine.		b. Querer es poder.
3. Knowledge is power.		c. Ver es creer.
4. Look before you leap.		d. Vivir para ver.
5. Where there's a will, there's a way.		e. El saber no ocupa lugar.
6. Live and learn.		f. El errar es humano; el perdonar es divino.

Worked Solutions

1. **c**   The verb *ver* means "to see."

2. **f**   The verb *errar* means "to err."

3. **e**   The verb *saber* means "to know."

4. **a**   The verb *mirar* means "to look."

5. **b**   The verb *querer* means "to wish" or "to want."

6. **d**   The verb *vivir* means "to live."

Derivations from Infinitives

Nouns can be derived from certain infinitives as follows:

1. The infinitive ending is dropped from an *-ar* verb, and *-a* or *-o* is added to the remaining stem:

ahorrar	to save	el ahorro	saving
anunciar	to announce	el anuncio	announcement
apoyar	to rest	el apoyo	support

ayudar	to help	la ayuda	help
bailar	to dance	el baile	dance
contar	to tell	el cuento	story
contar	to count	la cuenta	bill
dudar	to doubt	la duda	doubt
faltar	to need	la falta	mistake
practicar	to practice	la práctica	practice

2. The *-r* is dropped from an *-ar* verb, and *-ción* is added to the remaining stem:

acelerar	to accelerate	aceleración	acceleration
combinar	to combine	combinación	combination
declarar	to declare	declaración	declaration
exagerar	to exaggerate	exageración	exaggeration
frustrar	to frustrate	frustración	frustration
habitar	to inhabit	habitación	room
invitar	to invite	invitación	invitation
negociar	to do business with	negociación	negotiation
preparar	to prepare	preparación	preparation
separar	to separate	separación	separation

3. The *-r* is dropped from an *-ar, -er,* or *-ir* infinitive, and the suffix *-miento* is added to the remaining stem (note that *-cer* verbs change the final *-e* to *-i* before adding *-miento*):

asentar	to set up	asentamiento	settlement
tratar	to treat	tratamiento	treatment
conocer	to know	conocimiento	knowledge
crecer	to grow	crecimiento	growth
entender	to understand	entendimiento	understanding
establecer	to establish	establecimiento	establishment
nacer	to be born	nacimiento	birth
consentir	to consent	consentimiento	consent
descubrir	to discover	descubrimiento	discovery
sentir	to feel	sentimiento	feeling

4. The *-r* is dropped from an *-ar*, *-er*, or *-ir* infinitive, and the suffix *-ancia* is added for *-ar* verbs and the suffix *-encia* is added for *-er* and *-ir* verbs:

ignorar	to ignore	ignorancia	to ignore
importar	to be of importance	importancia	importance
tolerar	to tolerate	tolerancia	tolerance
vigilar	to watch over	vigilancia	vigilance
tender	to extend, to spread out	tendencia	tendency
competir	to compete	competencia	competition
exigir	to demand	exigencia	demand
existir	to exist	existencia	existence
insistir	to insist	insistencia	insistence
preferir	to prefer	preferencia	preference

5. The *-r* is dropped from an *-ar*, *-er*, or *-ir* infinitive, and the suffix *-ante* is added for *-ar* verbs and the suffix *-iente* is added for *-er* and *-ir* verbs to express "one who":

amar	to love	amante	lover
comerciar	to trade	comerciante	merchant
emigrar	to emigrate	emigrante	emigrant
restaurar	to restore	restaurante	restaurant
votar	to vote	votante	voter
corresponder	to correspond	correspondiente	correspondent
combatir	to fight	combatiente	fighter
expedir	to send	expediente	files, inquiry
remitir	to remit	remitente	sender
sobrevivir	to survive	sobreviviente	survivor

Adjectives can be derived from infinitives as follows:

6. The *-r* is dropped from the *-ar*, *-er*, or *-ir* infinitive, and *-able* is added for *-ar* verbs and *-ible* is added for *-er* or *-ir* verbs:

amar	to love	amable	kind
aplicar	to apply	aplicable	applicable
abominar	to hate	abominable	abominable
aceptar	to accept	aceptable	acceptable

comparar	to compare	comparable	comparable
desechar	to discard	desechable	disposable
creer	to believe	creíble	credible
temer	to be afraid of	temible	fearsome
corregir	to correct	corregible	rectifiable
preferir	to prefer	preferible	preferable

Example Problems

Give the Spanish infinitive and its meaning for each of the derivations.

> Example: el balance
>
> balancear/to balance

1. el abono

   Answer: abonar/to subscribe

   El abono is derived from the verb *abonar* (to subscribe). Drop the final *-o* from the noun and add *-ar*.

2. dirigible

   Answer: dirigir/to direct

   Dirigible is derived from the verb *dirigir* (to direct). Drop *-ible* from the adjective and add *-ir*.

3. el creyente

   Answer: creer/to believe

   El creyente is derived from the verb *creer* (to believe). Drop *-yente* from the noun and add *-er*.

Work Problems

Use these problems to give yourself additional practice.

Give the Spanish infinitive and its meaning for each of the derivations.

1. la correspondencia

2. sofocante

3. respetado

4. la anticipación

5. la planta

6. el corriente

7. preferido

8. el consentimiento

Worked Solutions

1. **corresponder/to correspond**   *La correspondencia* is derived from the verb *corresponder* (to correspond). Drop *-encia* from the noun and add *-er*.

2. **sofocar/to suffocate**   *Sofocante* is derived from the adjective *sofocar* (to suffocate). Drop *-ante* from the adjective and add *-ar*.

3. **respetar/to respect**   *Respetado* is derived from the verb *respetar* (to respect). Drop *-ado* from the adjective and add *-ar*.

4. **anticipar/to anticipate**   *La anticipación* is derived from the verb *anticipar* (to anticipate). Drop *-ción* from the noun and add *-r*.

5. **plantar/to plant**   *La planta* is derived from the verb *plantar* (to plant). Retain *-a* from the noun and add *-r*.

6. **correr/to run**   *El corriente* is derived from the verb *correr* (to run). Drop *-iente* from the noun and add *-er*.

7. **preferir/to prefer**   *Preferido* is derived from the verb *preferir* (to prefer). Drop *-ido* from the adjective and add *-ir*.

8. **consentir/to consent**   *El consentimiento* is derived from the verb *consentir* (to consent). Drop *-miento* from the noun and add *-ir*.

Infinitives Followed by Prepositions

In Spanish, the infinitive is the verb form that follows a preposition. Spanish verbs may require the preposition *a, de, en,* or *con* before the infinitive. Some Spanish verbs are followed immediately by the infinitive and no preposition should be used with them.

Spanish Verbs Requiring *A*

The following Spanish verbs are followed by *a* before an infinitive:

acercarse	to approach
acostumbrarse	to become accustomed
acudir	to go, to come
animar	to encourage
aprender	to learn

apresurarse	to hurry
aspirar	to aspire
atreverse	to dare
ayudar	to help
comenzar	to begin
convidar	to invite
correr	to run
decidirse	to decide
dedicarse	to devote oneself
disponerse	to get ready
echarse	to lie down, to move aside
empezar	to begin
enseñar	to teach
invitar	to invite
ir	to go
llegar	to succeed in
negarse (e→ie)	to refuse
obligar	to force
oponerse	to to oppose
ponerse	to begin
principiar	to begin
regresar	to return
resignarse	to resign oneself
salir	to go out
venir	to come
volver (o→ue)	to return (again)

El niño comienza a llorar.	The child starts to cry.
Ellos volvieron a jugar.	They played again.

Spanish Verbs Requiring *De*

The following Spanish verbs are followed by *de* before an infinitive:

acabar	to have just
acordarse (o→ue)	to remember to
alegrarse	to be glad
cansarse	to tire
cesar	to stop
deber	should
dejar	to stop
disfrutar	to enjoy
encargarse	to take charge of
gozar	to enjoy

ocuparse	to deal with
olvidarse	to forget
tratar	to try to

Los niños no se cansan de jugar.   Children do not get tired of playing.

Spanish Verbs Requiring *En*

The following Spanish verbs are followed by *en* before an infinitive:

consentir	to consent to
consistir	to consist of
convenir	to agree to
empeñarse	to insist on
insistir	to insist on
pensar	to think (to reflect)
tardar	to delay in

Yo insisto en pagar la cuenta   I insist on paying the check.

Spanish Verbs Requiring *Con*

The following Spanish verbs are followed by *con* before an infinitive:

amenazar	to threaten
conformarse	to be satisfied with
contar	to count on
soñar	to dream of

Él cuenta con recuperar su dinero.   He's counting on recovering his money.

Infinitives Requiring No Preposition

The following verbs are followed directly by an infinitive:

Spanish	English
deber	must (to have to)
dejar	to allow
desear	to want, to wish
esperar	to hope
hacer	to make (to have something done)
lograr	to succeed in
necesitar	to need
oír	to hear

Spanish	English
pensar	to intend
poder	to be able to
preferir	to prefer
pretender	to attempt
prometer	to promise
querer	to want, to wish
saber	to know (how)
ver	to see
Yo espero viajar.	I hope to travel.

Example Problems

Express what these people do by filling in the blank with a preposition, if necessary.

1. Diana aprende ____ jugar al fútbol.

   Answer: a

   The verb *aprender* is followed by the preposition *a*.

2. Salvador se ocupa ____ organizar su habitación.

   Answer: de

   The verb *ocuparse* is followed by the preposition *de*.

3. Marta debe ____ escribir una carta.

   Answer: none

   The verb *deber* is not followed by a preposition.

Work Problems

Use these problems to give yourself additional practice.

Complete the story about Gloria by filling in the blank with a preposition, if necessary.

Gloria se resigna ____₁ ser soltera. No puede ____₂ encontrar el hombre de sus sueños.

Sin embargo, un día Ramón la invita ____₃ salir con él al teatro. Ella no tarda ____₄

aceptar la invitación. Ella consiente ____₅ acompañarlo. Después de su primera cita con

Ramón, Gloria sueña ____₆ volver a verlo.

Worked Solutions

1. **a**   The verb *resignarse* is followed by the preposition *a*.

2. **none**   The verb *poder* is not followed by a preposition.

3. **a**   The verb *invitar* is followed by the preposition *a*.

4. **en**   The verb *tardar* is followed by the preposition *en*.

5. **en**   The verb *consentir* is followed by the preposition *en*.

6. **con**   The verb *soñar* is followed by the preposition *con*.

Prepositions Used Before Infinitives

Whereas English uses the present participle after certain prepositions, Spanish uses the infinitive. The following prepositions are generally used before a Spanish infinitive:

❑ *Al* (upon, on):

   Al entrar en casa, saludé a mis padres.

   Upon entering the house, I greeted my parents.

❑ *Antes de* (before):

   Antes de comer, hice mi tarea.

   Before eating, I did my homework.

❑ *Después de* (after):

   Después de descansar un rato, trabajé.

   After resting a while, I worked.

❑ *En* (on):

   Insistí en comer temprano.

   I insisted on eating early.

❑ *En lugar de* or *en vez de* (instead of):

   En lugar de (en vez de) estudiar, miré la televisión.

   Instead of studying, I watched television.

❑ *Sin* (without):

   Yo salí sin tomar mi paraguas.

   I went out without taking my umbrella.

Example Problems

Express what happened by completing the sentence in Spanish.

1. (Upon leaving) _____ de mi casa, encontré a mi amigo.

   Answer: Al salir

Use the preposition *al* to express "upon." Use the Spanish infinitive *salir* to express the English present participle "leaving."

2. (Before going) _____ al centro, hablé con él.

Answer: Antes de ir

Use the prepositional phrase *antes de* to express "before." Use the Spanish infinitive *ir* to express the English present participle "going."

3. (Instead of speaking) _____ de nuestras clases, hablamos de nuestros pasatiempos.

Answer: En vez de (en lugar de) hablar

Use the prepositional phrase *en vez de* or *en lugar de* to express "instead of." Use the Spanish infinitive *hablar* to express the English present participle "speaking."

Work Problems

Use these problems to give yourself additional practice.

Express what happened by completing the paragraph in Spanish.

(After leaving) _____ de la escuela, (instead of going) _____ a casa,
₁ ... ₂

fui a visitar a mis abuelos. (Without saying) _____ nada a mis padres me quedé en
₃

su casa por cuatro horas. Ellos insistieron (in giving me) _____ de comer. (Before
₄

returning) _____, telefoneé finalmente a mis padres, que tenían mucho miedo.
₅

(Upon arriving) _____ a casa tuve que explicar mi ausencia.
₆

Worked Solutions

1. **Después de salir** Use the prepositional phrase *después de* to express "after." Use the Spanish infinitive *salir* to express the English present participle "leaving."

2. **en vez de (en lugar de) ir** Use the prepositional phrase *en vez de* or *en lugar de* to express "instead of." Use the Spanish infinitive *ir* to express the English present participle "going."

3. **Sin decir** Use the preposition *sin* to express "without." Use the Spanish infinitive *decir* to express the English present participle "saying."

4. **en darme** Use the preposition *en* to express "in." Use the Spanish infinitive *dar* to express the English present participle "giving." Attach the indirect object pronoun *me* to the infinitive to express "to me."

5. **Antes de regresar** Use the prepositional phrase *antes de* to express "before." Use the Spanish infinitive *regresar* to express the English present participle "returning."

6. **Al llegar** Use the preposition *al* to express "upon." Use the Spanish infinitive *llegar* to express the English present participle "arriving."

Using an Infinitive Instead of the Subjunctive

An infinitive is used to avoid the subjunctive (see Chapter 14) in sentences where two clauses with the same subject can be combined to form one clause:

Ellos prefieren que ellos vayan al cine.

Ellos prefieren ir al cine.

They prefer going to the movies.

Example Problems

The students in Señor Rueda's class wrote Spanish compositions. Unfortunately many mistakes were made. Correct the grammatically incorrect sentences by replacing the subjunctive with the infinitive.

Example: Yo te llamo después de que yo regrese.

Yo te llamo después de regresar.

1. Yo tomo apuntes para que yo pueda recordarme de todo.

    Answer: Yo tomo apuntes para recordarme de todo.

    An infinitive is used to avoid the subjunctive in sentences with two clauses that have the same subject. Drop the phrase that begins *que yo pueda*.

2. Yo no me voy sin que yo termine mi trabajo.

    Answer: Yo no me voy sin terminar mi trabajo.

    An infinitive is used to avoid the subjunctive in sentences with two clauses that have the same subject. Drop the phrase that begins *que yo*. Use the infinitive *terminar* to replace the subjunctive form *termine*.

3. Yo me lavo los manos antes de que yo coma.

    Answer: Yo me lavo los manos antes de comer.

    An infinitive is used to avoid the subjunctive in sentences with two clauses that have the same subject. Drop the phrase that begins *de que yo*. Use the infinitive *comer* to replace the subjunctive form *coma*.

Work Problems

Use these problems to give yourself additional practice.

Continue to correct the grammatically incorrect sentences by replacing the subjunctive with the infinitive.

1. Yo te hablaré antes de que yo venga.

2. Yo no te escribiré sin que yo reciba cierta información.

3.   Yo leeré despacio para que yo comprenda todo.

4.   Yo no saldré sin que yo diga adiós a todo el mundo.

5.   Yo te telefonearé después de que yo haga el viaje.

6.   Yo te contaré la historia antes de que yo salga.

Worked Solutions

1.   **Yo te hablaré antes de venir.**   An infinitive is used instead of the subjunctive in sentences with two clauses that have the same subject. Drop the phrase that begins *que yo.* Use the infinitive *venir* to replace the subjunctive form *venga.*

2.   **Yo no te escribiré sin recibir cierta información.**   An infinitive is used instead of the subjunctive in sentences with two clauses that have the same subject. Drop the phrase that begins *que yo.* Use the infinitive *recibir* to replace the subjunctive form *reciba.*

3.   **Yo leeré despacio para comprender todo.**   An infinitive is used instead of the subjunctive in sentences with two clauses that have the same subject. Drop the phrase that begins *que yo.* Use the infinitive *comprender* to replace the subjunctive form *comprenda.*

4.   **Yo no saldré sin decir adiós a todo el mundo.**   An infinitive is used instead of the subjunctive in sentences with two clauses that have the same subject. Drop the phrase that begins *que yo.* Use the infinitive *decir* to replace the subjunctive form *diga.*

5.   **Yo te telefonearé despues de hacer el viaje.**   An infinitive is used instead of the subjunctive in sentences with two clauses that have the same subject. Drop the phrase that begins *que yo.* Use the infinitive *hacer* to replace the subjunctive form *haga.*

6.   **Yo te contaré la historia antes de salir.**   An infinitive is used instead of the subjunctive in sentences with two clauses that have the same subject. Drop the phrase that begins *que yo.* Use the infinitive *salir* to replace the subjunctive form *salga.*

The Perfect Infinitive

To form the perfect infinitive, take the infinitive of *haber* and add the past participle of the verb stating the action (see Chapter 13 for an explanation on the formation of the past participle):

> Habla bien el español para haber nacido en los Estados Unidos.
> He speaks Spanish well for having been born in the United States.

Example Problems

Express what Tomás did to receive awards at school.

> Example: Recibió premios. Estudió mucho.
>
> Recibió premios por haber estudiado mucho.

1.   Recibió premios. Sacó buenas notas.

     Answer: Recibió premios por haber sacado buenas notas.

     Use the infinitive of the verb *haber*. To form the past participle of the verb *sacar*, drop the -*ar* ending and add -*ado*.

2.   Recibió premios. Salió bien en sus exámenes.

     Answer: Recibió premios por haber salido bien en sus exámenes.

     Use the infinitive of the verb *haber*. To form the past participle of the verb *salir*, drop the -*ir* ending and add -*ido*.

3.   Recibió premios. Fue muy trabajador.

     Answer: Recibió premios por haber sido muy trabajador.

     Use the infinitive of the verb *haber*. To form the past participle of the verb *ser*, drop the -*er* ending and add -*ido*.

Work Problems

Express reasons why different men were famous.

1.   Fue conocido. Escribió libros.

2.   Fue conocido. Ganó premios científicos.

3.   Fue conocido. Descubrió una isla.

4.   Fue conocido. Ayudó a los desafortunados.

5.   Fue conocido. Pintó obras famosas.

6.   Fue conocido. Dirigió una orquesta sinfónica.

Worked Solutions

1.   **Fue conocido por haber escrito libros.**   Use the infinitive of the verb *haber*. The past participle of the verb *escribir* is irregular and must be memorized.

2.   **Fue conocido por haber ganado premios científicos.**   Use the infinitive of the verb *haber*. To form the past participle of the verb *ganar*, drop the -*ar* ending and add -*ado*.

3.   **Fue conocido por haber descubierto una isla.**   Use the infinitive of the verb *haber*. The past participle of the verb *describir* is irregular and must be memorized.

4. **Fue conocido por haber ayudado a los desafortunados.** Use the infinitive of the verb *haber*. To form the past participle of the verb *ayudar*, drop the *-ar* ending and add *-ado*.

5. **Fue conocido por haber pintado obras famosas.** Use the infinitive of the verb *haber*. To form the past participle of the verb *pintar*, drop the *-ar* ending and add *-ado*.

6. **Fue conocido por haber dirigido una orquesta sinfónica.** Use the infinitive of the verb *haber*. To form the past participle of the verb *dirigir*, drop the *-ir* ending and add *-ido*.

Chapter Problems

Problems

Complete each thought by using the appropriate verb.

1. El _____ idiomas es una ventaja.

2. El _____ ejercicios es bueno para la salud.

3. El _____ por el extranjero es interesante.

4. El _____ un instrumento musical ofrece horas de placer.

5. El _____ rápidamente puede causar accidentes.

Give the Spanish infinitive and its meaning for each of the derivations.

6. la abundancia

7. el aviso

8. el dependiente

9. la participación

10. el compartimiento

Complete the advertisement about joining a gym by filling in a preposition, if necessary.

No debe _____ resignarse _____ sufrir cuando quiere _____ bajar de peso.

11   12   13

Puede _____ contar _____ nosotros. Nos dedicaremos _____ preparar un

14   15   16

régimen saludable para Ud. No tarde Ud. _____ venir al gimnasio moderno y completo

17

que acabamos _____ construir. _____ firmar un contrato, le enseñaremos _____ hacer

18   19   20

ejercicios especializados.

Answers and Solutions

1. **Answer: saber**   Use the Spanish infinitive *saber* to express the English present participle "knowing." *Saber* is used to express knowing a fact.

2. **Answer: hacer**   Use the Spanish infinitive *hacer* to express the English present participle "doing."

3. **Answer: viajar**   Use the Spanish infinitive *viajar* to express the English present participle "traveling."

4. **Answer: tocar**   Use the Spanish infinitive *tocar* to express the English present participle "playing." *Tocar* is used to express playing a musical instrument.

5. **Answer: conducir**   Use the Spanish infinitive *conducir* to express the English present participle "driving."

6. **Answer: abundar/to abound**   *La abundancia* is derived from the verb *abundar* (to abound). Drop *-ancia* from the noun and add *-ar*.

7. **Answer: avisar/to notify**   *El aviso* is derived from the verb *avisar* (to notify). Drop *-o* from the noun and add *-ar*.

8. **Answer: depender/to depend**   *El dependiente* is derived from the verb *depender* (to depend). Drop *-iente* from the noun and add *-er*.

9. **Answer: participar/to participate**   *La participación* is derived from the verb *participar* (to participate). Drop *-ción* from the noun and add *-r*.

10. **Answer: compartir/to share**   *El compartimiento* is derived from the verb *compartir* (to share). Drop *-miento* from the noun and add *-r*.

11. **Answer: none**   The verb *deber* is not followed by a preposition.

12. **Answer: a**   The verb *resignarse* is followed by the preposition *a*.

13. **Answer: none**   The verb *querer* is not followed by a preposition.

14. **Answer: none**   The verb *poder* is not followed by a preposition.

15. **Answer: con**   The verb *contar* is followed by the preposition *con*.

16. **Answer: a**   The verb *dedicarse* is followed by the preposition *a*.

17. **Answer: en**   The verb *tardar* is followed by the preposition *en*.

18. **Answer: de**   The verb *acabar* is followed by the preposition *de*.

19. **Answer: Al**   The infinitive is preceded by the preposition *al*, which expresses "upon."

20. **Answer: a**   The verb *enseñar* is followed by the preposition *a*.

Supplemental Chapter Problems

Problems
Complete each thought by using the appropriate verb.

1. El _____ a los naipes es un pasatiempo divertido.

2. El _____ legumbres es necesario para la buena alimentación.

3. El _____ mucho dinero asegura la riqueza.

4. El _____ es la vocación del médico.

5. El _____ en bicicleta es un ejercicio aeróbico.

Give the Spanish infinitive and its meaning for each of the derivations.

6. el paso

7. el emigrante

8. el acompañamiento

9. la resistencia

10. la acumulación

Complete the paragraph about this person's morning by filling in a preposition, if necessary.

Yo trataba _____ prepararme para una entrevista. _____ levantarme, debía _____
$\quad$ 11 $\qquad$ 12 $\qquad$ 13

vestirme y ocuparme _____ muchas cosas. No tardé _____ preparme. No prestaba
$\quad$ 14 $\qquad$ 15

atención, y por eso, no vi _____ salir mi perro de mi apartamento. Yo oí _____ decir
$\quad$ 16 $\qquad$ 17

a una vecina que un perro andaba por el parque. Fui inmediatamente al parque y conté

_____ encontrarlo inmediatamente. ¡Qué buena suerte! Lo encontré diez minutos
$\quad$ 18

después _____ llegar allá. Me alegré muchísimo _____ verlo jugar con otros perros.
$\quad$ 19 $\qquad$ 20

Solutions

1. jugar (using an infinitive as a noun, p. 201)

2. comer (using an infinitive as a noun, p. 201)

3. ganar (using an infinitive as a noun, p. 201)

4. curar (using an infinitive as a noun, p. 201)

5. montar (using an infinitive as a noun, p. 201)

6. pasear/to stroll (derivations from infinitives, p. 202)

7. emigrar/to emigrate (derivations from infinitives, p. 202)

8. acompañar/to accompany (derivations from infinitives, p. 202)

9. resistir/to resist (derivations from infinitives, p. 202)

10. acumular/to accumulate (derivations from infinitives, p. 202)

11. de (Spanish verbs requiring *en,* p. 208)

12. Al (prepositions used before infinitives, p. 210)

13. none (infinitives requiring no preposition, p. 208)

14. de (Spanish verbs requiring *de,* p. 207)

15. en (Spanish verbs requiring *en,* p. 208)

16. none (infinitives requiring no preposition, p. 208)

17. none (infinitives requiring no preposition, p. 208)

18. con (Spanish verbs requiring *con,* p. 208)

19. de (Spanish verbs requiring *de,* p. 207)

20. de (Spanish verbs requiring *de,* p. 207)

Chapter 10
Preterit and Imperfect

The Preterit

The preterit is a past tense that expresses an action, event, or state of mind that occurred and was completed at a specific time in the past.

The Preterit of Regular Verbs

The preterit of regular verbs is formed by dropping the *-ar*, *-er*, or *-ir* infinitive endings and adding the preterit endings as follows:

		Yo	*Tú*	*Él, Ella, Ud.*	*Nosotros*	*Vosotros*	*Ellos, Ellas, Uds.*
-ar Verbs	trabaj~~ar~~	-é	-aste	-ó	-amos	-asteis	-aron
-er Verbs	corr~~er~~	-í	-iste	-ió	-imos	-isteis	-ieron
-ir Verbs	abr~~ir~~	-í	-iste	-ió	-imos	-isteis	-ieron

For example:

> Ayer yo trabajé. Mi amigo y yo comimos y después asistimos a un concierto.
>
> Yesterday I worked. My friend and I ate, then attended a concert.

The Preterit Tense of Spelling-Change Verbs

Verbs Ending in -car, -gar, and -zar

Verbs ending in *-car*, *-gar*, and *-zar* have the following changes only in the *yo* form of the preterit to preserve the original sound of the verb:

c → qu	*explicar* (to explain)	yo expliqué
g → gu	*jugar* (to play)	yo jugué
z → c	*comenzar* (to begin)	yo comencé

Verbs That Change I to Y

Except for the verb *traer* (to bring) and all verbs ending in *-guir* (which follow the rules for regular verbs for the formation of the preterit), verbs ending in a vowel when the infinitive *-er* or *-ir* ending is dropped change *i* to *y* in the third person singular (*él, ella, Ud.*) and plural (*ellos, ellas, Uds.*) forms. All other forms have an accented *i: í.*

	Yo	Tú	Él, Ella, Ud.	Nosotros	Vosotros	Ellos, Ellas, Uds.
leer	leí	leíste	leyó	leímos	leísteis	leyeron

Verbs ending in *-uir* (*concluir, destruir, sustituir,* and so on) follow the *i* to *y* change but do not accent the *i* in the *tú, nosotros,* or *vosotros* forms.

	Yo	Tú	Él, Ella, Ud.	Nosotros	Vosotros	Ellos, Ellas, Uds.
concluir	concluí	concluiste	concluyó	concluimos	concluisteis	concluyeron

The Preterit of Stem-Changing Verbs

Present-tense stem-changing verbs ending in *-ir* have a different stem change in the preterit. In the third person singular and plural forms, *e* changes to *i* and *o* changes to *u*:

	Yo	Tú	Él, Ella, Ud.	Nosotros	Vosotros	Ellos, Ellas, Uds.
m**e**ntir	mentí	mentiste	m**i**ntió	mentimos	mentisteis	m**i**ntieron
p**e**dir	pedí	pediste	p**i**dió	pedimos	pedisteis	p**i**dieron
d**o**rmir	dormí	dormiste	d**u**rmió	dormimos	dormisteis	d**u**rmieron

The verb *reír* (to laugh) and *sonreír* (to smile) follow the same changes but drop *e* in the stem of the third person singular (*él, ella, Ud.*) and third person plural (*ellos, ellas, Uds.*) forms and add accents to the *tú, nosotros,* and *vosotros* forms:

	Yo	Tú	Él, Ella, Ud.	Nosotros	Vosotros	Ellos, Ellas, Uds.
reír	reí	reíste	rió	reímos	reísteis	rieron

The Preterit of Irregular Verbs

Many verbs that are irregular in the present are also irregular in the preterit, and some may be grouped according to the changes they undergo.

Most irregular verbs in the preterit have these endings:

Yo	Tú	Él, ella, Ud.	Nosotros	Vosotros	Ellos, Ellas, Uds.
-e	-iste	-o	-imos	-isteis	-ieron (or *-jeron* if the stem ends in *j*)

The following verbs have an irregular stem in the preterit to which the preceeding endings are added:

Verb	Meaning	Preterit Stem
andar	to walk	anduv-
caber	to fit	cup-
estar	to be	estuv-
haber	to have (auxiliary verb)	hub-
hacer *	to make, to do	hic-
poder	to be able to	pud-
poner	to put	pus-
querer	to wish, to want	quis-
saber	to know	sup-
satisfacer *	to satisfy	satisfic-
tener	to have	tuv-
venir	to come	vin-

*In these verbs, c changes to z in the third person singular (él, ella, Ud.) form to maintain the original sound of the verb.

Here is an example of one of these verbs in a sentence: Yo hice mi tarea pero él no hizo nada. I did my homework, but he did nothing.

Verbs ending in -ducir and the verbs decir and traer have a j in the preterit stem and add the preterit endings for irregular verbs, except for the third person plural (ellos, ellas, Uds.), which uses the -eron ending.

Verb	Meaning	Preterit Stem
decir	to say, to tell	dij-
traer	to bring	traj-
producir	to produce	produj-

Dar and ver have the same irregular preterit endings, which are added to d- and v-:

Yo	Tú	Él, Ella, Ud.	Nosotros	Vosotros	Ellos, Ellas, Uds.
-i	-iste	-io	-imos	-isteis	-ieron

Ser (to be) and ir (to go) have the exact same preterit forms and are distinguishable by the context of the sentence:

Yo	Tú	Él, Ella, Ud.	Nosotros	Vosotros	Ellos, Ellas, Uds.
fui	fuiste	fue	fuimos	fuisteis	fueron

Use of the Preterit

Use the preterit:

❑ To express an action or event that began at a specific time in the past:

La fiesta comenzó a las siete. The party began at seven o'clock.

❑ To express an action or event that was completed at a specific time in the past:

Anoche fuimos al teatro. Last night we went to the theater.

❑ To express an action that was completed in the past within a specific time period:

Limpié la casa. I cleaned the house.

❑ To express a series of events that was completed within a definite time period in the past:

Fui al almacén, compré un regalo y regresé inmediatamente.

I went to the store, I bought a gift, and I returned home immediately.

Example Problems

Use the preterit to express what each person did on Sunday.

Example: yo/mirar la televisión
         Yo miré la televisión.

1. él/dormir hasta muy tarde

   Answer: Él durmió hasta muy tarde.

   For present-tense stem-changing verbs ending in -ir, o changes to u in the third person singular form.

2. tú/tener una fiesta

   Answer: Tú tuviste una fiesta.

   In the preterit stem, *tener* changes the *en* from the infinitive stem to *uv*. The second person singular preterit ending for an -er verb is -iste.

3. nosotros/hacer nuestras tareas

   Answer: Nosotros hicimos nuestras tareas.

   In the preterit stem, *hacer* changes the *a* from the infinitive stem to *i*. The first person plural preterit ending for an irregular -er verb is -imos.

4. yo/conducir al campo

   Answer: Yo conduje al campo.

   In the preterit stem, *conducir* (and other verbs ending in -ucir) adds a *j* after the *u* and drops the *c*. The first person singular preterit ending for this stem-changing verb is -e. Note that the accent that is normally used in the preterit is dropped.

5. Uds./andar por el parque

   Answer: Uds. anduvieron por el parque.

   In the preterit stem, *andar* adds *uv* to the infinitive stem *(and-)*. The third person plural preterit ending for an irregular verb is *-ieron*.

6. vosotros/poder visitar a vuestros amigos

   Answer: Vosotros pudisteis visitar a vuestros amigos.

   In the preterit stem, *poder* changes the *o* from the infinitive stem to *u*. The second person plural preterit ending for an *-er* verb is *-isteis*.

Work Problems

Use the preterit to express what the subject did yesterday.

Ayer yo (tener) _____ ganas de ir al cine. Yo (telefonear) _____ a mi amigo y le
                        1   2

(decir) _____ mis planes. Él les (pedir) _____ permiso a sus padres para
              3   4

acompañarme. Él (aceptar) _____ mi invitación. Yo (llegar) _____ a su casa a la
                                5   6

una. A la una y diez (empezar) _____ a llover. Mi amigo (decir) _____ que
                                      7   8

conducir con la lluvia era muy peligroso. De todos modos, yo (seguir) _____ mi ruta
                                                                              9

ordinaria. De repente, yo no (ver) _____ una curva y no (poder) _____ evitar lo
                                        10   11

que (pasar) _____. En este momento yo (ser) _____ presa del pánico. Yo (querer)
                  12   13

_____ evitar el otro coche, pero no (saber) _____ cómo. Desafortunadamente,
      14   15

mi coche (chocar) _____ con el otro. Yo (explicar) _____ el problema al otro
                        16   17

conductor. Yo (utilizar) _____ mi teléfono celular para llamar a la policía, que (venir)
                              18

_____ en seguida. El agente no me (dar) _____ una multa. Todo el mundo
      19   20

(concluir) _____ que no había mucho daño. Yo (prometer) _____ conducir más
                21   22

cuidadosamente. Mi amigo y yo (volver) _____ a mi casa, (comer) _____ algo y
                                              23   24

(mirar) _____ una película en la televisión.
              25

Worked Solutions

1. **tuve** In the preterit stem, *tener* changes the *en* from the infinitive stem to *uv*. The first person singular preterit ending for an irregular *-er* verb is *-e*.

2. **telefoneé** To conjugate regular *-ar* verbs in the preterit, drop the *-ar* ending and add *-é* as the first person singular ending.

3. **dije**   In the preterit stem, *decir* changes the *e* from the infinitive stem to *i*. A *j* is added after the *i*. The first person singular preterit ending is *-e*.

4. **pidió**   To conjugate stem-changing verbs ending in *-ir*, *e* changes to *i* in the third person singular form. Drop the *-ir* ending and add *-ió* as the third person singular ending.

5. **aceptó**   To conjugate regular *-ar* verbs in the preterit, drop the *-ar* ending and add *-ó* as the third person singular ending.

6. **llegué**   To conjugate spelling-change *-gar* verbs in the preterit, drop the *-ar* ending. For *yo*, change *g* to *gu* and add *-é* as the ending.

7. **empezó**   To conjugate spelling-change *-zar* verbs in the preterit, drop the *-ar* ending and add *-ó* as the third person singular ending.

8. **dijo**   In the preterit stem, *decir* changes the *e* from the infinitive stem to *i*. A *j* is added after the *i*. The third person singular preterit ending is *-o*.

9. **seguí**   To conjugate present-tense verbs ending in *-uir*, drop the *-ir* ending and add *-í* as the first person singular ending.

10. **vi**   *Ver* has irregular preterit endings that are added to the *v-* from the infinitive. The preterit ending for *yo* is an unaccented *-i*.

11. **pude**   In the preterit stem, *poder* changes the *o* from the infinitive stem to *u*. The first person singular preterit ending for an irregular *-er* verb is *-e*.

12. **pasó**   To conjugate regular *-ar* verbs in the preterit, drop the *-ar* ending and add *-ó* as the third person singular ending.

13. **fui**   The verb *ser* is irregular in the preterit and must be memorized. All forms start with *fu-*. The preterit ending for the *yo* form of this irregular verb is *-i*.

14. **quise**   In the preterit stem, *querer* changes the *e* from the infinitive stem to *i*. The *r* from the infinitive stem changes to *s* in the preterit. The first person singular preterit ending for an irregular *-er* verb is *-e*.

15. **supe**   In the preterit stem, *saber* changes the *ab* from the infinitive stem to *up*. The first person singular preterit ending for an irregular *-er* verb is *-e*.

16. **chocó**   To conjugate spelling-change *-car* verbs in the preterit, drop the *-ar* ending and add *-ó* as the third person singular ending.

17. **expliqué**   To conjugate spelling-change *-car* verbs in the preterit, drop the *-ar* ending. For *yo*, change *c* to *qu* and add *-é* as the ending.

18. **utilicé**   To conjugate spelling-change *-zar* verbs in the preterit, drop the *-zar* ending. For *yo*, change *z* to *c* and add *-é* as the ending.

19. **vino**   In the preterit stem, *venir* changes the *e* from the infinitive stem to *i*. The third person singular preterit ending for an irregular *-ir* verb is *-o*.

20. **dio**   *Dar* has irregular preterit endings that are added to the *d-* from the infinitive. The third person singular preterit ending is *-io*.

21. **concluyó**   To conjugate present-tense verbs ending in *-uir*, change *i* to *y* in the third person plural form. Drop the *-r* ending and add *-ó* as the third person singular ending.

22. **prometí**   To conjugate regular *-er* verbs in the preterit, drop the *-er* infinitive and add *-í* as the first person singular ending.

23. **volvimos**   To conjugate stem-changing verbs ending in *-er*, drop the *-er* ending and add *-imos* as the first person plural ending.

24. **comimos**   To conjugate regular *-er* verbs in the preterit, drop the *-er* infinitive and add *-imos* as the first person plural ending.

25. **miramos**   To conjugate regular *-ar* verbs in the preterit, drop the *-ar* ending and add *-amos* as the first person plural ending.

The Imperfect

The imperfect is a past tense that has no English grammatical equivalent. It expresses a continuing state or action in the past—an action that was taking place or that used to happen repeatedly over an indefinite period of time. The imperfect is used to describe scenes, settings, situations, or states in the past.

The imperfect of regular verbs is formed by dropping the *-ar*, *-er*, and *-ir* infinitive endings and adding the imperfect endings as follows:

		Yo	Tú	Él, Ella, Ud.	Nosotros	Vosotros	Ellos, Ellas, Uds.
-ar verbs	trabaj~~ar~~	-aba	-abas	-aba	-ábamos	-abais	-aban
-er and *-ir* verbs	corr~~er~~ abr~~ir~~	-ía	-ías	-ía	-íamos	-íais	-ían

All verbs in Spanish (including spelling-change, stem-changing, and most irregular verbs) form the imperfect in this manner except for three irregular verbs:

	Yo	Tú	Él, Ella, Ud.	Nosotros	Vosotros	Ellos, Ellas, Uds.
ir (to go)	iba	ibas	iba	íbamos	ibais	iban
ser (to be)	era	eras	era	éramos	erais	eran
ver (to see)	veía	veías	veía	veíamos	veíais	veían

Use of the Imperfect

Use the imperfect to

❑ Describe ongoing or continuous actions in the past (which may or may not have been completed) that lasted over an indefinite period of time:

Él jugaba con sus amigos. He was playing with his friends.

❑ Describe repeated or habitual actions that took place in the past:

Los sábados yo iba a casa de mis abuelos. On Saturdays, I used to go to my grandparents' house.

❑ Describe an action that continued for an unspecified period of time:

Viajábamos mucho. We used to travel a lot.

❑ Describe a person, place, thing, weather, time, day of the week, state of mind, or emotion in the past:

> Carlota era grande. Carlota was tall.

> Tenía quince años. He was 15 years old.

> Su casa era bonita. Her house was pretty.

> Hacía frío. It was cold.

> Era lunes. It was Monday.

> Yo pensaba que tú no venías. I thought you weren't coming.

> Tenía miedo. He was afraid.

❑ Describe simultaneous actions taking place at the same time in the past, generally indicated by the word *mientras* (while):

> El niño dormía mientras su madre preparaba la cena. The child was sleeping while his mother was preparing dinner.

❑ Describe a situation that was going on in the past when another action or event, expressed by the preterit, interrupted it:

> Yo leía cuando alguien llamó a la puerta. I was reading when someone knocked at the door.

❑ Narrate a story:

> Había (érase) una vez una niña que tenía pelo muy largo. Once upon a time there was a girl with very long hair.

❑ Substitute for the present in certain forms of courtesy:

> ¿Qué quería Ud.? What do you want?

❑ Substitute for the present when a modest tone is used:

> ¿Me llamaba Ud.? Are you calling me?

❑ To describe an action or event that began in the past and continued in the past by using *hacía* + time + *que* + imperfect or by using the imperfect + *desde hace* + expression of time:

> ¿Cuánto tiempo hacía que estaba enfermo? How long had he been sick?

> ¿Desde cuándo estaba enfermo?

> Estaba enfermo hacía dos días. He had been sick for two days.

> Estaba enfermo desde hacía dos días.

Example Problems

Use the imperfect to express what each person was doing when a storm broke out.

> Example: yo/mirar la televisión
> > Yo miraba la televisión.

1. yo/leer un libro

    Answer: Yo leía un libro.

    To conjugate regular -er verbs in the imperfect, drop the -er ending and add -ía as the first person singular ending.

2. él/trabajar

   Answer: Él trabajaba.

   To conjugate the regular -ar verb *trabajar* in the imperfect, drop the -ar ending and add -aba as the ending for *él*.

3. nosotros/conducir al centro

   Answer: Nosotros conducíamos al centro.

   To conjugate the verb *conducir* in the imperfect, drop the -ir ending and add -íamos as the first person plural ending.

4. tú/venir a visitarme

   Answer: Tú venías a visitarme.

   To conjugate the -ir verb *venir* in the imperfect, drop the -ir ending and add the second person singular ending (-ías).

5. vosotros/estar a punto de salir

   Answer: Vosotros estabais a punto de salir.

   To conjugate *estar* in the imperfect, drop the -ar ending and add -abais as the second person plural ending.

6. ellas/ir a los grandes almacenes

   Answer: Ellas iban a los grandes almacenes.

   To conjugate the verb *ir* in the imperfect, drop the -r from the infinitive ending and add -ban as the third person plural ending.

Work Problems

Use these problems to give yourself additional practice.

Use the imperfect to describe what happened.

(Ser) _____ el otoño. (Hacer) _____ mucho viento y las hojas ya (caer)
$\quad\quad\quad$ 1 $\quad\quad\quad\quad\quad\quad\quad$ 2

_____ de los árboles. Yo (correr) _____ a mi clase de español y (pensar)
$\quad$ 3 $\quad\quad\quad\quad\quad\quad\quad\quad\quad\quad$ 4

_____ en todo lo que (tener) _____ que hacer para salir bien en el examen.
$\quad$ 5 $\quad\quad\quad\quad\quad\quad\quad\quad\quad$ 6

(Estar) _____ muy inquieto porque (temer) _____ llegar tarde. Al mismo tiempo,
$\quad\quad\quad$ 7 $\quad\quad\quad\quad\quad\quad\quad\quad\quad\quad$ 8

una muchacha bellísima (avanzar) _____. Ella (tener) _____ pelo negro y largo y
$\quad\quad\quad\quad\quad\quad\quad\quad\quad$ 9 $\quad\quad\quad\quad\quad\quad\quad$ 10

ojos tan azules como el cielo. Ella (llevar) _____ un vestido del mismo color que sus
$\quad\quad\quad\quad\quad\quad\quad\quad\quad\quad$ 11

ojos. Además ella (parecerse) _____ a mi actriz favorita. Yo (creer) _____ que
$\quad\quad\quad\quad\quad\quad\quad\quad\quad$ 12 $\quad\quad\quad\quad\quad\quad\quad\quad$ 13

ella no (ir) _____ a verme y que no (querer) _____ hablarme. Yo (saber)
                  14   15

_____ que (desear) _____ salir con ella. (Esperar) _____ que ella
        16   17   18

(fijarse) _____ en mí. No (poder) _____ más pensar en mi examen.
              19   20

Worked Solutions

1. **Era**   To conjugate *ser* in the imperfect, use *er-* as the stem and add *-a* as the third person singular form.

2. **Hacía**   To conjugate *hacer* in the imperfect, drop the *-er* ending and add *-ía* as the third person singular ending.

3. **caían**   To conjugate *caer* in the imperfect, drop the *-er* ending and add *-ían* as the third person plural ending.

4. **corría**   To conjugate *correr* in the imperfect, drop the *-er* ending and add *-ía* as the first person singular ending.

5. **pensaba**   To conjugate *pensar* in the imperfect, drop the *-ar* ending and add *-aba* as the first person singular ending.

6. **tenía**   To conjugate *tener* in the imperfect, drop the *-er* ending and add *-ía* as the first person singular ending.

7. **Estaba**   To conjugate *estar* in the imperfect, drop the *-ar* ending and add *-aba* as the first person singular ending.

8. **temía**   To conjugate *temer* in the imperfect, drop the *-er* ending and add *-ía* as the first person singular ending.

9. **avanzaba**   To conjugate *avanzar* in the imperfect, drop the *-ar* ending and add *-aba* as the third person singular ending.

10. **tenía**   To conjugate *tener* in the imperfect, drop the *-er* ending and add *-ía* as the third person singular ending.

11. **llevaba**   To conjugate *llevar* in the imperfect, drop the *-ar* ending and add *-aba* as the third person singular ending.

12. **se parecía**   To conjugate *parecer* in the imperfect, drop the *-er* ending and add *-ía* as the third person singular ending. Add the reflexive pronoun *se*, which agrees with the subject pronoun.

13. **creía**   To conjugate *creer* in the imperfect, drop the *-er* ending and add *-ía* as the first person singular ending.

14. **iba**   To conjugate *ir* in the imperfect, drop the *-r* from the infinitive ending and add *-ba* as the third person singular ending.

15. **quería**   To conjugate *querer* in the imperfect, drop the *-er* ending and add *-ía* as the third person singular ending.

16. **sabía** To conjugate *saber* in the imperfect, drop the *-er* ending and add *-ía* as the first person singular ending.

17. **deseaba** To conjugate *desear* in the imperfect, drop the *-ar* ending and add *-aba* as the third person singular ending.

18. **Esperaba** To conjugate *esperar* in the imperfect, drop the *-ar* ending and add *-aba* as the third person singular ending.

19. **se fijaba** To conjugate *fijar* in the imperfect, drop the *-ar* ending and add *-aba* as the third person singular ending. Add the reflexive pronoun *se*, which agrees with the subject pronoun.

20. **podía** To conjugate *poder* in the imperfect, drop the *-er* ending and add *-ía* as the first person singular ending.

Comparing the Preterit and the Imperfect

The preterit expresses an action that was completed at a specific time in the past—whether or not that time is mentioned. The preterit tells what happened.

> Él jugó al béisbol (ayer). He played baseball (yesterday).

The imperfect describes an action that continued in the past over an indefinite period of time. The imperfect tells what was happening, what used to happen, or what would (meaning "used to") happen over time.

> Él jugaba al béisbol.   He used to play (would play, was playing) baseball.

Compare the two:

Preterit	Imperfect
Expresses specific actions or events that were started and completed at a definite time in the past (even if the time isn't mentioned): Él tocó la guitarra. (He played the guitar.)	Describes ongoing or continuous actions or events (what **was** happening) in the past (which may or may not have been completed): Él tocaba la guitarra. (He was playing the guitar.)
Expresses a specific action or event that occurred at a specific point in the past: Yo fui al parque esta mañana. (I went to the park this morning.)	Describes habitual or repeated actions in the past: Yo iba al parque cada mañana. (I used to go to the park every morning.)
Expresses a specific action or event that was repeated a stated number of times: Ese alumno respondió correctamente dos veces. (That student answered correctly two times.)	Describes a person, place, thing, or state of mind in the past: Él estaba orgulloso. (He was proud.)
Expresses a series of completed actions: Comí, hice mis tareas y miré la televisión. (I ate, did my homework, and watched television.) Expresses the beginning or the end of an action: Terminé mi trabajo a las nueve. (I finished my work at 9 o'clock.)	Expresses a time of day in the past: Era la una. (It was one o'clock.) Expresses simultaneous ongoing actions in the past: Él dormía mientras yo trabaja. (He was sleeping while I was working.

Some verbs have different meanings depending on whether they are used in the preterit or the imperfect:

conocer (to know)	La conocí en la fiesta.	I met her at the party. (for the first time)
	La conocía.	I knew her. (for a while)
poder (to be able to)	Podía tocar el piano.	He could play the piano. (all the time)
	Pudo tocar el piano.	He managed to play the piano. (finally was able to)
querer (to wish, want)	Quería hablarle.	I wanted to speak to him. (for a while)
	Quise hablarle.	I wanted to speak to him. (tried to)
	No quise hablarle.	I didn't want to speak to him. (refused)
saber (to know)	Sabíamos la verdad.	We knew the truth. (for a while)
	Supimos la verdad.	We knew the truth. (found out, discovered)
tener (to have)	Él tenía un telegrama.	He had a telegram. (was carrying it with him)
	Él tuvo un telegrama.	He had a telegram. (received)

Clues to the Preterit and the Imperfect

Certain words and expressions generally call for the use of the preterit because they specify a time period for a totally completed action, whereas others showing repeated or habitual actions indicate a need for the imperfect.

a menudo	often
anoche	last night
anteayer	the day before yesterday
antiguamente	formerly
a veces	sometimes
ayer	yesterday
ayer por la mañana (la tarde, la noche)	yesterday morning (afternoon, evening)
cada día	each (every) day
de repente	suddenly
de vez en cuando	from time to time
el año (mes) pasado	last year (month)
el otro día	the other day
el verano pasado	last summer
el viernes pasado	last Friday
en ese momento	at that time
en general	generally
finalmente	finally
frecuentemente	frequently
generalmente	generally
habitualmente	habitually
la semana pasada	last week
normalmente	normally
por fin	finally

primero	at first
siempre	always
todo el tiempo	all the time
todos los días (meses, años)	every day (month, year)
un día	one day
una vez, dos veces	once, twice
usualmente	usually

Example Problems

Use the correct form of the preterit or the imperfect to complete the story about the weather.

(Ser) _____ el domingo. Cuando yo (mirar) _____ por la ventana a las dos, yo
              1   2

(ver) _____ que (hacer) _____ muy mal tiempo. (Estar) _____ nevando y
          3   4   5

yo no (querer) _____ salir. Mientras yo (comer) _____ algo, (escuchar) _____
                   6   7   8

el pronóstico. El meteorólogo (decir) _____ que la ciudad (esperar) _____ un
                                          9   10

pie de nieve.

Answers and Solutions

1. **Answer: Era**

   The imperfect is used to express a day in the past. To conjugate *ser* in the imperfect, use *er-* as the stem and add *-a* for the third person singular form.

2. **Answer: miré**

   The preterit is used to tell what happened at a particular moment of time. To conjugate *mirar* in the preterit, drop the *-ar* ending and add *-é* as the first person singular ending.

3. **Answer: vi**

   The preterit is used to express an action that was completed. *Ver* has irregular preterit endings that are added to the *v-* from the infinitive. The first person singular preterit ending is an unaccented *-i*.

4. **Answer: hacía**

   The imperfect is used to describe a condition. To conjugate *hacer* in the imperfect, drop the *-er* ending and add *-ía* as the third person singular ending.

5. **Answer: Estaba**

   The imperfect is used to describe a condition. To conjugate *estar* in the imperfect, drop the *-ar* ending and add *-aba* as the third person singular ending.

6. **Answer: quería**

The imperfect is used to describe a state of mind. To conjugate *querer* in the imperfect, drop the *-er* ending and add *-ía* as the first person singular ending.

7. **Answer: comía**

The imperfect is used to describe what a person was doing. To conjugate *comer* in the imperfect, drop the *-er* ending and add *-ía* as the first person singular ending

8. **Answer: escuchaba**

The imperfect is used to describe what a person was doing. To conjugate *escuchar* in the imperfect, drop the *-ar* ending and add *-aba* as the first person singular ending.

9. **Answer: dijo**

The preterit is used to express an action that was completed in the past. In the preterit, *decir* changes the *e* from the infinitive stem to *i*. A *j* is added after the *i*. The third person singular preterit ending is *-o*.

10. **Answer: esperaba**

The imperfect is used to describe what was happening. To conjugate *esperar* in the imperfect, drop the *-ar* ending and add *-aba* as the third person singular ending.

Work Problems

Use these problems to give yourself additional practice.

Use the correct form of the preterit or the imperfect to complete the story about a phone call.

Yo (andar) _____ por el parque cuando de repente mi teléfono celular (sonar)
                    1

_____. Yo (contestar) _____ inmediatamente. (Ser) _____ mi amigo Roberto.
         2   3   4

Él (tener) _____ que darme un mensaje para nuestro amigo Ernesto a quien él no
              5

(poder) _____ contactar. Yo le (decir) _____: "Espera un momento," y (sacar)
           6   7

_____ un bolígrafo y un papel de mi bolsillo. Mientras Roberto (hablar) _____ yo
         8   9

(escribir) _____ toda la información.
              10

Worked Solutions

1. **andaba**   The imperfect is used to describe what a person was doing. To conjugate *andar* in the imperfect, drop the *-ar* ending and add *-aba* as the first person singular ending.

2. **sonó**   The preterit is used to express an action that was completed in the past. To conjugate *sonar* in the preterit, drop the *-ar* ending and add *-ó* as the third person singular ending.

3. **contesté**   The preterit is used to express an action that was completed in the past. To conjugate *contestar* in the preterit, drop the *-ar* ending and add *-é* as the first person singular ending.

4. **Era**   The imperfect is used to describe a condition. To conjugate *ser* in the imperfect, use *er-* as the stem and add *-a* for the third person singular form.

5. **tenía**   The imperfect is used to describe a condition. To conjugate *tener* in the imperfect, drop the *-er* ending and add *-ía* as the third person singular ending.

6. **podía**   The imperfect is used to describe a condition. To conjugate *poder* in the imperfect, drop the *-er* ending and add *-ía* as the third person singular ending.

7. **dije**   The preterit is used to express an action that was completed in the past. In the preterit, *decir* changes the *e* from the infinitive stem to *i*. A *j* is added after the *i*. The first person singular preterit ending is *-e*.

8. **saqué**   The preterit is used to express an action that was completed in the past. To conjugate spelling-change *-car* verbs in the preterit, drop the *-ar* ending. For *yo*, change *c* to *qu* and add *-é* as the ending.

9. **hablaba**   The imperfect is used to describe what a person was doing. To conjugate *hablar* in the imperfect, drop the *-ar* ending and add *-aba* as the third person singular ending.

10. **escribía**   The imperfect is used to describe what a person was doing. To conjugate *escribir* in the imperfect, drop the *-ir* ending and add *-ía* as the first person singular ending.

Chapter Problems

Problems
Use the correct form of the preterit or the imperfect to complete the story about a lucky man.

Cuando yo (ser) _____ joven yo (trabajar) _____ en una tienda dónde los
1   2

propietarios (vender) _____ billetes de lotería. Habitualmente, los viernes por la
3

noche, el señor Dudas (ir) _____ a la tienda para comprar un solo billete. Siempre
4

(decir) _____ que no (tener) _____ mucha suerte y no (querer) _____
5   6   7

malgastar su dinero. (Ser) _____ verdad. Nunca (ganar) _____ nada, pero nunca
8   9

(renunciar) _____ a jugar. Una noche me (preguntar) _____ mis números
10   11

favoritos. Yo (escoger) _____ los números al azar y se los (decir) _____ al señor.
12   13

Él los (escribir) _____ y (salir) _____ en seguida. Generalmente, se (anunciar)
14   15

_____ los números ganadores el sábado por la noche. Ese sábado no (poder)
16

_____ creer lo que (oír) _____ . Uno a uno, el locutor (repetir) _____ mis
17   18   19

números. (Ser) _____ fantástico. El lunes, el señor Dudas (venir) _____ a la
                    20   21

tienda. Él (sonreír) _____ y él (estar) _____ muy feliz. Él (ir) _____ a cobrar
                  22   23   24

veinticinco millones de dólares. (Ser) _____ un hombre muy honrado y me (dar)
                                    25

_____ la mitad de sus ganancias. Naturalmente, yo (estar) _____ muy
         26   27

asombrado y yo le (dar) _____ las gracias. Yo (tomar) _____ el dinero y (ayudar)
                     28   29

_____ a los pobres. También (comprarse) _____ algunas cosas extravagantes.
         30   31

Pero la riqueza no me (importar) _____ tanto como la generosidad de este
                              32

señor tan humilde.

Answers and Solutions

1. **Answer: era** The imperfect is used to describe an indefinite time in the past. To conjugate *ser* in the imperfect, use *er-* as the stem and add add *-a* for the third person singular form.

2. **Answer: trabajaba** The imperfect is used to describe what a person was doing. To conjugate *trabajar* in the imperfect, drop the *-ar* ending and add *-aba* as the first person singular ending.

3. **Answer: vendían** The imperfect is used to describe a habitual action in the past. To conjugate *vender* in the imperfect, drop the *-er* ending and add *-ían* as the third person plural ending.

4. **Answer: iba** The imperfect is used to describe a habitual action in the past. To conjugate *ir* in the imperfect, drop the *-r* from the infinitive ending and add *-ba* as the third person singular ending.

5. **Answer: decía** The imperfect is used to describe a habitual action in the past. To conjugate *decir* in the imperfect, drop the *-ir* ending and add *-ía* as the third person singular ending.

6. **Answer: tenía** The imperfect is used to describe a habitual action in the past. To conjugate *tener* in the imperfect, drop the *-er* ending and add *-ía* as the third person singular ending.

7. **Answer: quería** The imperfect is used to describe a state of mind. To conjugate *querer* in the imperfect, drop the *-er* ending and add *-ía* as the third person singular ending.

8. **Answer: Era** The imperfect is used to describe an indefinite time in the past. To conjugate *ser* in the imperfect, use *er-* as the stem and add add *-a* as the third person singular ending.

9. **Answer: ganaba** The imperfect is used to express a continuing action in the past. To conjugate *ganar* in the imperfect, drop the *-ar* ending and add *-aba* as the third person singular ending.

10. **Answer: renunció**   The preterit is used to express an action that was completed. To conjugate *renunciar* in the preterit, drop the *-ar* ending and add *-ó* as the third person singular ending.

11. **Answer: preguntó**   The preterit is used to express an action that was completed. To conjugate *preguntar* in the preterit, drop the *-ar* ending and add *-ó* as the third person singular ending.

12. **Answer: escogí**   The preterit is used to express an action that was completed. To conjugate *escoger* in the preterit, drop the *-er* ending and add *-í* as the first person singular ending.

13. **Answer: dije**   The preterit is used to express an action that was completed. In the preterit, *decir* changes the *e* from the infinitive stem to *i*. A *j* is added after the *i*. The first person singular preterit ending is *-e*.

14. **Answer: escribió**   The preterit is used to express an action that was completed. To conjugate *escribir* in the preterit, drop the *-ir* ending and add *-ió* as the third person singular ending.

15. **Answer: salió**   The preterit is used to express an action that was completed. To conjugate *salir* in the preterit, drop the *-ir* ending and add *-ió* as the third person singular ending.

16. **Answer: anunciaban**   The imperfect is used to describe a habitual action in the past. To conjugate *anunciar* in the imperfect, drop the *-ar* ending and add *-aban* as the third person plural ending.

17. **Answer: podía/pude**   The imperfect is used to describe a state of mind. To conjugate *poder* in the imperfect, drop the *-er* ending and add *-ía* as the first person singular ending. If, however, this action is viewed as completed on that particular Saturday, the preterit may be used.

18. **Answer: oía/oí**   The imperfect is used to describe an action that was taking place. To conjugate *oír* in the imperfect, drop the *-ir* ending and add *-ía* as the first person singular ending. If, however, this action is viewed as completed on that particular Saturday, the preterit is used. To conjugate *oír* in the preterit, drop the *-ir* ending and add *-í* as the first person singular ending.

19. **Answer: repitió**   The preterit is used to express an action that was completed. For stem-changing verbs ending in *-ir, e* changes to *i* in the third person singular form. Drop the *-ir* ending and add *-ió* as the third person singular ending.

20. **Answer: Era**   The imperfect is used to describe a condition. To conjugate *ser* in the imperfect, use *er-* as the stem and add *-a* as the third person singular ending.

21. **Answer: vino**   The preterit is used to express an action that was completed. In the preterit, *venir* changes the *e* from the infinitive stem to *i*. Drop the *-ir* ending and add an unaccented *-o* as the third person singular ending.

22. **Answer: sonreía**   The imperfect is used to describe a condition To conjugate *sonreír* in the imperfect, drop the *-ír* ending and add *-ía* as the third person singular ending.

23. **Answer: estaba**   The imperfect is used to describe a condition. To conjugate *estar* in the imperfect, drop the *-ar* ending and add *-aba* as the third person singular ending.

24. **Answer: iba**   The imperfect is used to describe what was happening. To conjugate *ir* in the imperfect, drop the *-r* from the infinitive ending and add *-ba* as the third person singular ending.

25. **Answer: Era**   The imperfect is used to describe a condition. To conjugate *ser* in the imperfect, use *er-* as the stem and add *-a* as the third person singular ending.

26. **Answer: dio**   The preterit is used to express an action that was completed. *Dar* has irregular preterit endings that are added to the *d-* from the infinitive. The third person singular preterit ending is *-io*.

27. **Answer: estaba**   The imperfect is used to describe a state of mind. To conjugate *estar* in the imperfect, drop the *-ar* ending and add *-aba* as the first person singular ending.

28. **Answer: di**   The preterit is used to express an action that was completed. *Dar* has irregular preterit endings that are added to the *d-* from the infinitive. The first person singular preterit ending is an unaccented *-i*.

29. **Answer: tomé**   The preterit is used to express an action that was completed. To conjugate *tomar* in the preterit, drop the *-ar* ending and add *-é* as the first person singular ending.

30. **Answer: ayudé**   The preterit is used to express an action that was completed. To conjugate *ayudar* in the preterit, drop the *-ar* ending and add *-é* as the first person singular ending.

31. **Answer: me compré**   The preterit is used to express an action that was completed. To conjugate *comprar* in the preterit, drop the *-ar* ending and add *-é* as the first person singular ending. Add the reflexive pronoun *me,* which agrees with the subject pronoun.

32. **Answer: importaba**   The imperfect is used to describe a state of mind. To conjugate *importar* in the imperfect, drop the *-ar* ending and add *-aba* as the third person singular ending.

Supplemental Chapter Problems

Problems

Use the correct form of the preterit or the imperfect to complete the story about a vacation.

Durante las vacaciones yo (ir) _____ a Las Vegas con unos amigos míos. Un día yo
                                    1

(querer) _____ salir solo. (Decidir) _____ visitar uno de los hoteles más famosos
           2   3

de la ciudad. (Tomar) _____ el desayuno y (salir) _____. (Seguir) _____ la
                        4   5   6

instrucciones del conserje y (ponerse) _____ en camino. (Haber) _____ mucha
                                        7   8

gente en las calles y (tener) _____ que caminar mucho. No (saber)_____ que las
                              9   10

avenidas (ser) _____ tan largas. Finalmente yo (llegar) _____ al hotel. Nunca
                11   12

(ver) _____ tantas tiendas y atracciones en un vestíbulo. Primero (sacar)_____
       13   14

algunas fotografías. Después (entrar) _____ en varias tiendas. Al mediodía (pensar)
　　　　　　　　　　　　　　　　　15

_____ en tomar algo a comer cuando de repente (encontrarme) _____ delante
　　16　　　　　　　　　　　　　　　　　　　　　　　　　　　　　　　　　　　　17

de un cine que (prometer) _____ un viaje extraordinario. Por solamente ocho dólares
　　　　　　　　　　　　　　18

yo (poder) _____ ver una película en tres dimensiones y en "realidad virtual." Yo
　　　　　19

(pagar) _____ y (entrar) _____. Yo (sentarme) _____, (abrocharme)
　　　　20　　　　　　　　　　21　　　　　　　　　　　　22

_____ el cinturón de seguridad, y (ponerse) _____ las gafas especiales. El
　23　　　　　　　　　　　　　　　　　　　　　　　　　24

espectáculo (comenzar) _____. Mientras yo lo (mirar) _____ yo (gritar) _____
　　　　　　　　　　　　　25　　　　　　　　　　　　　　　　26　　　　　　　　　　　27

de alegría. Por cinco minutos (participar) _____ en un viaje fenomenal a través el
　　　　　　　　　　　　　　　　　　　　28

espacio. No (creer) _____ a mis ojos. Cuando (regresar) _____ al hotel, les
　　　　　　　　29　　　　　　　　　　　　　　　　　　30

(describir) _____ mi aventura a mis amigos. Todos (tener) _____ celos de mí.
　　　　　31　　　　　　　　　　　　　　　　　　　　　　　　32

Solutions

1. fui (preterit of irregular verbs, p. 220; comparing the preterit and the imperfect, p. 229)

2. quería (use of the imperfect, p. 225; comparing the preterit and the imperfect, p. 229)

3. Decidí (preterit of regular verbs, p. 219; comparing the preterit and the imperfect, p. 229)

4. Tomé (preterit of regular verbs, p. 219; comparing the preterit and the imperfect, p. 229)

5. salí (preterit of regular verbs, p. 219; comparing the preterit and the imperfect, p. 229)

6. Seguí (preterit of stem-changing verbs, p. 220; preterit of spelling-change verbs, p. 219; comparing the preterit and the imperfect, p. 229)

7. me puse (preterit of irregular verbs, p. 220; comparing the preterit and the imperfect, p. 229)

8. Había (use of the imperfect, p. 225; comparing the preterit and the imperfect, p. 229)

9. tenía/tuve (depending on whether the action is viewed as ongoing or completed) (use of the imperfect, p. 225; preterit of regular verbs p. 219, comparing the preterit and the imperfect, p. 229)

10. sabía (use of the imperfect, p. 225; comparing the preterit and the imperfect, p. 229)

11. eran (use of the imperfect, p. 225; comparing the preterit and the imperfect, p. 229)

12. llegué (preterit of spelling-change verbs, p. 219; comparing the preterit and the imperfect, p. 229)

13. vi (preterit of irregular verbs, p. 220; comparing the preterit and the imperfect, p. 229)

14. saqué (preterit of spelling-change verbs, p. 219; comparing the preterit and the imperfect, p. 229)

15. entré (preterit of regular verbs, p. 219; comparing the preterit and the imperfect, p. 229)

16. pensaba (use of the imperfect, p. 225; comparing the preterit and the imperfect, p. 229)

17. me encontré (preterit of regular verbs, p. 219; comparing the preterit and the imperfect, p. 229)

18. prometía (use of the imperfect, p. 225; comparing the preterit and the imperfect, p. 229)

19. podía (use of the imperfect, p. 225; comparing the preterit and the imperfect, p. 229)

20. pagué (preterit of spelling-change verbs, p. 219; comparing the preterit and the imperfect, p. 229)

21. entré (preterit of regular verbs, p. 219; comparing the preterit and the imperfect, p. 229)

22. me senté (preterit of regular verbs, p. 219; comparing the preterit and the imperfect, p. 229)

23. me abroché (preterit of regular verbs, p. 219; comparing the preterit and the imperfect, p. 229)

24. me puse (preterit of irregular verbs, p. 220; comparing the preterit and the imperfect, p. 229)

25. comenzó (preterit of spelling-change verbs, p. 219; comparing the preterit and the imperfect, p. 229)

26. miraba (use of the imperfect, p. 225; comparing the preterit and the imperfect, p. 229)

27. gritaba (use of the imperfect, p. 225; comparing the preterit and the imperfect, p. 229)

28. participaba (use of the imperfect, p. 225; comparing the preterit and the imperfect, p. 229)

29. creía (use of the imperfect, p. 225; comparing the preterit and the imperfect, p. 229)

30. regresé (preterit of regular verbs, p. 219; comparing the preterit and the imperfect, p. 229)

31. describí (preterit of regular verbs, p. 219; comparing the preterit and the imperfect, p. 229)

32. tenían (use of the imperfect, p. 225; comparing the preterit and the imperfect, p. 229)

Chapter 11
The Future and the Conditional

Expressing the Future

The future may be expressed in Spanish as follows:

❏ By using the present tense of *ir* (to go) + *a* + an infinitive to express the immediate future.

Va a nevar esta tarde.   It's going to snow this afternoon.

❏ By using the future tense.

Nevará mañana.   It will snow tomorrow.

Note the difference as expressed by a time frame:

Present → Immediate Future → Future

The Future Tense of Most Verbs

The future tense tells what the subject will do or what action or event will take place in future time. In Spanish, all verbs—whether they have regular or irregular future stems—have the same future endings. In addition, there are no spelling or stem changes in the future tense.

The future tense in Spanish is formed by using the infinitive of the verb and its future endings, which correspond to the present tense endings of the auxiliary verb, *haber*:

	Yo	Tú	Él, Ella, Ud.	Nosotros	Vosotros	Ellos, Ellas, Uds.
-ar, -er, -ir Verbs	-é	-ás	-á	-emos	-éis	-án

Here are a couple examples in sentences:

Ella viajará con sus amigas.   She will travel with her friends.
¿Asistirán Uds. al concierto?   Will you go to the concert?

Verbs such as *oír* and *reír*, whose infinitive contains an accent mark, drop that accent in the future:

¿Oirá sonar Ud. el teléfono?   Will you hear the phone ring?
Ellos no reirán.   They won't laugh.

The Future Tense of Irregular Verbs

There are a few verbs that are irregular in the future. They have irregular future stems, which always end in *-r* or *-rr*. To form the future of irregular verbs, do one of three things:

❏ Drop *e* from the infinitive ending before adding the future endings:

Infinitive	Meaning	Future Stem
caber	to fit	cabr-
haber	to have(aux. verb)	habr-
poder	to be able	podr-
querer	to want	querr-
saber	to know	sabr-

❏ Drop *e* or *i* from the infinitive ending and replace the vowel with a *d* before adding the future endings:

Infinitive	Meaning	Future Stem
poner	to put	pondr-
salir	to leave	saldr-
tener	to have	tendr-
valer	to be worth	valdr-
venir	to come	vendr-

❏ Memorize the completely irregular stem and add the future endings:

Infinitive	Meaning	Future Stem
decir	to say	dir-
hacer	to make, to do	har-

Compounds of verbs that are irregular in the future (*predecir, deshacer, posponer, obtener,* and so on) are also irregular.

When to Use the Future Tense

Use the future:

❏ To express what will happen:

Harán un viaje este verano. They will take a trip this summer.

❏ To predict a future action or event:

Nevará esta noche. It will snow tonight.

❏ To express wonder, probability, conjecture, or vacillation in the present:

¿Qué hora será? I wonder what time it is.

Serán las tres. It's probably (it must be) three o'clock.

Alguien llama. ¿Quién será? Someone is calling. I wonder who it is.

¿Será mi amigo? I wonder if it's my friend.

¿Irá a darme flores Raúl? I wonder if Raúl is going to give me flowers.

❑ To express an expected action or resulting condition caused by a present action or event:

Si eres bueno te compraré un regalo. If you are good, I will buy you a present.

Si estudio mucho aprobaré el curso. If I study a lot, I will pass the course.

Note that the future, although implied, is not used after *si* (if).

Example Problems

Use the future tense to express what everyone will do this weekend to help around the house.

barrer	cortar	hacer
ir	sacar	sacudir

1. Nosotros _____ la basura.

   Answer: sacaremos

   To conjugate regular -*ar* verbs in the future, keep the -*ar* ending and add -*emos* as the ending for *nosotros*.

2. Yo _____ el césped.

   Answer: cortaré

   To conjugate regular -*ar* verbs in the future, keep the -*ar* ending and add -*é* as the ending for *yo*.

3. Uds. _____ los muebles.

   Answer: sacudirán

   To conjugate regular -*ir* verbs in the future, keep the -*ir* ending and add -*án* as the ending for *Uds.*

4. Tú _____ las camas.

   Answer: harás

   The verb *hacer* is irregular in the future and must be memorized. Use *har-* as the future stem and add -*ás* as the second person singular future ending.

5. Vosotros _____ de compras.

   Answer: iréis

   The verb *ir* is regular in the future. To conjugate *ir* in the future, keep the *ir* infinitive and add -*éis* as the ending for *vosotros*.

6. Él _____ el suelo.

   Answer: barrerá

   To conjugate regular -*er* verbs in the future, keep the -*er* ending and add -*á* the ending for *él*.

Work Problems

Use the future tense to express what the horoscope says for different people.

1. A Ud. le gusta mucho su puesto. Sin embargo, (valer) _____ la pena buscar otro empleo.

2. Su jefe le (poner) _____ mucho trabajo, que Ud. no (terminar) _____.

3. Ud. no (salir) ____ este fin de semana porque (estar) _____ enfermo.

4. Un antiguo amigo (venir) _____ a visitarlo a Ud.

5. Ud. (hacer) _____ un viaje importante durante el verano e (ir) _____ al extranjero.

6. Un amigo suyo le (decir) _____ un secreto personal que Ud. (revelar) _____.

7. Ud. (tener) _____ que ayudar a miembros de su familia que (necesitar) _____ dinero.

8. Ud. (saber) _____ que su mejor amigo le está diciendo mentiras.

9. Ud. (querer) _____ comprarle algo especial a su novia.

10. Ud. no (poder) _____ asistir a una conferencia importante porque (haber) _____ una tormenta.

11. Ud. (comprar) _____ algunas cosas que no (caber) _____ en su coche.

12. Ud. (recibir) _____ regalos que le (gustar) _____ mucho.

Worked Solutions

1. **valdrá**   The verb *valer* is irregular in the conditional. Drop *e* from the infinitive ending and replace it with a *d*. Add the third person singular future ending *(á)* to express "it will be worth."

2. **pondrá, terminará**   The verb *poner* is irregular in the future and must be memorized. Drop the *e* from the infinitive ending and replace it with a *d*. Add the third person singular future ending *(-á)* for *su jefe*. The verb *terminar* is regular in the future. To conjugate regular *-ar* verbs in the future, keep the *-ar* ending and add the third person singular future ending *(-á)* for *Ud*.

3. **saldrá, estará**   The verb *salir* is irregular in the future. Drop *i* from the infinitive ending and replace it with a *d*. Add the third person singular future ending *(-á)* for *Ud*. The verb *estar* is regular in the future. And add the third person singular future ending *(-á)* for *Ud*.

4. **vendrá**   The verb *venir* is irregular in the future. Drop *e* from the infinitive ending and replace it with a *d*. Add the third person singular future ending *(-á)* for *un amigo*.

5. **hará, irá**   The verb *hacer* is irregular in the future and must be memorized. Use *har-* as the future stem and add the third person singular future ending *(-á)* for *Ud*. The verb *ir* is regular in the future. Add the third person singular future ending *(-á)* for *Ud*.

6. **dirá, revelará**   The verb *decir* is irregular in the future and must be memorized. Use *dir-* as the future stem and add the third person singular future ending *(-á)* for *un amigo*. The

verb *revelar* is regular in the future. To conjugate regular *-ar* verbs in the future, keep the *-ar* ending and add the third person singular future ending *(-á)* for *Ud.*

7. **tendrá, necesitarán**   The verb *tener* is irregular in the future. Drop the *e* from the infinitive ending and replace it with a *d*. Add the third person singular future ending *(-á)* for *Ud.* The verb *necesitar* is regular in the future. To conjugate regular *-ar* verbs in the future, keep the *-ar* ending and add the third person plural future ending *(-án)* for *miembros.*

8. **sabrá**   The verb *saber* is irregular in the future. Drop the *e* from the infinitive ending. Add the third person singular future ending *(-á)* for *Ud.*

9. **querrá**   The verb *querer* is irregular in the future and must be memorized. Drop the *e* from the infinitive ending and add the third person singular future ending *(-á)* for *Ud.*

10. **podrá, habrá**   The verb *poder* is irregular in the future and must be memorized. Drop the *e* from the infinitive ending and add the third person singular future ending *(-á)* for *Ud.* The verb *haber* is irregular in the future and must be memorized. Drop the *e* from the infinitive ending and add the third person singular future ending *(-á)* for *una tormenta.*

11. **comprará, cabrán**   The verb *comprar* is regular in the future. To conjugate regular *-ar* verbs in the future, keep the *-ar* ending and add the third person singular future ending *(-á)* for *Ud.* The verb *caber* is irregular in the future and must be memorized. Drop the *e* from the infinitive ending and add the third person plural future ending *(-án)* for *algunas cosas.*

12. **recibirá, gustarán**   The verb *recibir* is regular in the future. To conjugate regular *-ir* verbs in the future, keep the *-ir* ending and add the third person singular future ending *(-á)* as the ending for *Ud.* The verb *gustar* is regular in the future. To conjugate regular *-ar* verbs in the future, keep the *-ar* ending and add the third person plural future ending *(-án)* for *los regalos* (which is the subject of *gustar*).

The Conditional

The conditional is not a tense, which shows a time period, such as the present, past, or future. The conditional is a mood that indicates what the subject "would" do or what "would" happen under certain circumstances or conditions. Because the conditional uses the same infinitive or irregular stem that is used to form the future, there are no spelling or stem changes for any verbs in the conditional. The endings for the conditional are the same as those for the imperfect of the auxiliary verb *haber*.

	Yo	**Tú**	**Él, Ella, Ud.**	**Nosotros**	**Vosotros**	**Ellos, Ellas, Uds.**
-ar, -er, -ir Verbs	-ía	-ías	-ía	-íamos	-íais	-ían

Here are a couple of examples:

¿Podrías ayudarme, por favor?   Could you help me, please?

Me dijeron que no vendrían mañana.   They told me they wouldn't come tomorrow.

The verbs that are irregular in the conditional have the same stem as they do in the future tense. Refer to the tables above for the stems for irregular verbs.

Uses of the Conditional

Use the conditional:

❑ To indicate a future action with respect to the past:

Eva me escribió que nos acompañaría al baile. Eva wrote to me that she would go with us to the dance.

Yo sabía que ella podría acompañarnos. I knew that she would be able to go with us.

❑ To express the result of a hypothetical condition (expressed in the imperfect subjunctive–see Chapter 15):

Si tuviera bastante dinero me compraría un castillo en España. If I had enough money, I would buy myself a castle in Spain.

❑ To express wonder, probability, conjecture, or vacillation in the past. Note that a subordinate clause in the past tense may be used or implied:

¿Qué hora sería cuando llamó? I wonder what time it was when he called?

Serían las tres (cuando llamó). It was probably (it must have been) three o'clock (when he called).

Alguien llamó. ¿Quién sería? Someone called. I wonder who it was?

¿Sería mi amigo? I wonder if it was my friend?

❑ To reinforce forms of courtesy, kindness, or modesty:

¿Desearía Ud. algo de comer? Would you like something to eat?

¿Le gustaría a Ud. ir al cine? Would you like to go to the movies?

Note that when "would" means "used to," use the imperfect:

Ellos iban al parque todos los días.

They would go to the park every day.

When "would" means "to be willing" or "to want," use the preterit of *querer:*

Él quiso esperar. He was willing (wanted) to wait.

Example Problems

Use the conditional to express what the people would do in the following situations.

1. Un amigo está enfermo.

(yo/prepararle sopa; María/ayudarlo; nosotros/hacerle sus compras)

Answers: Yo le prepararía sopa.

María lo ayudaría.

Nosotros le haríamos sus compras.

The verb *preparar* is regular in the conditional. To conjugate regular *-ar* verbs in the conditional, keep the *-ar* ending and add *-ía* as the ending for *yo.*

The verb *ayudar* is regular in the conditional. To conjugate regular *-ar* verbs in the conditional, keep the *-ar* ending and add *-ía* as the ending for *María.*

The verb *hacer* is irregular in the conditional and must be memorized. Use *har-* as the conditional stem and add the first person plural conditional ending (*-íamos*) for *nosotros*.

2. Un amigo viene a su casa.

(nosotros/decirle "bienvenido"; yo/invitarlo a entrar; mis padres/darle un sándwich)

Answers: Nosotros le diríamos "bienvenido."

Yo lo invitaría a entrar.

Mis padres le darían un sándwich.

The verb *decir* is irregular in the conditional and must be memorized. Use *dir-* as the conditional stem and add the first person plural conditional ending (*-íamos*) for *nosotros*.

The verb *invitar* is regular in the conditional. To conjugate regular *-ar* verbs in the conditional, keep the *-ar* ending and add *-ía* as the ending for *yo*.

The verb *dar* is regular in the conditional. Add *-ían* as the ending for *mis padres*.

3. Un amigo tiene problemas en su clase de matemáticas.

(yo/le aconsejar estudiar más; vosotros/explicarle todo; tú/mostrarle las reglas)

Answers: Yo le aconsejaría estudiar más.

Vosotros le explicaríais todo.

Tú le mostrarías las reglas.

The verb *aconsejar* is regular in the conditional. To conjugate regular *-ar* verbs in the conditional, keep the *-ar* ending and add *-ía* as the ending for *yo*.

The verb *explicar* is regular in the conditional. To conjugate regular *-ar* verbs in the conditional, keep the *-ar* ending and add *- íais* as the ending for *vosotros*.

The verb *mostrar* is regular in the conditional. To conjugate regular *-ar* verbs in the conditional, keep the *-ar* ending and add *-ías* as the ending for *tú*.

Work Problems

Ana and Luz would like to enroll in a summer program. Conjugate the verbs in parentheses into the conditional to complete the letter they have written.

Querido señor Rueda:

Un amigo mío y yo (desear) _____ hacer un viaje a México para estudiar y
                                    1

perfeccionar nuestras destrezas en español. ¿(valer) _____ la pena hacer eso?
                                                                2

(tener) _____ ganas de viajar en avión pero no nos (gustar) _____ pagar
            3   4

mucho por nuestros pasajes. ¿Cuánto (costar) _____ los pasajes más baratos?
                                                        5

Nosotros (inscribirse) _____ en cursos comprehensivos. (recibir) _____

crédito por los cursos. Nosotros (querer) _____ pasar seis semanas en su escuela.

(ser) _____ las alumnas más serias de su programa. Siempre (hacer) _____

todas las tareas e (ir) _____ a todas las clases. (estudiar) _____ todas las

noches y no (salir) _____ de noche. ¿Cuándo (empezar) _____ y cuándo

(terminar) _____ los cursos? ¿Dónde (vivir) _____? (Dormir) _____

en el dormitorio de la escuela? A decir verdad, (preferir) _____ vivir con una

familia mexicana. ¿(recomendar) _____ Ud. a una familia simpática? ¿(poder)

_____ Ud. escribirnos lo más pronto posible?

Ana García y Luz Rodríguez

Worked Solutions

1. **desearíamos**   The verb *desear* is regular in the conditional. To conjugate regular *-ar* verbs in the conditional, keep the *-ar* ending and add *-íamos* as the ending for *nosotros*.

2. **Valdría**   The verb *valer* is irregular in the conditional. Drop *e* from the infinitive ending and replace it with a *d*. Add the third person singular conditional ending (*-ía*) to express "it would be worth."

3. **Tendríamos**   The verb *tener* is irregular in the conditional. Drop the *e* from the infinitive ending and replace it with a *d*. Add the first person plural ending (*-íamos*) for *nosotros*.

4. **gustaría**   The verb *gustar* is regular in the conditional. To conjugate regular *-ar* verbs in the conditional, keep the *-ar* ending and add *-ía* as the ending for the subject of the verb, which is the infinitive *pagar*.

5. **costarían**   The verb *costar* is regular in the conditional. To conjugate regular *-ar* verbs in the conditional, keep the *-ar* ending and add *-ían* as the ending for *los pasajes*.

6. **nos inscribiríamos**   The verb *inscribir* is regular in the conditional. To conjugate regular *-ir* verbs in the conditional, keep the *-ir* ending and add *-íamos* as the ending for *nosotros*. Use the reflexive pronoun *nos*, which agrees with the verb.

7. **Recibiríamos**   The verb *inscribir* is regular in the conditional. To conjugate regular *-ir* verbs in the conditional, keep the *-ir* ending and add *-íamos* as the ending for *nosotros*.

8. **querríamos**   The verb *querer* is irregular in the conditional and must be memorized. Drop the *e* from the infinitive ending and add *-íamos* as the ending for *nosotros*.

9. **Seríamos**   The verb *ser* is regular in the conditional. Add *-íamos* as the ending for *nosotros*.

10. **haríamos**   The verb *hacer* is irregular in the conditional and must be memorized. Use *har-* as the conditional stem and add *-íamos* as the ending for *nosotros*.

11. **iríamos**   The verb *ir* is regular in the conditional. Add *-íamos* as the ending for *nosotros*.

12. **Estudiaríamos**   The verb *estudiar* is regular in the conditional. To conjugate regular *-ar* verbs in the conditional, keep the *-ar* ending and add *-íamos* as the ending for *nosotros*.

13. **saldríamos**   The verb *salir* is irregular in the conditional. Drop *i* from the infinitive ending and replace it with a *d*. Add *-íamos* as the ending for *nosotros*.

14. **empezarían**   The verb *empezar* is regular in the conditional. To conjugate regular *-ar* verbs in the conditional, keep the *-ar* ending and add *-ían* as the ending for *los cursos*.

15. **terminarían**   The verb *terminar* is regular in the conditional. To conjugate regular *-ar* verbs in the conditional, keep the *-ar* ending and add *-ían* as the ending for *los cursos*.

16. **viviríamos**   The verb *vivir* is regular in the conditional. To conjugate regular *-ir* verbs in the conditional, keep the *-ir* ending and add *-íamos* as the ending for *nosotros*.

17. **Dormiríamos**   The verb *dormir* is regular in the conditional. To conjugate regular *-ir* verbs in the conditional, keep the *-ir* ending and add *-íamos* as the ending for *nosotros*.

18. **preferiríamos**   The verb *preferir* is regular in the conditional. To conjugate regular *-ir* verbs in the conditional, keep the *-ir* ending and add *-íamos* as the ending for *nosotros*.

19. **Recomendaría**   The verb *recomendar* is regular in the conditional. To conjugate regular *-ar* verbs in the conditional, keep the *-ar* ending and add *-ía* as the ending for *Ud*.

20. **Podría**   The verb *poder* is irregular in the conditional and must be memorized. Drop the *e* from the infinitive ending and add *-ía* as the ending for *Ud*.

Chapter Problems

Problems

Use the future tense to express the promises the people make.

1. ella/no decir mentiras

2. nosotros/no oír música cuando trabajamos

3. Uds./no salir sin permiso

4. él/querer ayudar a todo el mundo

5. yo/no tener celos de nadie

6. tú/siempre hacer lo bueno

7. vosotros/no dejar las cosas para más tarde

8. Ud./no ser hipócrita

9. ellos/cumplir sus promesas

10. ellas/tener cuidado

Use the conditional to express what the person indicated in parentheses would choose.

> Example: visitar Europa o la América del Sur (ella)
>
> Ella visitaría Europa.

11. saber jugar al fútbol o tocar el piano (yo)

12. ser presidente o astronauta (él)

13. tener riqueza o buena salud (nosotros)

14. ver el mundo o la luna (ellas)

15. poder hablar español o francés (vosotros)

16. hacer un crucero o un viaje en avión (tú)

17. ir al teatro o al cine (Ud.)

18. comer pescado o pollo (ellos)

19. comprar un coche deportivo o una casa lujosa (ella)

20. vivir solo o en familia (Uds.)

Answers and Solutions

1. **Answer: Ella no dirá mentiras.**   The verb *decir* is irregular in the future and must be memorized. Use *dir-* as the future stem and add the third person singular future ending (*-á*) for *ella*.

2. **Answer: Nosotros no oiremos música cuando trabajamos.**   The verb *oír* is regular in the future. To conjugate regular *-ir* verbs in the future, keep the *-ir* ending and add *-emos* as the ending for *nosotros*.

3. **Answer: Uds. no saldrán sin permiso.**   The verb *salir* is irregular in the future. Drop *i* from the infinitive ending and replace it with a *d*. Add the third person plural future ending (*-án*) for *Uds*.

4. **Answer: Él querrá ayudar a todo el mundo.**   The verb *querer* is irregular in the future and must be memorized. Drop the *e* from the infinitive ending and add the third person singular future ending (*-á*) for *él*.

5. **Answer: Yo no tendré celos de nadie.**   The verb *tener* is irregular in the future. Drop the *e* from the infinitive ending and replace it with a *d*. Add the first person singular ending (*-é*) for *yo*.

6. **Answer: Tú siempre harás lo bueno.**   The verb *hacer* is irregular in the future and must be memorized. Use *har-* as the future stem and add the second person singular future ending (*-ás*) for *tú*.

7. **Answer: Vosotros no dejaréis las cosas para más tarde.**   The verb *dejar* is regular in the future. To conjugate regular *-ar* verbs in the future, keep the *-ar* ending and add *-éis* as the ending for *vosotros*.

8. **Answer: Ud. no será hipócrita.**   The verb *ir* is regular in the future. Add *-á* as the ending for *Ud.*

9. **Answer: Ellos cumplirán sus promesas.**   The verb *cumplir* is regular in the future. To conjugate regular *-ir* verbs in the future, keep the *-ir* ending and add *-án* as the ending for *ellos.*

10. **Answer: Ellas tendrán cuidado.**   The verb *tener* is irregular in the future. Drop the *e* from the infinitive ending and replace it with a *d.* Add the third person plural ending (*-án*) for *ellas.*

11. **Answer: Yo sabría . . .**   The verb *saber* is irregular in the conditional. Drop *e* from the infinitive ending. Add the first person singular conditional ending (*-ía*) for *yo.*

12. **Answer: Él sería . . .**   The verb *ser* is regular in the conditional. Add *-ía* as the ending for *él.*

13. **Answer: Nosotros tendríamos . . .**   The verb *tener* is irregular in the conditional. Drop the *e* from the infinitive ending and replace it with a *d.* Add the first person plural ending (*-íamos*) for *nosotros.*

14. **Answer: Ellas verían . . .**   The verb *ver* is regular in the conditional. Add *-ían* as the ending for *ellas.*

15. **Answer: Vosotros podríais . . .**   The verb *poder* is irregular in the conditional and must be memorized. Drop the *e* from the infinitive ending and add *-íais* as the ending for *vosotros.*

16. **Answer: Tú harías . . .**   The verb *hacer* is irregular in the conditional. Use *har-* as the conditional stem and add *-ías* as the ending for *tú.*

17. **Answer: Ud. iría . . .**   The verb *ir* is regular in the conditional. Add *-ía* as the ending for *Ud.*

18. **Answer: Ellos comerían . . .**   The verb *comer* is regular in the conditional. To conjugate regular *-er* verbs in the conditional, keep the *-er* ending and add *-ían* as the ending for *ellos.*

19. **Answer: Ella compraría . . .**   The verb *comprar* is regular in the conditional. To conjugate regular *-ar* verbs in the conditional, keep the *-ar* ending and add *-ía* as the ending for *ella.*

20. **Answer: Uds. vivirían . . .**   The verb *vivir* is regular in the conditional. To conjugate regular *-ir* verbs in the conditional, keep the *-ir* ending and add *-ían* as the ending for *Uds.*

Supplemental Chapter Problems

Problems

Use the future tense to complete the sentences about what will happen in school.

1. Si la clase hace una excursión, todo el mundo (caber) _____ en el autobús.

2. Si hay un examen, vosotros (tener) _____ que estudiar.

3. Si el profesor está ausente, (valer) _____ la pena obedecer al profesor suplente.

4. Si los alumnos desobedecen, el director (venir) _____ a la clase.

5. Si hay una fiesta, las muchachas (hacer) _____ los tacos.

6. Si el profesor hace preguntas difíciles, yo no (saber) _____ las respuestas.

7. Si los alumnos se comportan bien, ellos (querer) _____ una recompensa.

8. Si hay un simulacro de incendio, todo el mundo (salir) _____ de la escuela.

9. Si hay una prueba, tú (poner) _____ tus libros debajo de tu silla.

10. Si nieva mucho, nosotros (poder) _____ salir de la escuela temprano.

Use the conditional to express what would happen if people could do what they wanted.

11. Ud./no tener que trabajar

12. ellos/dormir mucho

13. tú/comer en los restaurantes más elegantes

14. ellas/comprar vestidos de última moda

15. vosotros/venir a visitarnos

16. yo/saber tocar el piano

17. tú/ser más fuerte

18. él/decir sus sentimientos íntimos a su novia

19. nosotros/poder hacer un crucero

20. mi casa/valer un millón de dólares

Solutions

1. cabrá (future tense of irregular verbs, p. 240)

2. tendréis (future tense of irregular verbs, p. 240)

3. valdrá (future tense of irregular verbs, p. 240)

4. vendrá (future tense of irregular verbs, p. 240)

5. harán (future tense of irregular verbs, p. 240)

6. sabré (future tense of irregular verbs, p. 240)

7. querrán (future tense of irregular verbs, p. 240)

8. saldrá (future tense of irregular verbs, p. 240)

9. pondrás (future tense of irregular verbs, p. 240)

10. podremos (future tense of irregular verbs, p. 240)

11. Ud. no tendría que trabajar. (the conditional, p. 243)

12. Ellos dormirían mucho. (the conditional, p. 243)

13. Tú comerías en los restaurantes más elegantes. (the conditional, p. 243)

14. Ellas comprarían vestidos de última moda. (the conditional, p. 243)

15. Vosotros vendríais a visitarnos. (the conditional, p. 243)

16. Yo sabría tocar el piano. (the conditional, p. 243)

17. Tú serías más fuerte. (the conditional, p. 243)

18. Él diría sus sentimientos íntimos a su novia. (the conditional, p. 243)

19. Nosotros podríamos hacer un crucero. (the conditional, p. 243)

20. Mi casa valdría un millón de dólares. (the conditional, p. 243)

Chapter 12
Gerunds and the Progressive Tenses

Gerunds

A Spanish gerund *(un gerundio)* is derived from a verb and expresses an action that is in the process of taking place. It may be the equivalent of an English present participle, which is used as an adjective that ends in *-ing*. A Spanish gerund may also be the equivalent of the English "by" or "while" + present participle.

Los alumnos están **escuchando** al profesor.	The students are **listening** to the teacher.
La alumna quien está **leyendo** es mi mejor amiga.	The student who is **reading** is my best friend.
Estudiando, se aprende mucho.	By (while) **studying,** one learns a lot.

An English gerund is used as a noun. A Spanish gerund, however, may not be used as a noun subject; rather, an infinitive is used:

Comer verduras es saludable.   **Eating** green vegetables is healthy.

The Formation of Gerunds

Gerunds of regular verbs are formed as follows:

❏ Drop *-ar* from *-ar* verb infinitive and add *-ando:*

❏ Drop *-er* or *-ir* from *-er* and *-ir* verb infinitives, respectively, and add *-iendo:*

Ending	Verb	Meaning	Past Participle	Meaning
-ar	trabajar	to work	trabajando	working
-er	comer	to eat	comiendo	eating
-ir	vivir	to live	viviendo	living

If an *-er* or *-ir* verb stem ends in a vowel, add *-yendo:*

caer (to fall)	ca*yendo*
destruir (to destroy)	destru*yendo*
creer (to believe)	cre*yendo*
leer (to read)	le*yendo*
oír (to hear)	o*yendo*
traer (to bring)	tra*yendo*

The following irregular and stem-changing *-ir* verbs change the stem vowel from *e* to *i* and from *o* to *u:*

co**le**gir (to collect)	col**i**giendo
d**e**cir (to say, to tell)	d**i**ciendo
div**e**rtir (to divert, to have fun)	div**i**rtiendo
m**e**ntir (to lie)	m**i**ntiendo
p**e**dir (to ask)	p**i**diendo
rep**e**tir (to repeat)	rep**i**tiendo
s**e**guir (to follow)	s**i**guiendo
s**e**ntir (to feel)	s**i**ntiendo
s**e**rvir (to serve)	s**i**rviendo
sug**e**rir (to suggest)	sug**i**riendo
v**e**nir (to come)	v**i**niendo
v**e**stir (to dress)	v**i**stiendo
d**o**rmir (to sleep)	d**u**rmiendo
m**o**rir (to die)	m**u**riendo

Three verbs with irregular gerunds are:

ir (to go)	yendo
poder (to be able)	pudiendo
reír (to laugh)	riendo

Example Problems

Express what people think and say by completing each sentence with the correct form of the verb in parentheses.

1. (By working) _____ ,se pone responsable.

    Answer: Trabajando

    Trabajar means "to work." To form the gerund of an *-ar* verb infinitive, drop the *-ar* ending and add *-ando.*

2. (Going) _____ al cine es muy divertido.

    Answer: Ir

A Spanish gerund may not be used as a noun subject; an infinitive is used instead. *Ir* expresses "going."

3. La niña que está (laughing) _____ es mi hermana.

Answer: riendo

Reír means "to laugh" and has an irregular gerund that must be memorized.

Work Problems

Express what a mother thinks and says about sports by completing each sentence with the correct form of the verb in parentheses.

1. (Playing) _____ al fútbol es muy divertido.

2. Mis hijos están (going out) _____ a jugar.

3. El muchacho quien está (throwing) _____ la pelota es mi hijo.

4. (By following) _____ las reglas del juego, se aprenden muchas lecciones importantes.

5. Mi esposo y yo estamos (watching) _____ el partido.

6. (Participating) _____ en un deporte es una actividad saludable.

Worked Solutions

1. **Jugar**   A Spanish gerund may not be used as a noun subject; an infinitive is used instead. *Jugar* expresses "playing."

2. **saliendo**   *Salir* means "to go out." To form the gerund of an -*ir* verb infinitive, drop the -*ir* ending and add -*iendo*.

3. **lanzando**   *Lanzar* means "to throw." To form the gerund of an -*ar* verb infinitive, drop the -*ar* ending and add -*ando*.

4. **Siguiendo**   *Seguir* means "to follow." A Spanish gerund expresses "by . . . -ing." To form the gerund of the stem-changing -*ir* verb *seguir,* change the stem vowel from *e* to *i*. Drop the -*ir* ending and add -*iendo*.

5. **mirando**   *Mirar* means "to watch." To form the gerund of an -*ar* verb infinitive, drop the -*ar* ending and add -*ando*.

6. **Participar**   A Spanish gerund may not be used as a noun subject; an infinitive is used instead. *Participar* expresses "participating."

The Present Progressive

The present tense (see Chapter 4) expresses an action or event that the subject generally does at a given time or that is habitual. The present progressive expresses an action or event that is in progress or that is continuing at a given time. The two elements necessary for the formation of the present progressive are:

❏ The present tense of the verb *estar:*

yo estoy   nosotros estamos

tú estás   vosotros estáis

él (ella, Ud.) está   ellos (ellas, Uds.) están

❏ The gerund of the verb, which expresses what the action is:

Ellos están cantando.

They are singing.

This simple equation shows you how the verb *estar* and the gerund of another verb compose the present progressive:

Present progressive = subject noun or pronoun + *estar* in present + gerund

The present progressive can also be formed by using the present tense of the verbs listed below + a gerund:

❏ *Seguir* (to keep on, to continue)

Él sigue hablando. He continues talking.

❏ *Continuar* (to continue)

Nosotros continuamos leyendo. We continue reading.

❏ *Ir* (to go)

El tiempo va cambiando. The weather is changing.

❏ *Venir* (to come)

Ella viene corriendo. She comes running.

❏ *Salir* (to go out)

Ellos salen riendo. They go out laughing.

❏ *Andar* (to walk)

El muchacho anda buscando a su amigo. The boy walks looking for his friend.

When attaching one pronoun to the gerund in the present progressive, count back three vowels from the end and add an accent:

Él está leyéndola.   He is reading it.
        3   2 1

When attaching two pronouns to the gerund in the present progressive, count back four vowels from the end and add an accent:

Ella estaba comprándoselos.   She was buying them for herself.
             4   3 2 1

Example Problems

Express what each person is doing while watching television by changing the sentence from the present to the present progressive.

1. Tú estudias.

    Answer: Tú estás estudiando.

    The *tú* form of *estar* is irregular. Drop the *-ar* ending and add *-ás*. To form the gerund of the *-ar* verb *estudiar*, drop the *-ar* ending and add *-ando*.

2. Ellos beben refrescos.

    Answer: Ellos están bebiendo refrescos.

    The *ellos* form of *estar* is irregular. Drop the *-ar* ending and add *-án*. To form the gerund of the *-er* verb *beber*, drop the *-er* ending and add *-iendo*.

3. Yo escribo mensajes por correo electrónico.

    Answer: Yo estoy escribiendo mensajes por correo electrónico.

    The *yo* form of *estar* is irregular. Drop the *-ar* ending and add *-oy*. To form the gerund of the *-ir* verb *escribir*, drop the *-ir* ending and add *–iendo*.

Work Problems

Express what each person is doing while Dad prepares dinner by changing the sentence from the present to the present progressive.

1. Mamá duerme.

2. Yo pongo la mesa.

3. Manolo y José divierten a los niños.

4. Tú escuchas las noticias.

5. Nosotros pedimos ayuda con nuestras tareas.

6. Vosotros leéis el periódico.

Worked Solutions

1. **Mamá está durmiendo.** The *ella* form of *estar* is irregular. Drop the *-ar* ending and add *-á*. *Dormir* is an *-ir* verb with an internal stem change. To form the gerund of *dormir*, change *o* to *u*, drop the *-ir* ending, and add *-iendo*.

2. **Yo estoy poniendo la mesa.** The *yo* form of *estar* is irregular. Drop the *-ar* ending and add *-oy*. *Poner* has a regular gerund. To form the gerund of an *-er* verb, drop the *-er* ending and add *-iendo*.

3. **Manolo y José están divirtiendo a los niños.**   The *ellos* form of *estar* is irregular. Drop the *-ar* ending and add *-án. Divertir* is an *-ir* verb with an internal stem change. To form the gerund of *divertir*, change *e* to *i*, drop the *-ir* ending, and add *-iendo.*

4. **Tú estás escuchando las noticias.**   The *tú* form of *estar* is irregular. Drop the *-ar* ending and add *-ás.* To form the gerund of the *-ar* verb *escuchar*, drop the *-ar* ending and add *-ando.*

5. **Nosotros estamos pidiendo ayuda con nuestras tareas.**   The *nosotros* form of *estar* is irregular. Drop the *-ar* ending and add *-amos. Pedir* is an *-ir* verb with an internal stem change. To form the gerund of *pedir*, change *e* to *i*, drop the *-ir* ending, and add *-iendo.*

6. **Vosotros estáis leyendo el periódico.**   The *vosotros* form of *estar* is irregular. Drop the *-ar* ending and add *-áis.* To form the gerund of the *-er* verb *leer*, whose stem ends in a vowel, drop the *-er* ending and add *-yendo.*

The Past Progressive

The past progressive tenses can be formed in the same manner as the present progressive. Use the preterit or imperfect form of the verb *estar* and add the gerund to express an action that was in progress in the past:

Past progressive = subject noun or pronoun + *estar* in preterit or imperfect + gerund

Los jóvenes estuvieron durmiendo toda la mañana.	The young people were sleeping all morning.
Sin embargo, ellos estaban trabajando a las dos.	They were working, however, at two o'clock.

The past progressive can also be formed with *seguir, continuar, ir, venir, salir,* and *andar:*

Ella continuó estudiando hasta las siete.	She continued studying until seven o'clock.
Ella seguía estudiando.	She continued studying.

Example Problems

Use the preterit or imperfect progressive to express what happened or what was happening last night.

1. Yo (was taking care) _____ a mi hermana menor.

   Answer: estaba cuidando

   Use the imperfect progressive to express what "was happening." For the imperfect *yo* form of *estar*, drop the *-ar* ending and add *-aba.* To form the gerund of the *-ar* verb *cuidar*, drop the *-ar* ending and add *-ando.*

2. Ellos (continued working) _____ hasta la medianoche.

   Answer: continuaron trabajando

   Use the preterit progressive to express what "happened." For the preterit *ellos* form of *continuar*, drop the *-ar* ending and add *-aron.* To form the gerund of the *-ar* verb *trabajar*, drop the *-ar* ending and add *-ando.*

3. Marisol (came back crying) _____.

    Answer: regresó llorando

    Use the preterit progressive to express what "happened." For the preterit *ella* form of *regresar*, drop the *-ar* ending and add *-ó*. To form the gerund of the *-ar* verb *llorar*, drop the *-ar* ending and add *-ando*.

4. Tú (were watching) _____ la televisión.

    Answer: estabas mirando

    Use the imperfect progressive to express what "was happening." For the imperfect *tú* form of *estar*, drop the *-ar* ending and add *-abas*. To form the gerund of the *-ar* verb *mirar*, drop the *-ar* ending and add *-ando*.

Work Problems

Use the preterit or imperfect progressive to express what happened or was happening on New Year's Eve.

1. El señor Nuñez (was sleeping) _____ toda la noche.

2. Después de la medianoche yo (continued dancing) _____.

3. A las tres de la madrugada, los camareros ya (were serving) _____ a sus clientes.

4. Tú (arrived running) _____ a casa a las dos de la madrugada.

5. Nosotros (went out laughing) _____ a las ocho.

6. Vosotros (were walking and whistling) _____.

7. Ellas (kept on singing) _____ hasta muy tarde.

8. Durante la noche, el tiempo (went on changing) _____.

Worked Solutions

1. **estuvo durmiendo**   Use the preterit progressive to express what "happened" for a specific time period. In the preterit stem, *estar* adds the *-uv* to the infinitive stem, *est-*. The third person singular preterit ending for an irregular verb is *-ieron*. *Dormir* is an *-ir* verb with an internal stem change. To form the gerund of *dormir*, change *o* to *u*, drop the *-ir* ending, and add *-iendo*.

2. **continuaba bailando**   Use the imperfect progressive to express what "was happening." For the imperfect *yo* form of *estar*, drop the *-ar* ending and add *-aba*. To form the gerund of the *-ar* verb *bailar*, drop the *-ar* ending and add *-ando*.

3. **estaban sirviendo**   Use the imperfect progressive to express what "was happening." For the imperfect *ellos* form of *estar*, drop the *-ar* ending and add *-aban*. *Servir* is an *-ir* verb with an internal stem change. To form the gerund of *servir*, change *e* to *i*, drop the *-ir* ending, and add *-iendo*.

4. **llegaste corriendo**   Use the preterit progressive to express what "happened." For the preterit *tú* form of *llegar*, drop the *-ar* ending and add *-aste*. To form the gerund of the *-er* verb *correr*, drop the *-er* ending and add *-iendo*.

5. **salimos riendo**   Use the preterit progressive to express what "happened." For the preterit *nosotros* form of *salir*, drop the *-ir* ending and add *-imos*. *Reír* is an irregular verb. To form the gerund of *reír*, drop the *-eír* ending and add *-iendo*.

6. **andabais silbando**   Use the imperfect progressive to express what "was happening." For the imperfect *vosotros* form of *andar*, drop the *-ar* ending and add *-abais*. To form the gerund of the *-ar* verb *silbar*, drop the *-ar* ending and add *-ando*.

7. **continuaron cantando**   Use the preterit progressive to express what "happened." For the preterit *ellas* form of *continuar*, drop the *-ar* ending and add *-aron*. To form the gerund of the *-ar* verb *cantar*, drop the *-ar* ending and add *-ando*.

8. **siguió cambiando**   Use the preterit progressive to express what "happened." The irregular verb *seguir* expresses "to go on." The preterit third person singular form of *seguir* is *siguió*. To form the gerund of the *-ar* verb *cambiar*, drop the *-ar* ending and add *-ando*.

The Future Progressive

The future progressive can be formed in the same manner as the present progressive. Use the future form of the verb *estar* (or any of the other verbs mentioned) and add the gerund to express an action that will be in progress in the future:

Future progressive = subject noun or pronoun + *estar* in future + gerund

Ellos estarán cantando después del examen.	They will be singing after the test.
Sus respuestas irán mejorándose.	His answers will keep getting better.

Example Problems

Use the future progressive to express what will be happening after school.

Example: ella/estar/caminar a casa
Ella estará caminando a casa.

1. los jóvenes/salir/correr

   Answer: Los jóvenes saldrán corriendo.

   The verb *salir* is irregular in the future. Drop *i* from the infinitive ending and replace it with a *d*. Add the third person plural future ending: *-án*. To form the gerund of the *-er* verb *correr*, drop the *-er* ending and add *-iendo*.

2. nosotros/venir a casa/charlar

   Answer: Nosotros vendremos charlando a casa.

   The verb *venir* is irregular in the future. Drop *e* from the infinitive ending and replace it with a *d*. Add the first person plural future ending: *-emos*. To fiorm the gerund of the *-ar* verb *charlar*, drop the *-ar* ending and add *-ando*.

3. tú/estar/tomar helado

   Answer: Tú estarás tomando helado.

   The verb *estar* is regular in the future. Add the second person singular future ending *-ás* to the infinitive. To form the gerund of the *-ar* verb *tomar*, drop the *-ar* ending and add *-ando*.

Work Problems

Use the future progressive to express what will be happening after the play is over.

1. los actores/estar/celebrar

2. nosotros/ir/sonreír

3. Ud./continuar/aplaudir

4. yo/andar/hablar de la obra

5. tú/salir/cantar

6. vosotros/seguir/repetir el diálogo

Worked Solutions

1. **Los actores estarán celebrando.** The verb *estar* is regular in the future. Add the third person plural future ending *-án* to the infinitive. To form the gerund of the *-ar* verb *celebrar*, drop the *-ar* ending and add *-ando*.

2. **Nosotros iremos sonriendo.** The verb *ir* is regular in the future. Add the first person plural future ending *-emos* to the infinitive. *Sonreír* is an irregular verb. To form the gerund of *-sonreír*, drop the *-eír* ending and add *-iendo*.

3. **Ud. continuará aplaudiendo.** The verb *continuar* is regular in the future. Add the third person singular future ending *-á* to the infinitive. To form the gerund of the *-ir* verb *aplaudir*, drop the *-ir* ending and add *-iendo*.

4. **Yo andaré hablando de la obra.** The verb *andar* is regular in the future. Add the first person singular future ending *-é* to the infinitive. To form the gerund of the *-ar* verb *hablar*, drop the *-ar* ending and add *-ando*.

5. **Tú saldrás cantando.** The verb *salir* is irregular in the future. Drop *i* from the infinitive ending and replace it with a *d*. Add the second person singular future ending: *-án*. To form the gerund of the *-ar* verb *cantar*, drop the *-ar* ending and add *-ando*.

6. **Vosotros seguiréis repitiendo el diálogo.** The verb *seguir* is regular in the future. Add the second person plural future ending *-éis* to the infinitive. *Repetir* is an *-ir* verb with an internal stem change. To form the gerund of *repetir*, change *e* to *i*, drop the *-ir* ending, and add *-iendo*.

The Conditional Progressive

The conditional progressive can be formed in the same manner as the present progressive. Use the conditional form of the verb *estar* (or any of the other verbs mentioned) and add the gerund to express an action that would be in progress under certain conditions. The condition in the clause following *si* (if) will be hypothetical and, therefore, will require a verb in the imperfect subjunctive (see Chapter 15):

Conditional progressive = subject noun or pronoun + *estar* in conditional + gerund in one clause

AND

si + subject noun or pronoun + verb in imperfect subjunctive in the other clause

Yo estaría viajando más si tuviera más dinero.   I would be traveling more if I had more money.

Example Problems

Use the conditional progressive to express what people would do if the weather were nice.

Si hiciera buen tiempo . . .

1.   tú (estar/caminar) _____ por el parque.

     Answer: estarías caminando

     The verb *estar* is regular in the conditional. To conjugate regular *-ar* verbs in the conditional, keep the *-ar* ending and add *-ías* as the ending for *tú*. To form the gerund of the *-ar* verb *caminar*, drop the *-ar* ending and add *-ando*.

2.   yo (andar/admirar) _____ el paisaje.

     Answer: andaría admirando

     The verb *andar* is regular in the conditional. To conjugate regular *-ar* verbs in the conditional, keep the *-ar* ending and add *-ía* as the ending for *yo*. To form the gerund of the *-ar* verb *admirar*, drop the *-ar* ending and add *-ando*.

3.   Uds. (continuar/describir) _____ la belleza de la naturaleza.

     Answer: continuarían describiendo

     The verb *continuar* is regular in the conditional. To conjugate regular *-ar* verbs in the conditional, keep the *-ar* ending and add *-ían* as the ending for *Uds*. To form the gerund of the *-ir* verb *describir*, drop the *-ir* ending and add *-iendo*.

Work Problems

Use the conditional progressive to express what people would do if there were a snowstorm.

Si hubiera una tormenta de nieve . . .

1.   yo no (estar/trabajar) _____.

2.   ella no (seguir/conducir) _____ su coche rápidamente.

3. nosotros no (llegar/sonreír) _____ a la escuela.

4. Uds. no (andar/buscar) _____ a otros amigos.

5. tú no (ir/correr) _____ por las calles.

6. vosotros no (salir/llevar) _____ solamente un suéter.

Worked Solutions

1. **estaría trabajando**   The verb *estar* is regular in the conditional. Add the first person singular conditional ending *-ía* to the infinitive. To form the gerund of the *-ar* verb *trabajar*, drop the *-ar* ending and add *-ando.*

2. **seguiría conduciendo**   The verb *seguir* is regular in the conditional. Add the third person singular conditional ending *-ía* to the infinitive. To form the gerund of the *-ir* verb *conducir*, drop the *-ir* ending and add *-iendo.*

3. **llegaríamos sonriendo**   The verb *llegar* is regular in the conditional. Add the first person plural conditional ending *-íamos* to the infinitive. *Sonreír* is an irregular verb. To form the gerund of *sonreír*, drop the *-eír* ending and add *-iendo.*

4. **andarían buscando**   The verb *andar* is regular in the conditional. Add the third person plural conditional ending *-ían* to the infinitive. To form the gerund of the *-ar* verb *buscar*, drop the *-ar* ending and add *-ando.*

5. **irías corriendo**   The verb *ir* is regular in the conditional. Add the second person singular conditional ending *-ías* to the infinitive. To form the gerund of the *-er* verb *correr*, drop the *-er* ending and add *-iendo.*

6. **saldríais llevando**   The verb *salir* is irregular in the conditional. Drop *i* from the infinitive ending and replace it with a *d*. Add the second person plural conditional ending: *-íais*. To form the gerund of the *-ar* verb *llevar*, drop the *-ar* ending and add *-ando.*

Chapter Problems

Problems
Use the present progressive to express what is happening on a Sunday afternoon.

1. una niña/estar/vestir a su muñeca

2. un muchacho/seguir/buscar su camión

3. yo/continuar/leer a los niños

4. Uds./estar/divertir/a la niña

5. los abuelos/venir/traer regalos

6. nosotros/salir/decir chistes

7. las tías/estar/oír las quejas de sus sobrinos

8. tú/estar/distribuir regalos a tus nietos

9. vosotros/estar/servir refrescos

10. los niños/estar/pedir permiso para salir

Express the actions of students by using the progressive tense of the verbs indicated in each sentence.

> Example: Trabajarán y no descansarán.
> Estarán trabajando y no estarán descansando.

11–12. Harán una prueba a la una y no almorzarán en la cafetería.

13–14. Estudiaron toda la noche y no jugaron a los naipes.

15–16. Aprenden mucho y no repiten sus errores.

17–18. Escribían las tareas a las tres y no miraban la televisión.

19–20. Si pudieran, nadarían en el mar y no asistirían a la escuela.

Answers and Solutions

1. **Answer: Una niña está visitiendo a su muñeca.**   The *ella* form of *estar* is irregular. Drop the *-ar* ending and add *-á*. *Vestir* is an *-ir* verb with an internal stem change. For the gerund of *vestir*, change the stem vowel from *e* to *i*. Drop the *-ir* ending and add *-iendo*.

2. **Answer: Un muchacho sigue buscando su camión.**   The third person singular form of *seguir* is irregular. *Seguir* has an internal change of *e* to *i* in all forms except *nosotros* and *vosotros*. Drop the *-ir* ending and add *-e*. To form the gerund of the *-ar* verb *escuchar*, drop the *-ar* ending and add *-ando*.

3. **Answer: Yo continúo leyendo a los niños.**   *Continuar* is an *-ar* verb with an accented *u* in all forms except *nosotros* and *vosotros*. Drop the *-ar* ending and add *-o*. To form the gerund of the *-er* verb *leer*, whose stem ends in a vowel, drop the *-er* ending and add *-yendo*.

4. **Answer: Uds. están divirtiendo a la niña.**   The *Uds.* form of *estar* is irregular. Drop the *-ar* ending and add *-án*. *Divertir* is an *-ir* verb with an internal stem change. To form the gerund of *divertir*, change *e* to *i*, drop the *-ir* ending, and add *-iendo*.

5. **Answer: Los abuelos vienen trayendo regalos.**   The stem-changing verb *venir* has an internal change of *e* to *ie* in all forms except *nosotros* and *vosotros*. Add the third person plural *-en* ending. To form the gerund of the *-er* verb *traer*, whose stem ends in a vowel, drop the *-er* ending and add *-yendo*.

6.   **Answer: Nosotros salimos diciendo chistes.**   The verb *salir* is regular in the *nosotros* form. Drop the *-ir* ending and add the first person plural ending: *-imos*. *Decir* is an *-ir* verb with an internal stem change. To form the gerund of *decir*, change *e* to *i*, drop the *-ir* ending, and add *-iendo*.

7.   **Answer: Las tías están oyendo las quejas de sus sobrinos.**   The *ellos* form of *estar* is irregular. Drop the *-ar* ending and add *-án*. To form the gerund of the *-ir* verb *oír*, whose stem ends in a vowel, drop the *-ir* ending and add *-yendo*.

8.   **Answer: Tú estás distribuyendo regalos a tus nietos.**   The *tú* form of *estar* is irregular. Drop the *-ar* ending and add *-ás*. To form the gerund of the *-ir* verb *distribuir*, whose stem ends in a vowel, drop the *-ir* ending and add *-yendo*.

9.   **Answer: Vosotros estáis sirviendo refrescos.**   The *vosotros* form of *estar* is irregular. Drop the *-ar* ending and add *-áis*. *Servir* is an *-ir* verb with an internal stem change. To form the gerund of *servir*, change *e* to *i*, drop the *-ir* ending, and add *-iendo*.

10.   **Answer: Los niños están pidiendo permiso para salir.**   The *ellos* form of *estar* is irregular. Drop the *-ar* ending and add *-án*. *Pedir* is an *-ir* verb with an internal stem change. To form the gerund of *pedir*, change *e* to *i*, drop the *-ir* ending, and add *-iendo*.

11–12.   **Answer: Estarán haciendo una prueba a la una y no estarán almorzando en la cafetería.**   The verb *estar* is regular in the future. Add the third person plural future ending *-án* to the infinitive. *Hacer* has a regular gerund. To form the gerund of an *-er* verb, drop the *-er* ending and add *-iendo*. To form the gerund of the *-ar* verb *almorzar*, drop the *-ar* ending and add *-ando*.

13–14.   **Answer: Estuvieron estudiando toda la noche y no estuvieron jugando a los naipes.**   Use the preterit progressive to express what "happened" for a specific time period. In the preterit stem, *estar* adds the *-uv* to the infinitive stem, *est-*. The third person singular preterit ending for an irregular verb is *-ieron*. To form the gerund of the *-ar* verb *estudiar*, drop the *-ar* ending and add *-ando*. To form the gerund of the *-ar* verb *jugar*, drop the *-ar* ending and add *-ando*.

15–16.   **Answer: Están aprendiendo mucho y no están repitiendo sus errores.**   The *ellos* form of *estar* in the present tense is irregular. Drop the *-ar* ending and add *-án*. To form the gerund of the *-er* verb *aprender*, drop the *-er* ending and add *-iendo*. *Repetir* is an *-ir* verb with an internal stem change. To form the gerund of *servir*, change *e* to *i*, drop the *-ir* ending, and add *-iendo*.

17–18.   **Answer: Estaban escribiendo las tareas a las tres y no estaban mirando la televisión.**   Use the imperfect progressive to express what "was happening." For the imperfect *ellos* form of *estar*, drop the *-ar* ending and add *-aban*. To form the gerund of the *-ir* verb *escribir*, drop the *-ir* ending and add *-iendo*. To form the gerund of the *-ar* verb *mirar*, drop the *-ar* ending and add *-ando*.

19–20.   **Answer: Si pudieran, estarían nadando en el mar y no estarían asistiendo a la escuela.**   The verb *estar* is regular in the conditional. Add the third person plural conditional ending *-ían* to the infinitive. To form the gerund of the *-ar* verb *nadar*, drop the *-ar* ending and add *-ando*. To form the gerund of the *-ir* verb *asistir*, drop the *-ir* ending and add *-iendo*.

Supplemental Chapter Problems

Problems

Use the present progressive to express what people are doing when their flight is delayed.

1. yo/estar/escuchar mis discos compactos

2. Uds./seguir/charlar

3. nosotros/continuar/pedir permiso para salir del avión

4. tú/estar/hacer un crucigrama

5. vosotros/estar/trabajar

6. ella/estar/comer un sándwich

7. un hombre/salir/decir tonterías

8. el piloto/estar/proveer información a los pasajeros

9. los niños/estar/dormir

10. la aeromoza/venir/servir bebidas

Express the habits of older people by using the progressive tense of the verbs indicated in each sentence.

> Example: Hablaban y no cantaban.
> Estaban hablando y no estaban cantando.

11–12. Toman el autobús y no conducen un coche.

13–14. Si pudieran, correrían rápidamente y no caminarían lentamente.

15–16. Comían a las cinco y no visitaban a sus amigos.

17–18. Durmieron toda la noche y no bailaron en un club.

19–20. Se relajarán a las nueve de la mañana y no trabajarán.

Solutions

1. Yo estoy escuchando mis discos compactos. (the formation of gerunds, p. 253; present progressive, p. 255)

2. Ud. sigue charlando. (the formation of gerunds, p. 253; present progressive, p. 255)

3. Nosotros continuamos pidiendo permiso para salir del avión. (the formation of gerunds, p. 253; present progressive, p. 255)

4. Tú estás haciendo un crucigrama. (the formation of gerunds, p. 253; present progressive, p. 255)

5. Vosotros estáis trabajando. (the formation of gerunds, p. 253; present progressive, p. 255)

6. Ella está comiendo un sándwich. (the formation of gerunds, p. 253; present progressive, p. 255)

7. Un hombre sale diciendo tonterías. (the formation of gerunds, p. 253; present progressive, p. 255)

8. El piloto está proveyendo información a los pasajeros. (the formation of gerunds, p. 253; present progressive, p. 255)

9. Los niños están durmiendo. (the formation of gerunds, p. 253; present progressive, p. 255)

10. La aeromoza viene sirviendo bebidas. (the formation of gerunds, p. 253; present progressive, p. 255)

11–12. Están tomando el autobús y no están conduciendo un coche. (the formation of gerunds, p. 253; present progressive, p. 255)

13–14. Si pudieran, estarían corriendo rápidamente y no estarían caminando lentamente. (the formation of gerunds, p. 253; conditional progressive, p. 262)

15–16. Estaban comiendo a las cinco y no estaban visitando a sus amigos. (the formation of gerunds, p. 253; past progressive, p. 258)

17–18. Estuvieron durmiendo toda la noche y no estuvieron bailando en un club. (the formation of gerunds, p. 253; past progressive, p. 258)

19–20. Se estarán relajando a las nueve de la mañana y no estarán trabajando. (the formation of gerunds, p. 253; future progressive, p. 260)

Chapter 13
Compound Tenses

The Difference between Simple and Compound Tenses

A verb tense can be classified as either simple (consisting of one verb form) or compound (consisting of an auxiliary, or helping, verb and a past participle). English has three simple tenses (past, present, and future) and three compound tenses (past perfect, present perfect, and future perfect). In Spanish, however, there are seven simple tenses and moods that have corresponding compound forms:

Simple Tense	*Compound Tense*
Present	*Present Perfect*
do/does; am/are/is	have + past participle
I speak.	I spoke (have spoken).
Yo hablo.	Yo he hablado.
Preterit	*Preterit Perfect*
did	had + past participle
I did speak.	I had spoken.
Yo hablé.	Yo hube hablado.
Imperfect	*Pluperfect*
was, used to	had + past participle
I was speaking.	I had spoken.
Yo hablaba.	Yo había hablado.
Future	*Future Perfect*
will	will have + past participle
I will speak.	I will have spoken.
Yo hablaré.	Yo habré hablado.
Conditional	*Conditional Perfect*
would	would have+ past participle
I would speak.	I would have spoken.

Yo hablaría.	Yo habría hablado.
Present Subjunctive	*Perfect (Past) Subjunctive*
may	may have + past participle
...that I may speak	...that I may have spoken
...que yo hable	...que yo haya hablado
Imperfect Subjunctive	*Pluperfect Subjunctive*
might	might have + past participle..that I might speak...that I might have spoken
que yo hablara (hablase)	...que yo hubiera (hubiese) hablado

Each simple tense can be identified by the specific endings for each subject noun or pronoun that are attached to a particular stem. These endings never change—even when the verb has a spelling or stem change or when the verb is irregular.

In Spanish, all compound (perfect) tenses or moods are formed by taking the corresponding simple tense of the auxiliary (helping) verb *haber* (to have) and adding the past participle of the action that was performed. Memorizing *haber* in all its forms enables you to construct all compound tenses.

Example Problems

Express what each person did by selecting the appropriate compound tense of the italicized verb.

1. Yo *comería* en este restaurante.

   a. habré comido b. habría comido c. he comido d. había comida

   Answer: b

   The italic verb is in the conditional. Use the conditional perfect: the conditional of *haber* + the past participle to form the compound tense.

2. Nosotros *reíamos*.

   a. habremos reído b. habríamos reído c. habíamos reído d. hemos reído

   Answer: c

   The italic verb is in the imperfect. Use the pluperfect: the imperfect of *haber* + the past participle to form the compound tense.

3. Ellos *corren* el maratón.

   a. hubieron corrido b. habrán corrido c. habían corrido d. han corrido

   Answer: d

   The italic verb is in the present. Use the present perfect: the present of *haber* + the past participle to form the compound tense.

Work Problems

Express what each person did by selecting the appropriate compound tense of the italicized verb.

1. Yo *leyó* un libro interestante.

   a. hube leído

   b. habré leído

   c. haya leído

   d. hubiera leído

2. Uds. *trabajaban* cuidadosamente.

   a. habrían trabajado

   b. han trabajado

   c. hubieron trabajado

   d. habían trabajado

3. Nosotros *iríamos* a la fiesta.

   a. hubieramos ido

   b. habremos ido

   c. habríamos ido

   d. hemos ido

4. Tú *viajarás* mucho.

   a. hayas viajado

   b. has viajado

   c. habría viajado

   d. habrás viajado

5. Es posible que ella *venga*.

   a. haya venido

   b. ha venido

   c. habría venido

   d. hube venido

Worked Solutions

1. **a.** The italic verb is in the preterit. Use the preterit perfect: the preterit of *haber* + the past participle to form the compound tense.

2. **d.** The italic verb is in the imperfect. Use the pluperfect: the imperfect of *haber* + the past participle to form the compound tense.

3. **c.** The italic verb is in the conditional. Use the conditional perfect: the conditional of *haber* + the past participle to form the compound tense.

4. **d.** The italic verb is in the future. Use the future perfect: the future of *haber* + the past participle to form the compound tense.

5. **a.** The italic verb is in the present subjunctive. Use the perfect (past) subjunctive: the present subjunctive of *haber* + the past participle to form the compound tense.

Past Participles of Regular and Irregular Verbs

Past participles of regular, spelling-change, and stem-changing verbs are formed as follows (except as noted below): Drop the *-ar* infinitive ending and add *-ado*, or drop the *-ir* or *-er* infinitive ending and add *-ido*.

Verb Ending	Verb	Meaning	Past Participle	Meaning
-ar	olvidar	to forget	olvidado	forgotten
-er	prometer	to promise	prometido	promised
-ir	decidir	to decide	decidido	decided

If an *-ir* or *-er* verb stem ends in a vowel, add an accent to the vowel before the *-do* ending:

Verb	Meaning	Past Participle	Meaning
caer	to fall	caído	fallen
creer	to believe	creído	believed
leer	to read	leído	read
oír	to hear	oído	heard
reír	to laugh	reído	laughed
traer	to bring	traído	brought

Irregular past participles must be memorized:

Verb	Meaning	Past Participle	Meaning
abrir	to open	abierto	opened
cubrir	to cover	cubierto	covered
decir	to tell, to say	dicho	said
escribir	to write	escrito	written
hacer	to make	hecho	made
freír	to fry	frito	fried
morir	to die	muerto	died
poner	to put	puesto	put

Verb	Meaning	Past Participle	Meaning
proveer	to provide	provisto	provided
resolver	to resolve	resuelto	resolved
romper	to break	roto	broken
satisfacer	to satisfy	satisfecho	satisfied
volver	to return	vuelto	returned
ver	to see	visto	seen

Note the following about the use of the past participle:

❏ The past participle always ends in -o when it follows *haber*:

Ella ha vivido en España. She has lived in Spain.

❏ The past participle remains invariable for the different subject pronouns:

Nosotras hemos recibido un mensaje electrónico. We have received an e-mail.

Ellos han recibido un mensaje electrónico. They have received an e-mail.

❏ The past participle cannot be separated from the helping verb:

Yo no he terminado el libro. I haven't finished the book.

Siempre ha faltado a sus promesas. He has always broken his promises.

Example Problems

Express what each person did by completing the sentence with the correct past participle.

1. (prometir) Él ha _____ de venir temprano.

   Answer: prometido

   To form the past participle of a regular –*ir* verb, drop the –*ir* infinitive ending and add –*ido*.

2. (comprar) Nosotros hemos _____ un coche nuevo.

   Answer: comprado

   To form the past participle of a regular –*ar* verb, drop the –*ar* infinitive ending and add –*ado*.

3. (oír) Los niños han _____ las noticias.

   Answer: oído

   To form the past participle of a regular –*ir* verb, drop the –*ir* infinitive ending and add –*ido*. If the –*ir* verb stem ends in a vowel, add an accent to the vowel before the *-do* ending.

Work Problems

Express what each person did by completing the sentence with the correct past participle.

1.　(traer) Él camarero ha _____ la cuenta.

2.　(decir) Nosotros hemos _____ la verdad.

3.　(romper) Los niños han _____ los juguetes.

4.　(hacer) Yo no he _____ mi tarea.

5.　(ver) Vosotros habéis _____ una película de ciencia ficción.

6.　(poner) Tú has _____ los libros en la estantería.

Worked Solutions

1.　**traído.**　To form the past participle of a regular –*ir* verb, drop the –*ir* infinitive ending and add –*ido*. If the –*ir* verb stem ends in a vowel, add an accent to the vowel before the -*do* ending.

2.　**dicho.**　The past participle of *decir* is irregular and must be memorized.

3.　**roto.**　The past participle of *romper* is irregular and must be memorized.

4.　**hecho.**　The past participle of *hacer* is irregular and must be memorized.

5.　**visto.**　The past participle of *ver* is irregular and must be memorized.

6.　**puesto.**　The past participle of *poner* is irregular and must be memorized.

The Present Perfect Tense

The present perfect tense expresses what "has happened." The present perfect tense is formed by taking the present tense of the auxiliary (helping) verb *haber* and adding the past participle of the action performed:

Present Tense of Haber	*Sample Past Participle*	*Meaning*
Yo **he**	descansado.	I **have** *rested*.
Tú **has**	comido.	You **have** *eaten*.
Él (ella, Ud.) **ha**	sufrido.	He (she, you) **has** (**have**) *suffered*.
Nosotros **hemos**	abierto la puerta.	We **have** *opened* the door.
Vosotros **habéis**	resuelto el problema.	You **have** *solved* the problem.
Ellos (ellas, Uds.) **han**	visto esa película.	They (you) **have** *seen* that movie.

Note the following about the present perfect:

❏ The present perfect tense is used to express an action that took place at no definite time in the past. This tense is also referred to as the past indefinite.

❏ The helping verb *haber* must be used in Spanish, even though English often omits this auxiliary verb:

　　He pagado la cuenta.　I (have) paid the bill.

Example Problems

It's springtime. Use the present perfect to express what people have done.

1. Yo (abrir) _____ la ventana.

   Answer: he abierto

   To form the present perfect of *abrir*, use the *yo* form of the present tense of the verb *haber* *(he)*. The past participle of the verb *abrir* is irregular and must be memorized: *abierto*.

2. Mi amigo y yo (ver) _____ la salida del sol.

   Answer: hemos visto

   To form the present perfect of *ver*, use the *nosotros* form of the present tense of the verb *haber (hemos)*. The past participle of the verb *ver* is irregular and must be memorized: *visto*.

3. Mi amigo y mi hermano (oír) _____ los pájaros.

   Answer: han oído

   To form the present perfect of *oír*, use the *ellos* form of the present tense of the verb *haber (han)*. Form the past participle of the verb *oír* by dropping the *-ir* ending and adding *-ido*. Because the stem of *oír* ends in a vowel, add an accent mark to the *i*.

Work Problems

Use these problems to give yourself additional practice.

Use the present perfect of the verbs in parentheses to express what people have done to break records.

1. Nosotros (trabajar) _____ veinticuatro horas sin dormir.

2. Ellos (comer) _____ diez tortas en una hora.

3. Tú (asistir) _____ a quince conciertos en una semana.

4. Yo (escribir) _____ mil mensajes por correo electrónico en ocho horas.

5. Vosotros (leer) _____ cien libros en un mes.

Worked Solutions

1. **hemos trabajado**   To form the present perfect of *trabajar*, use the *nosotros* form of the present tense of the verb *haber (hemos)*. Form the past participle of the verb *trabajar* by dropping the *-ar* ending and adding *-ado*.

2. **han comido**   To form the present perfect of *comer*, use the *ellos* form of the present tense of the verb *haber (han)*. Form the past participle of the verb *comer* by dropping the *-er* ending and adding *-ido*.

3. **has asistido**   To form the present perfect of *asistir*, use the *tú* form of the present tense of the verb *haber (has)*. Form the past participle of the verb *asistir* by dropping the *-ir* ending and adding *-ido*.

4. **he escrito**   To form the present perfect of *escribir*, use the *yo* form of the present tense of the verb *haber (he)*. The past participle of the verb *escribir* is irregular and must be memorized: *escrito*.

5. **habéis leído**   To form the present perfect of *leer*, use the *vosotros* form of the present tense of the verb *haber (habéis)*. Form the past participle of the verb *leer* by dropping the *-er* ending and adding *-ido*. Because the stem of *leer* ends in a vowel, add an accent mark to the *i*.

The Preterit Perfect and the Pluperfect Tenses

The preterit perfect tense expresses what "had happened." The preterit perfect tense is formed by taking the preterit tense of the auxiliary (helping) verb *haber* and adding the past participle of the action performed:

Preterit Tense of Haber	Sample Past Participle	Meaning
Yo **hube**	descansado.	I **had** *rested.*
Tú **hubiste**	comido.	You **had** *eaten.*
Él (ella, Ud.) **hubo**	sufrido.	He (she, you) **had** *suffered.*
Nosotros **hubimos**	abierto la puerta.	We **had** *opened* the door.
Vosotros **hubiseis**	resuelto el problema.	You **had** *solved* the problem.
Ellos (ellas, Uds.) **hubieron**	visto esa película.	They (you) **had** *seen* that movie.

Note the following about the use of the preterit perfect:

❑ The preterit perfect is used mainly in literary and historic writings to show that the action or event had just ended:

>   En cuanto hubimos llegado empezó a nevar. As soon as we had arrived it started to snow.

❑ The preterit perfect generally follows expressions such as:

cuando	when
apenas	hardly, scarcely
después (de) que	after
luego que	as soon as
en cuanto	as soon as
así que	as soon as
tan pronto como	as soon as

For example:

>   Tan pronto como ella se hubo dormido, el teléfono sonó.

>   As soon as she had fallen asleep, the phone rang.

❏ In conversation and informal writing, the preterit perfect is replaced by the pluperfect or the preterit tense:

> Tan pronto como se había dormido (se durmió), el teléfono sonó.

> As soon as she had fallen asleep, the phone rang.

The pluperfect tense expresses what "had happened." The pluperfect tense is formed by taking the imperfect tense of the auxiliary (helping) verb *haber* and adding the past participle of the action performed:

Imperfect Tense of Haber	Sample Past Participle	Meaning
Yo **había**	descansado.	I **had** rested.
Tú **habías**	comido.	You **had** eaten.
Él (ella, Ud.) **había**	sufrido.	He (she, you) **had** suffered.
Nosotros **habíamos**	abierto la puerta.	We **had** opened the door.
Vosotros **habíais**	resuelto el problema.	You **had** solved the problem.
Ellos (ellas, Uds.) **habían**	visto esa película.	They (you) **had** seen that movie.

Note the following about the use of the pluperfect:

❏ The pluperfect describes an action or event that was completed in the past before another action took place and is usually expressed by the English "had" + past participle. It is a tense that is chronologically further in the past than the preterit, as demonstrated in this timeline:

> ←   pluperfect   preterit   present perfect   present   →

> For example:

> Ellos habían vivido aquí antes.

> They had lived here before.

❏ Because the pluperfect is used in relation to another past action, that action is usually in the preterit or imperfect:

> Los alumnos ya se habían levantado cuando sonó el timbre.

> The students had already gotten up when the bell rang.

❏ When the pluperfect is used, it is not always necessary to have the other past action expressed:

> Él había dejado sus llaves en su abrigo.

> He had left his keys in his coat.

Example Problems

Use the pluperfect form of the appropriate verb from the list below to express what had happened to these people.

> descubrir
> oír
> recibir

1. Guillermo estaba orgulloso porque _____ un aumento de salario.

   Answer: había recibido

   To form the pluperfect of *recibir*, use the *él* form of the imperfect tense of the verb *haber* (*había*). Form the past participle of the verb *recibir* by dropping the *-ir* ending and adding *-ido*.

2. Yo sonreí porque _____ buenas noticias en la radio.

   Answer: había oído

   To form the pluperfect of *oír*, use the *yo* form of the imperfect tense of the verb *haber* (*había*). Form the past participle of the verb *oír* by dropping the *-ir* ending and adding *-ido*. Because the stem of *oír* ends in a vowel, add an accent mark to the *i*.

3. Tú estabas alegre porque _____ un billete de veinte dólares en la calle.

   Answer: habías descubierto

   To form the pluperfect of *oír*, use the *tú* form of the imperfect tense of the verb *haber* (*habías*). The past participle of the verb *descubrir* is irregular and must be memorized: *descubierto*.

Work Problems

Use these problems to give yourself additional practice.

Use the pluperfect form of the appropriate verb from the list below to express what had happened to these people.

devolver	morir
escribir	poner
hacer	romper

1. Tú te enfermaste porque tú no te _____ tu sombrero y tu bufanda.

2. Un niño gritaba porque sus amigos _____ su juguete.

3. Mi novio estaba muy contento porque yo le _____ una carta de amor.

4. Nosotros lloramos porque nuestro abuelo _____.

5. El profesor nos castigó porque nosotros no _____ nuestras tareas.

6. Ella se enojó porque vosotros no le _____ su dinero.

Worked Solutions

See above.

1. **habías puesto** To form the pluperfect of *poner*, use the *tú* form of the imperfect tense of the verb *haber* (*habías*). The past participle of the verb *poner* is irregular and must be

memorized: *puesto*. The *-se* attached to the infinitive indicates that the verb is reflexive. Place the reflexive pronoun *te*, which agrees with the subject, before the conjugated form of *haber*.

2. **habían roto**   To form the pluperfect of *romper*, use the *ellos* form of the imperfect tense of the verb *haber (habían)*. The past participle of the verb *romper* is irregular and must be memorized: *roto*.

3. **había escrito**·   To form the pluperfect of *escribir*, use the *yo* form of the imperfect tense of the verb *haber (había)*. The past participle of the verb *escribir* is irregular and must be memorized: *escrito*.

4. **había muerto**   To form the pluperfect of *morir*, use the *él* form of the imperfect tense of the verb *haber (había)*. The past participle of the verb *morir* is irregular and must be memorized: *muerto*.

5. **habíamos hecho**   To form the pluperfect of *hacer*, use the *nosotros* form of the imperfect tense of the verb *haber (habíamos)*. The past participle of the verb *hacer* is irregular and must be memorized: *hecho*.

6. **habíais devuelto**   To form the pluperfect of *poner*, use the *vosotros* form of the imperfect tense of the verb *haber (habíais)*. The past participle of the verb *devolver* is irregular and must be memorized: *devuelto*.

The Future Perfect Tense

The future perfect tense expresses what "will have happened." The future-perfect tense is formed by taking the future tense of the auxiliary (helping) verb *haber* and adding the past participle of the action performed. It is a tense that is chronologically closer to the present than the future:

←   present   immediate future   future perfect   future   →

Future Tense of Haber	Sample Past Participle	Meaning
Yo no **habré**	descansado suficientemente.	I **will** not **have** *rested* enough.
Tú **habrás**	comido demasiado.	You **will have** *eaten* too much.
Él (ella, Ud.) **habrá**	sufrido.	He (she, you) **will have** *suffered*.
Nosotros **habremos**	abierto la puerta primero.	We **will have** *opened* the door first.
Vosotros **habréis**	resuelto el problema.	You **will have** *solved* the problem.
Ellos (ellas, Uds.) **habrán**	visto esa película dos veces.	They (you) **will have** *seen* that movie twice.

Note the following about the future perfect tense:

❑ The future perfect expresses an action or event that will have taken place or will have been completed in the future before another action will take place. The adverb *ya* (already) is a clue indicating the use of the future perfect:

Para las cinco ya habré terminado de trabajar y podré salir contigo.

I will have already finished working by five o'clock and I'll be able to go out with you.

❑ The future perfect may be used to express probability or conjecture in the past:

¿Quién se habrá comido todas las galletitas?

Who could have eaten all the cookies?

I wonder who ate all the cookies?

Example Problems

Use the future perfect form of the verb in parentheses to express what will have happened before eight o'clock in the evening.

1. (pagar) Yo _____ todas mis cuentas.

Answer: habré pagado

To form the future perfect of *pagar*, use the *yo* form of the future tense of the verb *haber* (*habré*). Form the past participle of the verb *pagar* by dropping the *-ar* ending and adding *-ado*.

2. (comer) Nosotros _____.

Answer: habremos comido

To form the future perfect of *comer*, use the *nosotros* form of the future tense of the verb *haber* (*habremos*). Form the past participle of the verb *comer* by dropping the *-er* ending and adding *-ido*.

3. (subir) Ellos _____ a su cuarto.

Answer: habrán subido

To form the future perfect of *subir*, use the *ellos* form of the future tense of the verb *haber* (*habrán*). Form the past participle of the verb *subir* by dropping the *-ir* ending and adding *-ido*.

Work Problems

Use these problems to give yourself additional practice.

Use the future perfect of the verb in parentheses to express what will have happened before the end of the summer.

1. (aprender) Nosotros _____ a conducir un coche.

2. (ir) Yo _____ a América del Sur.

3. (recibir) Ud. _____ su bachillerato.

4. (dejar) Ellos _____ de fumar.

5. (crecer) Vosotros _____ cinco centímetros.

6. (cumplir) Tú _____ los veintiún años.

Worked Solutions

1. **habremos aprendido**   To form the future perfect of *comer*, use the *nosotros* form of the future tense of the verb *haber (habremos)*. Form the past participle of the verb *aprender* by dropping the *-er* ending and adding *-ido*.

2. **habré ido**   To form the future perfect of *ir*, use the *yo* form of the future tense of the verb *haber (habré)*. The past participle of the verb *ir* is *ido*.

3. **habrá recibido**   To form the future perfect of *comer*, use the *Ud.* form of the future tense of the verb *haber (habrá)*. Form the past participle of the verb *recibir* by dropping the *-er* ending and adding *-ido*.

4. **habrán dejado**   To form the future perfect of *dejar*, use the *ellos* form of the future tense of the verb *haber (habrán)*. Form the past participle of the verb *dejar* by dropping the *-ar* ending and adding *-ado*.

5. **habréis crecido**   To form the future perfect of *crecer*, use the *vosotros* form of the future tense of the verb *haber (habréis)*. Form the past participle of the verb *crecer* by dropping the *-er* ending and adding *-ido*.

6. **habrás cumplido**   To form the future perfect of *cumplir*, use the *tú* form of the future tense of the verb *haber (habrás)*. Form the past participle of the verb *cumplir* by dropping the *-ir* ending and adding *-ido*.

The Conditional Perfect

The conditional perfect expresses what "would have happened." The conditional perfect is formed by taking the conditional tense of the auxiliary (helping) verb *haber* and adding the past participle of the action performed:

Present Tense of Haber	Sample Past Participle	Meaning
Yo no **habría**	descansado suficientemente.	I **would** not **have** *rested* enough.
Tú **habrías**	comido demasiado.	You **would have** *eaten* too much.
Él (ella, Ud.) **habría**	sufrido.	He (she, you) **would have** *suffered*.
Nosotros **habríamos**	abierto la puerta primero.	We **would have** *opened* the door first.
Vosotros **habríais**	resuelto el problema.	You **would have** *solved* the problem.
Ellos (ellas, Uds.) **habrían**	visto esa película.	They (you) **would have** *seen* that movie.

Note the following about the conditional perfect tense:

❑ The conditional perfect expresses an action or event that would have taken place or would have been completed in the past:

  Yo les habría dado todo.

  I would have given them everything.

❑ The conditional perfect may be used to express probability or conjecture in the past:

  ¿Quién le habría mandado este paquete?

  I wonder who sent him this package?

  Who could have sent him this package?

Example Problems

Use the conditional perfect to express what people would have done had they had the time.

1. tú/ir al centro

   Answer: Tú habrías ido al centro.

   To form the conditional perfect of *ir*, use the *tú* form of the conditional tense of the verb *haber (habrías)*. The past participle of the verb *ir* is *ido*.

2. él/jugar al golf

   Answer: Él habría jugado al golf.

   To form the conditional perfect of *jugar*, use the *él* form of the conditional tense of the verb *haber (habría)*. Form the past participle of the verb *jugar* by dropping the *-ar* ending and adding *-ado*.

3. nosotros/leer una novela

   Answer: Nosotros habríamos leído una novela.

   To form the conditional perfect of *leer*, use the *nosotros* form of the conditional tense of the verb *haber (habríamos)*. Form the past participle of the verb *leer* by dropping the *-er* ending and adding *-ido*. Because the stem of *leer* ends in a vowel, add an accent mark to the *i*.

Work Problems

Use these problems to give yourself additional practice.

Use the conditional perfect to express what people would have done had they had the opportunity.

1. yo/recorrer todo el mundo

2. ella/partir para un safari en África

3. tú/aprender muchas lenguas extranjeras

4. vosotros/estudiar fotografía

5. él/pilotar un helicóptero

6. nosotros/hacer un viaje por el espacio

Worked Solutions

1. **Yo habría recorrido todo el mundo.** To form the conditional perfect of *recorrer*, use the *yo* form of the conditional tense of the verb *haber (habría)*. Form the past participle of the verb *correr* by dropping the *-er* ending and adding *-ido*.

2. **Ella habría partido para un safari en África.**   To form the conditional perfect of *partir*, use the *ella* form of the conditional tense of the verb *haber (habría)*. Form the past participle of the verb *partir* by dropping the *-ir* ending and adding *-ido*.

3. **Tú habrías aprendido muchas lenguas extranjeras.**   To form the conditional perfect of *aprender*, use the *tú* form of the conditional tense of the verb *haber (habrías)*. Form the past participle of the verb *aprender* by dropping the *-er* ending and adding *-ido*.

4. **Vosotros habríais estudiado fotografía.**   To form the conditional perfect of *estudiar*, use the *vosotros* form of the conditional tense of the verb *haber (habríais)*. Form the past participle of the verb *estudiar* by dropping the *-ar* ending and adding *-ado*.

5. **Él habría pilotado un helicóptero.**   To form the conditional perfect of *pilotar*, use the *él* form of the conditional tense of the verb *haber (habría)*. Form the past participle of the verb *pilotar* by dropping the *-ar* ending and adding *-ado*.

6. **Nosotros habríamos hecho un viaje por el espacio.**   To form the conditional perfect of *hacer*, use the *nosotros* form of the conditional tense of the verb *haber (habríamos)*. The past participle of the verb *hacer* is irregular and must be memorized: *hecho*.

The Present Perfect (Past) Subjunctive

The present perfect subjunctive expresses what "may have happened." The present perfect subjunctive is formed by taking the present subjunctive form of the auxiliary (helping) verb *haber* and adding the past participle of the action performed. See Chapter 14 for a full discussion.

The Pluperfect Subjunctive

The pluperfect subjunctive expresses what "might have happened." The pluperfect subjunctive is formed by taking the imperfect subjunctive form of the auxiliary (helping) verb *haber* and adding the past participle of the action performed. See Chapter 15 for a full discussion.

Other Uses of the Past Participle

Past participles may also be used in the following ways:

❑ As adjectives that agree in number and gender with the nouns they modify:

Buscamos una piscina cubierta. We are looking for an indoor pool.

❑ With *estar* to express a condition that is the result of an action:

Las ventanas están abiertas. The windows are open.

❑ With *ser* (see Chapter 18) to express the passive voice:

El coche fue reparado por mi padre. The car was repaired by my father.

❑ To form a noun from a verb:

Infinitive	*Meaning*	*Noun*	*Meaning*
comer	to eat	la comida	the meal
correr	to run	la corrida	the running (of bulls)
entrar	to enter	la entrada	the entrance

(continued)

Infinitive	Meaning	Noun	Meaning
ir	to go	la ida	the one-way trip
llegar	to arrive	la llegada	the arrival
mirar	to look at	la mirada	the look
salir	to go out	la salida	the exit
volver	to return	la vuelta	the return trip

For example:

La comida es deliciosa. The meal is delicious.

Example Problems

Describe the scene.

1. The table is set.

   Answer: La mesa está puesta.

   A past participle may be used with *estar* to express a condition that is the result of an action. Use *la mesa* to express "the table." The third person singular form of *estar* is irregular. Drop the *-ar* ending and add *-á*. The verb *poner* is used idiomatically to express "to set" the table. The past participle of the verb *poner* is irregular and must be memorized. Used as an adjective, the past participle must agree in number and gender with the feminine singular noun it is describing: *puesta*.

2. Lunch is prepared.

   Answer: El almuerzo está preparado.

   A past participle may be used with *estar* to express a condition that is the result of an action. Use *el almuerzo* to express "lunch." The masculine singular definite article must be used before a noun used in a general sense. The third person singular form of *estar* is irregular. Drop the *-ar* ending and add *-á*. Form the past participle of the verb *preparar* by dropping the *-ar* ending and adding *-ado*. Used as an adjective, the past participle must agree in number and gender with the masculine singular noun it is describing: *preparado*.

3. The children are seated in order to eat.

   Answer: Los niños están sentados para comer.

   A past participle may be used with *estar* to express a condition that is the result of an action. Use *los niños* to express "the children." The third person plural form of *estar* is irregular. Drop the *-ar* ending and add *-án*. Form the past participle of the verb *sentar* by dropping the *-ar* ending and adding *-ado*. Used as an adjective, the past participle must agree in number and gender with the masculine plural noun it is describing: *sentados*. Use the preposition *para* to express purpose: "in order to." The preposition is followed by the infinitive: *comer* (to eat).

Work Problems

Use these problems to give yourself additional practice.

Describe the room.

1. The bed is made.

2. The door is shut.

3. The windows are open.

4. The dresses are hung in the closet.

5. The television is turned off.

6. The light is turned on.

Worked Solutions

1. **La cama está hecha.**   A past participle may be used with *estar* to express a condition that is the result of an action. Use *la cama* to express "the bed." The third person singular form of *estar* is irregular. Drop the *-ar* ending and add *-á*. The past participle of the verb *hacer* is irregular and must be memorized. Used as an adjective, the past participle must agree in number and gender with the feminine singular noun it is describing: *hecha*.

2. **La puerta está cerrada.**   Use *la puerta* to express "the door." The third person singular form of *estar* is irregular. Drop the *-ar* ending and add *-á*. Form the past participle of the verb *cerrar* by dropping the *-ar* ending and adding *-ado*. Used as an adjective, the past participle must agree in number and gender with the feminine singular noun it is describing: *cerrada*.

3. **Las ventanas están abiertas.**   Use *las ventanas* to express "the windows." The third person plural form of *estar* is irregular. Drop the *-ar* ending and add *-án*. The past participle of the verb *abrir* is irregular and must be memorized. Used as an adjective, the past participle must agree in number and gender with the feminine plural noun it is describing: *abiertas*.

4. **Los vestidos están colgados en el ropero.**   A past participle may be used with *estar* to express a condition that is the result of an action. Use *los vestidos* to express "the dresses." The third person plural form of *estar* is irregular. Drop the *-ar* ending and add *-án*. Form the past participle of the verb *colgar* (to hang) by dropping the *-ar* ending and adding *-ado*. Used as an adjective, the past participle must agree in number and gender with the masculine plural noun it is describing: *colgados*. Use the preposition *en* to express purpose: "in." Use *el ropero* to express "the closet."

5. **El televisor está apagado.**   Use *el televisor* to express "the television set." The third person singular form of *estar* is irregular. Drop the *-ar* ending and add *-á*. Form the past participle of the verb *apagar* (to turn off) by dropping the *-ar* ending and adding *-ado*. Used as an adjective, the past participle must agree in number and gender with the masculine singular noun it is describing: *apagado*.

6. **La luz está encendida.**   Use *la luz* to express "the light." The third person singular form of *estar* is irregular. Drop the *-ar* ending and add *-á*. Form the past participle of the verb *encender* (to turn on) by dropping the *-er* ending and adding *-ido*. Used as an adjective,

the past participle must agree in number and gender with the feminine singular noun it is describing: *encendida*.

Verbs with Two Past Participles

Some verbs have one participle that is used with compound tenses and another that is used as an adjective:

Infinitive	Participle for Compound Tenses	Meaning	Participle Used as an Adjective	Meaning
completar	completado	completed	completo	complete
confesar	confesado	confessed	confeso	confessed
confundir	confundido	confused	confuso	confused
convencer	convencido	convinced	convicto	convinced
corromper	corrompido	corrupted	corrupto	corrupt
descalzar	descalzado	barefoot	descalzo	barefoot
despertar	despertado	awakened	despierto	awake
difundir	difundido	spread	disfuso	diffused
elegir	elegido	elected	electo	elected
expresar	expresado	expressed	expreso	express
extender	extendido	extended	extenso	extensive
limpiar	limpiado	cleaned	limpio	clean
llenar	llenado	filled	lleno	full
secar	secado	dried	seco	dry
suspender	suspendido	suspended	suspenso	suspended
sustituir	sustituido	substituted	sustituto	substituted
vaciar	vaciado	emptied	vacío	empty

For example:

He limpiado la casa.   I cleaned the house.
Tengo una casa limpia.   I have a clean house.

Example Problems

Use the correct form of the present perfect or the adjective to complete each thought.

1. (elegir) Los votantes _____ al presidente. Es el presidente _____.

   Answer: han elegido, electo

   Use the present perfect to express that the voters have elected the president. To form the present perfect of *elegir*, use the *ellos* form of the present tense of the verb *haber (han)*.

Form the past participle of the verb *elegir* by dropping the *-ir* ending and adding *-ido*. To express that the president is elected, use the past participle as an adjective (which must agree with the masculine singular noun *presidente*): *electo*.

2. (confundir) Estoy un poco _____. La situación me _____.

Answer: confuso (-a), ha confundido

To express that you are a little confused, use the past participle as an adjective (which must agree with the singular pronoun *yo*): *confuso (-a)*. Use the present perfect to express that the situation has confused you. To form the present perfect of *confundir*, use the third person singular form of the present tense of the verb *haber (ha)*. Form the past participle of the verb *confundir* by dropping the *-ir* ending and adding *-ido*.

3. (difundir) La noticia está _____ porque ellos la _____.

Answer: difusa, han difundido

To express that the news is spread, use the past participle as an adjective (which must agree with the feminine singular noun *noticia*): *difusa*. Use the present perfect to express that the news has been spread. To form the present perfect of *difundir*, use the third person plural form of the present tense of the verb *haber (han)*. Form the past participle of the verb *difundir* by dropping the *-ir* ending and adding *-ido*.

Work Problems

Use these problems to give yourself additional practice.

Use the correct form of the present perfect or the adjective to complete each thought.

1. (limpiar) La casa está _____ porque tú la _____.

2. (llenar) Yo _____ las tazas de café y ahora ellas están _____.

3. (despertar) Los niños están _____ porque él los _____.

4. (secar) Ellos _____ los platos y ahora los platos están _____.

5. (extender) Él _____ el mantel y ahora el mantel está _____.

6. (completar) El trabajo está _____, porque nosotros lo _____.

Worked Solutions

1. **limpia, has limpiado** To express that the house is clean, use the past participle as an adjective (which must agree with the feminine singular noun *casa*): *limpia*. Use the present perfect to express that you have cleaned the house. To form the present perfect of *limpiar*, use the second person singular form of the present tense of the verb *haber (has)*. Form the past participle of the verb *limpiar* by dropping the *-ar* ending and adding *-ado*.

2. **he llenado, llenas** Use the present perfect to express that you have filled the glasses. To form the present perfect of *llenar*, use the first person singular form of the present tense of the verb *haber (he)*. Form the past participle of the verb *llenar* by dropping the *-ar*

ending and adding *-ado*. To express that the glasses are full, use the past participle as an adjective (which must agree with the feminine plural noun *tazas*): *llenas*.

3. **despiertos, ha despertado**	To express that the children are awake, use the past participle as an adjective (which must agree with the masculine plural noun *niños*): *despiertos*. Use the present perfect to express that he "has awakened" them. To form the present perfect of *despertar*, use the third person singular form of the present tense of the verb *haber (ha)*. Form the past participle of the verb *despertar* by dropping the *-ar* ending and adding *-ado*.

4. **han secado, secos**	Use the present perfect to express that they have dried the plates. To form the present perfect of *secar*, use the third person plural form of the present tense of the verb *haber (han)*. Form the past participle of the verb *secar* by dropping the *-ar* ending and adding *-ado*. To express that the plates are dry, use the past participle as an adjective (which must agree with the masculine plural noun *platos*): *secos*.

5. **ha extendido, extenso**	Use the present perfect to express that he "has spread out" the tablecloth. To form the present perfect of *extender*, use the third person singular form of the present tense of the verb *haber (ha)*. Form the past participle of the verb *extender* by dropping the *-er* ending and adding *-ido*. To express that the tablecloth is spread, use the past participle as an adjective (which must agree with the masculine singular noun *mantel*): *extenso*.

6. **completo, hemos completado**	To express that work is complete, use the past participle as an adjective (which must agree with the masculine singular noun *trabajo*): *completo*. Use the present perfect to express that we "have completed" it. To form the present perfect of *completar*, use the first person plural form of the present tense of the verb *haber (hemos)*. Form the past participle of the verb *completar* by dropping the *-ar* ending and adding *-ado*.

The Perfect Participle

The perfect participle shows that one action occurred before another. To form the perfect participle, take the gerund of *haber* and add the past participle:

Habiendo entrado en el cuarto, encendió la luz. Having entered the room, he turned on the light.

Example Problems

Use the perfect participle of the verb in parentheses to express what happened.

1. (Beber) _____ el refresco, lavó el vaso.

	Answer: Habiendo bebido

	To form the perfect participle, use the gerund of *haber*. To form the gerund of *haber*, drop the *-er* ending and add *-iendo*. Form the past participle of the verb *beber* by dropping the *-er* ending and adding *-ido*.

2. (Entrar) _____, cerró las ventanas.

Answer: Habiendo entrado

To form the perfect participle, use the gerund of *haber*. To form the gerund of *haber*, drop the -*er* ending and add -*iendo*. Form the past participle of the verb *entrar* by dropping the -*ar* ending and adding -*ado*.

3. (Apagar) _____ la luz, se acostó.

Answer: Habiendo apagado

To form the perfect participle, use the gerund of *haber*. To form the gerund of *haber*, drop the -*er* ending and add -*iendo*. Form the past participle of the verb *apagar* by dropping the -*ar* ending and adding -*ado*.

Work Problems

Use these problems to give yourself additional practice.

Use the perfect participle to express what happened.

1. (Volver) _____ a casa, se quitó el abrigo.

2. (Cortar) _____ las legumbres, las puso en la ensalada.

3. (Preparar) _____ la cena, se sentó a comer.

4. (Comer) _____, se sentó a leer el periódico.

5. (Abrir) _____ el correo, pagó sus cuentas.

6. (Terminar) _____ su trabajo, descansó.

Worked Solutions

1. **Habiendo vuelto** To form the perfect participle, use the gerund of *haber*. To form the gerund of *haber*, drop the -*er* ending and add -*iendo*. The past participle of the verb *volver* is irregular and must be memorized: *vuelto*.

2. **Habiendo cortado** To form the perfect participle, use the gerund of *haber*. To form the gerund of *haber*, drop the -*er* ending and add -*iendo*. Form the past participle of the verb *cortar* by dropping the -*ar* ending and adding -*ado*.

3. **Habiendo preparado** To form the perfect participle, use the gerund of *haber*. To form the gerund of *haber*, drop the -*er* ending and add -*iendo*. Form the past participle of the verb *preparar* by dropping the -*ar* ending and adding -*ado*.

4. **Habiendo comido** To form the perfect participle, use the gerund of *haber*. To form the gerund of *haber*, drop the -*er* ending and add -*iendo*. Form the past participle of the verb *comer* by dropping the -*er* ending and adding -*ido*.

5. **Habiendo abierto**   To form the perfect participle, use the gerund of *haber*. To form the gerund of *haber*, drop the *-er* ending and add *-iendo*. The past participle of the verb *abrir* is irregular and must be memorized: *abierto*.

6. **Habiendo terminado**   To form the perfect participle, use the gerund of *haber*. To form the gerund of *haber*, drop the *-er* ending and add *-iendo*. Form the past participle of the verb *terminar* by dropping the *-ar* ending and adding *-ado*.

Chapter Problems

Problems

Use the correct compound tense to express the accomplishments of these people.

1. Yo (have succeeded) _____.

2. Tú (had traveled) _____ por países extranjeros.

3. Ella (will not have read) _____ demasiados libros.

4. Nosotros (would have received) _____ premios.

5. Juan y yo (hadn't seen) _____ muchos monumentos.

6. Ud. (will have memorized) _____ los poemas.

7. Ellos (would have resolved) _____ el problema.

8. Nosotros (have become) _____ famosos.

9. Yo (will have written) _____ muchos libros.

10. Uds. (had studied) _____ arquitectura.

11. Él (hasn't made) _____ malas decisiones.

12. Yo (wouldn't have broken) _____ ningunas promesas.

Use the past participle of the appropriate verb from the list below as an adjective to describe the picnic.

animar	hacer
cubrir	llenar
descalzar	romper
freír	sentar

13. Los niños _____ corren por el parque.

14. Una niña tiene la pierna _____.

15. Un muchacho lleva un suéter _____ a mano.

16. Todo el mundo está muy _____.

17. Los padres están _____ en la hierba.

18. La mesa está _____ con un mantel.

19. Van a comer pollo _____.

20. Los platos están _____ de comida sabrosa.

Answers and Solutions

1. **Answer: he tenido éxito**   "Has" or "have" and a past participle indicates that the present perfect is needed. *Tener éxito* means "to succeed." To form the present perfect of *tener*, use the *yo* form of the present tense of the verb *haber (he)*. Form the past participle of the verb *tener* by dropping the *-er* ending and adding *-ido*.

2. **Answer: habías viajado**   "Had" and a past participle indicates that the pluperfect is needed. *Viajar* means "to travel." To form the pluperfect of *viajar*, use the *tú* form of the imperfect tense of the verb *haber (habías)*. Form the past participle of the verb *viajar* by dropping the *-ar* ending and adding *-ado*.

3. **Answer: no habrá leído**   "Will have" and a past participle indicates that the future perfect is needed. *Leer* means "to read." To form the future perfect of *leer*, use the *ella* form of the future tense of the verb *haber (habrá)*. Form the past participle of the verb *leer* by dropping the *-er* ending and adding *-ido*. Because the stem of *leer* ends in a vowel, add an accent mark to the *i*.

4. **Answer: habríamos recibido**   "Would have" and a past participle indicates that the conditional perfect is needed. *Recibir* means "to receive." To form the conditional perfect of *recibir*, use the *nosotros* form of the conditional tense of the verb *haber (habríamos)*. Form the past participle of the verb *recibir* by dropping the *-ir* ending and adding *-ido*.

5. **Answer: no habíamos visto**   "Had" and a past participle indicates that the pluperfect is needed. *Ver* means "to see." To form the pluperfect of *ver*, use the *nosotros* form of the imperfect tense of the verb *haber (habíamos)*. The past participle of the verb *ver* is irregular and must be memorized: *visto*.

6. **Answer: habrá aprendido de memoria**   "Will have" and a past participle indicates that the future perfect is needed. *Aprender de memoria* means "to memorize." To form the future perfect of *aprender*, use the *Ud.* form of the future tense of the verb *haber (habrá)*. Form the past participle of the verb *aprender* by dropping the *-er* ending and adding *-ido*.

7. **Answer: habrían resuelto**   "Would have" and a past participle indicates that the conditional perfect is needed. *Resolver* means "to solve." To form the conditional perfect of *resolver*, use the *ellos* form of the conditional tense of the verb *haber (habrían)*. The past participle of the verb *resolver* is irregular and must be memorized: *resuelto*.

8. **Answer: nos hemos hecho**   "Has" or "have" and a past participle indicates that the present perfect is needed. *Hacerse* means "to become." To form the present perfect of *hacer*, use the *nosotros* form of the present tense of the verb *haber (hemos)*. The past participle of the verb *hacer* is irregular and must be memorized: *hecho*. The *-se* attached to the infinitive indicates that a reflexive pronoun that agrees with the subject must be used. Place the reflexive pronoun *nos* before the conjugated form of *haber*.

9. **Answer: habré escrito**   "Will have" and a past participle indicates that the future perfect is needed. *Escribir* means "to write." To form the future perfect of *escribir*, use the *yo* form

of the future tense of the verb *haber (habré)*. The past participle of the verb *escribir* is irregular and must be memorized: *escrito*.

10. **Answer: habían estudiado**   "Had" and a past participle indicates that the pluperfect is needed. *Estudiar* means "to study." To form the pluperfect of *estudia*, use the *Uds*. form of the imperfect tense of the verb *haber (habían)*. Form the past participle of the verb *estudiar* by dropping the *-ar* ending and adding *-ado*.

11. **Answer: no ha tomado**   "Has" or "have" and a past participle indicates that the present perfect is needed. *Tomar una decisión* means "to make a decision." To form the present perfect of *tomar*, use the *él* form of the present tense of the verb *haber (ha)*. Form the past participle of the verb *tomar* by dropping the *-ar* ending and adding *-ado*.

12. **Answer: no habría roto**   "Would have" and a past participle indicates that the conditional perfect is needed. *Romper* means "to break." To form the conditional perfect of *romper*, use the *yo* form of the conditional tense of the verb *haber (habría)*. The past participle of the verb *romper* is irregular and must be memorized: *roto*.

13. **Answer: descalzos**   *Descalzar* means "without shoes." To express that the children are barefoot, use the past participle as an adjective (which must agree with the masculine plural noun *niños*): *descalzos*.

14. **Answer: rota**   *Romper* means "to break." To express that the leg is broken, use the past participle as an adjective (which must agree with the feminine singular noun *pierna*): *rota*.

15. **Answer: hecho**   *Hacer* means "to make." To express that the sweater is handmade, use the past participle as an adjective (which must agree with the masculine singular noun *suéter*): *hecho*.

16. **Answer: animado**   *Animar* means "to liven up." To express that everyone is lively, use the past participle as an adjective (which must agree with the masculine singular noun *mundo*): *animado*.

17. **Answer: sentados**   *Sentar* means "to seat." To express that they are seated, use the past participle as an adjective (which must agree with the masculine plural noun *padres*): *sentados*.

18. **Answer: cubierta**   *Cubrir* means "to cover." To express that the table is covered, use the past participle as an adjective (which must agree with the feminine singular noun *mesa*): *cubierta*.

19. **Answer: frito**   *Freír* means "to fry." To express that the chicken is fried, use the past participle as an adjective (which must agree with the masculine singular noun *pollo*): *frito*.

20. **Answer: llenos**   *Llenar* means "to fill." To express that the plates are full, use the past participle as an adjective (which must agree with the masculine plural noun *platos*): *llenos*.

Supplemental Chapter Problems

Problems
Use the correct compound tense to express what these people have done at the office.

1.   Tú (wouldn't have foreseen) _____ el error.

2.   Yo (will not have put) _____ todo en su sitio.

3.   Uds. (had described) _____ la situación perfectamente bien.

4.   Ella (has finished) _____ el proyecto.

5.   Tú (hadn't chosen) _____ la mejor respuesta.

6.   Nosotros (wouldn't have concluded) _____ ese asunto.

7.   Él (will have saved) _____ mil dólares.

8.   Clara y yo (haven't heard) _____ todo.

9.   Ellas (will have communicated) _____ sus ideas al jefe.

10.   Ud. (would have consented) _____ en estudiar.

11.   Nosotros (hadn't understood) _____ sus objeciones.

12.   Yo (haven't explained) _____ las reglas.

Use the past participle of the appropriate verb from the list below as an adjective to describe the concert.

abrir	admirar	conocer
cubrir	entusiasmar	proveer
vaciar	vender	

13.   Todos los billetes están _____. No hay más.

14.   No hay asientos _____.

15.   Todas las puertas están _____.

16.   El público está _____. Grita y aplaude.

17.   La escena está _____ de flores.

18.   Los programas _____ hablan del grupo.

19.   Los músicos son muy famosos, es decir son muy_____ por todo el mundo.

20.   Van a tocar canciones _____ por todos.

Solutions

1.   no habrías previsto (conditional perfect, p. 281, past participles of irregular verbs, p. 272)

2.   no habré puesto (future perfect, p. 279, past participles of irregular verbs, p. 272)

3. habían descrito (the preterit perfect and the pluperfect tenses, p. 276, past participles of irregular verbs, p. 272)

4. ha terminado (present perfect tense, p. 274, past participles of regular verbs, p. 272)

5. no habías escogido (the preterit perfect and the pluperfect tenses, p. 276, past participles of regular verbs, p. 272)

6. no habríamos concluido (conditional perfect, p. 281, past participles of regular verbs, p. 272)

7. habrá ahorrado (future perfect tense, p. 279, past participles of regular verbs, p. 272)

8. no hemos oído (present perfect tense, p. 274, past participles of irregular verbs, p. 272)

9. habrán comunicado (future perfect tense, p. 279, past participles of regular verbs, p. 272)

10. habría consentido (conditional perfect, p. 281, past participles of regular verbs, p. 272)

11. no habíamos comprendido (the preterit perfect and the pluperfect tenses, p. 276, past participles of regular verbs, p. 272)

12. no he explicado (present perfect tense, p. 274, past participles of regular verbs, p. 272)

13. vendidos (past participles of regular verbs, p. 272; other uses of the past participle, p. 283)

14. vacíos (past participles of regular verbs, p. 272; other uses of the past participle, p. 283)

15. abiertas (past participles of irregular verbs, p. 272; other uses of the past participle, p. 283)

16. entusiasmado (past participles of regular verbs, p. 272; other uses of the past participle, p. 283)

17. cubierta (past participles of irregular verbs, p. 272; other uses of the past participle, p. 283)

18. provistos (past participles of irregular verbs, p. 272; other uses of the past participle, p. 283)

19. conocidos (past participles of regular verbs, p. 272; other uses of the past participle, p. 283)

20. admiradas (past participles of regular verbs, p. 272; other uses of the past participle, p. 283)

Chapter 14
The Present and Present Perfect Subjunctive

The Present Subjunctive

The present subjunctive expresses actions or events that take place in the present or the future. The subjunctive mood expresses unreal, hypothetical, or unsubstantiated conditions or situations resulting from doubt, wishes, needs, desires, feelings, emotions, speculation, or supposition.

Forming the Subjunctive

The present subjunctive of regular verbs is formed by dropping the -o from the *yo* form of the present tense and adding the subjunctive endings:

	Present	*Yo*	*Tú*	*Él, Ella, Ud.*	*Nosotros*	*Vosotros*	*Ellos, Ellas, Uds.*
-*ar* Verbs	trabajo	-e	-es	-e	-emos	-éis	-en
-*er* Verbs	corro	-a	-as	-a	-amos	-áis	-an
-*ir* Verbs	abro	-a	-as	-a	-amos	-áis	-an

Here are some examples in sentences:

> Es importante que Ud. trabaje mañana.
> It's important that you work tomorrow.
> Es posible que los alumnos no comprendan la lección.
> It's possible that the students don't understand the lesson.
> El jefe quiere que yo asista a esa conferencia.
> The boss wants me to attend that conference.

Example Problems

Use the subjunctive to express the advice being given to and by older people.

Es importante que . . .

1. (escuchar) tú _____ los consejos de tu médico.

   Answer: escuches

   To conjugate regular -*ar* verbs in the present subjunctive, drop the -*ar* ending and add -*es* as the ending for *tú*.

2. (correr) ellas no _____ muy rápidamente.

   Answer: corran

   To conjugate regular -*er* verbs in the present subjunctive, drop the -*er* ending and add -*an* as the ending for *ellas*.

3. (escribir) yo _____ mi testamento.

   Answer: escriba

   To conjugate regular -*ir* verbs in the present subjunctive, drop the -*ir* ending and add -*a* as the ending for *yo*.

Work Problems

Use these problems to give yourself additional practice.

Use the subjunctive to continue to express advice being given to and by older people.

Es importante que . . .

1. (esconderse) él no_____ en su casa.

2. (pretender) nosotros siempre _____ ser jóvenes.

3. (resistirse) ellos _____ a sentirse viejos.

4. (aguardar) tú _____ la calma.

5. (temer) vosotros no _____ la muerte.

6. (telefonear) yo _____ a mi familia a menudo.

Worked Solutions

1. **se esconda**   To conjugate regular -*er* verbs in the present subjunctive, drop the -*er* ending and add -*a* the ending for *él*. Additionally, the -*se* ending indicates that the verb *esconderse* is reflexive. Place the reflexive pronoun *se*, which agrees with the subject, before the conjugated verb.

2. **pretendamos**   To conjugate regular -*er* verbs in the present subjunctive, drop the -*er* ending and add -*amos* as the ending for *nosotros*.

3. **se resistan** To conjugate regular *-ir* verbs in the present subjunctive, drop the *-ir* ending and add *-an* as the ending for *ellos*. Additionally, the *-se* ending indicates that the verb *resistirse* is reflexive. Place the reflexive pronoun *se*, which agrees with the subject, before the conjugated verb.

4. **aguardes** To conjugate regular *-ar* verbs in the present subjunctive, drop the *-ar* ending and add *-es* as the ending for *tú*.

5. **temáis** To conjugate regular *-er* verbs in the present subjunctive, drop the *-er* ending and add *-ais* as the ending for *vosotros*.

6. **telefonee** To conjugate regular *-ar* verbs in the present subjunctive, drop the *-ar* ending and add *-e* as the ending for *yo*.

Irregular in the Present Tense *Yo* Form Verbs

Some verbs that are irregular in the *yo* form of the present tense form the subjunctive in the same manner as regular verbs: Drop the final *-o* from the irregular *yo* form and add the appropriate subjunctive ending:

Infinitive	Meaning	Subjunctive Stem
caber	to fit	quep̶e̶
caer	to fall	caig̶e̶
decir	to say, to tell	dig̶e̶
hacer	to make	hag̶e̶
incluir	to include	incluy̶e̶
oír	to hear	oig̶e̶
poner	to put	pong̶e̶
salir	to go out	salg̶e̶
tener	to have	teng̶e̶
valer	to be worth	valg̶e̶
venir	to come	veng̶e̶
ver	to see	ve̶e̶

Example Problems

Use the present subjunctive to express what the teacher tells the students it is necessary for them to do.

Es necesario que Uds. . . .

1. no salir de la clase sin permiso

   Answer: Es necesario que Uds. no salgan de la clase sin permiso.

   Salir is a verb that is irregular in its present tense *yo* form. To form the subjunctive, take the *yo* form *(salgo)*, drop the *-o*, and add *-an* as the ending for *Uds.*

2. tener cuidado en clase

   Answer: Es necesario que Uds. tengan cuidado en clase.

   Tener is a verb that is irregular in its present tense *yo* form. To form the subjunctive, take the *yo* form *(tengo)*, drop the *-o*, and add *-an* as the ending for *Uds.*

3. contribuir a la clase

   Answer: Es necesario que Uds. contribuyan a la clase.

   Contribuir is a verb that is irregular in its present tense *yo* form. To form the subjunctive, take the *yo* form *(contribuyo)*, drop the *-o*, and add *-an* as the ending for *Uds.*

Work Problems

Use these problems to give yourself additional practice.

Use the present subjunctive to express what the teacher tells the students it is necessary for them to do.

Es necesario que Uds. . . .

1. no caerse en el patio de recreo

2. caber todos en la clase de arte

3. no decir mentiras

4. ver bien las reglas escritas en la pizarra

5. valer mucho como alumnos

6. hacer todo el trabajo escolar

Worked Solutions

1. **Es necesario que Uds. no se caigan en el patio de recreo.**   *Caer* is a verb that is irregular in its present tense *yo* form. To form the subjunctive, take the *yo* form *(caigo)*, drop the *-o*, and add *-an* as the ending for *Uds.* Additionally, the *-se* ending indicates that the verb *caerse* is reflexive. Place the reflexive pronoun *se*, which agrees with the subject, before the conjugated verb.

2. **Es necesario que Uds. quepan todos en la clase de arte.**   *Caber* is a verb that is irregular in its present tense *yo* form. To form the subjunctive, take the *yo* form *(quepo)*, drop the *-o*, and add *-an* as the ending for *Uds.*

3. **Es necesario que Uds. no digan mentiras.**   *Decir* is a verb that is irregular in its present tense *yo* form. To form the subjunctive, take the *yo* form *(digo)*, drop the *-o*, and add *-an* as the ending for *Uds.*

4. **Es necesario que Uds. vean bien las reglas escritas en la pizarra.**   *Ver* is a verb that is irregular in its present tense *yo* form. To form the subjunctive, take the *yo* form *(veo)*, drop the *-o*, and add *-an* as the ending for *Uds.*

5. **Es necesario que Uds. valgan mucho como alumnos.**   *Valer* is a verb that is irregular in its present tense *yo* form. To form the subjunctive, take the *yo* form *(valgo)*, drop the *-o*, and add *-an* as the ending for *Uds.*

6. **Es necesario que Uds. hagan el trabajo escolar.**   *Hacer* is a verb that is irregular in its present tense *yo* form. To form the subjunctive, take the *yo* form *(hago)*, drop the *-o*, and add *-an* as the ending for *Uds.*

Spelling Changes in the Present Subjunctive

In the present subjunctive, verbs ending in *-car, -gar,* and *-zar* undergo the same change that occurs in the *yo* form of the preterit:

-car verbs: *c → qu*
-gar verbs: *g → gu*
-zar verbs: *z → c*

Infinitive	Meaning	Subjunctive Stem
buscar	to look for	busqué
pagar	to pay	pagué
avanzar	to advance	avancé

Verbs ending in *-cer/-cir, -ger/-gir,* and *-guir* (but not *-uir*) undergo the same change that occurs in the *yo* form of the present:

consonant + *-cer/-cir* verbs: *c → z*
vowel + *-cer/-cir* verbs: *c → zc*
-ger/-gir verbs: *g → j*
-guir verbs: *gu → g*

Infinitive	Meaning	Subjunctive Stem
vencer	to conquer	venzo
esparcir	to spread out	esparzo
conocer	to know	conozco
traducir	to translate	traduzco
coger	to seize	cojo
dirigir	to direct	dirijo
distinguir	to distinguish	distingo

Stem Changes in the Present Subjunctive

The changes that stem-changing *-ar, -er,* and *-ir* verbs undergo in the present subjunctive are often—but not always—the same changes they undergo in the present. Changes in the stem occur in all persons but *nosotros* and *vosotros*.

Verb Type	Stem Change	Subjunctive Stems	
-ar and -er	**e to ie**	**Yo, Tú, Él, Ellos, Ellas, Uds.**	**Nosotros/Vosotros**
pensar (to think)	yo pienso	piens-	pens-
defender (to defend)	yo defiendo	defiend-	defend-
	o to ue	**Yo, Tú, Él, Ellos, Ellas, Uds.**	**Nosotros/Vosotros**
mostrar (to show)	yo muestro	muestr-	mostr-
poder (to be able to)	yo puedo	pued-	pod-
-ir	**e to ie**	**Yo, Tú, Él, Ellos, Ellas, Uds.**	**Nosotros/Vosotros**
mentir (lie)	yo miento	mient-	mint-
	o to ue	**Yo, Tú, Él, Ellos, Ellas, Uds.**	**Nosotros/Vosotros**
morir (to die)	yo muero	muer-	mur-
	e to i	**Yo, Tú, Él, Ellos, Ellas, Uds.**	**Nosotros/Vosotros**
servir (to serve)	yo sirvo	sirv-	sirv-

Accent marks are used in the *-iar* and *-uar* verbs listed below in all forms but *nosotros*:

  enviar (to send)   yo envío   env-   -íe, -íes, -íe, -iemos, -iéis, -íen

Like *enviar*:

  confiar (en)   to rely (on), to confide (in)
  espiar   to spy
  fiarse (de)   to trust
  guiar   to guide
  resfriarse   to catch a cold
  variar   to vary

  continuar (to continue)   yo continúo   contin- **-úe, -úes, -úe**, -uemos, -uéis, **-úen**

Like *continuar*:

  actuar   to act
  graduarse   to graduate

For verbs ending in *-uir* (but not *-guir*), a *y* is inserted after the *u* in all forms of the present subjunctive:

  incluir (to include)   yo incluyo   incluy- -a, -as, -a, -amos, -áis, -an

Example Problems

Express that what a parent tells a babysitter is essential.

Example: tú/llegar temprano
Es esencial que tú llegues temprano.

1. Roberto/no utilizar tijeras

   Answer: Es esencial que Roberto no utilice tijeras.

   Utilizar is a spelling-change verb that is irregular in its preterit tense *yo* form: *z* changes to *c*. To form the subjunctive, take the *yo* form *(utilicé)*, drop the *-é*, and add *-e* as the subjunctive ending for *Roberto (él)*.

2. los niños/no desobedecer

   Answer: Es esencial que los niños no desobedezcan.

   Desobedecer is a spelling-change "vowel + -cer" verb that is irregular in its present tense *yo* form: *c* changes to *zc*. To form the subjunctive, take the *yo* form *(desobedezco)*, drop the *-o*, and add *-an* as the subjunctive ending for *los niños (ellos)*.

3. yo/te pagar bastante dinero

   Answer: Es esencial que yo te pague bastante dinero.

   Pagar is a spelling-change verb that is irregular in its preterit tense *yo* form: *g* changes to *gu*. To form the subjunctive, take the *yo* form *(pagué)*, drop the *-é*, and add *-e* as the subjunctive ending for *yo*.

Work Problems

Use these problems to give yourself additional practice.

Express the other things that the parent tells the babysitter are essential (see the previous example).

1. Eva/no sacar todas sus muñecas

2. tú/no conducir los niños a la tienda

3. Eva/no coger todos los juguetes

4. todos/distinguir entre lo bueno y lo malo

5. los niños/no esparcir sus juguetes por todo el suelo

6. Roberto/no fingir tener hambre

Worked Solutions

1. **Es esencial que Eva no saque todas sus muñecas.** *Sacar* is a spelling-change verb that is irregular in its preterit tense *yo* form: *c* changes to *qu*. To form the subjunctive, take the *yo* form *(saqué)*, drop the *-é*, and add *-e* as the subjunctive ending for *Eva*.

2. **Es esencial que tú no conduzcas los niños a la tienda.**   *Conducir* is a spelling-change "vowel + *-cir*" verb that is irregular in its present tense *yo* form: *c* changes to *zc*. To form the subjunctive, take the *yo* form *(conduzco)*, drop the *-o*, and add *-as* as the subjunctive ending for *tú*.

3. **Es esencial que Eva no coja todos los juguetes.**   *Coger* is a spelling-change *-ger* verb that is irregular in its present tense *yo* form: *g* changes to *j*. To form the subjunctive, take the *yo* form *(cojo)*, drop the *-o*, and add *-a* as the subjunctive ending for *Eva*.

4. **Es esencial que todos distingan entre lo bueno y lo malo.**   *Distinguir* is a spelling-change *-guir* verb that is irregular in its present-tense *yo* form: *gu* changes to *g*. To form the subjunctive, take the *yo* form *(distingo)*, drop the *-o*, and add *-an* as the subjunctive ending for *todos*.

5. **Es esencial que los niños no esparzan sus juguetes por todo el suelo.**   *Esparcir* is a spelling-change "consonant + *-cir*" verb that is irregular in its present tense *yo* form: *c* changes to *z*. To form the subjunctive, take the *yo* form *(esparzo)*, drop the *-o*, and add *-an* as the subjunctive ending for *los niños*.

6. **Es esencial que Roberto no finja tener hambre.**   *Fingir* is a spelling-change *-gir* verb that is irregular in its present tense *yo* form: *g* changes to *j*. To form the subjunctive, take the *yo* form *(finjo)*, drop the *-o*, and add *-a* as the subjunctive ending for *Roberto*.

Irregular Verbs in the Present Subjunctive

Verbs that follow no rules for the formation of the subjunctive must be memorized. The most common irregular verbs are

dar (to give): dé, des, dé, demos, deis, den

estar (to be): esté, estés, esté, estemos, estéis, estén

haber (to have – auxiliary verb): haya, hayas, haya, hayamos, hayáis, hayan

ir (to go): vaya, vayas, vaya, vayamos, vayáis, vayan

saber (to know): sepa, sepas, sepa, sepamos, sepáis, sepan

ser (to be): sea, seas, sea, seamos, seáis, sean

Using the Present Subjunctive

The subjunctive is used if:

❑ The sentence contains two different clauses with two different subjects.

❑ The clauses are joined by *que* (that), which is followed by the subjunctive.

❑ The main clause shows wishing, need, emotion, or doubt, among other things.

A **clause** is a group of words (containing a subject and a verb) that is part of a sentence. An independent, or main, clause can stand by itself as a simple sentence. A dependent, or subordinate, clause cannot stand by itself.

Example Problems

Using the present subjunctive, express what a person must do to prepare for a big exam.

Example: reflejar antes de escribir

Es preciso que Ud. refleje antes de escribir.

1. pensar profundamente

   Answer: Es preciso que Ud. piense profundamente.

   Pensar is a stem-changing *-ar* verb that undergoes the same changes in the present subjunctive as in the present. The stem vowel changes from *e* to *ie* in all forms except *nosotros* and *vosotros*. To form the subjunctive, take the *yo* form *(pienso)*, drop the *-o*, and add *-e* as the ending for *Ud*.

2. saber salir bien en un examen

   Answer: Es preciso que Ud. sepa salir bien en un examen.

   Saber has an irregular subjunctive stem *(sep-)*, which must be memorized. Add *-a* as the subjunctive ending for *Ud*.

3. no estar nervioso

   Answer: Es preciso que Ud. no esté nervioso.

   Estar has irregular subjunctive forms that must be memorized. Add *-é* as the subjunctive ending for *Ud*.

Work Problems

Use these problems to give yourself additional practice.

Using the present subjunctive, express other things a person has to do to prepare for a big exam (see the preceding example).

1. entender todo

2. poder concentrarse en sus estudios

3. no temblar de miedo durante el examen

4. continuar estudiando hasta el día del examen

5. ser inteligente

6. intuir ciertas respuestas

Worked Solutions

1. **Es preciso que Ud. entienda todo.**   *Entender* is a stem-changing verb that has an internal change from *e* to *ie* in the *yo* form of the present. To form the subjunctive, take the *yo* form *(entiendo)*, drop the *-o*, and add *-a* as the subjunctive ending for *Ud*.

2. **Es preciso que Ud. pueda concentrarse en sus estudios.**   *Poder* is a stem-changing verb that has an internal change from *o* to *ue* in the *yo* form of the present. To form the

subjunctive, take the *yo* form *(puedo)*, drop the *-o*, and add *-a* as the subjunctive ending for *Ud*.

3. **Es preciso que Ud. no tiemble de miedo durante el examen.**   *Temblar* is a stem-changing verb that has an internal change from *e* to *ie* in the *yo* form of the present. To form the subjunctive, take the *yo* form *(tiemblo)*, drop the *-o*, and add *-e* as the subjunctive ending for *Ud*.

4. **Es preciso que Ud. continúe estudiando hasta el día del examen.**   *Continuar* is a stem-changing verb that has an accent added to the *u* in the *yo*, *tú*, *él*, and *ellos* forms. To form the subjunctive, take the *yo* form *(continúo)*, drop the *-o*, and add *-e* as the subjunctive ending for *Ud*.

5. **Es preciso que Ud. sea inteligente.**   *Ser* has an irregular subjunctive stem *(se-)*, which must be memorized. Add *-a* as the subjunctive ending for *Ud*.

6. **Es preciso que Ud. intuya ciertas respuestas.**   *Intuir* is a stem-changing verb. A *y* is inserted after the *u* in all forms of the present subjunctive for verbs ending in *-uir*. Add *-a* as the subjunctive ending for *Ud*.

The Subjunctive after Impersonal Expressions

The subjunctive is used after impersonal expressions that show wishing, emotion, need, necessity, uncertainty, possibility, probability, or doubt, among other things. Many impersonal expressions begin with *es* (it is), are followed by an adjective, and then use *que* to express "that" before the independent (main) clause. Others are third person singular verb forms that are followed by *que*.

English	Spanish
it is absurd that	es absurdo que
it is advisable	conviene que
it is amazing that	es asombroso que
it is amusing that	es divertido que
it is bad that	es malo que
it is better that	es mejor que, más vale que
it is curious that	es curioso que
it is difficult that	es difícil que
it is doubtful that	es dudoso que
it is easy that	es fácil que
it is enough that	es suficiente que, basta que
it is essential that	es esencial que
it is fair that	es justo que
it is fitting that	es conveniente que
it is good that	es bueno que
it is imperative that	es imperativo que
it is important that	es importante que, importa que
it is impossible that	es imposible que
it is improbable that	es improbable que
it is incredible that	es increíble que
it is indispensable that	es indispensable que

it is interesting that	es interesante que
it is ironic that	es irónico que
it is natural that	es natural que
it is necessary that	es necesario que, es preciso que, es menester que
it is nice that	es bueno que
it is a pity that	es lástima que
it is possible that	es posible que
it is preferable that	es preferible que
it is probable that	es probable que
it is rare that	es raro que
it is regrettable that	es lamentable que
it seems untrue that	parece mentira que
it is strange that	es extraño que
it is surprising that	es sorprendiente que
it is unfair that	es injusto que
it is urgent that	es urgente que
it is useful that	es útil que

When using the subjunctive in English, people often omit the word "that." In Spanish, however, *que* must always be used to join the two clauses. Here are examples showing how the subjunctive is used in the clause following an impersonal expression. Note that the subjunctive is used with these expressions even when they are negated:

Es posible que ellos vengan mañana.	It is possible (that) they will come tomorrow.
Es dudoso que yo pueda ayudarte.	It is doubtful (that) I will be able to help you.
No es urgente que me telefonees.	It isn't urgent that you call me.

The subjunctive is used after *tal vez* (perhaps) and *quizás* (perhaps) when doubt or uncertainty are implied. When certainty is expressed, the indicative is used:

Tal vez (Quizás) compre ese coche.

Perhaps I'll buy that car.

Si no saliste bien en tus exámenes, tal vez tienes que estudiar más.

If you didn't do well on your tests, perhaps you need to study more.

Certain impersonal expressions show certainty and, therefore, require the indicative:

English	**Spanish**
it is certain, it is sure	es cierto
it is clear	es claro
it is evident	es evidente
it is exact	es exacto
it is obvious	es obvio
it is sure	es seguro
it is true	es verdad
it seems	parece

Es evidente que ella estará contenta.   It is evident that she will be happy.

Es cierto que él sale.   It is certain that he is going out.

In the negative, however, these expressions show doubt or denial and, thus, require the subjunctive:

No es evidente que ella esté contenta.   It is not evident that she will be happy.

No es cierto que él salga.   It isn't certain that he is going out.

Example Problems

Express what a tour guide tells people. Use the correct form of the present subjunctive or the present indicative.

1. (sacar) Es natural que Uds. _____ muchas fotografías.

   Answer: saquen

   The impersonal expression *es natural que* takes the subjunctive to show the probable nature of the act. *Sacar* is a spelling-change verb that is irregular in its preterit tense *yo* form: *c* changes to *qu*. To form the subjunctive, take the *yo* form *(saqué)*, drop the *-é*, and add *-en* as the subjunctive ending for *Uds*.

2. (estar) Es evidente que todo el mundo _____ contento.

   Answer: está

   The expression *es evidente que* takes the indicative because it shows certainty. *Estar* is irregular in the present tense. Drop the *-ar* ending and add *-á* as the ending for *todo el mundo*.

3. (mostrar) Es importante que yo les _____ a todos los monumentos famosos.

   Answer: muestre

   The expression *es importante que* takes the subjunctive because it shows need. *Mostrar* is a stem-changing *-ar* verb that undergoes the same changes in the present subjunctive as in the present. The stem vowel changes from *o* to *-ue* in all forms except *nosotros* and *vosotros*. To form the subjunctive, take the *yo* form *(muestro)*, drop the *-o*, and add *-e* as the ending for *yo*.

Work Problems

Use these problems to give yourself additional practice.

Young people are at a club meeting. Express what they say to each other. Use the correct form of the present subjunctive or the present indicative.

1. (venir) Es posible que Julio _____ con Sergio.

2. (organizar) Es necesario que yo _____ nuestra próxima reunión.

3. (preferir) Es cierto que todos los miembros _____ hablar español.

4. (poder) Es bueno que nosotros _____ hacer una fiesta.

5. (trabajar) Es claro que tú _____ mucho.

6. (buscar) Es útil que nosotros _____ más miembros.

Worked Solutions

1. **venga**   The expression *es posible que* takes the subjunctive because it shows probability. *Venir* is a verb that is irregular in its present tense *yo* form. To form the subjunctive, take the *yo* form *(vengo)*, drop the -*o*, and add -*a* as the third person singular ending.

2. **organice**   The expression *es necesario que* takes the subjunctive because it shows need. *Organizar* is a spelling-change verb that is irregular in its preterit tense *yo* form: *z* changes to *c*. To form the subjunctive, take the *yo* form *(organicé)*, drop the -*é*, and add -*e* as the subjunctive ending for *yo*.

3. **prefieren**   The expression *es cierto que* takes the indicative because it shows certainty. *Preferir* is spelling-change -*ir* verb whose internal *e* changes to *ie* in all forms of the present except *nosotros* and *vosotros*. Drop the -*ir* ending and add -*en* as the third person plural ending.

4. **podamos**   The expression *es bueno que* takes the subjunctive because it shows an opinion and not a certainty. *Poder* is a stem-changing -*er* verb that undergoes the same changes in the present subjunctive as in the present. The stem vowel changes from *o* to *ue* in all forms except *nosotros* and *vosotros*. To form the subjunctive, take the *nosotros* form of the present *(podemos)*, drop the -*emos*, and add -*amos* as the ending for *nosotros*.

5. **trabajas**   The expression *es claro que* takes the indicative because it shows certainty. *Trabajar* is a regular verb in the present tense. Drop the -*ar* ending and add -*as* the ending for *tú*.

6. **busquemos**   The expression *es útil que* takes the subjunctive because it shows opinion and not a certainty. *Buscar* is a spelling-change verb that is irregular in its preterit tense *yo* form: *c* changes to *qu*. To form the subjunctive, take the *yo* form *(busqué)*, drop the -*é*, and add -*emos* as the subjunctive ending for *nosotros*.

The Subjunctive after Verbs of Wishing, Emotion, Need, and Doubt

The subjunctive is used in the dependent clause introduced by *que* when the main clause expresses not only wishing, emotion, need, or doubt, but also other related activities such as advice, command, demand, desire, hope, permission, preference, prohibition, request, suggestion, or wanting, as shown below:

Spanish	English
aconsejar	to advise
alegrarse (de)	to be glad, to be happy
avergonzarse de	to be ashamed of
desear	to desire, to wish, to want
dudar	to doubt

enfadarse	to become angry
enojarse	to become angry
esperar	to hope
exigir	to require, to demand
insistir	to insist
lamentar	to regret
mandar	to command, to order
necesitar	to need
negar	to deny
ojalá que . . .	if only . . .
ordenar	to order
pedir	to ask for, to request
permitir	to permit
preferir	to prefer
prohibir	to forbid
querer	to wish, to want
reclamar	to demand
recomendar	to recommend
requerir	to require
rogar	to beg, to request
sentir	to be sorry, to regret
solicitar	to request
sorprenderse de	to be surprised
sugerir	to suggest
suplicar	to beg, to plead
temer	to fear
tener miedo de	to fear

Here are a couple of examples in sentences:

Quiero que Uds. me acompañen al consultorio del doctor.
I want you to accompany me to the doctor's office.
Yo les pido que me ayuden.
I ask them to help me.
Ojalá que Ud. no pierdan el partido.
I hope you don't lose the match!

Note that when doubt is negated, the indicative is used:

Yo no dudo que él tendrá éxito.   I don't doubt that he will succeed.

When certainty is negated or questioned, the subjunctive is used:

Ella no piensa que él sea serio.   She doesn't think that he is serious.
¿No crees que ellos no vengan?   Don't you believe that they aren't coming?

Using the Subjunctive after Certain Adjectives Showing Emotion

When one clause of a sentence contains *estar* followed by an adjective expressing feelings or emotions + *de que,* the subjunctive is used in the second clause. These adjectives include

alegre	happy
asombrado (-a)	astonished, surprised
asustado (-a)	afraid
avergonzado (-a)	embarrassed, ashamed
contento (-a)	happy
encantado (-a)	delighted
enfadado (-a)	displeased
enojado (-a)	angry
fastidiado (-a)	bothered
feliz	happy
furioso (-a)	furious
infeliz	unhappy
irritado (-a)	irritated
lisonjeado (-a)	flattered
orgulloso (-a)	proud
triste	sad

Here are a couple of examples in sentences:

Sus padres están contentos de que ella estudie el español.

Her parents are happy that she is studying Spanish.

Estoy alegre de que tú vayas a la corrida de toros conmigo.

I'm happy that you are going to the bullfight with me.

Example Problems

Express what a person says to a roommate after work. Use the correct form of the present subjunctive or the present indicative.

1. (venir) Me alegro de que nuestros amigos no _____ esta noche.

   Answer: vengan

   The subjunctive is used after a verb showing emotion. *Venir* is a verb that is irregular in its present tense *yo* form. To form the subjunctive, take the *yo* form *(vengo)*, drop the *-o,* and add *-an* as the third person plural ending.

2. (poder) Estoy contento de que Juan y tú_____ ayudarme.

   Answer: puedan

   The subjunctive is used after an adjective showing emotion. *Poder* is a stem-changing verb that has an internal change from *o* to *ue* in the *yo* form of the present. To form the subjunctive, take the *yo* form *(puedo)*, drop the *-o*, and add *-an* as the subjunctive ending for *Uds. (Juan y tú)*.

3. (estar) No dudo que tú _____ cansado también.

Answer: estás

The indicative is used when there is no doubt. *Estar* is irregular in the present tense. Drop the *-ar* ending and add *-as* as the ending for *tú*.

Work Problems

Use these problems to give yourself additional practice.

Express what people say about the accomplishments of others. Use the correct form of the present subjunctive or the present indicative.

1. (recibir) Estamos asombrados de que ella _____ tanto dinero como premio.

2. (ser) Pienso que tú _____ famoso.

3. (tener) Está contento de que su hijo _____ éxito en sus negocios.

4. (merecer) No creen que ella _____ este premio.

5. (mostrar) Quiero que Ud. me _____ sus medallas.

6. (estar) Ojalá que Uds. _____ orgullosos de sus logros.

Worked Solutions

1. **reciba** The subjunctive is used after adjectives showing emotion. To conjugate regular *-ir* verbs in the present subjunctive, drop the *-ir* ending and add *-a* as the ending for *yo*.

2. **eres** The indicative is used when the verb pensar is used affirmatively, because this construction is construed as showing that there is certainty in the mind of the speaker. The irregular present tense of the verb *ser* must be memorized. Use *eres* for the *tú* form of the verb.

3. **tenga** The subjunctive is used after adjectives showing emotion. *Tener* is a verb that is irregular in its present tense *yo* form. To form the subjunctive, take the *yo* form *(tengo)*, drop the *-o*, and add *-a* as the third person singular ending.

4. **merezca** The subjunctive is used when there is doubt. *Merecer* is a spelling-change "vowel + *-cer*" verb that is irregular in its present tense *yo* form: *c* changes to *zc*. To form the subjunctive, take the *yo* form *(merezco)*, drop the *-o*, and add *-a* as the subjunctive ending for *ella*.

5. **muestre** The subjunctive is used after a verb showing a wish. *Mostrar* is a stem-changing *-ar* verb that undergoes the same changes in the present subjunctive as in the present. The stem vowel changes from *o* to *ue* in all forms except *nosotros* and *vosotros*. To form the subjunctive, take the *yo* form *(muestro)*, drop the *-o*, and add *-e* as the ending for *Ud*.

6. **estén** The subjunctive is used after a verb showing a wish. *Estar* has irregular subjunctive forms that must be memorized. Add *-én* as the subjunctive ending for *Uds*.

Using the Subjunctive after Certain Conjunctions

The subjunctive is used with conjunctions that express time, purpose, condition, concession, negation, or fear. Some conjunctions always take the subjunctive, whereas others take the subjunctive only when the speaker wishes to convey doubt or uncertainty. When using conjunctions and the subjunctive, both clauses may contain the same subject.

The subjunctive is always used with the following conjunctions:

a condición de que	on condition that
a menos que	unless
a no ser que	unless
antes de que	before
con tal que	provided that
en caso de que	in case that
para que	in order that
por miedo a que	for fear that
sin que	without

Here are a couple of examples in sentences:

Yo le ayudaré a condición de que Ud. me pague.
I will help you on condition that you pay me.
Mis niños no salen de noche sin que yo lo sepa.
My children don't go out at night without my knowing it.

The subjunctive is used with the following conjunctions only if the action has not as yet occurred. In such cases, the subjunctive refers to future events that are considered uncertain. These conjunctions are followed by the indicative when referring to past or present events. When applicable, the subjunctive form of the verb can be translated as "may":

así que	even if
aunque	although, even if, even though
cuando	when
de manera que	so that
de modo que	so that
después de que	after
en cuanto	as soon as
hasta que	until
luego que	as soon as
mientras (que)	while
tan pronto como	as soon as

Here are a couple of examples in sentences:

Aunque cueste mucho dinero, yo compraré esa casa.
Although it costs (may cost) a lot of money, I am going to buy that house.
(The price of the house is uncertain.)

Aunque costó mucho dinero, yo compré esa casa.

Although it cost a lot of money, I bought that house.

(I knew the price before I made the purchase.)

Él me telefoneará en cuanto él llegue a casa.

He will call me as soon as he arrives home.

(The time of his arrival is uncertain.)

Siempre me telefonea en cuanto llega a casa.

He always calls me when he arrives home.

(This is customary.)

Example Problems

Express what this person says about himself. Use the correct form of the present subjunctive or the present indicative.

1. Aunque yo no _____ las películas de ciencia ficción, te acompañaré al cine.
   (preferir)

   Answer: prefiera

   The subjunctive is used when *aunque* refers to a future action. *Preferir* is a stem-changing *-ir* verb that undergoes the same changes in the present subjunctive as in the present. The stem vowel changes from *e* to *ie* in all forms except *nosotros* and *vosotros*. To form the subjunctive, take the *yo* form *(prefiero)*, drop the *-o,* and add *-a* as the ending for *yo.*

2. Nunca escribo un cheque, a menos que _____ bastante dinero en mi cuenta.
   (tener)

   Answer: tenga

   The subjunctive is always used with *a menos que. Tener* is a verb that is irregular in its present tense *yo* form. To form the subjunctive, take the *yo* form *(tengo),* drop the *-o,* and add *-a* as the ending for *yo.*

3. Conduzco demasiado rápidamente, de modo que _____ muchas multas.
   (recibir)

   Answer: recibo

   The present indicative is used when *de modo que* refers to a present action. *Recibir* is a regular *-ir* verb. Drop the *-ir* ending and add *-o* as the ending for *yo.*

Work Problems

Use these problems to give yourself additional practice.

Express more of what this person says about himself. Use the correct form of the present subjunctive or the present indicative.

1. Nunca salgo de noche sin que mis padres lo _____.
    (saber)

2. Siempre dejo un mensaje en el buzón de voz cuando _____ ayuda.
    (necesitar)

3. Yo pagaré mis cuentas en cuanto yo _____ más dinero.
    (ganar)

4. Yo telefoneo a mis amigos porque _____ invitarles a una fiesta.
    (querer)

5. Tengo que explicar mi retraso al jefe antes de que yo _____ al trabajo.
    (llegar)

Worked Solutions

1. **sepan**   The subjunctive is always used with *sin que*. *Saber* has an irregular subjunctive stem *(sep-),* which must be memorized. Add *-an* as the third person plural subjunctive ending.

2. **necesito**   The present indicative is used with *cuando* when it refers to a present action. To form the present tense of the regular verb *necesitar,* drop the *-ar* ending and add *-o* as the ending for *yo*.

3. **gane**   The subjunctive is always used with *en cuanto.* To conjugate regular *-ar* verbs in the present subjunctive, drop the *-ar* ending and add *-e* as the ending for *yo*.

4. **quiero**   The present indicative is used with *porque* when the present is implied. *Querer* has an internal stem change from *e* to *ie* in all forms except *nosotros* and *vosotros*. Drop the *-er* ending and add *-o* for *yo*.

5. **llegue**   The subjunctive is always used with *antes de que*. *Llegar* is a spelling-change verb that is irregular in its preterit tense *yo* form: *g* changes to *gu*. To form the subjunctive, take the *yo* form *(llegué),* drop the *-é,* and add *-e* as the subjunctive ending for *yo*.

The Subjunctive after Indefinites

The subjunctive is used after indefinites or compounds of *-quiera + que:*

comoquiera	however
cualquier (-a)	whatever, any
cuandoquiera	whenever
(a-) dondequiera	wherever
por + adjective/adverb + que	however, no matter how, as
quienquiera	whoever

Here are a couple of examples in sentences:

Quienquiera que sea, no respondas.

Whoever it is, don't answer.

Por trabajador que él sea, no gana mucho dinero.

As hardworking as he is, he doesn't earn a lot of money.

The Subjunctive in Relative Clauses

The subjunctive is used in relative clauses if the person or thing in the main clause is indefinite, is desired but not yet attained, or is nonexistent or whose existence is doubtful. If, however, the person or thing exists, the indicative is used: Note that these constructions, although grammatically correct, tend to be awkward and can be replaced by simpler sentences.

Busco una casa que sea grande. (Busco una casa grande.)

I'm looking for a big house.

(It is unclear that such a house exists.)

Tengo una casa que es grande. (Tengo una casa grande.)

I have a house that is big.

(The house exists.)

The Subjunctive in Third Person Commands

The subjunctive is used in third person singular or plural commands:

¡Que viva la reina!   Long live the queen!

¡Que sean felices!   Let them (May they) be happy!

Avoiding the Subjunctive

For simplicity and for ease in speaking, try to avoid the subjunctive whenever possible. When the subjects of both clauses are the same, *que* is omitted and the infinitive replaces the subjunctive:

Yo insisto en que tú me digas la verdad.   I insist that you tell me the truth.

Yo insisto en decir la verdad.   I insist on telling the truth.

The verbs *dejar* (to allow), *hacer* (to make, to do), *mandar* (to order), *permitir* (to permit), and *prohibir* (to forbid) may be followed by either the subjunctive or the infinitive:

She orders him to leave.

Ella lo manda que salga.

Ella lo manda salir.

My parents forbid me to drive at night.

Mis padres me prohiben que conduzca de noche.

Mis padres me prohiben conducir de noche.

Example Problems

Express in Spanish what the different people say. Use the correct form of the present subjunctive or the present indicative.

1. Long live the president!

    Answer: ¡Que viva el presidente!

    The subjunctive is used in third person commands. Begin the command with *que*. Give the subjunctive of *vivir*. To conjugate regular *-ir* verbs in the present subjunctive, drop the *-ir* ending and add *-a* as the third person singular for *yo*. Use *el presidente* to express "the president."

2. I'm looking for an employee that knows Spanish.

    Answer: Busco a un empleado que sepa el español.

    The subjunctive is used in a relative clause when something is indefinite. The verb *buscar* express "to look for." Drop the *-ar* ending and add *-o* for the *yo* form. Use *el empleado* to express "the employee." Use *que* to express "that." Give the subjunctive of *saber*. *Saber* has an irregular subjunctive stem *(sep-)*, which must be memorized. Add *-a* as the third person singular subjunctive ending. Use *el español* to express "Spanish." The definite article must be used with a noun being used in a general sense.

3. I won't speak to him, whoever he may be.

    Answer: No le hablaré, quienquiera que sea.

    The subjunctive is used after indefinites or compounds of *-quiera + que*. Use *no* to express "no." Use *le* to express "to him." Give the future of the verb *hablar*. Use the infinitive and add *-é* as the future ending for *yo*. Use *quienquiera que* to express "whomever." *Ser* has an irregular subjunctive stem *(se-)*, which must be memorized. Add *-a* as the third person singular subjunctive ending.

4. My parents forbid me to smoke.

    Answer: Mis padres prohiben que yo fume. Mis padres me prohiben fumar.

    The subjunctive or the indicative may be used with the verb *prohibir*. Use *Mis padres* to express "my parents." Use the present tense of the *prohibir*. Drop the *-ir* ending and add *-en* for the third person plural ending. Use *me* to express "me." Use *que* to express "that." Give the subjunctive of *fumar*. To conjugate regular *-ar* verbs in the present subjunctive, drop the *-ar* ending and add *-e* as the third person singular for *yo*. Alternatively, use the infinitive directly after *prohiben*.

Work Problems

Use these problems to give yourself additional practice.

Express in Spanish what the different people say at the office. Use the correct form of the present subjunctive or the present indicative.

1. Let her hear the truth!

2. I have an office that is very modern.

3. Whenever they come, we will see them.

4. I want to arrive on time.

5. Let the men do it!

6. I need a mechanic who has a lot of experience.

7. No matter how easy the job, he won't do it.

8. They allow me to leave early on Friday.

Worked Solutions

1. **¡Que oiga la verdad!**   The subjunctive is used in third person commands. Begin the command with *que*. Give the subjunctive of *oír*. *Oír* is a verb that is irregular in its present tense *yo* form. To form the subjunctive, take the *yo* form *(oigo)*, drop the *-o*, and add *-a* as the third person singular ending. Use *la verdad* to express "the truth."

2. **Tengo una oficina (que es) muy moderna.**   The indicative is used when there is no uncertainty. *Tener* is a verb that is irregular in its present tense *yo* form: *tengo*. Use *una oficina* to express "an office." Use *que* to express "that." *Ser* is an irregular verb that must be memorized. Use *es* for the third person singular. Use *muy* to express "very." Use the feminine singular adjective *moderna* to express "modern" and describe the feminine singular noun *oficina*.

3. **Cuandoquiera que vengan, los veremos.**   The subjunctive is used after indefinites or compounds of *-quiera + que*. Use *cuandoquiera que* to express "whenever." Give the subjunctive of *venir*. *Venir* is a verb that is irregular in its present tense *yo* form. To form the subjunctive, take the *yo* form *(vengo)*, drop the *-o*, and add *-an* as the ending for *ellos*. Use *los* to express "them." Give the future of the verb *ver*. Use the infinitive and add *-emos* as the future ending for *nosotros*.

4. **Quiero llegar a tiempo.**   The indicative is used after a verb showing "wishing" or "wanting" when there is only one clause. *Querer* has an internal stem change from *e* to *ie* in all forms except *nosotros* and *vosotros*. Drop the *-er* ending and add *-o* for *yo*. Use the infinitive *llegar* to express "to arrive" immediately after the conjugated verb. Use *a tiempo* to express "on time."

5. **¡Que los hombres lo hagan!**   The subjunctive is used in third person commands. Begin the command with *que*. Use *los hombres* to express "the men." Use *lo* to express "it." Give the subjunctive of *hacer*. *Hacer* is a verb that is irregular in its present tense *yo* form. To form the subjunctive, take the *yo* form *(hago)*, drop the *-o*, and add *-an* as the third person plural ending.

6. **Necesito un mecánico que tenga mucha experiencia.**   The subjunctive is used in a relative clause when something is indefinite. The verb *necesitar* expresses "to need." Drop the *-ar* ending and add *-o* for the *yo* form. Use *un mécanico* to express "a mechanic." Use *que* to express "that." Give the subjunctive of *tener*. *Tener* is a verb that is irregular in its present tense *yo* form. To form the subjunctive, take the *yo* form *(tengo)*, drop the *-o*, and add *-a* as the third person singular ending. Use the feminine singular adjective *mucha* to express "a lot of" before the feminine singular noun *experiencia* (experience).

7. **Por fácil que sea el puesto, él no lo hará.**   The subjunctive is used after indefinites. Use *por* + adjective to express "however." Use *fácil* to express "easy." *Ser* has an irregular

subjunctive stem (se-), which must be memorized. Add -a as the third person singular subjunctive ending. Use *el puesto* to express "the job." Use *él* to express "he." Use *no* before the conjugated verb to express that he will not do this job. Give the future of the verb *hacer*. Use the irregular future stem *har-* and add -á as the future ending for *él*. Use *lo* to express "it."

8. **Dejan que yo salga temprano el viernes./Me dejan salir temprano el viernes.**   The subjunctive or the indicative may be used with the verb *dejar*. Use the present tense of *dejar*. Drop the -ar ending and add -an for the third person plural ending. Use *que* to express "that." Use *yo* to express "I." Give the subjunctive of *salir*. *Salir* is a verb that is irregular in its present tense *yo* form. To form the subjunctive, take the *yo* form (salgo), drop the -o, and add -a as the ending for *yo*. Use *temprano* to express "early." Use *el viernes* to express "on Friday." Alternatively, use the present tense of *dejar*. Use *me* to express "me." Use the infinitive *salir* directly after *dejan*.

Forming and Using the Present Perfect Subjunctive

The present perfect subjunctive generally refers to a completed action and expresses what "may have happened." The present perfect subjunctive is formed by taking the present subjunctive form of the auxiliary (helping) verb *haber* and adding the past participle of the action performed.

Present Subjunctive of Haber	*Sample Past Participle*	*Meaning*
que yo **haya**	descansado	that I (may **have**) *rested*
que tú **hayas**	comido	that you (may **have** *eaten*) ate
que él (ella, Ud.) **haya**	sufrido	that he (she, you) (may **have**) *suffered*
que nosotros **hayamos**	abierto la puerta	that we (may **have**) *opened* the door
que vosotros **hayáis**	resuelto el problema	that you (may **have**) *resolved* the problem
que ellos (ellas, Uds). **hayan**	visto esa película	that they (you) (may **have** *seen*) saw that movie

Here are a couple of examples in sentences:

Sus padres esperan que él haya hecho todas sus tareas.
His parents hope that he did (may have done) all his homework.
Estoy contenta de que Uds. hayan venido.
I am happy that you came.

Example Problems

Express what people did when they went on a trip. Use the present perfect subjunctive:

1. es menester/Ud./hacer un itinerario

   Answer: Es menester que Ud. haya hecho un itinerario.

   The expression *es menester que* takes the subjunctive because it shows need. To form the present perfect subjunctive, use the present subjunctive of the helping verb *haber* and the past participle of *hacer*. *Haber* is irregular in the present subjunctive. Its stem is *hay-*. Add *-a* as the ending for *Ud*. The past participle of *hacer* is irregular and must be memorized: *hecho*.

2. no creer/nosotros/consultar el horario de vuelos

Answer: No cree que nosotros hayamos consultado el horario de vuelos.

The expression *no cree* takes the subjunctive because it shows doubt. To form the present perfect subjunctive, use the present subjunctive of the helping verb *haber* and the past participle of *consultar*. *Haber* is irregular in the present subjunctive. Its stem is *hay-*. Add *-amos* as the ending for *nosotros*. To form the past participle of the regular verb *consultar*, drop the *-ar* ending and add *-ado*.

3. es bueno/yo/escoger un hotel lujoso

Answer: Es bueno que yo haya escogido un hotel lujoso.

The expression *es bueno que* takes the subjunctive because it shows an opinion. To form the present perfect subjunctive, use the present subjunctive of the helping verb *haber* and the past participle of *escoger*. *Haber* is irregular in the present subjunctive. Its stem is *hay-*. Add *-a* as the ending for *yo*. To form the past participle of the verb *escoger*, drop the *-er* ending and add *-ido*.

Work Problems

Use these problems to give yourself additional practice.

Express other things people had to do when they went on a trip. Use the present perfect subjunctive.

1. es importante/yo/ir al banco a cambiar mi dinero

2. es bueno/nosotros/tener nuestros pasaportes en mano

3. es natural/tú/hacer una reservación en un hotel

4. es probable/Uds./estar en el aeropuerto dos horas antes del vuelo

5. es extraño que/él/traer un guía consigo

6. es útil/vosotros/comprar vuestros billetes en el Internet

Worked Solutions

1. **Es importante que yo haya ido al banco a cambiar mi dinero.** The expression *es importante que* takes the subjunctive because it shows opinion. To form the present perfect subjunctive, use the present subjunctive of the helping verb *haber* and the past participle of *ir*. *Haber* is irregular in the present subjunctive. Its stem is *hay-*. Add *-a* as the ending for *yo*. The past participle of *ir* is *ido*.

2. **Es bueno que nosotros hayamos tenido nuestros pasaportes en mano.** The expression *es bueno que* takes the subjunctive because it shows an opinion. To form the present perfect subjunctive, use the present subjunctive of the helping verb *haber* and the past

participle of *tener*. *Haber* is irregular in the present subjunctive. Its stem is *hay-*. Add -*amos* as the ending for *nosotros*. The past participle of *tener* is regular. Drop the -*er* ending and add -*ido*.

3. **Es natural que tú hayas hecho una reservación en un hotel.** The expression *es natural que* takes the subjunctive because it shows opinion. To form the present perfect subjunctive, use the present subjunctive of the helping verb *haber* and the past participle of *hacer*. *Haber* is irregular in the present subjunctive. Its stem is *hay-*. Add -*as* as the ending for *tú*. The past participle of *hacer* is irregular and must be memorized: *hecho*.

4. **Es probable que Uds. hayan estado en el aeropuerto dos horas antes del vuelo.** The expression *es probable que* takes the subjunctive because it shows probability. To form the present perfect subjunctive, use the present subjunctive of the helping verb *haber* and the past participle of *estar*. *Haber* is irregular in the present subjunctive. Its stem is *hay-*. Add -*an* as the ending for *Uds*. The past participle of *estar* is regular. Drop the -*ar* ending and add -*ado*.

5. **Es extraño que él haya traído un guía consigo.** The expression *es extraño que* takes the subjunctive because it shows opinion. To form the present perfect subjunctive, use the present subjunctive of the helping verb *haber* and the past participle of *traer*. *Haber* is irregular in the present subjunctive. Its stem is *hay-*. Add -*a* as the ending for *él*. The past participle of *traer* is formed by dropping the -*er* ending and adding -*ido*. Because the stem of *traer* ends in a vowel, an accent must be added to the *i: traído*.

6. **Es útil que vosotros hayáis comprado vuestros billetes en el Internet.** The expression *es útil que* takes the subjunctive because it shows opinion. To form the present perfect subjunctive, use the present subjunctive of the helping verb *haber* and the past participle of *comprar*. *Haber* is irregular in the present subjunctive. Its stem is *hay-*. Add -*áis* as the ending for *vosotros*. The past participle of *comprar* is regular. Drop the -*ar* ending and add -*ado*.

Chapter Problems

Problems

Complete the story about a boss looking for an employee by using the correct form of the present subjunctive, present perfect subjunctive, present indicative or the infinitive.

El señor Hidalgo, presidente de la compañía San Pedro busca a una empleada que (ser)

_____ trabajadora, que (tener) _____ paciencia, que (saber) _____ utilizar
　　　1　　　　　　　　　　　　　　　2　　　　　　　　　　　　　　　3

un ordenador y que (poder) _____ calcular bien. Hoy, Gisela López tiene una cita
　　　　　　　　　　　　　4

con él a las once. Aunque ella (estar) _____ en la oficina temprano, tiene que
　　　　　　　　　　　　　　　　　　　5

esperarlo por lo menos media hora. No está contenta de que él (estar) _____ tarde.
　　　　　　　　　　　　　　　　　　　　　　　　　　　　　　　　　　　　6

Es evidente que ella (ponerse) _____ cada vez más nerviosa. Ella sabe que (deber)
　　　　　　　　　　　　　　　7

_____ quedarse tranquila para no (hacer) _____ errores durante la envista y
　　8　　　　　　　　　　　　　　　　　　　　　　　9

no (decir) _____ tonterías. Mientras (esperar) _____ ella lee una revista.
　　　　　　　10　　　　　　　　　　　　　　　　　11

Finalmente ella oye decir al señor Hidalgo: "Que Gisela López (ir) _____ a la sala de
                                                                    12

conferencia y que (traer) _____ su historial con ella. Es importante que yo (hacer)
                            13

_____ esta entrevista inmediatamente." Tan pronto como Gisela (entrar) _____
  14   15

en la sala, empieza a contestar las preguntas del señor Hidalgo. Ella teme (parecer)

_____ incapaz de hacer el trabajo, pero es verdad que ella (salir) _____ bien
  16   17

en la entrevista. Después, el señor Hidalgo exclama, "Encontré a una muchacha que

(ser) _____ muy inteligente y trabajadora. Me alegro de que ella (venir)
        18

_____." El señor Hidalgo le ofrece el puesto a Gisela y le dice: "Cualquiera que
  19

(ser) _____ sus demandas, las discutiremos." Gisela dice que (querer) _____
        20   21

el puesto a condición de que (conseguir) _____ un buen salario y (recibir)
                                            22

_____ por lo menos dos semanas de vacaciones. El señor Hidalgo piensa que
  23

Gisela (ser) _____ una muchacha razonable. Él está muy alegre de que ella
              24

(obtener) _____ el puesto.
            25

Answers and Solutions

1. **Answer: sea**   The subjunctive is used in a relative clause when something is indefinite. *Ser* has an irregular subjunctive stem *(se-)*, which must be memorized. Add *-a* as the third person singular subjunctive ending.

2. **Answer: tenga**   The subjunctive is used in a relative clause when something is indefinite. *Tener* is a verb that is irregular in its present tense *yo* form. To form the subjunctive, take the *yo* form *(tengo)*, drop the *-o*, and add *-a* as the third person singular ending.

3. **Answer: sepa**   The subjunctive is used in a relative clause when something is indefinite. *Saber* has an irregular subjunctive stem *(sep-)*, which must be memorized. Add *-a* as the third person singular subjunctive ending.

4. **Answer: pueda**   The subjunctive is used in a relative clause when something is indefinite. *Poder* is a stem-changing verb that has an internal change from *o* to *ue* in the *yo* form of the present. To form the subjunctive, take the *yo* form *(puedo)*, drop the *-o*, and add *-a* for the third person singular subjunctive ending.

5. **Answer: está**   The indicative is used when *aunque* refers to a present action. *Estar* is irregular in the present tense. Drop the *-ar* ending and add *-a* as the ending for the third person singular ending.

6. **Answer: esté**   The subjunctive is used after a verb showing emotion. *Estar* has irregular subjunctive forms that must be memorized. Add *-é* as the subjunctive ending for *él*.

7. **Answer: se pone**   The indicative is used when there is certainty. *Poner* is regular in the present in all forms except *yo*. Drop the *-er* ending and add *-e* for *ella*. The infinitive *ponerse* indicates that the verb is used reflexively. Use the third person singular reflexive pronoun *se* before the verb.

8. **Answer: debe**   The indicative is used when there is certainty. Drop the *-er* infinitive ending and add *-e* for *ella*.

9. **Answer: hacer**   The infinitive is used after the preposition *para*.

10. **Answer: decir**   The infinitive is used after the preposition *para*.

11. **Answer: espera**   The indicative is used when *mientras* refers to a present action. Drop the *-ar* ending and add *-a* for *ella*.

12. **Answer: vaya**   The subjunctive is used in a third person command. *Ir* has an irregular subjunctive stem *(vay-)*, which must be memorized. Add *-a* as the subjunctive ending for *Gisela López (ella)*.

13. **Answer: traiga**   The subjunctive is used in a third person command. *Traer* is a verb that is irregular in its present tense *yo* form. To form the subjunctive, take the *yo* form *(traigo)*, drop the *-o*, and add *-a* as the third person singular ending.

14. **Answer: haga**   The subjunctive is used after an impersonal expression showing opinion. *Hacer* is a verb that is irregular in its present tense *yo* form. To form the subjunctive, take the *yo* form *(hago)*, drop the *-o*, and add *-a* as the ending for *yo*.

15. **Answer: entra**   The indicative is used when *tan pronto como* refers to a present action. Drop the *-ar* ending and add *-a* for *Gisela (ella)*.

16. **Answer: parecer**   The indicative is used when there is only one clause. Use the infinitive after the conjugated form of *temer*.

17. **Answer: sale**   *Salir* is regular in the present in all forms except *yo*. The indicative is used when there is certainty. Drop the *-ir* ending and add *-e* for *ella*.

18. **Answer: es**   The indicative is used in a relative clause when the person or thing exists. *Ser* is irregular in all forms of the present and must be memorized. Use *es* for the third person singular.

19. **Answer: haya venido**   The past subjunctive is used after a verb showing emotion, when the past is implied. To form the present perfect subjunctive, use the present subjunctive of the helping verb *haber* and the past participle of *venir*. *Haber* is irregular in the present subjunctive. Its stem is *hay-*. Add *-a* as the ending for *ella*. The past participle of *venir* is regular. Drop the *-ir* ending and add *-ido*.

20. **Answer: sean**   The subjunctive is used after indefinites. *Ser* has an irregular subjunctive stem *(se-)*, which must be memorized. Add *-an* as the third person plural subjunctive ending that agrees with *sus demandas*.

21. **Answer: quiere**   The indicative is used after *decir* when an order is not being given. *Querer* has an internal stem change from *e* to *ie* in all forms except *nosotros* and *vosotros*. Drop the *-er* ending and add *-e* for *Gisela (ella)*.

22. **Answer: consiga**   The subjunctive is always used after the conjunction *a condición de que*. *Conseguir* is a stem-changing *-uir* verb that undergoes the same changes in the present subjunctive as in the present tense. The stem vowel changes from *e* to *i* in all forms except *nosotros* and *vosotros*. To form the subjunctive, take the *yo* form *(consigo)*, drop the *-o*, and add *-a* as the ending for *ella*.

23. **Answer: reciba**   The subjunctive is always used after the conjunction *a condición de que*. To conjugate regular *-ir* verbs in the present subjunctive, drop the *-ir* ending and add *-a* as the ending for *ella*.

24. **Answer: es**   The indicative is used with the verb *pensar* to show a degree of certainty. The verb *ser* is irregular in the present and must be memorized. Use *es* for the third person singular.

25. **Answer: haya obtenido**   The past subjunctive is used after an adjective showing emotion when the past is implied. To form the present perfect subjunctive, use the present subjunctive of the helping verb *haber* and the past participle of *obtener*. *Haber* is irregular in the present subjunctive. Its stem is *hay-*. Add *-a* as the ending for *ella*. The past participle of *obtener* is regular. Drop the *-er* ending and add *-ido*.

Supplemental Chapter Problems

Problems

Complete the story about a boy who has to move by using the correct form of the present subjunctive, present perfect subjunctive, infinitive, or present indicative.

Miguel tiene que (mudarse) _____. Aunque le (gustar) _____ mucho su
                                  1   2

apartamento, no puede quedarse en él porque el propietario ha vendido la casa. Es

necesario que Miguel (buscar) _____ un nuevo domicilio en seguida. Esta vez
                                      3

quiere comprar su propio apartamento que (ser) _____ limpio y que (tener)
                                                      4

_____ todas la conveniencias modernas. Por ejemplo, él quiere que el edificio
     5

(estar) _____ en el centro, pero que (dar) _____ al río. Es importante que
             6   7

(poder) _____ caminar a las tiendas. Tiene muchos muebles. Es necesario que todo
            8

(caber) _____ en su nueva residencia. Es claro que Miguel (ser) _____
            9   10

exigente y que no quiere (aceptar) _____ algo inferior. Él conoce a una agente
                                    11

que (querer) _____ ayudarlo pero teme que ella no (comprender) _____ bien
             12   13

sus deseos y que no lo (tomar) _____ en serio. La agente saldrá con Miguel
                              14

cuandoquiera que (estar) _____ listo. Miguel insiste en que ellos (salir) _____
                            15   16

el sábado próximo. La agente le dice, "Ojalá que Ud. (encontrar) _____ lo que Ud.
                                                               17

(necesitar) _____ rápidamente. Van a un edificio nuevo para ver los apartamentos.

<small>18</small>

El gerente les dice: "Que (entrar) _____ Ud." En cuanto que Miguel (ver)

<small>19</small>

_____ el primer apartamento, sabe lo que (desear) _____. Es sorprendente

<small>20</small> <small>21</small>

que no (costar) _____ demasiado. No hay duda que Miguel (tener) _____

<small>22</small> <small>23</small>

mucha suerte. Él tomará el apartmento, con tal de que lo (pagar) _____ ahora

<small>24</small>

mismo. Los padres y los amigos de Miguel no creen que él (conseguir) _____ un

<small>25</small>

apartamento tan fácilmente.

Solutions

1. mudarse (using the present subjunctive, p. 302)

2. gusta (using the subjunctive after certain conjunctions, p. 311)

3. busque (spelling changes in the present subjunctive, p. 299; the subjunctive after impersonal expressions, p. 304)

4. sea (irregular verbs in the present subjunctive; p. 302, the subjunctive in relative clauses, p. 314)

5. tenga (irregular in the present tense *yo* form verbs; p. 297, the subjunctive in relative clauses, p. 314)

6. esté (irregular verbs in the present subjunctive; p. 302, the subjunctive after verbs of wishing, emotion, need, and doubt, p. 307)

7. dé (irregular verbs in the present subjunctive, p. 302; the subjunctive after verbs of wishing, emotion, need, and doubt, p. 307)

8. pueda (stem changes in the present subjunctive, p. 299; the subjunctive after impersonal expressions, p. 304)

9. quepa (irregular verbs in the present subjunctive, p. 302; the subjunctive after impersonal expressions, p. 304)

10. es (the subjunctive after impersonal expressions, p. 304)

11. aceptar (using the present subjunctive, p. 302)

12. quiere (the subjunctive in relative clauses, p. 314)

13. comprenda (forming the subjunctive, p. 295; the subjunctive after verbs of wishing, emotion, need, and doubt, p. 307)

14. tome (forming the subjunctive, p. 295; the subjunctive after verbs of wishing, emotion, need, and doubt, p. 307)

15. esté (forming the subjunctive, p. 295; the subjunctive after indefinites, p. 313)

16. salgan (irregular in the present-tense *yo* form verbs, p. 297; the subjunctive after verbs of wishing, emotion, need, and doubt, p. 307)

17. encuentre (forming the subjunctive, p. 295; the subjunctive after verbs of wishing, emotion, need, and doubt, p. 307)

18. necesita (using the present subjunctive, p. 302)

19. entre (forming the subjunctive, p. 295; the subjunctive in third person commands, p. 314)

20. ve (irregular verbs in the present subjunctive, p. 302; the subjunctive after certain conjunctions, p. 311)

21. desea (using the present subjunctive, p. 302)

22. cueste (stem changes in the present subjunctive, p. 299; the subjunctive after impersonal expressions, p. 304)

23. tiene (the subjunctive after verbs of wishing, emotion, need, and doubt, p. 307)

24. pague (spelling changes in the present subjunctive, p. 299; the subjunctive after certain conjunctions, p. 311)

25. haya conseguido (forming and using the present perfect subjunctive, p. 317)

Chapter 15
The Imperfect and the Pluperfect Subjunctive

The Imperfect Subjunctive

Like the present subjunctive, the imperfect subjunctive is a mood that expresses unreal, hypothetical, or unsubstantiated conditions or situations resulting from doubt, wishes, needs, desires, feelings, emotions, speculation, or supposition. Unlike the present subjunctive, which is used in the dependent clause when the verb in the main clause is in the present, present perfect, future, or imperative, the imperfect subjunctive is used in the dependent clause when the verb in the main clause is in the preterit, imperfect, conditional, or pluperfect tense.

The Imperfect Subjunctive of Regular and Irregular Verbs

In Spanish, the imperfect subjunctive has two possible endings, referred to as the -ra (more commonly used) and the -se endings. Either of these endings may be used for any verb. The imperfect subjunctive of regular verbs is formed by dropping -ron from the *ellos* form of the preterit tense and by adding the subjunctive endings.

The -ra endings are added as follows (Note that an accent is added to the a or the e before the –ramos or -semos ending of the *nosotros* form of the verb):

	-ar Verbs	*-er Verbs*	*-ir Verbs*
Ellos Form of the Preterit	compraron (they bought)	aprendieron (they learned)	escribieron (they wrote)
Yo	compra**ra**	aprendie**ra**	escribie**ra**
Tú	compra**ras**	aprendie**ras**	escribie**ras**
Él, Ella, Ud.	compra**ra**	aprendie**ra**	escribie**ra**
Nosotros	comprá**ramos**	aprendié**ramos**	escribié**ramos**
Vosotros	compra**rais**	aprendie**rais**	escribie**rais**
Ellos, Ellas, Uds.	compra**ran**	aprendie**ran**	escribie**ran**

Here are some examples in sentences:

Insistieron en que ella trabajara.	They insisted that she work.
Yo temía que Uds. no comprendieran.	I was afraid that you wouldn't understand.
Él quería que yo partiera.	He wanted me to leave.

The -se endings are added as follows:

	-ar Verbs	-er Verbs	-ir Verbs
Ellos Form of the Preterit	compra~~ron~~ (they bought)	aprendie~~ron~~ (they learned)	escribie~~ron~~ (they wrote)
Yo	compra**se**	aprendie**se**	escribie**se**
Tú	compra**ses**	aprendie**ses**	escribie**ses**
Él, Ella, Ud.	compra**se**	aprendie**se**	escribie**se**
Nosotros	comprá**semos**	aprendié**semos**	escribié**semos**
Vosotros	compra**seis**	aprendie**seis**	escribie**seis**
Ellos, Ellas, Uds.	compra**sen**	aprendie**sen**	escribie**sen**

Here are the same examples given above, but with the -se endings rather than the -ra endings:

Insistieron en que ella trabajase.	They insisted that she work.
Yo temía que Uds. no comprendiesen.	I was afraid that you wouldn't understand.
Él quería que yo partiese.	He wanted me to leave.

Example Problems

Express why the teacher was happy with the progress of her students.

Se alegró de que . . .

1. yo/responder con entusiasmo

   Answer: Se alegró de que yo respondiera (respondiese) con entusiasmo.

   The imperfect subjunctive of regular verbs is formed by dropping -ron from the *ellos* form of the preterit tense. Form the third person plural preterit of a regular -er verb by dropping the -er ending and adding -ieron. Drop -ron and add -ra or -se for the *yo* form of the imperfect subjunctive.

2. nosotros/decidir estudiar seriamente

   Answer: Se alegró de que nosotros decidiéramos (decidiésemos) estudiar seriamente.

   The imperfect subjunctive of regular verbs is formed by dropping -ron from the *ellos* form of the preterit tense. Form the third person plural preterit of a regular -ir verb by dropping the -ir ending and adding -ieron. Drop -ron and add an accent on the vowel *(e)* preceding the -ramos or -semos ending for the *nosotros* form of the imperfect subjunctive.

3. Uds./contestar mucho en clase.

    Answer: Se alegró de que Uds. contestaran (contestasen) mucho en clase.

    The imperfect subjunctive of regular verbs is formed by dropping *-ron* from the *ellos* form of the preterit tense. Form the third person plural preterit of a regular *-ar* verb by dropping the *-ar* ending and adding *-aron*. Drop *-ron* and add *-ran* or *-sen* for the *Uds.* form of the imperfect subjunctive.

Work Problems

Use these problems to give yourself additional practice.

Express more reasons why the teacher was happy with the progress of her students.

Se alegró de que . . .

1. nosotros/aprender mucho

2. vosotros/hablar español todo el tiempo

3. yo/escribir poemas en español

4. él/estudiar el vocabulario todos los días

5. tú/asistir al club de español

6. ellas/comprender las lecciones

Solutions

1. **Se alegró de que nosotros aprendiéramos (aprendiésemos) mucho.**   The imperfect subjunctive of regular verbs is formed by dropping *-ron* from the *ellos* form of the preterit tense. Form the third person plural preterit of a regular *-er* verb by dropping the *-er* ending and adding *-ieron*. Drop *-ron* and add an accent on the vowel *(e)* preceding the *-ramos* or *-semos* ending for the *nosotros* form of the imperfect subjunctive.

2. **Se alegró de que vosotros hablarais (hablaseis) español todo el tiempo.**   The imperfect subjunctive of regular verbs is formed by dropping *-ron* from the *ellos* form of the preterit tense. Form the third person plural preterit of a regular *-ar* verb by dropping the *-ar* ending and adding *-aron*. Drop *-ron* and add *-rais* or *-seis* for the *vosotros* form of the imperfect subjunctive.

3. **Se alegró de que yo escribiera (escribiese) poemas en español.**   The imperfect subjunctive of regular verbs is formed by dropping *-ron* from the *ellos* form of the preterit tense. Form the third person plural preterit of a regular *-ir* verb by dropping the *-ir* ending and adding *-ieron*. Drop *-ron* and add *-ra* or *-se* for the *yo* form of the imperfect subjunctive.

4. **Se alegró de que él estudiara (estudiase) el vocabulario todos los días.**   The imperfect subjunctive of regular verbs is formed by dropping *-ron* from the *ellos* form of the preterit tense. Form the third person plural preterit of a regular *-ar* verb by dropping the *-ar* ending and adding *-aron*. Drop *-ron* and add *-ra* or *-se* for the *él* form of the imperfect subjunctive.

5. **Se alegró de que tú asistieras (asistieses) al club de español.**　The imperfect subjunctive of regular verbs is formed by dropping *-ron* from the *ellos* form of the preterit tense. Form the third person plural preterit of a regular *-ir* verb by dropping the *-ir* ending and adding *-ieron*. Drop *-ron* and add *-ras* or *-ses* for the *tú* form of the imperfect subjunctive.

6. **Se alegró de que ellas comprendieran (comprendiesen) las lecciones.**　The imperfect subjunctive of regular verbs is formed by dropping *-ron* from the *ellos* form of the preterit tense. Form the third person plural preterit of a regular *-er* verb by dropping the *-er* ending and adding *-ieron*. Drop *-ron* and add *-ran* or *-sen* for the *ellas* form of the imperfect subjunctive.

The Imperfect Subjunctive of Verbs with Spelling Changes

Verbs ending in *-car, -gar, -zar, -cer/-cir* (except those ending in *-ducir*), *-ger/-gir*, and *-guir* are formed like regular verbs in the imperfect subjunctive: Drop *-ron* from the third person plural preterit form and add the appropriate ending:

Verb	Meaning	Ellos Form of the Preterit	Imperfect Subjunctive Stem
buscar	to look for	busca~~ron~~	busca-
pagar	to pay	paga~~ron~~	paga-
comenzar	to begin	comenza~~ron~~	comenza-
conocer	to know	conocie~~ron~~	conocie-
convencer	to convince	convencie~~ron~~	convencie-
escoger	to choose	escogie~~ron~~	escogie-
dirigir	to direct	dirigie~~ron~~	dirigie-
distinguir	to distinguish	distinguie~~ron~~	distinguie-

Note these exceptions to the rule:

❑ Verbs ending in *-uir* (but not *-guir*) change the third person plural form *(ellos)* from *-ieron* to *-yeron* in the preterit and, therefore, in the imperfect subjunctive as well.

❑ Verbs ending in vowel + *-er/-ir* change the third person plural form *(ellos)* from *-ieron* to *-yeron* in the preterit and, therefore, in the imperfect subjunctive as well.

Verb	Meaning	Ellos Form of the Preterit	Imperfect Subjunctive Stem
sustituir	to substitute	sustituye~~ron~~	sustituye-
caer	to fall	caye~~ron~~	caye-
leer	to read	leye~~ron~~	leye-
oír	to hear	oye~~ron~~	oye-

Here are some examples in sentences:

Era importante que ellos llegaran (llegasen) a tiempo.

It was important that they arrive on time.

El profesor quería que el alumno leyera (leyese) en voz alta.

The teacher wanted the student to read aloud.

Example Problems

Express what was necessary for the people to do at work.

1. (oír) Era necesario que él _____ las explicaciones de los otros.

   Answer: oyera (oyese)

   The imperfect subjunctive is formed by dropping -ron from the *ellos* form of the preterit tense. Verbs ending in a vowel when the -ir ending is dropped change *i* to *y* in the third person plural and add -eron. Drop -ron and add -ra or -se for the *él* form of the imperfect subjunctive.

2. (obedecer) Era necesario que los empleados _____ las reglas.

   Answer: obedecieran (obedeciesen)

   The imperfect subjunctive is formed by dropping -ron from the *ellos* form of the preterit tense. Verbs ending in -cer are regular in the preterit. Form the third person plural preterit of a regular -er verb by dropping the -er ending and adding -ieron. Drop -ron and add -ran or -sen for the third person plural form of the imperfect subjunctive.

3. (exigir) Era necesario que yo _____ mucho de los otros empleados.

   Answer: exigiera (exigiese)

   The imperfect subjunctive is formed by dropping -ron from the *ellos* form of the preterit tense. Verbs ending in -gir are regular in the preterit. Form the third person plural preterit of a regular -ir verb by dropping the -ir ending and adding -ieron. Drop -ron and add -ra or -se for the *yo* form of the imperfect subjunctive.

Work Problems

Use these problems to give yourself additional practice.

Express what the boss told the workers was important.

1. (explicar) Era importante que Uds. _____ su retraso.

2. (alzar) Era importante que Ud. _____ la voz.

3. (investigar) Era importante que yo _____ esos problemas.

4. (leer) Era importante que nosotros _____ esa correspondencia con cuidado.

5. (distribuir) Era importante que vosotros _____ esos folletos.

6. (escoger) Era importante que tú _____ un plan de acción definitivo.

Worked Solutions

1. **explicaran (explicasen)**   The imperfect subjunctive is formed by dropping -ron from the *ellos* form of the preterit tense. Verbs ending in -car are regular in the preterit. Form the

third person plural preterit of a regular *-ar* verb by dropping the *-ar* ending and adding *-aron*. Drop *-ron* and add *-ran* or *-sen* for the *Uds.* form of the imperfect subjunctive.

2. **alzara (alzase)**   The imperfect subjunctive is formed by dropping *-ron* from the *ellos* form of the preterit tense. Verbs ending in *-zar* are regular in the preterit. Form the third person plural preterit of a regular *-ar* verb by dropping the *-ar* ending and adding *-aron*. Drop *-ron* and add *-ra* or *-se* for the *Ud.* form of the imperfect subjunctive.

3. **investigara (investigase)**   The imperfect subjunctive is formed by dropping *-ron* from the *ellos* form of the preterit tense. Verbs ending in *-gar* are regular in the preterit. Form the third person plural preterit of a regular *-ar* verb by dropping the *-ar* ending and adding *-aron*. Drop *-ron* and add *-ra* or *-se* for the *yo* form of the imperfect subjunctive.

4. **leyéramos (leyésemos)**   The imperfect subjunctive is formed by dropping *-ron* from the *ellos* form of the preterit tense. Verbs ending in a vowel when the *-ir* ending is dropped change *i* to *y* in the third person plural and add *-eron*. Drop *-ron* and add an accent on the vowel *(e)* preceding the *-ramos* or *-semos* ending for the *nosotros* form of the imperfect subjunctive.

5. **distribuyerais (distribuyeseis)**   The imperfect subjunctive is formed by dropping *-ron* from the *ellos* form of the preterit tense. Verbs ending in a vowel when the *-ir* ending is dropped change *i* to *y* in the third person plural and add *-eron*. Drop *-ron* and add *-rais* or *-seis* for the *vosotros* form of the imperfect subjunctive.

6. **escogieras (escogieses)**   The imperfect subjunctive is formed by dropping *-ron* from the *ellos* form of the preterit tense. Verbs ending in *-ger* are regular in the preterit. Form the third person plural preterit of a regular *-er* verb by dropping the *-er* ending and adding *-ieron*. Drop *-ron* and add *-ras* or *-ses* for the *tú* form of the imperfect subjunctive.

The Imperfect Subjunctive of Verbs with Stem Changes

Only *-ir* verbs whose stems change from *e* to *ie*, *e* to *i*, or *o* to *ue* in the present change their stems from *e* to *i* in the preterit in the third person plural *(ellos)* form, as well as in the imperfect subjunctive.

Verb	Meaning	Ellos Form of the Present	Ellos Form of the Preterit	Imperfect Subjunctive Stem
mentir	to lie	mienten	mintieron	mintier-
pedir	to ask for	piden	pidieron	pidie-
dormir	to sleep	duermen	durmieron	durmie-

The verb *reír* changes as follows:

Verb	Meaning	Ellos Form of the Present	Ellos Form of the Preterit	Imperfect Subjunctive Stem
reír	to laugh	ríen	rieron	rie-

Here are some examples in sentences:

Ellos nos miraban como si nosotros mintiéramos (mintiésemos).
They looked at us as if we were lying.

Era necesario que los niños durmieran (durmiesen) mucho.

It was necessary that the children sleep a lot.

Example Problems

Express what was surprising.

1. Era sorprendente que ella _____ al final de la novela.
   (morir)

   Answer: muriera (muriese)

   The imperfect subjunctive is formed by dropping -ron from the *ellos* form of the preterit tense. Present tense stem-changing verbs ending in -ir change o to u and add -ieron in the third person plural preterit. Drop -ron and add -ra or -se for the *ella* form of the imperfect subjunctive.

2. Era sorprendente que Uds. _____.
   (disentir)

   Answer: disintieran (disintiesen)

   The imperfect subjunctive is formed by dropping -ron from the *ellos* form of the preterit tense. Present tense stem-changing verbs ending in -ir change e to i and add -ieron in the third person plural preterit. Drop -ron and add -ran or -sen for the *Uds.* form of the imperfect subjunctive.

3. Era sorprendente que tú _____ esa investigación.
   (impedir)

   Answer: impidieras (impidieses)

   The imperfect subjunctive is formed by dropping -ron from the *ellos* form of the preterit tense. Present tense stem-changing verbs ending in -ir change e to i and add -ieron in the third person plural preterit. Drop -ron and add -ras or -ses for the *tú* form of the imperfect subjunctive.

Work Problems

Use these problems to give yourself additional practice.

Express other things that were surprising.

1. Era sorprendente que tú _____.
   (mentir)

2. Era sorprendente que él _____ en los asuntos de sus amigos.
   (interferir)

3. Era sorprendente que nosotros _____ hasta el mediodía.
   (dormir)

4. Era sorprendente que yo _____ con mi hermano.
   (competir)

5. Era sorprendente que Uds. _____ el problema.
       (presentir)

6. Era sorprendente que vosotros _____ a ayudar a Pablo.
       (consentir)

Worked Solutions

1. **mintieras (mintieses)**   The imperfect subjunctive is formed by dropping -*ron* from the *ellos* form of the preterit tense. Present tense stem-changing verbs ending in -*ir* change *e* to *i* and add -*ieron* in the third person plural preterit. Drop -*ron* and add -*ras* or -*ses* for the *tú* form of the imperfect subjunctive.

2. **interfiriera (interfiriese)**   The imperfect subjunctive is formed by dropping -*ron* from the *ellos* form of the preterit tense. Present tense stem-changing verbs ending in -*ir* change *e* to *i* and add -*ieron* in the third person plural preterit. Drop -*ron* and add -*ra* or -*se* for the *él* form of the imperfect subjunctive.

3. **durmiéramos (durmiésemos)**   The imperfect subjunctive is formed by dropping -*ron* from the *ellos* form of the preterit tense. Present tense stem-changing verbs ending in -*ir* change *o* to *u* and add -*ieron* in the third person plural preterit. Drop -*ron* and add an accent on the vowel (*e*) preceding the -*ramos* or -*semos* ending for the *nosotros* form of the imperfect subjunctive.

4. **compitiera (compitiese)**   The imperfect subjunctive is formed by dropping -*ron* from the *ellos* form of the preterit tense. Present tense stem-changing verbs ending in -*ir* change *e* to *i* and add -*ieron* in the third person plural preterit. Drop -*ron* and add -*ra* or -*se* for the *yo* form of the imperfect subjunctive.

5. **presintieran (presintiesen)**   The imperfect subjunctive is formed by dropping -*ron* from the *ellos* form of the preterit tense. Present tense stem-changing verbs ending in -*ir* change *e* to *i* and add -*ieron* in the third person plural preterit. Drop -*ron* and add -*ran* or -*sen* for the *Uds.* form of the imperfect subjunctive.

6. **consintierais (consintieseis)**   The imperfect subjunctive is formed by dropping -*ron* from the *ellos* form of the preterit tense. Present tense stem-changing verbs ending in -*ir* change *e* to *i* and add -*ieron* in the third person plural preterit. Drop -*ron* and add -*rais* or -*seis* for the *vosotros* form of the imperfect subjunctive.

The Imperfect Subjunctive of Irregular Verbs

Verbs that are irregular in the preterit are also irregular in the imperfect subjunctive. The following verbs have an irregular stem in the preterit to which the -*ra* or -*se* endings are added:

Verb	Meaning	Ellos Form of the Preterit	Imperfect Subjunctive Stem
andar	to walk	anduvieron	anduvie-
caber	to fit	cupieron	cupie-
dar	to give	dieron	die-
estar	to be	estuvieron	estuvie-
haber	to have (auxiliary verb)	hubieron	hubie-

Verb	Meaning	Ellos Form of the Preterit	Imperfect Subjunctive Stem
hacer	to make, to do	hicie~~ron~~	hicie-
ir	to go	fue~~ron~~	fue-
poder	to be able to	pudie~~ron~~	pudie-
poner	to put	pusie~~ron~~	pusie-
querer	to wish, to want	quisie~~ron~~	quisie-
saber	to know	supie~~ron~~	supie-
satisfacer	to satisfy	satisficie~~ron~~	satisficie-
ser	to be	fue~~ron~~	fue-
tener	to have	tuvie~~ron~~	tuvie-
venir	to come	vinie~~ron~~	vinie-
ver	to see	vie~~ron~~	vie-

Verbs ending in *-ducir* and the verbs *decir* and *traer* have a *j* in the preterit stem:

Verb	Meaning	Ellos Form of the Preterit	Imperfect Subjunctive Stem
decir	to say, to tell	dije~~ron~~	dije-
traer	to bring	traje~~ron~~	traje-
conducir	to drive	conduje~~ron~~	conduje-

Here are some examples in sentences:

Me alegré de que tu hermano viniera a mi fiesta.
I was happy that your brother came to my party.
No salí de noche sin que mis padres lo supieran (supiesen).
I didn't go out at night unless my parents knew about it.

Example Problems

Express what Mrs. Muñoz was looking for.

Example: buscaba a una persona/decirle el futuro
Buscaba a una persona que le dijera (dijese) el futuro.

1. buscaba a un músico/poder tocar la guitarra

   Answer: Buscaba a un músico que pudiera (pudiese) tocar la guitarra.

   The imperfect subjunctive is formed by dropping *-ron* from the *ellos* form of the preterit tense. The irregular preterit stem of *poder* is *pud-*. Form the third person plural preterit by adding *-ieron*. Drop *-ron* and add *-ra* or *-se* for the third person singular form of the imperfect subjunctive.

2. buscaba a un médico/venir a su casa

    Answer: Buscaba a un médico que viniera (viniese) a su casa.

    The irregular preterit stem of *venir* is *vin-*. Form the third person plural preterit by adding *-ieron*. Drop *-ron* and add *-ra* or *-se* for the third person singular form of the imperfect subjunctive.

3. buscaba a un piloto/hacer un viaje a África

    Answer: Buscaba a un piloto que hiciera (hiciese) un viaje a África.

    The irregular preterit stem of *hacer* is *hic-*. Form the third person plural preterit by adding *-ieron*. Drop *-ron* and add *-ra* or *-se* for the third person singular form of the imperfect subjunctive.

Work Problems

Use these problems to give yourself additional practice.

Express what other things Mrs. Muñoz was looking for (see the previous example).

1. buscaba a un juez/ser indulgente

2. buscaba a un abogado/decir la verdad

3. buscaba a un chofer/conducir bien

4. buscaba a un mecánico/saber reparar su coche

5. buscaba a un secretario/tener paciencia

6. buscaba a un psiquiatra/dar buenos consejos

Worked Solutions

1. **Buscaba a un juez que fuera (fuese) indulgente.**   The irregular preterit stem of *ser* is *fu-*. Form the third person plural preterit by adding *-eron*. Drop *-ron* and add *-ra* or *-se* for the third person singular form of the imperfect subjunctive.

2. **Buscaba a un abogado que dijera (dijese) la verdad.**   The irregular preterit stem of *decir* is *dij-*. Form the third person plural preterit by adding *-eron*. Drop *-ron* and add *-ra* or *-se* for the third person singular form of the imperfect subjunctive.

3. **Buscaba a un chofer que condujera (condujese) bien.**   The irregular preterit stem of *conducir* is *conduj-*. Form the third person plural preterit by adding *-eron*. Drop *-ron* and add *-ra* or *-se* for the third person singular form of the imperfect subjunctive.

4. **Buscaba a un mecánico que supiera (supiese) reparar su coche.**   The irregular preterit stem of *saber* is *sup-*. Form the third person plural preterit by adding *-ieron*. Drop *-ron* and add *-ra* or *-se* for the third person singular form of the imperfect subjunctive.

5. **Buscaba a un secretario que tuviera (tuviese) paciencia.** The irregular preterit stem of *tener* is *tuv-*. Form the third person plural preterit by adding *-ieron*. Drop *-ron* and add *-ra* or *-se* for the third person singular form of the imperfect subjunctive.

6. **Buscaba a un psiquiatra que diera (diese) buenos consejos.** The irregular preterit stem of *decir* is *di-*. Form the third person plural preterit by adding *-ieron*. Drop *-ron* and add *-ra* or *-se* for the third person singular form of the imperfect subjunctive.

Forming the Pluperfect Subjunctive of All Verbs

The pluperfect subjunctive expresses what "might have happened" and generally refers to a completed action. The pluperfect subjunctive is formed by taking the imperfect subjunctive form of the auxiliary (helping) verb *haber* and adding the past participle of the action performed.

Present Subjunctive of Haber	Sample Past Participle	Meaning
que yo **hubiera (hubiese)**	descansado	that I had (might have) *rested*
que tú **hubieras (hubieses)**	comido	that you had (might have) *eaten*
que él (ella, Ud.) **hubiera (hubiese)**	sufrido	that he (she, you) had (might have) *suffered*
que nosotros **hubiéramos (hubiésemos)**	abierto la puerta	that we had (might have) *opened* the door
que vosotros **hubierais (hubieseis)**	resuelto el problema	that you had (might have) *resolved* the problem
que ellos (ellas, Uds). **hubieran (hubiesen)**	visto esa película	that they (you) had (might have) *seen* that movie

Here are a couple of examples in sentences:

No creíamos que ese artista hubiera (hubiese) pintado un cuadro tan feo.
We didn't believe that that artist had (might have) painted such an ugly picture.
Mi amigo me telefoneó antes de que yo me hubiera (hubiese) despertado.
My friend phoned me before I had awakened.

Example Problems

Express what the boss had feared.

Temía que . . .

1. Uds. no (completar) _____ el trabajo.

Answer: hubieran (hubiesen) completado

The pluperfect subjunctive is formed by taking the imperfect subjunctive form of the auxiliary (helping) verb *haber* and adding the past participle of the action performed. The irregular preterit stem of *haber* is *hub-*. Form the third person plural preterit by adding *-ieron*. Drop *-ron* and add *-ran* or *-sen* for the *Uds.* form of the imperfect subjunctive. To form the past participle of *completar*, drop the *-ar* ending and add *-ado*.

2.   yo no (resolver) _____ el problema.

Answer: hubiera (hubiese) resuelto

The pluperfect subjunctive is formed by taking the imperfect subjunctive form of the auxiliary (helping) verb *haber* and adding the past participle of the action performed. The irregular preterit stem of *haber* is *hub-*. Form the third person plural preterit by adding *-ieron*. Drop *-ron* and add *-ra* or *-se* for the *yo* form of the imperfect subjunctive. The past participle of *resolver* is irregular and must be memorized: *resuelto*.

3.   nosotros no (cumplir) _____ nuestra promesa.

Answer: hubiéramos (hubiésemos) cumplido

The pluperfect subjunctive is formed by taking the imperfect subjunctive form of the auxiliary (helping) verb *haber* and adding the past participle of the action performed. The irregular preterit stem of *haber* is *hub-*. Form the third person plural preterit by adding *-ieron*. Drop *-ron* and add an accent on the vowel *(e)* preceding the *-ramos* or *-semos* ending for the *nosotros* form of the imperfect subjunctive. To form the past participle of *cumplir*, drop the *-ir* ending and add *-ido*.

Work Problems

Use these problems to give yourself additional practice.

Express what the Ricardos feared.

Temían que . . .

1.   Yo (estar) _____ enfermo.

2.   Los muchachos (perder) _____ su dinero.

3.   Nosotros (sufrir) _____ .

4.   Elena (recibir) _____ una triste noticia.

5.   Vosotros (fumar) _____ .

6.   Tú (decir) _____ mentiras.

Worked Solutions

1.   **hubiera (hubiese) estado**   The pluperfect subjunctive is formed by taking the imperfect subjunctive form of the auxiliary (helping) verb *haber* and adding the past participle of the action performed. The irregular preterit stem of *haber* is *hub-*. Form the third person plural preterit by adding *-ieron*. Drop *-ron* and add *-ra* or *-se* for the *yo* form of the imperfect subjunctive. To form the past participle of *estar*, drop the *-ar* ending and add *-ado*.

2.   **hubieran (hubiesen) perdido**   The pluperfect subjunctive is formed by taking the imperfect subjunctive form of the auxiliary (helping) verb *haber* and adding the past participle of the action performed. The irregular preterit stem of *haber* is *hub-*. Form the third person plural preterit by adding *-ieron*. Drop *-ron* and add *-ran* or *-sen* for the third

person plural form of the imperfect subjunctive. To form the past participle of *perder*, drop the *-er* ending and add *-ido*.

3. **hubiéramos (hubiésemos) sufrido** The pluperfect subjunctive is formed by taking the imperfect subjunctive form of the auxiliary (helping) verb *haber* and adding the past participle of the action performed. The irregular preterit stem of *haber* is *hub-*. Form the third person plural preterit by adding *-ieron*. Drop *-ron* and add an accent on the vowel (e) preceding the *-ramos* or *-semos* ending for the *nosotros* form of the imperfect subjunctive. To form the past participle of *sufrir*, drop the *-ir* ending and add *-ido*.

4. **hubiera (hubiese) recibido** The pluperfect subjunctive is formed by taking the imperfect subjunctive form of the auxiliary (helping) verb *haber* and adding the past participle of the action performed. The irregular preterit stem of *haber* is *hub-*. Form the third person plural preterit by adding *-ieron*. Drop *-ron* and add *-ra* or *-se* for the third person singular form of the imperfect subjunctive. To form the past participle of *recibir*, drop the *-ir* ending and add *-ido*.

5. **hubierais (hubieseis) fumado** The pluperfect subjunctive is formed by taking the imperfect subjunctive form of the auxiliary (helping) verb *haber* and adding the past participle of the action performed. The irregular preterit stem of *haber* is *hub-*. Form the third person plural preterit by adding *-ieron*. Drop *-ron* and add *-rais* or *-seis* for the *vosotros* form of the imperfect subjunctive. To form the past participle of *fumar*, drop the *-ar* ending and add *-ado*.

6. **hubieras (hubieses) dicho** The pluperfect subjunctive is formed by taking the imperfect subjunctive form of the auxiliary (helping) verb *haber* and adding the past participle of the action performed. The irregular preterit stem of *haber* is *hub-*. Form the third person plural preterit by adding *-ieron*. Drop *-ron* and add *-ras* or *-ses* for the *tú* form of the imperfect subjunctive. The past participle of *decir* is irregular and must be memorized: *dicho*.

Using the Imperfect Subjunctive and Pluperfect Subjunctive

Generally, the same rules that apply to the use of the present subjunctive also apply to the use of the imperfect subjunctive. The tense of the verb in the main clause determines the tense of the subjunctive verb in the dependent clause.

The imperfect subjunctive and pluperfect subjunctive may be used in dependent clauses when the verb in the main clause is in the imperfect, preterit, pluperfect, or conditional.

Verb in Main Clause	Verb in Dependent Clause
Present	Present Subjunctive
Present Perfect	or
Future	Present Perfect (Past) Subjunctive
Command	Imperfect Subjunctive
Imperfect	or
Preterit	Pluperfect Subjunctive
Pluperfect	
Conditional	

Here are some examples with the present, the imperfect subjunctive, and the pluperfect subjunctive in the dependent clauses:

Ud. manda que entren.	You tell them to enter.
Ud. ha mandado que entren.	You have told them to enter.
Ud. mandará que entren.	You will tell them to enter.
Mándeles que entren.	Tell them to enter.
Ud. mandaba que entraran (entrasen).	You were telling them to enter.
Ud. mandó que entraran (entrasen).	You told them to enter.
Ud. había mandado que entraran (entrasen).	You had told them to enter.
Ud. mandaría que entraran (entrasen).	You would tell them to enter.
Ud. insistía en que lo hubieran (hubiesen) hecho.	You were insisting that they had done it.
Ud. insistió en que lo hubieran (hubiesen) hecho.	You insisted that they had done it.
Ud. había insistido en que lo hubieran (hubiesen) hecho.	You had insisted that they had done it.
¿Creería Ud. que lo hubieran (hubiesen) hecho?	Would you believe that they had done it?

The imperfect subjunctive or pluperfect subjective is also used after the expression *como si* (as if):

Sus padres lo miraron como si hubiera (hubiese) dicho una mentira.

His parents looked at him as if he had told a lie.

Ellas me hablaban como si yo fuera una niña.

They spoke to me as if I were a child.

The imperfect subjunctive is used after the expression *ojalá (que)* (meaning "I wish," "I hope," or "If only" when referring to a hypothetical situation). The pluperfect subjunctive is used after *ojalá (que)* to express a contrary-to-fact situation in the past:

Ojalá que yo pudiera (pudiese) cantar.

I wish I could sing.

Ojalá que yo supiera (supiese) bailar.

If I only knew how to dance.

Ojalá que yo hubiera (hubiese) estado aquí cuando ellos llegaron.

I wish I had been here when they arrived.

Ojalá que ellos hubieran (hubiesen) hablado conmigo.

If only they had spoken with me.

The *-ra* ending of the imperfect subjunctive is often substituted for the conditional of *deber* (to have to), *querer* (to want to), and *poder* (to be able to) to soften the sentence and to be extremely polite:

Quisiera acompañarlos a la fiesta.	I would like to accompany you to the party.
Debieras tener más confianza.	You should be more confident.
Pudiera continuar.	You may continue.

Example Problems

Express this person's thoughts in Spanish.

1. If only you (formal singular) had understood the problem.

   Answer: Ojalá que Ud. hubiera (hubiese) comprendido el problema.

   Use *ojalá que* to express "if only." Use *comprender* to express "to understand." Use the pluperfect subjunctive to refer to express a contrary-to-fact situation in the past. The pluperfect subjunctive is formed by taking the imperfect subjunctive form of the auxiliary (helping) verb *haber* and adding the past participle of the action performed. The irregular preterit stem of *haber* is *hub-*. Form the third person plural preterit by adding *-ieron*. Drop *-ron* and add *-ra* or *-se* for the *Ud.* form of the imperfect subjunctive. To form the past participle of *comprender*, drop the *-er* ending and add *-ido*. Use *el problema* to express "the problem."

2. They should go out more often.

   Answer: Debieran salir más frecuentemente.

   The imperfect subjunctive (*-ra* form only) is often substituted for the conditional of *deber* to express what "should" be done and to soften the sentence. The imperfect subjunctive of regular verbs is formed by dropping *-ron* from the *ellos* form of the preterit tense. Form the third person plural preterit of a regular *-er* verb by dropping the *-er* ending and adding *-ieron*. Drop *-ron* and add *-ra* for the third person-plural form of the imperfect subjunctive. Use *más* to express "more." Use *frecuentemente* to express "frequently."

3. I hoped they would arrive sooner.

   Answer: Yo esperaba que ellos llegaran (llegasen) más pronto.

   The subjunctive is used after verbs showing hope. Use the imperfect of the verb *esperar* to show that the subject "was hoping." Drop the *-ar* ending and add *-aba* for the *yo* ending. Use *que* to express "that." Use the imperfect subjunctive to express "would" in the past. The imperfect subjunctive of regular verbs is formed by dropping *-ron* from the *ellos* form of the preterit tense. Form the third person plural preterit of a regular *-ar* verb by dropping the *-ar* ending and adding *-aron*. Drop *-ron* and add *-ran* or *-sen* for the third person plural form of the imperfect subjunctive. Use *más pronto* to express "sooner."

Work Problems

Use these problems to give yourself additional practice.

Express this person's thoughts in Spanish.

1. He called before she had returned home.

2. It was necessary that we go out immediately.

3. If only I had known how to speak Spanish.

4. I would like to go to Spain.

5. I was looking for a teacher who had studied in a Spanish-speaking country.

6. They talk as if they are rich.

Worked Solutions

1. **Él llamó antes de que ella hubiera (hubiese) regresado a casa.** Use the preterit of *llamar* (to call) to express the completed past action. Drop the *-ar* ending and add *-ó* for the *él* form. The conjunction *antes de que* always requires the use of the subjunctive. Use the pluperfect subjunctive to express what had happened in the past. The pluperfect subjunctive is formed by taking the imperfect subjunctive form of the auxiliary (helping) verb *haber* and adding the past participle of the action performed. The irregular preterit stem of *haber* is *hub-*. Form the third person plural preterit by adding *-ieron*. Drop *-ron* and add *-ra* or *-se* for the *ella* form of the imperfect subjunctive. To form the past participle of *regresar*, drop the *-ar* ending and add *-ado*.

2. **Era necesario que saliéramos (saliésemos) inmediatamente.** Use the imperfect of *ser* to express what "was" necessary. *Ser* is irregular in the imperfect. Use *er-* as the stem and add *-a* for the third person singular ending. Use the imperfect subjunctive to express the simple past. The imperfect subjunctive of regular verbs is formed by dropping *-ron* from the *ellos* form of the preterit tense. Form the third person plural preterit of a regular *-ir* verb by dropping the *-ir* ending and adding *-ieron*. Drop *-ron* and add an accent on the vowel *(e)* preceding the *-ramos* or *-semos* ending for the *nosotros* form of the imperfect subjunctive. Use *inmediatamente* to express "immediately."

3. **Ojalá que yo hubiera (hubiese) sabido hablar español.** Use *ojalá que* to express "if only." The pluperfect subjunctive is used after *ojalá que* when referring to a hypothetical situation. The pluperfect subjunctive is formed by taking the imperfect subjunctive form of the auxiliary (helping) verb *haber* and adding the past participle of the action performed. The irregular preterit stem of *haber* is *hub-*. Form the third person plural preterit by adding *-ieron*. Drop *-ron* and add *-ra* or *-se* for the first person singular form of the imperfect subjunctive. To form the past participle of *saber*, drop the *-er* ending and add *-ido*. Use *hablar* to express "speak." Use *español* to express "Spanish."

4. **Quisiera ir a España.** The imperfect subjunctive (*-ra* form only) is often substituted for the conditional of *querer* to soften the sentence. The irregular preterit stem of *querer* is *quis-*. Form the third person plural preterit by adding *-ieron*. Drop *-ron* and add *-ra* or *-se* for the third person singular form of the imperfect subjunctive. Use *ir* to express "to go." Use *a España* to express "to Spain."

5. **Buscaba a un profesor que hubiera (hubiese) estudiado en un país de habla española.** Use the imperfect of the verb *buscar* to show that the subject "was looking." Drop the *-ar* ending and add *-aba* for the *yo* ending. Use *un profesor* to express "a teacher." Use *que* to express "that." The subjunctive is used in relative clauses that show uncertainty. Use the pluperfect subjunctive to express "had studied." The pluperfect subjunctive is formed by taking the imperfect subjunctive form of the auxiliary (helping) verb *haber* and adding the past participle of the action performed. The irregular preterit stem of *haber* is *hub-*. Form the third person plural preterit by adding *-ieron*. Drop *-ron* and add *-ra* or *-se* for the third person singular form of the imperfect subjunctive. To form the past participle of *estudiar*, drop the *-ar* ending and add *-ado*. Use *en* to express "in." Use *un país* to express "a country." Use *de habla española* to express "Spanish-speaking."

6. **Hablan como si fueran (fuesen) ricos.** Use the present tense of the verb *hablar* to express "to speak." Drop the *-ar* ending and add *-an* for the third person plural form. Use *como si* to express "as if." Use the imperfect subjunctive to express "were." The irregular preterit stem of *ser* is *fu-*. Form the third person plural preterit by adding *-eron*. Drop *-ron* and add *-ran* or *-sen* for the third person plural form of the imperfect subjunctive. Use the masculine plural adjective *ricos* to express "rich" to describe the masculine plural subject.

Conditional Sentences

A conditional sentence consists of a condition, an "if" clause (*si* clause), and a result (main clause). Two basic conditions exist: "real" conditions and "unreal" (or "contrary-to-fact") conditions.

Real Conditions

Real conditions exist, are certain, or are likely to occur. Use the indicative after *si* to express a real condition:

> Dígame si quiere jugar al tenis esta tarde.
>
> Tell me if you want to play tennis this afternoon.
>
> Si tú me enviaste una invitación, yo no la recibí.
>
> If you sent me an invitation, I didn't receive it.

Contrary-to-Fact Conditions

Contrary-to-fact conditions or situations do not actually exist or have not occurred. To express something that is contrary-to-fact (not true) at the present time or something that was contrary-to-fact in the past, Spanish uses the imperfect or pluperfect subjunctive, respectively. The imperfect subjunctive expresses that something is not expected to happen but might happen in the future and is translated by "should" or "were to." The pluperfect subjunctive expresses that something was not expected to happen but might have happened and is translated by "should have" or "were to have." Note that the result, or main, clause is usually (but not always) expressed by the conditional or the conditional perfect.

Time	Tense of Si Clause	Tense of Result Clause
Present	Imperfect Subjunctive (-*ra* or -*se* form)	Conditional (preferred in simple tenses) or Imperfect Subjunctive (-*ra* form only)
Past	Pluperfect Subjunctive (-*ra* or -*se* form)	Conditional Perfect or Pluperfect Subjunctive (-*ra* form only)

Here are a couple of examples in sentences:

> Si tú ahorraras (ahorrases) mucho dinero, podrías (pudieras) comprar ese coche.
>
> If you saved (were to save) a lot of money, you could buy that car.
>
> Si tú hubieras (hubieses) ahorrado mucho dinero, habrías (hubieras) podido comprar ese coche.
>
> If you had saved (were to have saved) a lot of money, you could have bought that car.

Example Problems

Complete each thought about people's prerogatives with the correct form of the verb.

1. Si yo ganara la lotería, yo me _____ una casa grande.

    a. comprase

    b. compraría

    c. compraba

    d. hubiera comprado

Answer: b

When a contrary-to-fact condition exists, if the tense of the *si* clause is the imperfect subjunctive, the tense of the result clause is the conditional.

2. Si nosotros_____ el dinero, nosotros habríamos hecho un viaje a Europa.

    a. hubiéramos tenido

    b. hayamos tenido

    c. tenemos

    d. tendríamos

Answer: a

When a contrary-to-fact condition exists, if the tense of the result clause is the conditional perfect, the tense of the *si* clause is the pluperfect subjunctive.

3. Si ella recibe una beca, ella _____ a la universidad.

    a. iría

    b. hubiera ido

    c. vaya

    d. irá

Answer: d

When a real condition exists, the indicative is used. The future expresses that she will go to the university if she receives a scholarship.

Work Problems

Use these problems to give yourself additional practice.

Complete each thought about a day off with the correct form of the verb.

1. Si tú _____ un abrigo, tú tendrás calor.

    a. llevaste

    b. hubiera llevado

    c. lleves

    d. llevas

2. Si yo _____ nadar en el mar, yo habría ido al mar.

    a. querría

    b. habría querido

    c. quiera

    d. hubiera querido

3. Si nosotros tuviéramos bastante dinero, nosotros _____ a las montañas.

    a. iríamos

    b. hubiéramos ido

    c. iremos

    d. vayamos

4. Si ella _____ a jugar al tenis, ella practicaría con Uds.

    a. aprenda

    b. aprendiera

    c. aprende

    d. habría aprendido

5. Si vosotros _____ dormir al aire libre, vosotros habrías comprado un saco de dormir.

    a. habríais querido

    b. hubierais querido

    c. querrías

    d. queráis

6. Si Uds. escuchan el pronóstico del tiempo, Uds. _____ que tiempo hace.

    a. sepan

    b. sabrían

    c. sabrán

    d. hubieran sabido

Worked Solutions

1. **d**   When a real condition exists, the indicative is used. The present expresses that if you wear a coat, you will be warm.

2. **d**   When a contrary-to-fact condition exists, if the tense of the result clause is the conditional perfect, the tense of the *si* clause is the pluperfect subjunctive.

3. **a**   When a contrary-to-fact condition exists, if the tense of the *si* clause is the imperfect subjunctive, the tense of the result clause is the conditional.

4. **b**   When a real condition exists, the indicative is used. The present expresses that if she learns to play tennis, she will practice with you.

5. **b** When a contrary-to-fact condition exists, if the tense of the result clause is the conditional perfect, the tense of the *si* clause is the pluperfect subjunctive.

6. **c** When a real condition exists, the indicative is used. The future expresses that you will know what the weather is like if you listen to the weather report.

Chapter Problems

Problems

Express what each person would do under the circumstances described.

> Example: Isabel sale de la escuela. Tiene hambre. Se compra un helado.
> Si Isabel tuviera (tuviese) hambre, se compraría un helado.

1. Carlota no es una muchacha muy aplicada. Ella sale muy bien en sus exámenes. Ella grita de alegría.

2. El señor Padilla siempre se viste con mucho cuidado. Él deja caer una taza de café en su traje. Él no está contento.

3. Enrique es un muchacho muy débil. Sus compañeros de clase lo molestan. Él no los escucha.

4. La señora Marcos siempre llega temprano a la oficina. Un día ella llega tarde. El director no le dice nada.

5. El señor Cruz es muy distraído. Se pone el sombrero en la cabeza. No puede encontrarlo.

Express how this person lived.

> Vivió como si . . .
> Example: (no) estar contento
> Vivió como si (no) hubiera (hubiese) estado contento.

6. ser rey del mundo

7. no sufrir de nada

8. no tener miedo de la muerte

9. conocer a todo el mundo

10. ganar mucho dinero

Express what a counselor at school says to a student.

11. You (formal singular) should try to do well.

12. I wish you (formal singular) had come to see me sooner.

13. The principal insisted that I call you.

14. I would like to help you.

15. You may begin to speak.

Express how the people react to the different situations by completing each sentence with the correct form of the verb in parentheses.

16. Si yo (ser) _____ famoso, yo sería rico.

17. Si Ud. (hacer) _____ un error, Ud. lo habría corregido.

18. Si un amigo mío (faltar) a _____ una cita conmigo, yo le telefonearía.

19. Si tú (lavar) _____ mi coche, yo te pagaré.

20. Si nosotros no (encontrar)_____ nuestros pasaportes perdidos, nosotros hubiéramos ido a la embajada americana.

Answers and Solutions

1. **Answer: Si Carlota saliera (saliese) muy bien en sus exámenes, ella gritaría de alegría.**
When a contrary-to-fact condition exists, if the tense of the *si* clause is the imperfect subjunctive, the tense of the result clause is the conditional. The imperfect subjunctive of regular verbs is formed by dropping -*ron* from the *ellos* form of the preterit tense. Form the third person plural preterit of a regular -*ir* verb by dropping the -*ir* ending and adding -*ieron*. Drop -*ron* and add -*ra* or -*se* for the *ella* form of the imperfect subjunctive. The verb *gritar* is regular in the conditional. To conjugate regular -*ar* verbs in the conditional, keep the -*ar* ending and add -*ía* as the ending for *ella*.

2. **Answer: Si el señor Padilla dejara (dejase) caer una taza de café en su traje, él no estaría contento.**   When a contrary-to-fact condition exists, if the tense of the *si* clause is the imperfect subjunctive, the tense of the result clause is the conditional. The imperfect subjunctive of regular verbs is formed by dropping -*ron* from the *ellos* form of the preterit tense. Form the third person plural preterit of a regular -*ar* verb by dropping the -*ar* ending and adding -*aron*. Drop -*ron* and add -*ra* or -*se* for the third person singular form of the imperfect subjunctive. The verb *estar* is regular in the conditional. To conjugate regular -*ar* verbs in the conditional, keep the -*ar* ending and add -*ía* as the ending for *él*.

3. **Answer: Si sus compañeros de clase lo molestaran (molestasen), Enrique no los escucharía.**   When a contrary-to-fact condition exists, if the tense of the *si* clause is the imperfect subjunctive, the tense of the result clause is the conditional. The imperfect subjunctive of regular verbs is formed by dropping -*ron* from the *ellos* form of the preterit tense. Form the third person plural preterit of a regular -*ar* verb by dropping the -*ar* ending and adding -*aron*. Drop -*ron* and add -*ran* or -*sen* for the third person plural form of the imperfect subjunctive. The verb *escuchar* is regular in the conditional. To conjugate regular -*ar* verbs in the conditional, keep the -*ar* ending and add -*ía* as the ending for the third person singular.

4. **Answer: Si la señora Marcos llegara (llegase) tarde, el director no le diría nada.**
When a contrary-to-fact condition exists, if the tense of the *si* clause is the imperfect subjunctive, the tense of the result clause is the conditional. The imperfect subjunctive of regular verbs is formed by dropping -*ron* from the *ellos* form of the preterit tense. Form the third person plural preterit of a regular -*ar* verb by dropping the -*ar* ending and adding -*aron*. Drop -*ron* and add -*ra* or -*se* for the third person singular form of the imperfect subjunctive. The verb *decir* is irregular in the conditional and must be memorized. Use

dir- as the conditional stem and add the third person singular conditional ending *(-ía)* for *el director.*

5. **Answer: Si el señor Cruz se pusiera (pusiese) el sombrero en la cabeza, no podría encontrarlo.** When a contrary-to-fact condition exists, if the tense of the *si* clause is the imperfect subjunctive, the tense of the result clause is the conditional. To form the imperfect subjunctive, use the irregular preterit stem of *poner: pus-.* Form the third person plural preterit by adding *-ieron.* Drop *-ron* and add *-ra* or *-se* for the third person singular form of the imperfect subjunctive. The verb *poder* is irregular in the conditional and must be memorized. Drop the *e* from the infinitive ending and add *-ía* as the ending for the third person singular.

6. **Answer: Vivió como si hubiera (hubiese) sido rey del mundo.** After *como si,* use the pluperfect subjunctive to express the past. The pluperfect subjunctive is formed by taking the imperfect subjunctive form of the auxiliary (helping) verb *haber* and adding the past participle of the action performed. The irregular preterit stem of *haber* is *hub-.* Form the third person plural preterit by adding *-ieron.* Drop *-ron* and add *-ra* or *-se* for the third person singular form of the imperfect subjunctive. The past participle of *ser* is irregular and must be memorized: *sido.*

7. **Answer: Vivió como si no hubiera (hubiese) sufrido de nada.** After *como si,* use the pluperfect subjunctive to express the past. The pluperfect subjunctive is formed by taking the imperfect subjunctive form of the auxiliary (helping) verb *haber* and adding the past participle of the action performed. The irregular preterit stem of *haber* is *hub-.* Form the third person plural preterit by adding *-ieron.* Drop *-ron* and add *-ra* or *-se* for the third person singular form of the imperfect subjunctive. To form the past participle of *sufrir,* drop the *-ir* ending and add *-ido.*

8. **Answer: Vivió como si no hubiera (hubiese) tenido miedo de la muerte.** After *como si,* use the pluperfect subjunctive to express the past. The pluperfect subjunctive is formed by taking the imperfect subjunctive form of the auxiliary (helping) verb *haber* and adding the past participle of the action performed. The irregular preterit stem of *haber* is *hub-.* Form the third person plural preterit by adding *-ieron.* Drop *-ron* and add *-ra* or *-se* for the third person singular form of the imperfect subjunctive. To form the past participle of *tener,* drop the *-er* ending and add *-ido.*

9. **Answer: Vivió como si hubiera (hubiese) conocido a todo el mundo.** After *como si,* use the pluperfect subjunctive to express the past. The pluperfect subjunctive is formed by taking the imperfect subjunctive form of the auxiliary (helping) verb *haber* and adding the past participle of the action performed. The irregular preterit stem of *haber* is *hub-.* Form the third person plural preterit by adding *-ieron.* Drop *-ron* and add *-ra* or *-se* for the third person singular form of the imperfect subjunctive. To form the past participle of *conocer,* drop the *-er* ending and add *-ido.*

10. **Answer: Vivió como si hubiera (hubiese) ganado mucho dinero.** After *como si,* use the pluperfect subjunctive to express the past. The pluperfect subjunctive is formed by taking the imperfect subjunctive form of the auxiliary (helping) verb *haber* and adding the past participle of the action performed. The irregular preterit stem of *haber* is *hub-.* Form the third person plural preterit by adding *-ieron.* Drop *-ron* and add *-ra* or *-se* for the third person singular form of the imperfect subjunctive. To form the past participle of *ganar,* drop the *-ar* ending and add *-ado.*

11. **Answer: Debiera tratar de salir bien.** The imperfect subjunctive (*-ra* form only) is often substituted for the conditional of *deber* to express what "should" be done and to soften the sentence. The imperfect subjunctive of regular verbs is formed by dropping *-ron* from the *ellos* form of the preterit tense. Form the third person plural preterit of a regular *-er*

verb by dropping the *-er* ending and adding *-ieron*. Drop *-ron* and add *-ra* for the *Ud.* form of the imperfect subjunctive. Use the infinitive *tratar* to express "to try" immediately after the conjugated form of *deber*. The verb *tratar* is followed by the preposition *de*, which is followed by the term *salir bien* to express "to do well."

12. **Answer: Ojalá que hubiera (hubiese) venido a verme más pronto.**   Use *ojalá que* to express "if only." Use the pluperfect subjunctive to express a contrary-to-fact situation in the past. The pluperfect subjunctive is formed by taking the imperfect subjunctive form of the auxiliary (helping) verb *haber* and adding the past participle of the action performed. The irregular preterit stem of *haber* is *hub-*. Form the third person plural preterit by adding *-ieron*. Drop *-ron* and add *-ra* or *-se* for the third person singular form of the imperfect subjunctive. Use *venir* to express "to come." To form the past participle of *venir*, drop the *-ir* ending and add *-ido*. *Venir* is followed by the preposition *a*. Use the infinitive *ver* to express "to see" immediately after the preposition. Use *me* to express "me". Attach *me* to the infinitive. Alternatively, *me* may be placed before the helping verb: *hubiera (hubiese)*. Use *más pronto* to express "sooner".

13. **Answer: El director insistió en que yo lo llamara (llamase) a Ud.**   Use *el director* to express "the principal". Use the preterit of the verb *insistir* (to insist) to express the completed action. Drop the *-ir* ending and add *-ió* for the third person singular form. *Insistir* is followed by the preposition *en*. Use *que* to express "that." The imperfect subjunctive is used after verbs that show a request in the past. The imperfect subjunctive of regular verbs is formed by dropping *-ron* from the *ellos* form of the preterit tense. Form the third person plural preterit of a regular *-ar* verb by dropping the *-ar* ending and adding *-aron*. Drop *-ron* and add *-ra* or *-se* for the *yo* of the imperfect subjunctive.

14. **Answer: Quisiera ayudarle a Ud.**   The imperfect subjunctive (*-ra* form only) is often substituted for the conditional of *querer* to soften the sentence. The irregular preterit stem of *querer* is *quis-*. Form the third person plural preterit by adding *-ieron*. Drop *-ron* and add *-ra* or *-se* for the third person singular form of the imperfect subjunctive. Use the infinitive *ayudar* to express "to help" immediately after the preposition. Use *le* to express "you." Attach *le* to the infinitive. Alternatively, *le* may be placed before the conjugated verb: *quisiera*. Use *a Ud.* to clarify "you."

15. **Answer: Pudiera empezar a hablar.**   The imperfect subjunctive (*-ra* form only) is often substituted for the conditional of *poder* to soften the sentence. The irregular preterit stem of *poder* is *pud-*. Form the third person plural preterit by adding *-ieron*. Drop *-ron* and add *-ra* for the third person singular form of the imperfect subjunctive. Use the infinitive *empezar* to express "to begin" immediately after the infinitive. *Empezar* is followed by the preposition *a*. Use the infinitive *hablar* to express "to speak" immediately after the preposition.

16. **Answer: fuera (fuese)**   When a contrary-to-fact condition exists, if the tense of the result clause is the conditional, the tense of the *si* clause is the imperfect subjunctive. To form the imperfect subjunctive, take the irregular preterit stem of *ser*: *fu-*. Form the third person plural preterit by adding *-eron*. Drop *-ron* and add *-ra* or *-se* for the *yo* form of the imperfect subjunctive.

17. **Answer: hubiera (hubiese) hecho**   When a contrary-to-fact condition exists, if the tense of the result clause is the conditional perfect, the tense of the *si* clause is the pluperfect subjunctive. The pluperfect subjunctive is formed by taking the imperfect subjunctive form of the auxiliary (helping) verb *haber* and adding the past participle of the action performed. The irregular preterit stem of *haber* is *hub-*. Form the third person plural preterit by adding *-ieron*. Drop *-ron* and add *-ra* or *-se* for the *Ud.* form of the imperfect subjunctive. The past participle of *hacer* is irregular and must be memorized: *hecho*.

18. **Answer: faltara (faltase)**　When a contrary-to-fact condition exists, if the tense of the *si* clause is the imperfect subjunctive, the tense of the result clause is the conditional. The imperfect subjunctive of regular verbs is formed by dropping *-ron* from the *ellos* form of the preterit tense. Form the third person plural preterit of a regular *-ar* verb by dropping the *-ar* ending and adding *-aron*. Drop *-ron* and add *-ra* or *-se* for the third person singular form of the imperfect subjunctive.

19. **Answer: lavas**　When a real condition exists, the indicative is used. The future expresses that if you wash my car, I will pay you.

20. **Answer: hubiéramos (hubiésemos) encontrado**　When a contrary-to-fact condition exists, if the tense of the result clause is the conditional perfect, the tense of the *si* clause is the pluperfect subjunctive. The pluperfect subjunctive is formed by taking the imperfect subjunctive form of the auxiliary (helping) verb *haber* and adding the past participle of the action performed. The irregular preterit stem of *haber* is *hub-*. Form the third person plural preterit by adding *-ieron*. Drop *-ron* and add an accent on the vowel *(e)* preceding the *-ramos* or *-semos* ending for the *nosotros* form of the imperfect subjunctive. To form the past participle of *encontrar*, drop the *-ar* ending and add *-ado*.

Supplemental Chapter Problems

Problems

Express what each person would do under the circumstances described (see the previous example).

1. Julia tiene miedo de los perros. Ella ve a un perro. Corre.

2. La señora Martín es muy vanidosa. Tiene el pelo gris. Llora.

3. Rogelio es un muchacho muy serio. Sus amigos le gastan una broma. Él se enoja.

4. Mauricio quiere salir con Bárbara. Ella le escribe una carta de amor. Él le telefonea.

5. Lorenzo tiene una discusión desagradable con Esteban. Esteban lo invita a pelear. Lorenzo no acepta.

Express how this person spent money by using the pluperfect subjunctive (see the previosu example).

　　Gastó dinero como si . . .

6. ser millionario

7. ganar la lotería

8. no tener deudas

9. no estar inquieto

10. heredar una fortuna

Express what a person interviewing you says.

11. You may come in.

12. You should speak more slowly.

13. I would like to ask you some questions.

14. I doubted that you saw our ad.

15. I wish you had called me sooner.

Express how the people react to the different situations by completing each sentence with the correct form of the verb in parentheses.

16. Si yo (arreglar) _____ mi cuarto, yo podré salir esta noche.

17. Si ella (aprender)_____ el español, ella habría viajado a España.

18. Si un amigo tuyo te (decepcionar) _____, tu te pondrías furioso.

19. Si ellos (tener) _____ hambre, ellos comerían en un restaurante italiano.

20. Si nosotros (ganar) _____ la lotería, nosotros hubiéramos dejado de trabajar.

Solutions

1. Si Julia viera (viese) a un perro, ella correría. (the imperfect subjunctive of regular and irregular verbs, p. 325; conditional sentences, p. 341; contrary-to-fact conditions, p. 341)

2. Si la señora Martín tuviera (tuviese) el pelo gris, ella lloraría. (the imperfect subjunctive of regular and irregular verbs, p. 325; conditional sentences, p. 341; contrary-to-fact conditions, p. 341)

3. Si sus amigos le gastaran (gastasen) una broma, Rogelio se enojaría. (the imperfect subjunctive of regular and irregular verbs, p. 325; conditional sentences, p. 341; contrary-to-fact conditions, p. 341)

4. Si Bárbara le escribiera (escribiese) una carta de amor, Mauricio le telefonearía. (the imperfect subjunctive of regular and irregular verbs, p. 325; conditional sentences, p. 341; contrary-to-fact conditions, p. 341)

5. Si Esteban lo invitara (invitase) a pelear, Lorenzo no aceptaría. (the imperfect subjunctive of regular and irregular verbs, p. 325; conditional sentences, p. 341; contrary-to-fact conditions, p. 341)

6. Gastó dinero como si hubiera sido millonario. (the imperfect subjunctive, p. 325; using the imperfect subjunctive and pluperfect subjunctive, p. 337)

7. Gastó dinero como si hubiera ganado la lotería. (the imperfect subjunctive, p. 325; using the imperfect subjunctive and pluperfect subjunctive, p. 337)

8. Gastó dinero como si no hubiera tenido deudas. (the imperfect subjunctive, p. 325; using the imperfect subjunctive and pluperfect subjunctive, p. 337)

9. Gastó dinero como si no hubiera estado inquieto. (the imperfect subjunctive, p. 325; using the imperfect subjunctive and pluperfect subjunctive, p. 337)

10. Gastó dinero como si hubiera heredado una fortuna. (the imperfect subjunctive, p. 325; using the imperfect subjunctive and pluperfect subjunctive, p. 337)

11. Pudiera entrar. (forming the pluperfect subjunctive of all verbs, p. 335; using the imperfect subjunctive and pluperfect subjunctive, p. 337)

12. Debiera hablar más despacio. (forming the pluperfect subjunctive of all verbs, p. 335; using the imperfect and pluperfect subjunctive, p. 337)

13. Quisiera hacerle algunas preguntas a Ud.. (forming the pluperfect subjunctive of all verbs, p. 335; using the imperfect subjunctive and pluperfect subjunctive, p. 337)

14. Yo dudé que Ud. hubiera visto nuestro anuncio. (the imperfect subjunctive, p. 325; using the imperfect subjunctive and pluperfect subjunctive, p. 337)

15. Ojalá que me hubiera (hubiese) llamado más pronto. (the imperfect subjunctive, p. 325; using the imperfect subjunctive and pluperfect subjunctive, p. 337)

16. arreglo (conditional sentences, p. 341; real conditions, p. 341)

17. hubiera aprendido (conditional sentences, p. 341; contrary-to-fact conditions, p. 341; forming the pluperfect subjunctive of all verbs, p. 335)

18. decepcionara (decepcionase) (conditional sentences, p. 341; contrary-to-fact conditions, p. 341; the imperfect subjunctive, p. 325)

19. tuvieran (conditional sentences, p. 341; contrary-to-fact conditions, p. 341; the imperfect subjunctive, p. 325)

20. hubiéramos ganado (conditional sentences, p. 341; contrary-to-fact conditions, p. 341; forming the pluperfect subjunctive of all verbs, p. 335)

Chapter 16
The Imperative

The imperative is a mood used to give a command. Just as in English, the subject of most commands is understood to be "you." There are four ways to express "you" in Spanish, depending on whether the speaker is being formal (polite) or informal (familiar) or whether the speaker is addressing one or more than one person.

	Singular	Plural
Informal (familiar)	tú	vosotros
Formal (polite)	usted (Ud.)	(ustedes) Uds.

Formal Commands

A speaker addresses formal, or polite, commands to people who are older or who are unfamiliar to the speaker. The subject of the command is *Ud.* (if one person is being addressed) or *Uds.* (if more than one person is being addressed).

In Spanish, the use of the subject pronoun in the command is optional. When the subject pronoun is not used, the verb form being used identifies the subject.

Regular Verbs

To form an affirmative or a negative command with any verb when *Ud.* or *Uds.* is the subject, use the present subjunctive of the *Ud.* or *Uds.* form of that verb. To form the present subjunctive:

1. Drop the final *-o* from the *yo* form of the present tense.

2. For infinitives ending in *-ar,* add *-e* for *Ud.* and *-en* for *Uds.*

   For infinitives ending in *-er* or *-ir,* add *-a* for *Ud.* and *-an* for *Uds.*

Infinitive	*Affirmative*	*Negative*	*Meaning*
-ar: trabajar (to work)	trabaje(n) (Ud.)(s.)	no trabaje(n) (Ud.)(s)	(don't) work
-er: comer (to eat)	coma(n) (Ud.)(s.)	no coma(n) (Ud.)(s)	(don't) eat
-ir: escribir (to write)	escriba(n) (Ud.)(s.)	no escriba(n) (Ud.)(s)	(don't) write

An inverted exclamation mark (¡) may be placed at the beginning of an emphasized command with a regular exclamation mark (!) placed at the end:

¡Hablen (Uds.) más despacio!   Speak slower!

¡No lea (Ud.) tan rápidamente!   Don't read so quickly!

Spelling-Change, Stem-Changing, and Irregular Verbs

Most spelling-change, all stem-changing, and all irregular *yo* form verbs form the affirmative and negative imperative by using the present subjunctive of the *Ud.* or *Uds.* form of that verb. Exceptions to this rule include spelling-change verbs that end in *-car*, *-gar*, or *-zar*. For these verbs only, the present subjunctive is formed by dropping the final *-é* from the *yo* form of the preterit tense and adding *-e* for *Ud.* and *-en* for *Uds.*

¡Explique la regla!	Explain the rule!
¡Pague la cuenta!	Pay the bill!
¡No avance!	Don't advance!

Formal Commands for Irregular *Yo* Form Verbs			
Infinitive	**Affirmative**	**Negative**	**Meaning**
decir	diga(n) (Ud.)(s)	no diga(n) (Ud.)(s)	(don't) tell (don't) say
hacer	haga(n) (Ud.)(s)	no haga(n) (Ud.)(s)	(don't) do
oír	oiga(n) (Ud.)(s)	no oiga(n) (Ud.)(s)	(don't) hear
poner	ponga(n) (Ud.)(s)	no ponga(n) (Ud.)(s)	(don't) put
salir	salga(n) (Ud.)(s)	no salga(n) (Ud.)(s)	(don't) leave
tener	tenga(n) (Ud.)(s)	no tenga(n) (Ud.)(s)	(don't) have (don't) be (in certain idiomatic expressions)
traer	traiga(n) (Ud.)(s)	no traiga(n) (Ud.)(s)	(don't) bring
valer	valga(n) (Ud.)(s)	no valga(n) (Ud.)(s)	(don't) be worth
venir	venga(n) (Ud.)(s)	no venga(n) (Ud.)(s)	(don't) come

Formal Commands for Spelling-Change Verbs			
Infinitive	**Affirmative**	**Negative**	**Meaning**
bus**c**ar	bus**que**(n) (Ud.)(s)	no bus**que**(n) (Ud.)(s)	(don't) look for
lle**g**ar	lle**gue**(n) (Ud.)(s)	no lle**gue**(n) (Ud.)(s)	(don't) arrive
trope**z**ar	trope**ce**(n) (Ud.)(s)	no trope**ce**(n) (Ud.)(s)	(don't) stumble
ven**c**er	ven**za**(n) (Ud.)(s)	no ven**za**(n) (Ud.)(s)	(don't) conquer
obede**c**er	obede**zca**(n) (Ud.)(s)	no obede**zca**(n) (Ud.)(s)	(don't) obey
zur**c**ir	zur**za**(n) (Ud.)(s)	no zur**za**(n) (Ud.)(s)	(don't) mend
condu**c**ir	condu**zca**(n) (Ud.)(s)	no condu**zca**(n) (Ud.)(s)	(don't) drive
esco**g**er	esco**ja**(n) (Ud.)(s)	no esco**ja**(n) (Ud.)(s)	(don't) choose
diri**g**ir	diri**ja**(n) (Ud.)(s)	no diri**ja**(n) (Ud.)(s)	(don't) direct
distin**gu**ir	distin**ga**(n) (Ud.)(s)	no distin**ga**(n) (Ud.)(s)	(don't) distinguish

Formal Commands for Stem-Changing Verbs			
Infinitive	*Affirmative*	*Negative*	*Meaning*
cerrar	cierre(n) (Ud.)(s)	no cierre(n) (Ud.)(s)	(don't) close
mostrar	muestre(n) (Ud.)(s)	no muestre(n) (Ud.)(s)	(don't) show
perder	pierda(n) (Ud.)(s)	no pierda(n) (Ud.)(s)	(don't) lose
devolver	devuelva(n) (Ud.)(s)	no devuelva(n) (Ud.)(s)	(don't) give back
advertir	advierta(n) (Ud.)(s)	no advierta(n) (Ud.)(s)	(don't) warn
dormir	duerma(n) (Ud.)(s)	no duerma(n) (Ud.)(s)	(don't) sleep
servir	sirva(n) (Ud.)(s)	no sirva(n) (Ud.)(s)	(don't) serve
guiar	guíe(n) (Ud.)(s)	no guíe(n) (Ud.)(s)	(don't) guide
actuar	actúe(n) (Ud.)(s)	no actúe(n) (Ud.)(s)	(don't) act
concluir	concluya(n) (Ud.)(s)	no concluya(n) (Ud.)(s)	(don't) conclude

Formal Commands for Irregular Verbs			
Infinitive	*Affirmative*	*Negative*	*Meaning*
dar	dé (den) (Ud.)(s)	no dé (den) (Ud.)(s)	(don't) give
estar	esté(n) (Ud.)(s)	no esté(n) (Ud.)(s)	(don't) be
ir	vaya(n) (Ud.)(s)	no vaya(n) (Ud.)(s)	(don't) go
saber	sepa(n) (Ud.)(s)	no sepa(n) (Ud.)(s)	(don't) know
ser	sea(n) (Ud.)(s)	no sea(n) (Ud.)(s)	(don't) be

Here are two examples:

¡(No) Cierre las ventanas!   (Don't) Close the windows!

¡(No) Vayan a la farmacia!   (Don't) Go to the drugstore!

Example Problems

Express the advice an older teacher gives a new staff member.

1. (servir) _____ de ejemplo a los alumnos.

Answer: Sirva

To form a command with *Ud.*, use the present subjunctive of the verb. The present tense of the stem-changing verb *servir* changes the internal *e* to *i*. To form the present subjunctive for *servir*, drop the final *-o* from the *yo* form of the present tense *(sirvo)* and add *-a*.

2. (ofrecer) _____ su ayuda.

Answer: Ofrezca

To form a command with *Ud.*, use the present subjunctive of the verb. The present tense of the stem-changing verb *ofrecer* changes the *c* to *zc* in the *yo* form. To form the present subjunctive for *ofrecer*, drop the final *-o* from the *yo* form of the present tense *(ofrezco)* and add *-a*.

3. (explicar) _____ bien las reglas.

Answer: Explique

To form a command with *Ud.*, use the present subjunctive of the verb. To form the present subjunctive for the spelling-change verb *explicar*, drop the final *-é* from the *yo* form of the preterit tense *(expliqué)* and add *-e*.

Work Problems

Use these problems to give yourself additional practice.

Continue expressing the advice of the seasoned teacher:

1. (dar) _____ consejos.

2. (tener) _____ sentido del humor.

3. (perder) No _____ la paciencia.

4. (conducir) _____ la clase en español.

5. (castigar) _____ a los alumnos distraídos.

6. (asentar) _____ a los alumnos por orden alfabético.

7. (demostrar) _____ su interés en la materia.

8. (corregir) _____ los errores de los alumnos.

Worked Solutions

1. **Dé** To form a command with *Ud.*, use the present subjunctive of the verb. The present subjunctive for the verb *dar* is irregular and must be memorized. Note that the *Ud.* form has an accented *-é*.

2. **Tenga** To form a command with *Ud.*, use the present subjunctive of the verb. To form the present subjunctive for the irregular verb *tener*, drop the final *-o* from the *yo* form of the present tense *(tengo)* and add *-a*.

3. **pierda** To form a command with *Ud.*, use the present subjunctive of the verb. The present tense of the stem-changing verb *perder* changes the internal *e* to *ie*. To form the present subjunctive for *perder*, drop the final *-o* from the *yo* form of the present tense *(pierdo)* and add *-a*.

4. **Conduzca**   To form a command with *Ud.*, use the present subjunctive of the verb. The present tense of the stem-changing verb *conducir* changes the *c* to *zc* in the *yo* form. To form the present subjunctive for *conducir*, drop the final *-o* from the *yo* form of the present tense *(conduzco)* and add *-a*.

5. **Castigue**   To form a command with *Ud.*, use the present subjunctive of the verb. To form the present subjunctive for the spelling-change verb *castigar*, drop the final *-é* from the *yo* form of the preterit tense *(castigué)* and add *-e*.

6. **Asiente**   To form a command with *Ud.*, use the present subjunctive of the verb. The present tense of the stem-changing verb *asentar* changes the internal *e* to *ie*. To form the present subjunctive for *asentar*, drop the final *-o* from the *yo* form of the present tense *(asiento)* and add *-e*.

7. **Demuestre**   To form a command with *Ud.*, use the present subjunctive of the verb. The present tense of the stem-changing verb *demostrar* changes the internal *o* to *ue*. To form the present subjunctive for *demostrar*, drop the final *-o* from the *yo* form of the present tense *(demuestro)* and add *-e*.

8. **Corrija**   To form a command with *Ud.*, use the present subjunctive of the verb. The present tense of the spelling-change verb *corregir* changes the *g* to *j*. To form the present subjunctive for *corregir*, drop the final *-o* from the *yo* form of the present tense *(corrijo)* and add *-a*.

Informal Commands

Informal or familiar commands are addressed to friends, peers, family members, or pets. Use *tú* if one person is being addressed or *vosotros* if more than one person is being addressed. The *vosotros* command is used primarily in Spain. In Latin American countries, the *Uds.* form is used exclusively for informal plural commands.

Informal Singular Commands with *Tú*

To form an affirmative command with any verb when *tú* is the subject, use the *tú* form of the present indicative and drop the final *-s* (which results in the *él* form of the present indicative). A few irregular verbs have irregular informal affirmative command forms and must be memorized.

To form a negative command with any verb when *tú* is the subject (except for the *-car*, *-gar*, and *-zar* verbs mentioned above, in which the final *-é* is dropped from the *yo* form of the preterit), use the present subjunctive *tú* form. To form the present subjunctive:

1. Drop the final *-o* from the *yo* form of the present tense.

2. For infinitives ending in *-ar*, add *-es* for the *tú* form.

    For infinitives ending in *-er* or *-ir*, add *-as* for the *tú* form.

Informal Singular Commands for Regular Verbs			
Infinitive	*Affirmative*	*Negative*	*Meaning*
trabajar	trabaja (tú)	no trabajes (tú)	(don't) work
comer	come (tú)	no comas (tú)	(don't) eat
escribir	escribe (tú)	no escribas (tú)	(don't) write

Informal Singular Commands for Irregular *Yo* Form Verbs

Infinitive	Affirmative	Negative	Meaning
oír	oye (tú)	no oigas (tú)	(don't) hear
traer	trae (tú)	no traigas (tú)	(don't) bring

Informal Singular Commands for Spelling-Change Verbs

Infinitive	Affirmative	Negative	Meaning
buscar	busca (tú)	no busques (tú)	(don't) look for
llegar	llega (tú)	no llegues (tú)	(don't) arrive
tropezar	tropieza (tú)	no tropieces (tú)	(don't) stumble
vencer	vence (tú)	no venzas (tú)	(don't) conquer
obedecer	obedece (tú)	no obedezcas (tú)	(don't) obey
zurcir	zurce (tú)	no zurzas (tú)	(don't) mend
conducir	conduce (tú)	no conduzcas (tú)	(don't) drive
escoger	escoge (tú)	no escojas (tú)	(don't) choose
dirigir	dirige (tú)	no dirijas (tú)	(don't) direct
distinguir	distingue (tú)	no distingas (tú)	(don't) distinguish

Informal Singular Commands for Stem-Changing Verbs

Infinitive	Affirmative	Negative	Meaning
cerrar	cierra (tú)	no cierres (tú)	(don't) close
mostrar	muestra (tú)	no muestres (tú)	(don't) show
perder	pierde (tú)	no pierdas (tú)	(don't) lose
devolver	devuelve (tú)	no devuelvas (tú)	(don't) give back
advertir	advierte (tú)	no adviertas (tú)	(don't) warn
dormir	duerme (tú)	no duermas (tú)	(don't) sleep
servir	sirve (tú)	no sirvas (tú)	(don't) serve
guiar	guía (tú)	no guíes (tú)	(don't) guide
actuar	actúa (tú)	no actúes (tú)	(don't) act
concluir	concluye (tú)	no concluyas (tú)	(don't) conclude

Informal Singular Commands for Irregular Verbs			
Infinitive	*Affirmative*	*Negative*	*Meaning*
decir	di (tú)	no digas (tú)	(don't) tell
hacer	haz (tú)	no hagas (tú)	(don't) do
ir	ve (tú)	no vayas (tú)	(don't) go
poner	pon (tú)	no pongas (tú)	(don't) put
salir	sal (tú)	no salgas (tú)	(don't) leave
ser	sé (tú)	no seas (tú)	(don't) be
tener	ten (tú)	no tengas (tú)	(don't) have (don't) be
valer	val *or* vale (tú)	no valgas (tú)	(don't) be worth
venir	ven (tú)	no vengas (tú)	(don't) come

Here are two examples, using both affirmative and negative commands. Note that *tú* is generally not used when issuing an informal command:

| ¡Sirve pollo! | ¡No sirvas pollo! | (Don't) Serve chicken! |
| ¡Sé optimista! | ¡No seas optimista! | (Don't) Be optimistic! |

Example Problems

Express what the director of the school play is saying to individual students.

> Example: no hablar en voz baja, sino en voz alta
> No hables en voz baja. Habla en voz alta.

1. no volver a la escuela a las seis, sino a las siete

Answer: No vuelvas a la escuela a las seis. Vuelve a las siete.

To form a negative command with *tú*, use the present subjunctive *tú* form. To form the present subjunctive for the stem-changing verb *volver*, change the internal *o* to *ue* (the same change made for the present indicative *yo* form). Drop the *-er* ending and add the present subjunctive ending for *tú (-as)*. To negate the command, put *no* before the conjugated verb. To form an affirmative command with *tú*, drop the final *-s* from the second person singular present indicative form of *tú (vuelves)*.

2. no actuar de manera cómica, sino de manera seria

Answer: No actúes de manera cómica. Actúa de manera seria.

To form a negative command with *tú*, use the present subjunctive *tú* form. To form the present subjunctive for the spelling-changing verb *actuar*, change the internal *u* to *ú* (the same change made for the present indicative *yo* form). Drop the *-ar* ending and add the present subjunctive ending for *tú (-es)*. To negate the command, put *no* before the conjugated verb. To form an affirmative command with *tú*, drop the final *-s* from the second person singular present indicative form of *tú (actúas)*.

3. no venir a la escuela solo, sino con tus amigos

Answer: No vengas a la escuela solo. Ven con tus amigos.

To form a negative command with *tú*, use the present subjunctive *tú* form. Take the irregular *yo* form of the present tense *(vengo)*. Drop the *-o* and add the *tú* form subjunctive ending *(-as)*. To negate the command, put *no* before the conjugated verb. The informal affirmative command form of *venir* is irregular and must be memorized: *ven*.

Work Problems

Use these problems to give yourself additional practice.

Continue to express what the director of the school play is saying to individual students. Follow the example given previously.

1. no hacer el papel del príncipe, sino el del rey

2. no ser cantante, sino bailarina

3. no tocar el violín, sino el piano

4. no ir a la derecha, sino a la izquierda

5. no poner las sillas, sino los folletos

6. no cerrar las ventanas, sino la puerta

7. no llegar tarde, sino temprano

8. no obedecer a Carlos, sino a Julio

Worked Solutions

1. **No hagas el papel del príncipe. Haz el papel del rey.**   To form a negative command with *tú*, use the present subjunctive *tú* form. Take the irregular *yo* form of the present tense *(hago)*. Drop the *-o* and add the *tú* form subjunctive ending *(-as)*. To negate the command, put *no* before the conjugated verb. The informal affirmative command form of *hacer* is irregular and must be memorized: *haz*.

2. **No seas cantante. Sé bailarina.**   To form a negative command with *tú*, use the present subjunctive *tú* form. Take the irregular stem of the subjunctive *(se-)*. Add the *tú* form subjunctive ending *(-as)*. To negate the command, put *no* before the conjugated verb. The informal affirmative command form of *ser* is irregular and must be memorized: *sé*.

3. **No toques el violín. Toca el piano.**   To form a negative command with *tú*, use the present subjunctive *tú* form. To form the present subjunctive for the spelling-change verb *tocar*, change *c* to *qu* (the same change made for the preterit indicative *yo* form). Drop the *-ar* ending and add the present subjunctive ending for *tú (-es)*. To negate the command, put *no* before the conjugated verb. To form an affirmative command with *tú*, drop the final *-s* from the second person singular present indicative form of *tú (tocas)*.

4. **No vayas a la derecha. Ve a la izquierda.**   To form a negative command with *tú*, use the present subjunctive *tú* form. The irregular present subjunctive stem of *ir* is *vay-*. Add

the *tú* form subjunctive ending *(-as)*. To negate the command, put *no* before the conjugated verb. The informal affirmative command form of *venir* is irregular and must be memorized: *ve*.

5. **No pongas las sillas. Pon los folletos.**   To form a negative command with *tú*, use the present subjunctive *tú* form. Take the irregular *yo* form of the present tense *(pongo)*. Drop the *-o* and add the *tú* form subjunctive ending *(-as)*. To negate the command, put *no* before the conjugated verb. The informal affirmative command form of *poner* is irregular and must be memorized: *pon*.

6. **No cierres las ventanas. Cierra la puerta.**   To form a negative command with *tú*, use the present subjunctive *tú* form. To form the present subjunctive for the stem-changing verb *cerrar*, change the internal *e* to *ie* (the same change made for the present indicative *yo* form). Drop the *-ar* ending and add the present subjunctive ending for *tú (-es)*. To negate the command, put *no* before the conjugated verb. To form an affirmative command with *tú*, drop the final *-s* from the second person singular present indicative form of *tú (cierras)*.

7. **No llegues tarde. Llega temprano.**   To form a negative command with *tú*, use the present subjunctive *tú* form. To form the present subjunctive for the spelling-change verb *llegar*, change *g* to *gu* (the same change made for the preterit indicative *yo* form). Drop the *-ar* ending and add the present subjunctive ending for *tú (-es)*. To negate the command, put *no* before the conjugated verb. To form an affirmative command with *tú*, drop the final *-s* from the second person singular present indicative form of *tú (llegas)*.

8. **No obedezcas a Carlos. Obedece a Julio.**   To form a negative command with *tú*, use the present subjunctive *tú* form. To form the present subjunctive for the spelling-change verb *parecer*, change the *c* to *zc* (the same change made for the present indicative *yo* form). Drop the *-er* ending and add the present subjunctive ending for *tú (-as)*. To negate the command, put *no* before the conjugated verb. To form an affirmative command with *tú*, drop the final *-s* from the second person singular present indicative form of *tú (pareces)*.

Informal Plural Commands with *Vosotros (Vosotras)*

To form an affirmative command with any verb when *vosotros* is the subject, drop the final *-r* of the infinitive and add *-d*.

To form a negative command with any verb when *vosotros* is the subject, use the present subjunctive *vosotros* form. To form the present subjunctive:

1. Drop the final *-o* from the *yo* form of the present tense.

2. For infinitives ending in *-ar*, add *-éis* for the *vosotros* form.

   For infinitives ending in *-er* or *-ir*, add *-áis* for the *vosotros* form.

Informal Plural Commands for Regular Verbs			
Infinitive	*Affirmative*	*Negative*	*Meaning*
trabajar	trabajad (vosotros)	no trabajéis (vosotros)	(don't) work
comer	comed (vosotros)	no comáis (vosotros)	(don't) eat
escribir	escribid (vosotros)	no escribáis (vosotros)	(don't) write

Informal Plural Commands for Irregular *Yo* Form Verbs

Infinitive	Affirmative	Negative	Meaning
oír	oíd (vosotros)	no oigáis (vosotros)	(don't) hear
traer	traed (vosotros)	no traigáis (vosotros)	(don't) bring

Informal Plural Commands for Spelling-Change Verbs

Infinitive	Affirmative	Negative	Meaning
buscar	buscad (vosotros)	no busquéis (vosotros)	(don't) look for
llegar	llegad (vosotros)	no lleguéis (vosotros)	(don't) arrive
tropezar	tropezad (vosotros)	no tropecéis (vosotros)	(don't) stumble
vencer	venced (vosotros)	no venzáis (vosotros)	(don't) conquer
obedecer	obedeced (vosotros)	no obedezcáis (vosotros)	(don't) obey
zurcir	zurcid (vosotros)	no zurzáis (vosotros)	(don't) mend
conducir	conducid (vosotros)	no conduzcáis (vosotros)	(don't) drive
escoger	escoged (vosotros)	no escojáis (vosotros)	(don't) choose
dirigir	dirigid (vosotros)	no dirijáis (vosotros)	(don't) direct
distinguir	distinguid (vosotros)	no distingáis (vosotros)	(don't) distinguish

Informal Plural Commands for Stem-Changing Verbs

Infinitive	Affirmative	Negative	Meaning
cerrar	cerrad (vosotros)	no cerréis (vosotros)	(don't) close
mostrar	mostrad (vosotros)	no mostréis (vosotros)	(don't) show
perder	perded (vosotros)	no perdáis (vosotros)	(don't) lose
devolver	devolved (vosotros)	no devolváis (vosotros)	(don't) give back
advertir	advertid (vosotros)	no advirtáis (vosotros)	(don't) warn
dormir	dormid (vosotros)	no durmáis (vosotros)	(don't) sleep
servir	servid (vosotros)	no sirváis (vosotros)	(don't) serve
guiar	guiad (vosotros)	no guiéis (vosotros)	(don't) guide
actuar	actuad (vosotros)	no actuéis (vosotros)	(don't) act
concluir	concluid (vosotros)	no concluyáis (vosotros)	(don't) conclude

Informal Plural Commands for Irregular Verbs			
Infinitive	**Affirmative**	**Negative**	**Meaning**
decir	decid (vosotros)	no digáis (vosotros)	(don't) tell
hacer	haced (vosotros)	no hagáis (vosotros)	(don't) do
ir	id (vosotros)	no vayáis (vosotros)	(don't) go
poner	poned (vosotros)	no pongáis (vosotros)	(don't) put
salir	salid (vosotros)	no salgáis (vosotros)	(don't) leave
ser	sed (vosotros)	no seáis (vosotros)	(don't) be
tener	tened (vosotros)	no tengáis (vosotros)	(don't) have (don't) be (in certain idiomatic expressions)
valer	valed (vosotros)	no valgáis (vosotros)	(don't) be worth
venir	venid (vosotros)	no vengáis (vosotros)	(don't) come

Here are two examples, using both affirmative and negative commands:

¡Devolved su dinero!   ¡No devolváis su dinero!   (Don't) Give back his money!

¡Poned la mesa!   ¡No pongáis la mesa!   (Don't) Set the table!

Example Problems

Express what Gloria says to her grandparents who are ill.

Example: tomar: leche (no)/agua (sí)

No toméis leche. Tomad agua.

1. salir: a menudo (no)/raramente (sí)

    Answer: No salgáis a menudo. Salid raramente.

    To form a negative command with *vosotros*, use the present subjunctive *vosotros* form. To form the present subjunctive, drop the final *-o* from the *yo* form of the irregular present tense for *salir: salgo*. To negate the command, put *no* before the conjugated verb. For an infinitive ending in *-ir*, add *-áis*. To form an affirmative command with *vosotros*, drop the final *-r* from the infinitive and add *-d*.

2. comer: pollo (sí)/carne (no)

    Answer: Comed pollo. No comáis carne.

    To form an affirmative command with *vosotros*, drop the final *-r* from the infinitive and add *-d*. To form a negative command with *vosotros*, use the present subjunctive *vosotros* form. To form the present subjunctive, drop the final *-o* from the *yo* form of the present tense and, for infinitives ending in *-er*, add *-áis*. To negate the command, put *no* before the conjugated verb.

3.   ser: pesimista (no)/optimista (sí)

    Answer: No seáis pesimistas. Sed optimistas.

To form a negative command with *vosotros*, use the present subjunctive *vosotros* form. To form the present subjunctive of the irregular verb *ser*, use *se-* as the subjunctive stem. This stem is irregular and must be memorized. Add the *vosotros* subjunctive ending *(-áis)*. To negate the command, put *no* before the conjugated verb. To form an affirmative command with *vosotros*, drop the final *-r* from the infinitive and add *-d*.

Work Problems

Use these problems to give yourself additional practice.

1.   tener: miedo (no)/paciencia (sí)

2.   ir: al jardín (sí)/al centro (no)

3.   hacer: lo menos posible (sí)/mucho (no)

4.   atender: lo más innecesario (no)/lo más urgente (sí)

5.   concluir: lo peor (no)/lo mejor (sí)

6.   exigir: la verdad (sí)/mentiras (no)

Worked Solutions

1.   **No tengáis miedo. Tened paciencia.**   To form a negative command with *vosotros*, use the present subjunctive *vosotros* form. To form the present subjunctive, drop the final *-o* from the *yo* form of the irregular present tense for *tener: tengo.* For an infinitive ending in *-ir*, add *-áis*. To negate the command, put *no* before the conjugated verb. To form an affirmative command with *vosotros*, drop the final *-r* from the infinitive and add *-d*.

2.   **Id al jardín. No vayáis al centro.**   To form an affirmative command with *vosotros*, drop the final *-r* from the infinitive and add *-d*. To form a negative command with *vosotros*, use the present subjunctive *vosotros* form. To form the present subjunctive of the irregular verb *ir*, use *vay-* as the subjunctive stem. This stem is irregular and must be memorized. Add the *vosotros* subjunctive ending *-áis*. To negate the command, put *no* before the conjugated verb.

3.   **Haced lo menos posible. No hagáis mucho.**   To form an affirmative command with *vosotros*, drop the final *-r* from the infinitive and add *-d*. To form a negative command with *vosotros*, use the present subjunctive *vosotros* form. To form the present subjunctive, drop the final *-o* from the *yo* form of the irregular present tense for *hacer: hago.* For an infinitive ending in *-ir*, add *-áis*. To negate the command, put *no* before the conjugated verb.

4.   **No atendáis lo más innecesario. Atended lo más urgente.**   To form a negative command with *vosotros*, use the present subjunctive *vosotros* form. To form the present subjunctive, drop the final *-o* from the *yo* form of the present tense and, for infinitives ending in *-er*, add *-áis*. To negate the command, put *no* before the conjugated verb. To form an affirmative command with *vosotros*, drop the final *-r* from the infinitive and add *-d*.

5. **No concluyáis lo peor. Concluid lo mejor.**   To form an affirmative command with *vosotros*, drop the final *-r* from the infinitive and add *-d*. To form a negative command with *vosotros*, use the present subjunctive *vosotros* form. The present tense of the spelling-changing verb *concluir* adds *y* after *u*. To form the present subjunctive for *concluir*, drop the final *-o* from the *yo* form of the present tense *(concluyo)* and add the ending for *vosotros* *(-áis)*.

6. **Exigid la verdad. No exijáis mentiras.**   To form an affirmative command with *vosotros*, drop the final *-r* from the infinitive and add *-d*. To form a negative command with *vosotros*, use the present subjunctive *vosotros* form. The present tense of the spelling-changing verb *exigir* changes the *g* to *j*. To form the present subjunctive for *exigir*, drop the final *-o* from the *yo* form of the present tense *(exijo)* and add the ending for *vosotros* *(-áis)*.

Indirect Commands

Indirect commands are usually expressed by *que* + the third person singular or plural form of the present subjunctive:

¡Que venga Jorge la semana próxima!	Let Jorge come next week!
¡Que se despierte ella!	Let her wake up!
¡Que coman ellos!	Let them eat!
¡Que no lo hagan ellas!	Let them not do it!

"Let us" (or "Let's") can be expressed in two ways:

❑ Use *vamos a* + infinitive (or noun) in the affirmative and *no vayamos a* + infinitive (or noun) in the negative:

Vamos a bailar.	Let's dance.
No vayamos a cantar.	Let's not sing.
Vamos al cine.	Let's go to the movies.
No vayamos al teatro.	Let's not go to the theater.

Note: This is the method always used to express "let's" with the verb *ir* (to go).

❑ Use the *nosotros* form of the subjunctive:

Bailemos.	Let's dance.
No cantemos.	Let's not sing.

Example Problems

Express what your friends say when you have an afternoon free.

1. Let Jorge drive.

    Answer: Que conduzca Jorge.

    Indirect commands are usually expressed by *que* + the third person singular or plural form of the present subjunctive. Begin the command with *que*. Use *conducir* to express "to drive." To form a third person singular command, use the present subjunctive of the verb. The present tense of the stem-changing verb *conducir* changes the *c* to *zc* in the *yo* form. To form the third person singular present subjunctive for *conducir*, drop the final *-o* from the *yo* form of the present tense *(ofrezco)* and add *-a*. The verb is followed by the subject: *Jorge*.

2. Let's go to the park to play basketball.

   Answer: Vamos al parque a jugar al baloncesto.

   Use *vamos a* + an infinitive to express "Let's." Use *al parque* to express "to the park." Use *jugar* to express "to play." *Jugar* is followed by the preposition *a* before the name of a sport. *A* contracts with *el* to become *al* before the masculine singular *baloncesto* (basketball).

3. Let's play until six o'clock.

   Answer: Juguemos hasta las seis./Vamos a jugar hasta las seis.

   "Let's" can also be expressed by using the *nosotros* form of the subjunctive. Use *jugar* to express "to play." To form the present subjunctive for the spelling-change verb *jugar*, change *g* to *gu* (the same change made for the preterit indicative *yo* form). Drop the *-ar* ending and add the present subjunctive ending for *nosotros* (*-emos)*. Use *hasta* to express "until." Use *las seis* to express "six o'clock."

Work Problems

Use these problems to give yourself additional practice.

Express what your friends say when you are planning a party together.

1. Let's have a party.

2. Let's organize our ideas.

3. Let Mariana and Ana send the invitations.

4. Let's serve sandwiches.

5. Let's make decorations.

6. Let Julio choose the music.

Worked Solutions

1. **Vamos a tener una fiesta./Tengamos una fiesta.**   Use *vamos a* + an infinitive to express "Let's." Use *tener* to express "to have." Use *una fiesta* to express "a party." Let's" can also be expressed by using the *nosotros* form of the subjunctive. Use *tener* to express "to have." To form the present subjunctive for the irregular verb *tener*, take the irregular *yo* form of the present tense: *tengo*. Drop the final *-o* and add the present subjunctive ending for *nosotros* (*-amos)*.

2. **Vamos a organizar nuestras ideas./Organicemos nuestras ideas.**   Use *vamos a* + an infinitive to express "Let's." Use *organizar* to express "to organize." Use the feminine plural possessive adjective *nuestras* to express "our" before the feminine plural noun *ideas*. "Let's" can also be expressed by using the *nosotros* form of the subjunctive. Use *organizar* to express "to organize." To form the present subjunctive for the spelling-change verb *organizar*, drop the final *-é* from the *yo* form of the preterit tense (*organicé*) and add the present subjunctive ending for *nosotros* (*-emos)*.

3. **Que envíen las invitaciones Mariana y Ana.**   Indirect commands are usually expressed by *que* + the third person singular or plural form of the present subjunctive. Begin the command with *que*. Use *enviar* to express "to send." To form a third person plural command, use the present subjunctive of the verb. The present tense of the spelling-changing verb *enviar* changes the *i* to *í* in the *yo* form. To form the third person plural present subjunctive for *enviar*, drop the final -*o* from the *yo* form of the present tense *envío* and add the present subjunctive ending for *ellas* (-*en*). Use *las invitaciones* to express "the invitations." The verb is followed by the subject: *Mariana y Ana.*

4. **Vamos a servir sándwiches./Sirvamos sándwiches.**   Use *vamos a* + an infinitive to express "Let's." Use *servir* to express "to serve." Use *sándwiches* to express "sandwiches." "Let's" can also be expressed by using the *nosotros* form of the subjunctive. Use *servir* to express "to serve." To form the present subjunctive for the stem-changing verb *servir*, change the internal *e* to *i* (the same change made for the present indicative *yo* form) and add the present subjunctive ending for *nosotros* (-*amos*).

5. **Vamos a hacer decoraciones./Hagamos decoraciones.**   Use *vamos a* + an infinitive to express "Let's." Use *hacer* to express "to make." Use *decoraciones* to express "decorations." "Let's" can also be expressed by using the *nosotros* form of the subjunctive. Use *hacer* to express "to make." To form the present subjunctive for the irregular verb *hacer*, take the irregular *yo* form of the present tense: *hago*. Drop the final -*o* and add the present subjunctive ending for *nosotros* (-*amos*).

6. **Que Julio escoja la música.**   Indirect commands are usually expressed by *que* + the third person singular or plural form of the present subjunctive. Begin the command with *que*. Use *escoger* to express "to choose." To form a third person singular command, use the present subjunctive of the verb. The present tense of the spelling-changing verb *escoger* changes the *g* to *j* in the *yo* form. To form the third person singular present subjunctive for *escoger*, drop the final -*o* from the *yo* form of the present tense (*escojo*) and add -*a*. Use *la música* to express "the music." The verb is followed by the subject: *Julio.*

Object Pronouns with Commands

In Spanish, direct objects, indirect objects, and reflexive pronouns precede negative commands and follow and are attached to affirmative commands.

Traígalo (Ud.).	Bring it.	No lo traiga (Ud.).	Don't bring it.
Traíganlo (Uds.).	Bring it.	No lo traigan (Uds.).	Don't bring it.
Tráelo (tú).	Bring it.	No lo traigas (tú).	Don't bring it.
Traedlo (vosotros).	Bring it.	No lo traigáis (vosotros).	Don't bring it

The stressed vowel normally requires an accent mark when the command form (not including any pronoun that may be attached to the end of it) has more than one syllable:

Affirmative: Dígame su nombre.   Dime tu nombre.   Tell me your name.

               3 2 1

Cepíllese los dientes.   Cepíllate los dientes.   Brush your teeth.
 3 2   1   3 2 1

Note that diphthongs (two vowels that are pronounced as one sound) count as one vowel:

Siéntala. Siéntela.   Feel it.
 3 2 1   3 2 1

Also note that when two object pronouns are attached to a multisyllabic verb, it is necessary to count back four vowels:

Tráigamelo.   Bring it to me.
  4 3 2 1

No accent is required in the negative:

No nos repita las reglas.   Don't repeat the rules to us.

When forming the informal plural *(vosotros)* command, the final *-d* is dropped before adding *-os* for all verbs except *ir:*

levantarse	→	levantad – *d* + *os*	→	¡Levantaos!	Get up!
sentarse	→	sentad – *d* + *os*	→	¡Sentaos!	Sit!
BUT:					
irse	→	id + *os*	→	¡Idos!	Go!

When forming the informal plural *(vosotros)* command when *-os* is added to an *-ir* reflexive verb (see Chapter 17), an accent mark must be added:

| vestirse | → | vestid – *d* + *os* | → | ¡Vestíos! | Get dressed! |

When expressing the affirmative "let's" with a reflexive verb, the final *-s* of the *nosotros* ending is dropped before adding the reflexive pronoun (see Chapter 17):

vamos + nos =¡Vámonos!   ¡Let's go!
sentemos + nos = ¡Sentémonos!   ¡Let's sit!

Example Problems

You are going to the movies. Express what different people say.

Example: (Uds./el refresco) Don't buy it for me.
No me lo compren.

1. (vosotros) Have fun.

   Answer: Divertíos.

   Use the reflexive verb *divertirse* to express "to have fun." When forming the informal plural *(vosotros)* command, the final *-d* is dropped before adding the reflexive pronoun *os*. When *-os* is added to an *-ir* reflexive verb, an accent mark must be added to the preceding *-i*.

2. (tú/la crítica) Show it to me.

   Answer: Muéstramela.

   Use the verb *mostrar* to express "to show." To form the informal singular affirmative command, use the *tú* form of the present indicative without the final *-s. Mostrar* is a stem-changing verb whose internal *o* changes to *ue* in all forms except *nosotros* and *vosotros.*

Use *me* to express "to me." Use *la* to express "it" when referring to the feminine singular direct object: *la crítica*. When there are two object pronouns in a sentence, the indirect object precedes the direct object. In an affirmative command, both pronouns follow the verb and are attached to it. Because two pronouns are attached, count back four vowels and add an accent.

3. (Ud./los billetes) Don't give them to her.

   Answer: No se los dé.

   Use the verb *dar* to express "to give." To form a negative formal command with *Ud.*, use the present subjunctive form of the verb. *Dar* is irregular in the present subjunctive and must be memorized: *dé*. Use *le* to express "to her" Use *los* to express "them" when referring to the masculine plural direct object: *los billetes*. When there are two object pronouns in a sentence, the indirect object precedes the direct object. *Le* changes to *se* before *los*. In a negative command, the pronouns precede the conjugated verb.

Work Problems

Use these problems for additional practice.

Express what is said by different people at a bridal shower.

1. (tú/las mentiras) Don't tell them to her.

2. (nosotros) Let's get married.

3. (Ud./el rumor) Don't repeat it to us.

4. (tú) Brush your hair.

5. (Uds./la invitación) Don't send it to them.

6. (vosotros) Say goodbye to each other with a kiss.

Worked Solutions

1. **No se las digas.**   Use the verb *decir* to express "to tell." To form a negative command with *tú,* use the present subjunctive *tú* form. Take the irregular *yo* form of the present tense *(digo).* Drop the *-o* and add the *tú* form subjunctive ending *(-as).* To negate the command, put *no* before the conjugated verb. Use *le* to express "to her." Use *las* to express "them" when referring to the feminine plural direct object: *las mentiras.* When there are two object pronouns in a sentence, the indirect object precedes the direct object. *Le* changes to *se* before *las*. In a negative command, the pronouns precede the conjugated verb.

2. **¡Vamos a casarnos!/¡Casémonos!**   Use *vamos a* + an infinitive to express "Let's." Use the reflexive verb *casarse* to express "to get married." Use the reflexive pronoun *nos* to agree with the subject *nosotros*. When there are two verbs, attach the pronoun to the infinitive. Alternatively, the pronoun may precede the conjugated verb: *Nos vamos a casar.* "Let's" can also be expressed by using the *nosotros* form of the subjunctive. To form the present subjunctive for *casar,* drop the final *-o* from the *yo* form of the present

tense *(caso)* and add the present subjunctive ending for *nosotros (-emos)*. Use the reflexive pronoun *nos* with the subject *nosotros*. In an affirmative command, the pronoun follows the verb and is attached to it. The final *-s* of the *nosotros* ending is dropped before adding the reflexive pronoun. Because there is only one pronoun attached, count back three vowels and add an accent.

3. **No nos lo repita.** Use the verb *repetir* to express "to repeat." To form a negative formal command with *Ud.*, use the present subjunctive form of the verb. *Repetir* is a stem-changing verb whose internal *e* changes to *i*. The third person singular subjunctive ending is *-a*. Use *nos* to express "to us." Use *lo* to express "it" when referring to the masculine singular direct object: *el rumor*. When there are two object pronouns in a sentence, the indirect object precedes the direct object.

4. **Cepíllate el pelo.** Use the reflexive verb *cepillarse* to express "to brush." Use the reflexive pronoun *te* to agree with the subject *tú*. To form an affirmative command with *tú*, drop the final *-s* from the second person singular present indicative form of *tú* *(cepillas)*. In an affirmative command, the pronoun follows the verb and is attached to it. Because there is only one pronoun attached, count back three vowels and add an accent. Use *el pelo* to express "your hair." Note that the definite article (rather than the possessive adjective) is used when the possessor is clear.

5. **No se la envíen.** Use the verb *enviar* to express "to send." To form a negative formal command with *Uds.*, use the present subjunctive form of the verb. *Enviar* is a spelling-change verb whose internal *i* changes to *í*. The third person plural subjunctive ending is *-en*. Use *les* to express "to them." Use *la* to express "it" when referring to the feminine singular direct object: *la invitación*. When there are two object pronouns in a sentence, the indirect object precedes the direct object. *Les* changes to *se* before *la*. In a negative command, the pronouns precede the conjugated verb.

6. **Despedíos con un beso.** To form an affirmative command with *vosotros*, drop the final *-r* from the infinitive and add *-d*. This *-d* is dropped when the reflexive pronoun *os* is added and attached to the end of the command form. When *-os* is added to an *-ir* reflexive verb, an accent must be added to the preceding *-r*. Use *con* to express "with." *Un beso* expresses "a kiss."

Chapter Problems

Problems

Suggest what you and your friends can do on vacation.

Example: salir
Salgamos.

1. ir al mar

2. hacer el alpinismo

3. dar una caminata

4. tener una fiesta

5. jugar al vóleibol

6. ver un espectáculo

7. conducir al campo

8. correr por el parque

9. sacar fotografías

10. escoger una buena película

Express the advice that one friend gives to another about writing a composition.

> Example: (no) escribir con un lápiz
> Escribe con un lápiz.
> No escribas con un lápiz.

11. no empezar inmediatamente

12. organizar tus ideas

13. pensar profundamente antes de escribir

14. no leer rápidamente

15. no pedir ayuda a nadie

16. hacer un esquema

17. no estar distraído

18. tener confianza

19. verificar tu gramática

20. no escoger un tema demasiado difícil

Answers and Solutions

1. **Answer: Vamos al mar.**   Use *vamos a* + a noun to express "Let's" when the verb is *ir* (to go).

2. **Answer: Hagamos el alpinismo.**   To form the present subjunctive for the irregular verb *hacer*, take the irregular *yo* form of the present tense: *hago*. Drop the final *-o* and add the present subjunctive ending for *nosotros* (*-amos*).

3. **Answer: Demos una caminata.**   The present subjunctive for the irregular verb *dar* is irregular and must be memorized. Use the first person plural present subjunctive ending for *nosotros* (*-emos*).

4. **Answer: Tengamos una fiesta.**   To form the present subjunctive for the irregular verb *tener*, take the irregular *yo* form of the present tense: *tengo*. Drop the final *-o* and add the present subjunctive ending for *nosotros* (*-amos*).

5. **Answer: Juguemos al vóleibol.** The spelling-changing verb *jugar* changes the *g* to *gu* in the *yo* form of the preterit. To form the present subjunctive for *jugar*, drop the final *-é* from the *yo* form of the preterit tense *(jugué)* and add the present subjunctive ending for *nosotros (-emos)*.

6. **Answer: Veamos un espectáculo.** To form the present subjunctive for the irregular verb *ver*, take the irregular *yo* form of the present tense: *veo*. Drop the final *-o* and add the present subjunctive ending for *nosotros (-amos)*.

7. **Answer: Conduzcamos al campo.** The spelling-changing verb *conducir* changes the *c* to *zc* in the *yo* form of the present. To form the present subjunctive for *conducir*, drop the final *-o* from the *yo* form of the present tense *(conduzco)* and add the present subjunctive ending for *nosotros (-amos)*.

8. **Answer: Corramos por el parque.** To form the present subjunctive for *correr*, drop the final *-o* from the *yo* form of the present tense *(corro)* and add the present subjunctive ending for *nosotros (-amos)*.

9. **Answer: Saquemos fotografías.** The spelling-changing verb *sacar* changes the *c* to *qu* in the *yo* form of the preterit. To form the present subjunctive for *sacar*, drop the final *-é* from the *yo* form of the preterit tense *(saqué)* and add the present subjunctive ending for *nosotros (-emos)*.

10. **Answer: Escojamos una buena película.** The present tense of the spelling-changing verb *escoger* changes the *g* to *j* in the *yo* form. To form the present subjunctive for *escoger*, drop the final *-o* from the *yo* form of the present tense *(escojo)* and add the present subjunctive ending for *nosotros (-amos)*.

11. **Answer: No empieces inmediatamente.** To form a negative command with *tú*, use the present subjunctive *tú* form. To form the present subjunctive for the stem-changing verb *empezar*, change the internal *e* to *ie* (the same change made for the present indicative *yo* form). Additionally, *empezar* requires a spelling change of *z* to *c* (the same change made for the preterit indicative *yo* form). Drop the *-ar* ending and add the present subjunctive ending for *tú (-es)*. To negate the command, put *no* before the conjugated verb.

12. **Answer: Organiza tus ideas.** To form an affirmative command with *tú*, drop the final *-s* from the second person singular present indicative form of *tú (organizas)*.

13. **Answer: Piensa profundamente antes de escribir.** To form an affirmative command with *tú*, drop the final *-s* from the second person singular present indicative form of *tú* by changing the internal *e* to *ie (piensas)*.

14. **Answer: No leas rápidamente.** To form a negative command with *tú*, use the present subjunctive *tú* form. Drop the *-er* ending and add the present subjunctive ending for *tú (-as)*. To negate the command, put *no* before the conjugated verb.

15. **Answer: No pidas ayuda a nadie.** To form a negative command with *tú*, use the present subjunctive *tú* form. To form the present subjunctive for the stem-changing verb *pedir*, change the internal *e* to *i* (the same change made for the present indicative *yo* form). Drop the *-ir* ending and add the present subjunctive ending for *tú (-as)*. To negate the command, put *no* before the conjugated verb.

16. **Answer: Haz un esquema.** The informal affirmative command form of *hacer* is irregular and must be memorized: *haz*.

17. **Answer: No estés distraído.**   To form a negative command with *tú*, use the present subjunctive *tú* form. Drop the *-ar* ending and add the irregular present subjunctive ending for *tú (-és)*. To negate the command, put *no* before the conjugated verb.

18. **Answer: Ten confianza.**   The informal affirmative command form of *tener* is irregular and must be memorized: *ten.*

19. **Answer: Verifica tu gramática.**   To form an affirmative command with *tú*, drop the final *-s* from the second person singular present indicative form of *tú (verificas)*.

20. **Answer: No escojas un tema demasiado difícil.**   To form a negative command with *tú*, use the present subjunctive *tú* form. To form the present subjunctive of the verb for the spelling-change verb *corregir*, change the internal *g* to *j* (the same change made for the present indicative *yo* form). Drop the *-er* ending and add the present subjunctive ending for *tú (-as).*

Supplemental Chapter Problems

Problems

Suggest what you and your brothers and sisters can do to do help around the house (see the previous example).

1. poner la mesa

2. hacer recados

3. sacudir los muebles

4. planchar la ropa

5. ir a la farmacia

6. dar de comer al perro

7. pagar las cuentas

8. organizar la ropa en los roperos

9. secar los platos

10. recoger los objetos del suelo

Express the advice one friend gives to another about being a good friend (see the previous example).

11. dar apoyo a tus amigos

12. nunca mentir

13. no tener celos de nadie

14. ser honesto

15. estar listo a ayudarlos

16. explicar tus sentimientos a tus amigos

17. no juzgar a tus amigos

18. no desconfiar de ellos

19. simpatizar con ellos

20. no competir con ellos

Solutions

1. Pongamos la mesa. (indirect commands, p. 363)

2. Hagamos recados. (indirect commands, p. 363)

3. Sacudamos los muebles. (indirect commands, p. 363)

4. Planchemos la ropa. (indirect commands, p. 363)

5. Vamos a la farmacia. (indirect commands, p. 363)

6. Demos de comer al perro. (indirect commands, p. 363)

7. Paguemos las cuentas. (indirect commands, p. 363)

8. Organicemos la ropa en los roperos. (indirect commands, p. 363)

9. Sequemos los platos. (indirect commands, p. 363)

10. Recojamos los objetos del suelo. (indirect commands, p. 363)

11. Da apoyo a tus amigos. (informal singular commands with *tú*, p. 355)

12. Nunca mientas. (informal singular commands with *tú*, p. 355)

13. No tengas celos de nadie. (informal singular commands with *tú*, p. 355)

14. Sé honesto. (informal singular commands with *tú*, p. 355)

15. Está listo a ayudarlos. (informal singular commands with *tú*, p. 355)

16. Explica tus sentimientos a tus amigos. (informal singular commands with *tú*, p. 355)

17. No juzgues a tus amigos. (informal singular commands with *tú*, p. 355)

18. No desconfíes de ellos. (informal singular commands with *tú*, p. 355)

19. Simpatiza con ellos. (informal singular commands with *tú*, p. 355)

20. No compitas con ellos. (informal singular commands with *tú*, p. 355)

Chapter 17
Reflexive Verbs

Recognizing Reflexive Verbs

An infinitive (the form ending in *-ar, -er,* or *-ir*) that ends in *-se* indicates that a verb is reflexive in Spanish. A reflexive verb is one in which the action is performed by the subject on itself. A reflexive verb has a reflexive pronoun as its object (direct or indirect). The subject (which may, as with other verbs, be omitted) and the reflexive pronoun refer to the same person or thing:

(Yo) Me llamo Margarita.	My name is Margarita. (I call myself Margarita.)
(Ella) Se lava el pelo.	She washes her hair.

In some instances, a verb may have both a reflexive and a non-reflexive form. A verb that can be reflexive may be used without a reflexive pronoun if the action is performed upon or for someone else, in which case the verb is no longer considered reflexive:

Él <u>se</u> lava.	He washes himself.
Él lava su coche.	He washes his car.

Some common reflexive verbs include (bold letters indicate a spelling change or irregularity):

Verb	Meaning
abrocharse	to fasten
aburrirse	to become bored
ac**o**rdarse (de)	to remember
ac**o**starse	to go to bed, to lie down
afeitarse	to shave
aho**gar**se	to drown, to suffocate
alegrarse (de)	to be glad
apoderarse (de)	to take possession (of)
apresurarse (a)	to hurry
aprovecharse (de)	to avail oneself (of), to profit (by)
apurarse	to get upset, to worry, to hurry (Latin American countries)
arrep**e**ntirse (de)	to repent
asegurarse (de)	to make sure
asustarse	to become frightened
atreverse (a)	to dare
bañarse	to bathe oneself
burlarse (de)	to make fun of
callarse	to be silent

cambiarse	to change (clothing),
cansarse	to become tired
casarse	to get married
cepillarse	to brush one's hair or teeth
colo**car**se	to place oneself
conven**cer**se (de)	to convince oneself (of)
cuidarse (de)	to take care of (to worry about)
darse	to give in
decidirse (a)	to make up one's mind
desanimarse	to get discouraged
desayunarse	to have breakfast
desmayarse	to faint
des**pedir**se	to say goodbye, take leave of
des**per**tarse	to wake up
di**ve**rtirse	to have fun
d**o**rmirse	to fall asleep
ducharse	to take a shower
ejercitarse (en)	to train (in)
empeñarse (en)	to insist (on)
enfadarse (con)	to get angry (with)
engañarse	to be mistaken; to kid, delude, or deceive oneself
enojarse	to become angry
enterarse (de)	to find out about
equivocarse	to be mistaken
escaparse	to escape
esconderse (de)	to hide (from)
fiarse (de)	to trust
figurarse	to imagine
fijarse (en)	to notice
hacerse (a)(con)	to become
irse	to go away, to leave
lavarse	to wash oneself
levantarse	to get up (when the entire body is involved)
llamarse	to be called, to be named
maquillarse	to put on makeup
marcharse	to go away
mojarse	to get wet
m**o**verse	to move
ne**g**arse (de)	to refuse (to)
olvidarse (de)	to forget
pararse (a)	to stop
pare**cer**se (a)	to resemble
pasearse	to go for a walk
peinarse	to comb one's hair
pelearse (con)	to fight (with)

ponerse	to put on, to become, to place oneself, to become
preocuparse	to worry
protegerse	to protect oneself
quedarse	to remain
quejarse (de)	to complain (about)
quitarse	to remove, to take off (one's clothes)
reírse (de)	to laugh at
relajarse	to relax
resfriarse	to catch a cold
romperse	to break (a part of one's body)
secarse	to dry oneself
sentarse	to sit down
sentirse	to feel
tratarse (de)	to concern
vestirse	to get dressed

Reflexive Pronouns

Reflexive verbs and verbs used reflexively are conjugated in all tenses with the reflexive pronoun that agrees with the subject. These pronouns generally, but not always, precede the conjugated verb. The verb is then conjugated according to its family (-ar, -er, or -ir), taking into account any irregularities or spelling and/or stem changes (bold letters indicate these irregularities and changes):

Infinitive	Subject	Reflexive Pronoun	Conjugation
despertarse (to awaken)	yo	me	me despierto
acordarse (to remember)	tú	te	te acuerdas
desvestirse (to get undressed)	él, ella, Ud.	se	se desviste
ponerse (to put on, to become)	nosotros	nos	nos ponemos
irse (to go away)	vosotros	os	os vais
despedirse (to take leave of)	ellos, ellas, Uds.	se	se despiden

Here are two examples in sentences:

Nos divertimos muchísimo en la clase de español.   We have a good time in Spanish class.
Siempre me despierto temprano.   I always wake up early.

Example Problems

Express what happens in the López household. Complete the sentences by filling in the reflexive pronoun where needed.

1. Los padres ___ despiertan y entonces ___ despiertan a sus niños.

    Answer: Los padres se despiertan y entonces despiertan a sus niños.

The reflexive pronoun is needed before the first verb because the subject, *los padres*, is acting upon itself: "The parents" are waking up by "themselves." The third person plural reflexive pronoun is *se*.

The second verb is not used reflexively because the subject is acting upon someone else: "The parents" are waking up their children.

2. Tú ___ preparas el desayuno para toda la familia y entonces ___ preparas para ir a la escuela.

   Answer: Tú preparas el desayuno para toda la familia y entonces te preparas para ir a la escuela .

   The first verb is not used reflexively because the subject is acting upon someone else: "You" are preparing the breakfast for the entire family.

   The reflexive pronoun is needed before the second verb because the subject, *tú*, is acting upon itself: "You" are preparing yourself to go to school. The reflexive pronoun for *tú* is *te*.

Work Problems

The day unfolds in the López household. Complete the sentences by filling in the reflexive pronoun where needed.

1. La madre ___ viste a sus hijos y después ___ viste.

2. Él ___ compra un helado y luego ___ compra un helado a su hermana.

3. Tú ___ pones el abrigo y después ___ pones tus libros en tu mochila.

4. Uds. ___ bañan al perro y más tarde ___bañan.

5. Yo ___ peino a mi hermana y después ___ peino.

6. Vosotros ___ cuidáis y luego vosotros ___ cuidáis a vuestros hermanos.

Worked Solutions

1. **La madre viste a sus hijos y después se viste.** The first verb is not used reflexively because the subject is acting upon someone else: "She" is dressing her children. The reflexive pronoun is needed before the second verb because the subject, *la madre,* is acting upon itself: "She" is dressing herself. The reflexive pronoun for *ella* is *se*. The second verb is not used reflexively because the subject is acting upon someone else: "She" is dressing her children.

2. **Él se compra un helado y luego compra un helado a su hermana.** The reflexive pronoun is needed before the first verb because the subject, *él,* is acting upon itself: "He" is buying an ice cream for himself. The reflexive pronoun for *él* is *se*. The second verb is not used reflexively because the subject is acting upon someone else: "He" is buying an ice cream for his sister.

3. **Tú te pones el abrigo y después pones tus libros en tu mochila.** The reflexive pronoun is needed before the first verb because the subject, *tú,* is acting upon itself: "You" are putting on your coat. The reflexive pronoun for *tú* is *te*. The second verb is not used

reflexively because the subject is acting upon something else: "You" are putting your books in your backpack.

4. **Uds. bañan al perro y más tarde Uds. se bañan.**   The first verb is not used reflexively because the subject is acting upon someone else: "You" are bathing the dog. The reflexive pronoun is needed before the second verb because the subject, *Uds.*, is acting upon itself: "You" are bathing yourself. The reflexive pronoun for *Uds.* is *se*.

5. **Yo peino a mi hermana y después me peino.**   The first verb is not used reflexively because the subject is acting upon someone else: "I" am combing my sister's hair. The reflexive pronoun is needed before the second verb because the subject, *Yo*, is acting upon itself: "I" am combing my hair. The reflexive pronoun for *yo* is *me*.

6. **Vosotros os cuidáis y luego cuidáis a vuestros hermanos.**   The reflexive pronoun is needed before the first verb because the subject, *vosotros*, is acting upon itself: "You" are taking care of yourself. The reflexive pronoun for *vosotros* is *os*. The second verb is not used reflexively because the subject is not acting upon itself: "You" are taking care of your brothers.

Verbs Used Reflexively in Spanish but Not in English

Some verbs are always reflexive in Spanish even though they are not necessarily used reflexively in English. Bold letters indicate a spelling change or irregularity:

Verb	Meaning
acercarse a	to approach
ac**o**rdarse (de)	to remember
apoderarse de	to take possession (of)
apresurarse a	to hurry
aprovecharse (de)	to take advantage of
arrepentirse (de)	to repent, to regret
atreverse (a)	to dare (to)
asustarse	to get frightened
burlarse de	to make fun of
desayunarse	to eat breakfast
empeñarse en	to insist (on)
enterarse de	to find out about
escaparse (de)	to escape (from)
fiarse de	to trust
figurarse	to imagine
fijarse (en)	to notice
ir**se**	to go away
n**e**garse (a)	to refuse (to)
olvidarse (de)	to forget
pasearse	to stroll
pare**cer**se a	to resemble

quejarse (de)	to complain (about)
reírse de	to laugh at
tratarse (de)	to be a matter of

Here are two examples in sentences:

| Él se ríe de sus amigos. | He laughs at his friends. |
| Me paseaba por el parque. | I was strolling through the park. |

Example Problems

Express the following opinions in Spanish.

1. (take care of myself) Yo_____ bien.

Answer: me cuido

Use *cuidarse* to express "to take care of oneself." The reflexive pronoun for *yo* is *me*. Place the reflexive pronoun before the conjugated verb. Drop the -*ar* infinitive ending and add the ending for *yo* (-*o*).

2. (forget) Tú _____ de todo.

Answer: te olvidas

Use *olvidarse* to express "to forget." The reflexive pronoun for *tú* is *te*. Place the reflexive pronoun before the conjugated verb. Drop the -*ar* infinitive ending and add the ending for *tú* (-*as*).

3. (becomes bored) Ella _____ fácilmente.

Answer: se aburre

Use *aburrirse* to express "to become bored." The reflexive pronoun for *ella* is *se*. Place the reflexive pronoun before the conjugated verb. Drop the -*ir* infinitive ending and add the ending for *ella* (-*e*).

Work Problems

Use these problems to give yourself additional practice.

Express the following opinions in Spanish.

1. (look like) Yo _____ a mi madre.

2. (refuses) Él _____ a escuchar.

3. (become angry) Nosotros _____ a menudo.

4. (notice) Tú _____ en todo.

5. (take advantage) Ellos _____ de cada oportunidad.

6. (complain) Vosotros _____ mucho.

Worked Solutions

1. **me parezco**   Use *parecerse* to express "to look like." The reflexive pronoun for *yo* is *me*. Place the reflexive pronoun before the conjugated verb. *Parecerse* is a spelling-change verb that changes *c* to *zc* in the *yo* form of the present tense. Drop the *-er* infinitive ending and add the ending for *yo* (*-o*).

2. **se niega**   Use *negarse* to express "to refuse." The reflexive pronoun for *él* is *se*. Place the reflexive pronoun before the conjugated verb. *Negarse* is a stem-changing verb that changes *e* to *ie* in all forms except *nosotros* and *vosotros*. Drop the *-ar* infinitive ending and add the ending for *él* (*-a*).

3. **nos enfadamos**   Use *enfadarse* to express "to become angry." The reflexive pronoun for *nosotros* is *nos*. Place the reflexive pronoun before the conjugated verb. Drop the *-ar* infinitive ending and add the ending for *nosotros* (*-amos*).

4. **te fijas**   Use *fijarse* to express "to notice." The reflexive pronoun for *tú* is *te*. Place the reflexive pronoun before the conjugated verb. Drop the *-ar* infinitive ending and add the ending for *tú* (*-as*).

5. **se aprovechan**   Use *aprovecharse* to express "to take advantage." The reflexive pronoun for *ellos* is *se*. Place the reflexive pronoun before the conjugated verb. Drop the *-ar* infinitive ending and add the ending for *ellos* (*-an*).

6. **os quejáis**   Use *quejarse* to express "to complain." The reflexive pronoun for *vosotros* is *os*. Place the reflexive pronoun before the conjugated verb. Drop the *-ar* infinitive ending and add the ending for *vosotros* (*-áis*).

Verbs with Special Reflexive Meanings

Some Spanish verbs have different meanings depending on whether or not they are used reflexively (irregularities and spelling and stem changes appear in bold):

General Form	*General Meaning*	*Reflexive Form*	*Reflexive Meaning*
aburrir	to bore	aburrirse	to become bored
ac**o**rdar	to agree	ac**o**rdarse de	to remember
ac**o**star	to put to bed	ac**o**starse	to go to bed, to lie down
bañar	to bathe (someone)	bañarse	to bathe oneself
cansar	to tire	cansarse	to become tired
colocar	to place (something)	colocarse	to place oneself, to get a job
d**o**rmir	to sleep	d**o**rmirse	to fall asleep
enfadar	to anger, to irritate	enfadarse (con)	to get angry, to get annoyed
engañar	to deceive	engañarse	to be mistaken; to kid, delude, or deceive oneself
esconder	to hide (something)	esconderse	to hide oneself

(continued)

General Form	General Meaning	Reflexive Form	Reflexive Meaning
ir	to go	**ir**se	to go away
levantar	to raise (something)	levantarse	to get up
llamar	to call	llamarse	to be called, to call oneself
parar	to stop (something)	pararse	to stop oneself, to get up
po**ner**	to put (something)	po**ner**se	to put (something on), to become, to place oneself
quitar	to remove	quitarse	to take off
s**e**ntar	to seat	s**e**ntarse	to sit down

Note how the verbs are used differently depending on whether or not they are reflexive:

Yo baño a mi perro.	I bathe my dog.
Me baño.	I bathe myself.
Pone el sombrero en la mesa.	He puts his hat on the table.
Se pone un sombrero.	He puts on a hat.

Example Problems

Complete the sentences by filling in the reflexive pronoun where needed to express what different people do.

1. (enfadar/enfadarse) Tú _____ cuando _____ a tu amigo.

    Answer: te enfadas, enfadas

    The reflexive verb is needed before the first verb because the subject, *tú*, is acting upon itself: "You" get angry with yourself. The reflexive pronoun for *tú* is *te*. The second verb is not used reflexively because the subject is acting upon someone else: "You" anger your friend. To conjugate *enfadar*, drop the *-ar* ending and add the ending for *tú (-as)*.

2. (levantar/levantarse) Yo _____la voz cuando _____.

    Answer: levanto, me levanto

    The reflexive verb is needed before the second verb because the subject, *yo*, is acting upon itself: "I" get up. The reflexive pronoun for *yo* is *me*. The verb *levantar* is only used reflexively when referring to the entire body. The first verb is not used reflexively because the subject is not raising its entire body: "I" raise my voice. To conjugate *levantar*, drop the *-ar* ifinitive ending and add the ending for *yo (-o)*.

3. (esconder/esconderse) Los ladrones _____ el dinero y luego _____.

    Answer: esconden/se esconden

    The reflexive verb is needed before the second verb because the subject, *los ladrones (ellos)*, is acting upon itself: "They" hide themselves. The reflexive pronoun for *ellos* is *se*. The first verb is not used reflexively because the subject is acting upon something else:

"They" hide the money. To conjugate *esconder,* drop the *-er* ending and add the ending for *ellos (-en).*

Work Problems

Use these problems to give yourself additional practice.

Complete the sentences by filling in the reflexive verb where needed to express what different people do.

1. (cambiar/cambiarse) Él _____ la camisa por otra de talla diferente y luego _____ de ropa.

2. (secar/secarse) Yo _____ a mi niño y luego _____.

3. (divertir/divertirse) Nosotros _____ a nuestros niños y luego _____.

4. (afeitar/afeitarse) Tú _____ y más tarde _____ a tu hermano.

5. (ir/irse) Uds. _____ del aeropuerto y luego _____ a casa.

6. (dar/darse) Ella _____ un grito cuando _____ contra la esquina de la mesa.

Worked Solutions

1. **cambia, se cambia**   The reflexive verb is needed before the second verb because the subject, *él,* is acting upon itself: "He" changes his clothes. The reflexive pronoun for *él* is *se.* The first verb is not used reflexively because the subject is acting upon something else: "He" is exchanging the shirt for another one of different size. To conjugate *levantar,* drop the *-ar* ending and add the ending for *él (-a).*

2. **seco, me seco**   The reflexive verb is needed before the second verb because the subject, *yo,* is acting upon itself: "I" dry myself. The reflexive pronoun for *yo* is *me.* The first verb is not used reflexively because the subject is acting upon someone else: "I" am drying my child. To conjugate *secar,* drop the *-ar* ending and add the ending for *yo (-o).*

3. **divertimos, nos divertimos**   The reflexive verb is needed before the second verb because the subject, *nosotros,* is acting upon itself: "We" have fun. The reflexive pronoun for *nosotros* is *nos.* The first verb is not used reflexively because the subject is acting upon someone else: "We" are amusing our children. *Divertir* is a stem-changing verb that changes *e* to *ie* in all forms except *nosotros* and *vosotros.* Drop the *-ir* ending and add the ending for *nosotros (-imos).*

4. **te afeitas, afeitas**   The reflexive verb is needed before the first verb because the subject, *tú,* is acting upon itself: "You" shave yourself. The reflexive pronoun for *tú* is *te.* The second verb is not used reflexively because the subject is acting upon someone else: "You" shave your brother. To conjugate *afeitar,* drop the *-ar* ending and add the ending for *tú (-as).*

5. **se van, van**   The reflexive verb is needed before the first verb because the subject, *Uds.,* is acting upon itself: "You" leave the airport. The reflexive pronoun for *Uds.* is *se.* The second verb is not used reflexively because the subject is acting upon something else: "You" go home. The verb *ir* is irregular in all forms. The third person plural form is *van.*

6. **da, se da** The reflexive verb is needed before the second verb because the subject, *ella*, is acting upon itself: "She" bumps into the corner of the table. The reflexive pronoun for *ella* is *se*. The first verb is not used reflexively because the subject is not acting upon itself: "She" screams. Although *dar* is irregular in the first person singular form, the rest of the verb is regular. To conjugate *dar*, drop the *-ar* ending and add the ending for *ella* (*-a*).

Idioms with Reflexive Verbs

Some popular idiomatic expressions are formed with reflexive verbs (bold indicates irregularities or spelling or stem changes):

Idiom	Meaning
aburrir**se** como una ostra	to be bored stiff
a**co**star**se** con las gallinas	to go to bed early
aho**garse** en un vaso de agua	to make a mountain out of a molehill
andar**se** con chiquitas	to beat around the bush
cal**e**ntar**se** la cabeza por	to agonize about something
en**co**ntrar**se** con la horma de su zapato	to meet one's match
estrujar**se** el cerebro (la mollera)	to rack one's brains
guardar**se** un as en la manga	to have an ace up one's sleeve
meter**se** en belenes	to get into trouble
quedar**se** tan ancho	to feel pleased with oneself
romper**se** la cabeza	to rack one's brains
s**o**ltar**se** la melena	to let one's hair down
vender**se** como rosquilla	to sell like hotcakes

Example Problems

Give an idiom that expresses each idea below.

1. Tú te preocupas de algo no muy importante. Tú _____.

   Answer: te ahogas en un vaso de agua

   If you worry about things that aren't very important, you make a mountain out of a molehill. The reflexive pronoun for *tú* is *te*. To conjugate *preocupar*, drop the *-ar* ending and add the ending for *tú* (*-as*).

2. Ud. nunca dice lo que quiere decir. Ud. _____.

   Answer: se anda con chiquitas

   If you never say what you want to say, you beat around the bush. The reflexive pronoun for *Ud.* is *se*. To conjugate *andar*, drop the *-ar* ending and add the ending for *Ud.* (*-a*).

3. Yo nunca digo a nadie todas mis ideas. De esa manera yo _____.

   Answer: me guardo un as en la manga

   If I never tell anyone all of my ideas, I have an ace up my sleeve. The reflexive pronoun for *yo* is *me*. To conjugate *guardar*, drop the *-ar* ending and add the ending for *yo* (*-o*).

Work Problems

Use these problems to give yourself additional practice.

Give an idiom that expresses each idea below.

1. Uds. son inteligentes. Ellos son tan inteligentes como Uds. Uds. _____.

2. Estamos a punto de dormirnos porque miramos un programa no muy interesante. Nosotros _____.

3. Son las ocho de la noche, pero ya quieres dormir. Tú _____.

4. Yo salgo muy bien en mis exámenes. Yo _____.

5. Ella no sabe la respuesta a la pregunta. Por eso, ella _____.

6. Esta panadería vende muchos pasteles. Es decir, los pasteles _____.

Worked Solutions

1. **se encuentran con la horma de su zapato**   If you are intelligent and they are as intelligent as you, you meet your match. The reflexive pronoun for *Uds.* is *se. Encontrar* is a stem-changing verb that changes *o* to *ue* in all forms except *nosotros* and *vosotros*. Drop the *-ar* ending and add the ending for *Uds.* (*-an*).

2. **nos aburrimos como una ostra**   If we are on the verge of falling asleep while watching a television show that isn't very interesting, we are bored stiff. The reflexive pronoun for *nosotros* is *nos*. To conjugate *aburrir*, drop the *-ir* ending and add the ending for *nosotros* (*-imos*).

3. **te acuestas con las gallinas**   If you go to bed at eight o'clock in the evening, you go to bed early. The reflexive pronoun for *tú* is *te. Acostar* is a stem-changing verb that changes *o* to *ue* in all forms except *nosotros* and *vosotros*. Drop the *-ar* ending and add the ending for *tú* (*-as*).

4. **me quedo tan ancho**   If I do well on my tests, I feel pleased with myself. The reflexive pronoun for *yo* is *me*. To conjugate *quedar*, drop the *-ar* ending and add the ending for *yo* (*-o*).

5. **se rompe la cabeza/se estruja el cerebro**   If she doesn't know the answer to a question, she racks her brains for the answer. The reflexive pronoun for *ella* is *se*. To conjugate *romper*, drop the *-er* ending and add the ending for *ella* (*-e*). Alternatively, to conjugate *estrujar*, drop the *-ar* ending and add the ending for *ella* (*-a*).

6. **se venden como rosquillas**   If this pastry shop sells a lot of pastries, the pastries sell like hotcakes. The reflexive pronoun for *los pasteles* is *se*. To conjugate *vender*, drop the *-er* ending and add the ending for *los pasteles* (*-en*).

Reflexive Verbs in Simple Tenses

Reflexive pronouns in affirmative and negative sentences generally precede the verb in simple tenses:

Tense	Example	Meaning
Present	(Yo) No me levanto tarde.	I don't get up late.
Preterit	(Él) Se hizo médico.	He became a doctor.
Imperfect	(Nosotros) Nos relajábamos.	We were relaxing.
Future	¿No se acordará ella de su nombre?	Won't she remember his name?
Conditional	¿No te maquillarías cada día?	Wouldn't you put on makeup every day?
Subjunctive	Es necesario que me vista ahora.	It is necessary for me to get dressed now.
Imperfect Subjunctive	Era imperativo que él se fuera (se fuese).	It was imperative that he go away.

Example Problems

Complete each thought with the correct form and tense of the verb.

1. Es importante que Ud. _____ cada día.
   (eat breakfast)

   Answer: se desayune

   The present subjunctive is needed after the phrase *es importante que*. The reflexive verb *desayunarse* means "to eat breakfast." To form the present subjunctive for *desayunar*, drop the final *-o* from the *yo* form of the present tense *(desayuno)* and add *-e* as the third person plural ending. The reflexive pronoun for *Ud.* is *se*. Place the reflexive pronoun before the conjugated verb.

2. Él _____ de sus amigos.
   (was making fun of)

   Answer: se burlaba

   Use the imperfect to express what "was happening" in the past. The reflexive verb *burlarse* means "to make fun of." Drop the *-ar* ending and add *-aba* as the imperfect ending for *él*. The reflexive pronoun for *él* is *se*. Place the reflexive pronoun before the conjugated verb.

3. Yo _____ en casa hoy.
   (will stay)

   Answer: me quedaré

   Use the future to express what "will happen." The reflexive verb *quedarse* means "to stay." To form the future, add *-é* to the infinitive as the ending for *yo*. The reflexive pronoun for *yo* is *me*. Place the reflexive pronoun before the conjugated verb.

Work Problems

Use these problems to give yourself additional practice.

Complete each thought with the correct form and tense of the verb.

1. Yo no _____.
   (will not become frightened)

2. No era necesario que ellos _____.
   (hurry)

3. ¿_____ cuando yo te llamé?
   (were you taking a shower)

4. Nosotros _____ enfermos ayer por la tarde.
   (became)

5. ¿_____ Ud. de recibir este regalo?
   (wouldn't you be happy)

6. Es urgente que tú _____ de la fecha.
   (remember)

Worked Solutions

1. **me asustaré**   Use the future to express what "will happen." The reflexive verb *asustarse* means "to become frightened." To form the future, add *-é* to the infinitive as the ending for *yo*. The reflexive pronoun for *yo* is *me*. Place the reflexive pronoun before the conjugated verb.

2. **se apresuraran/se apresurasen**   The imperfect subjunctive is needed to express the past after the phrase *era necesario que*. The reflexive verb *apresurarse* means "to hurry." To form the imperfect subjunctive for *apresurar*, take the third person plural preterit form: *apresuraron*. Drop the *-ron* ending and add either *-ran* or *-sen* as the ending for *ellos*. The reflexive pronoun for *ellos* is *se*. Place the reflexive pronoun before the conjugated verb.

3. **Te duchabas**   Use the imperfect to express what "was happening" in the past. The reflexive verb *ducharse* means "to take a shower." To form the imperfect, drop the *-ar* ending and add *-abas* as the ending for *tú*. The reflexive pronoun for *tú* is *te*. Place the reflexive pronoun before the conjugated verb.

4. **nos pusimos**   Use the imperfect to express "what happened" at a particular moment in the past and was completed. The reflexive verb *ponerse* means "to become." The preterit stem of *poner* is irregular and must be memorized: *pus-*. Add the preterit ending for *nosotros*: *-imos*. The reflexive pronoun for *nosotros* is *nos*. Place the reflexive pronoun before the conjugated verb.

5. **No se alegraría**   Use the conditional to express what "would happen." The reflexive verb *alegrarse* means "to become happy." To form the conditional, add *-ía* to the infinitive as the ending for *Ud*. The reflexive pronoun for *Ud*. is *se*. Place the reflexive pronoun before the conjugated verb. Put *no* before the reflexive pronoun to negate the question.

6. **te acuerdes**   The present subjunctive is needed after the phrase *es urgente que*. The reflexive verb *acordarse* means "to remember." The present subjunctive for the stem-changing verb *acordar* changes *o* to *ue* in all forms except *nosotros* and *vosotros* (the same changes that occur in the present). Drop the final *-o* from the *yo* form of the present

tense *(acuerdo)* and add *-es* as the ending for *tú*. The reflexive pronoun for *tú* is *te*. Place the reflexive pronoun before the conjugated verb.

Reflexive Verbs in Compound Tenses

The reflexive pronouns in affirmative and negative sentences generally precede the verb in simple tenses:

Tense	Example	Meaning
Present Perfect	¿Todavía no se ha vestido?	Hasn't he gotten dressed yet?
Pluperfect	(Yo) No me había paseado aquí antes.	I hadn't taken a walk here before.
Future Perfect	¿Se habrá olvidado de la fecha?	I wonder if he has forgotten the date.
Conditional Perfect	(Ud.) Se habría preocupado de eso.	You probably worried about that.
Present Perfect Subjunctive	Es importante que tú te hayas fijado en ella.	It is important that you noticed her.
Pluperfect Subjunctive	Él esperaba que nos hubiéramos (hubiesemos) divertido.	He hoped that we had had fun.

Example Problems

Choose the sentence that expresses each thought in Spanish.

1. Has she gotten up?

    a. ¿Se había levantado?
    b. ¿Se habrá levantado?
    c. ¿Se ha levantado?
    d. ¿Se hará levantado?

    Answer: c

    The present perfect expresses what "has happened."

2. You probably were mistaken.

    a. Te habrías engañado.
    b. Te habrás engañado.
    c. Te hubiste engañado.
    d. Te había engañado.

    Answer: a

    The conditional perfect expresses what probably took place in the past.

3. I hadn't noticed her before.

   a. No me hubiera fijado en ella.

   b. No me había fijado en ella.

   c. No me habré fijado en ella.

   d. No me he fijado en ella.

   Answer: b

   The pluperfect expresses what "had happened" in the past.

Work Problems

Use these problems to give yourself additional practice.

Choose the sentence that expresses each thought in Spanish.

1. I wonder if he has made up his mind.

   a. ¿Se habrá decidido?

   b. ¿Se habría decidido?

   c. ¿Se ha decidido?

   d. ¿Se hubo decidido?

2. Haven't you put on your makeup?

   a. ¿No se hubiera maquillado?

   b. ¿No se habría maquillado?

   c. ¿No se ha maquillado?

   d. ¿No se haya maquillado?

3. The car hadn't stopped at the corner.

   a. El coche no se habrían parado en la esquina.

   b. El coche no se habrán parado en la esquina.

   c. El coche no se había parado en la esquina.

   d. El coche no se han parado en la esquina.

4. It was fair that he became rich.

   a. Era justo que él se haya hecho rico.

   b. Era justo que él se hubiera hecho rico.

   c. Era justo que él se ha hecho rico.

   d. Era justo que él se había hecho rico.

5. I wanted you to have relaxed.

    a. Yo quería que tú te hayas relajado.

    b. Yo quería que tú te habías relajado.

    c. Yo quería que tú te habrías relajado.

    d. Yo quería que tú te hubieras relajado.

6. I hadn't dared speak to him.

    a. No me he atrevido a hablarle.

    b. No me habría atrevido a hablarle.

    c. No me había atrevido a hablarle.

    d. No me habré atrevido a hablarle.

Worked Solutions

1. **a** The future perfect expresses wonderment in the present.

2. **c** The present perfect expresses what "has happened."

3. **c** The pluperfect expresses what "had happened" in the past.

4. **b** A form of the subjunctive is needed after the phrase *era justo que*. The imperfect subjunctive expresses what the subject did.

5. **d** A form of the subjunctive is needed after the verb *quería + que*. The pluperfect subjunctive expresses what the subject "has done."

6. **c** The pluperfect expresses what "had happened" in the past.

Other Uses of Reflexive Verbs

In progressive tenses, the reflexive pronoun may be placed either before the conjugated verb form or after the gerund and attached to it, in which case an accent mark is placed on the stressed vowel of the verb:

Tense	Example	Meaning
Present	Ella **se** está bañando.	She is taking a bath.
	Ella está bañándo**se**.	
Preterit	Ud. no **se** estuvo duchando hasta las seis.	You weren't taking a shower until six o'clock
	Ud. no estuvo duchándo**se** hasta las seis.	
Imperfect	Él **se** estaba afeitando.	He was shaving.
	Él estaba afeitándo**se**.	

Tense	Example	Meaning
Future	Ellos **se** estarán quejando por una semana.	They will be complaining for a week.
	Ellos estarán quejándo**se** por una semana.	
Conditional	**Nos** estaríamos divirtiendo si pudiéramos.	We would have been having fun if we could.
	Estaríamos divirtiéndo**nos** si pudiéramos.	

When only one pronoun follows the verb, count back three vowels from the end and add an accent:

> No estoy relajándome.
>   3   2   1

When two pronouns follow the verb, count back four vowels and add an accent.

> Estoy cepillándome el pelo. Estoy cepillándomelo.
>   3   2   1   4   3   2 1

When used with an infinitive (that is, when there is one subject but two verbs), the reflexive pronoun may be placed either before the conjugated verb form or after the infinitive and attached to it:

I can't fall asleep now.	No **me** puedo dormir ahora.
	No puedo dormir**me** ahora.

She is going to go to bed soon.	**Se** va a acostar pronto.
	Va a acostar**se** pronto.

When used with a command, the reflexive pronoun precedes a negative command but follows and is attached to an affirmative command. When one pronoun is attached, count back three vowels and add an accent. When two pronouns are attached, count back four vowels and add an accent:

No se acuesten tarde.	Don't go to bed late.
Acuéstense temprano.	Go to bed early.

   3 2 1

Lávate el pelo.	Wash your hair.

  3 2 1

Lávatelo.	Wash it.

 4 3 2 1

Plural reflexive constructions may express reciprocal action corresponding to "each other" and "one another" in English:

Nos abrazamos.	We hug one another (each other).

Use *uno a otro (una a otra)* or *el uno al otro (la una a la otra)* (each other) to clarify or reinforce the meaning of the reflexive pronoun:

Ellos se respetan.	They respect themselves. *or* They respect each other.
Ellos se respetan el uno al otro. (uno a otro)	They respect each other.

Reflexive verbs are frequently used to express the passive voice when the agent (person performing the action) isn't mentioned and the subject is a thing (not a person):

Aquí se habla español.   Spanish is spoken here.

Se venden flores en una florería.   They sell flowers in a flower shop.

The reflexive pronoun *se* can substitute for the indefinite subject *uno:*

Uno no puede entrar sin pagar.   One can't enter without paying.

No se puede entrar sin pagar.

Example Problems

As you go for a walk, express what you want and what you see in Spanish.

1. (I want to go for a walk) _____ por el parque.

     Answer: Quiero pasearme/Me quiero pasear

     A. Use the *yo* form *(quiero)* of the irregular verb *querer* to express "to want." *Querer* undergoes an internal stem change from *e* to *ie* in all forms except *nosotros* and *vosotros*. Drop the *-er* ending and add *-o* as the ending for *yo*. Because there is only one subject and two verbs, *querer* is conjugated and *pasearse*, the verb expressing "to go for a walk" remains in the infinitive. The reflexive pronoun for *yo* is *me*. Attach the reflexive pronoun to the infinitive of the verb, *pasear*.

     B. The reflexive pronoun for *yo* is *me*. Place the reflexive pronoun before the conjugated form of *querer (quiero)*.

2. (is making fun of) Ese muchacho _____ de esas muchachas.

     Answer: está burlándose/se está burlando

     A. Use the third person singular form of the irregular verb *estar* to express the present progressive tense: *está*. Form the gerund of *burlar* by dropping the *-ar* ending and adding *-ando*. The third person singular reflexive pronoun is *se*. Attach the reflexive pronoun to the gerund of the verb, *burlando*. Count back three vowels and add an accent.

     B. The third person singular reflexive pronoun is *se*. Place the reflexive pronoun before the conjugated form of *estar (está)*. Form the gerund of *burlar* by dropping the *-ar* ending and adding *-ando*.

3. (They sell) _____ postres deliciosos en esa pastelería.

     Answer: Se venden

     The reflexive pronoun *se* may be used to express the passive voice when the subject is a thing. Because *postres* is plural, the third person plural form of the verb is needed. The third person plural reflexive pronoun is *se*. Conjugate the verb *vender*. Drop the *-er* ending and add the third person plural ending *(-en)*.

4. (help each other) Esos muchachos _____ a cuidar a los niños.

     Answer: se ayudan (uno a otro) (el uno al otro)

The phrase "each other" shows reciprocal action and calls for the use of a reflexive construction. The third person plural reflexive pronoun is *se*. Place the reflexive pronoun before the conjugated verb. Drop the *-ar* ending and add the third person plural ending *(-an)*. For clarity, the expression *uno a otro* (or *el uno al* otro) may be added.

Work Problems

Use these problems to give yourself additional practice.

Elena and Roberto are getting married. Use a reflexive construction to express what is said about them.

1. (You can hear) _____ cantar los pájaros.

2. (are going to get married) Elena y Roberto _____.

3. (remained) Ellos siempre _____ en su pueblo.

4. (One can understand) _____ su alegría.

5. (They have argued) Nunca _____.

6. (was becoming) Elena _____ nerviosa sin causa.

7. (They love each other) _____ de todo corazón.

8. (Relax) Sus amigos les dicen: _____.

9. (Don't worry) Otros dicen: _____.

10. (want to go away) Después de las bodas ellos _____ de su pueblo por un rato.

Worked Solutions

1. **Se puede oír**   The reflexive pronoun *se* can be used before the irregular verb *poder* (to be able to). This reflexive expression can substitute for the indefinite subject *uno* when used in an indefinite sense and can express "one (you, they, and so on) can." *Poder* undergoes an internal stem change from *o* to *ue* in all forms except *nosotros* and *vosotros*. Drop the *-er* ending and add *-e* as the ending that would be used for *uno*. The verb *oír* means "to hear."

2. **van a casarse/se van a casar**

    A. Use the *ellos* form *(van)* of the irregular verb *ir* to express "to go." The conjugated form of *ir* is followed by the preposition *a*. Because there is only one subject and two verbs, *ir* is conjugated and the second verb remains in the infinitive. The reflexive verb *casar* means "to get married." The reflexive pronoun for *ellos* is *se*. Attach the reflexive pronoun to the infinitive of the verb, *casar*.

    B. The reflexive pronoun for *ellos* is *se*. Place the reflexive pronoun before the conjugated form of *ir (van)*. Add the preposition *a*, then the infinitive of the verb.

3. **se quedaban**   Use the imperfect tense to show that they always remained faithful to each other. The reflexive pronoun for *ellos* is *se*.

4. **Se puede comprender**   The reflexive pronoun *se* can be used before the irregular verb *poder* (to be able to). This reflexive expression can substitute for the indefinite subject *uno* when used in an indefinite sense and can express "one (you, they, and so on) can." *Poder* undergoes an internal stem change from *o* to *ue* in all forms except *nosotros* and *vosotros*. Drop the *-er* ending and add *-e* as the ending that would be used for *uno*. The verb *comprender* means "to understand."

5. **se han peleado**   The reflexive verb *pelearse* means "to argue." To form the present perfect of *pelear*, take the *ellos* form of the present tense of the verb *haber (han)*. Form the past participle of the verb *pelear* by dropping the *-ar* ending and adding *-ado*. Place the reflexive pronoun before the conjugated helping verb *han*.

6. **estaba poniéndose/se estaba poniendo**

   A. Use the third person singular form of the irregular verb *estar* to express the imperfect progressive tense: *estaba*. The reflexive verb *ponerse* means "to become." Form the gerund of *poner* by dropping the *-er* ending and adding *-iendo*. The third person singular reflexive pronoun is *se*. Attach the reflexive pronoun to the gerund of the verb: *poniendo*. Count back three vowels and add an accent.

   B. The third person singular reflexive pronoun is *se*. Place the reflexive pronoun before the conjugated form of *estar (estaba)*. Form the gerund of *poner* by dropping the *-er* ending and adding *-iendo*.

7. **se aman**   The phrase "each other" shows reciprocal action and calls for the use of a reflexive construction. The reflexive verb *amarse* means "to love each other." The third person plural reflexive pronoun for *ellos* is *se*. Place the reflexive pronoun before the conjugated verb. Drop the *-ar* ending and add the third person plural ending *(-an)*.

8. **Relájense**   The reflexive verb *relajarse* means "to relax." To form a command with *Uds.*, use the present subjunctive of the verb. To form the present subjunctive for *relajar*, drop the final *-o* from the *yo* form of the present tense *(relajo)* and add *-en* as the third person plural ending. In an affirmative command, the reflexive pronoun follows the verb and is attached to it. Count back three vowels and add an accent.

9. **No se preocupen**   The reflexive verb *preocuparse* means "to worry." To form a command with *Uds.*, use the present subjunctive of the verb. To form the present subjunctive for *preocupar*, drop the final *-o* from the *yo* form of the present tense *(preocupo)* and add *-en* as the third person plural ending. In a negative command, the reflexive pronoun precedes the verb.

10. **quieren irse/se quieren ir**

    A. Use the *ellos* form *(quieren)* of the irregular verb *querer* to express "to want." *Querer* undergoes an internal stem change from *e* to *ie* in all forms except *nosotros* and *vosotros*. Drop the *-er* ending and add *-en* as the ending for *ellos*. Because there is only one subject but two verbs, *querer* is conjugated and *irse*, the verb expressing "to go away," remains in the infinitive. The reflexive pronoun for *ellos* is *se*. Attach the reflexive pronoun to the infinitive of the verb, *ir*.

B. The reflexive pronoun for *ellos* is *se*. Place the reflexive pronoun before the conjugated form of *querer (quieren)*.

Chapter Problems

Problems

Express what people were doing when the phone rang.

1. (bañarse) Yo_____.

2. (desayunarse) Nosotros _____.

3. (maquillarse) Ella_____.

4. (peinarse) Uds._____.

5. (vestirse) Tú_____.

Express what happens as a result of an accident.

   Example: Ud./pensar/acercarse a la escena
   Ud. piensa acercarse a la escena.

6. él/ir/desmayarse

7. nosotros/poder/cuidarse

8. ellas/querer/sentarse

9. tú/deber/callarse

10. yo/preferir/irse de la escena

Express what a mother says to her child who is going on a ski trip.

11. (Don't break) _____ la pierna.

12. (Put on)_____ tu abrigo cuando hace frío.

13. (Remember) _____ de tener cuidado.

14. (Take a shower) _____ todos los días.

15. (Don't get wet) _____ cuando esquíes.

Complete the sentences by filling in the reflexive verb where needed to express what different people did yesterday at three o'clock.

16. (poner/ponerse) Tú_____ la mesa y _____ un delantal.

17. (preparer/prepararse) Nosotros _____ la cena y _____ a salir.

18. (sentir/sentirse) Uds. _____ mal porque _____ dolores en la espalda.

19. (colocarse/colocar) Yo _____ en mi cuarto y _____ el póster en la pared.

20. (esconder/esconderse) Ella_____ sus joyas y _____.

Answers and Solutions

1. **Answer: estaba bañándome/me estaba bañando**

A. Use the first person singular form of the irregular verb *estar* to express the imperfect progressive tense: *estaba*. Form the gerund of *bañar* by dropping the *-ar* ending and adding *-ando*. The reflexive pronoun for *yo* is *me*. Attach the reflexive pronoun to the gerund of the verb: *bañando*. Count back three vowels and add an accent.

B. The reflexive pronoun for *yo* is *me*. Place the reflexive pronoun before the conjugated form of *estar (estaba)*. Form the gerund of *bañar* by dropping the *-ar* ending and adding *-ando*.

2. **Answer: estábamos desayunándonos/nos estábamos desayunando**

A. Use the first person plural form of the irregular verb *estar* to express the imperfect progressive tense: *estábamos*. Form the gerund of *desayunar* by dropping the *-ar* ending and adding *-ando*. The reflexive pronoun for *nosotros* is *nos*. Attach the reflexive pronoun to the gerund of the verb: *desayunando*. Count back three vowels and add an accent.

B. The reflexive pronoun for *nosotros* is *nos*. Place the reflexive pronoun before the conjugated form of *estar (estábamos)*. Form the gerund of *desayunar* by dropping the *-ar* ending and adding *-ando*.

3. **Answer: estaba maquillándose/se estaba maquillando**

A. Use the third person singular form of the irregular verb *estar* to express the imperfect progressive tense: *estaba*. Form the gerund of *maquillar* by dropping the *-ar* ending and adding *-ando*. The reflexive pronoun for *ella* is *se*. Attach the reflexive pronoun to the gerund of the verb: *maquillando*. Count back three vowels and add an accent.

B. The reflexive pronoun for *ella* is *se*. Place the reflexive pronoun before the conjugated form of *estar (estaba)*. Form the gerund of *maquillar* by dropping the *-ar* ending and adding *-ando*.

4. **Answer: estaban peinándose/se estaban peinando**

A. Use the third person plural form of the irregular verb *estar* to express the imperfect progressive tense: *estaban*. Form the gerund of *peinar* by dropping the *-ar* ending and adding *-ando*. The reflexive pronoun for *Uds.* is *se*. Attach the reflexive pronoun to the gerund of the verb: *peinando*. Count back three vowels and add an accent.

B. The reflexive pronoun for *Uds.* is *se*. Place the reflexive pronoun before the conjugated form of *estar (estaban)*. Form the gerund of *peinar* by dropping the *-ar* ending and adding *-ando*.

5. **Answer: estabas vistiéndote/te estabas vistiendo**

    A. Use the second person singular form of the irregular verb *estar* to express the imperfect progressive tense: *estabas*. *Vestir* is a stem-changing *-ir* verb that changes the stem vowel from *e* to *i* when forming the gerund. Drop the *-ir* ending and adding *-iendo*. The reflexive pronoun for *tú* is *te*. Attach the reflexive pronoun to the gerund of the verb: *vistiendo*. Count back three vowels and add an accent.

    B. The reflexive pronoun for *tú* is *te*. Place the reflexive pronoun before the conjugated form of *estar* (*estabas*). *Vestir* is a stem-changing *-ir* verb that changes the stem vowel from *e* to *i* when forming the gerund. Drop the *-ir* ending and adding *-iendo*.

6. **Answer: Él va a desmayarse.** Use the *él* form of the irregular verb *ir* (*va*). The conjugated form of *ir* is followed by the preposition *a*. Because there is only one subject but two verbs, *ir* is conjugated and the second verb remains in the infinitive. The reflexive pronoun for *él* is *se*. Attach the reflexive pronoun to the infinitive of the verb: *desmayar*.

7. **Answer: Nosotros podemos cuidarnos.** Use the *nosotros* form of the irregular verb *poder* (*podemos*). *Poder* undergoes an internal stem change of *o* to *ue* in all forms except *nosotros* and *vosotros*. Because there is only one subject but two verbs, *poder* is conjugated and the second verb remains in the infinitive. The reflexive pronoun for *nosotros* is *nos*. Attach the reflexive pronoun to the infinitive of the verb: *cuidar*.

8. **Answer: Ellas quieren sentarse.** Use the *ellas* form of the irregular verb *querer* (*quieren*). *Querer* undergoes an internal stem change of *e* to *ie* in all forms except *nosotros* and *vosotros*. Because there is only one subject but two verbs, *querer* is conjugated and the second verb remains in the infinitive. The reflexive pronoun for *ellas* is *se*. Attach the reflexive pronoun to the infinitive of the verb: *sentar*.

9. **Answer: Tú debes callarte.** Use the *tú* form of the verb *deber* (*debes*). Drop the *-er* ending and add *-es* for the *tú* form. Because there is only one subject but two verbs, *deber* is conjugated and the second verb remains in the infinitive. The reflexive pronoun for *tú* is *te*. Attach the reflexive pronoun to the infinitive of the verb: *callar*.

10. **Answer: Yo prefiero irme de la escena.** Use the *yo* form of the irregular verb *preferir* (*prefiero*). *Preferir* undergoes an internal stem change of *e* to *ie* in all forms except *nosotros* and *vosotros*. Because there is only one subject but two verbs, *preferir* is conjugated and the second verb remains in the infinitive. The reflexive pronoun for *yo* is *me*. Attach the reflexive pronoun to the infinitive of the verb: *ir*.

11. **Answer: No te rompas** Use the verb *romperse* to express "to break." To form a negative command with *tú*, use the present subjunctive *tú* form. To form the present subjunctive for the regular verb *romper*, drop the final *-er* infinitive ending and add the present subjunctive ending for *tú* (*-as*). In a negative command, the reflexive pronoun precedes the verb.

12. **Answer: Ponte** Use the verb *ponerse* to express "to put on." The informal affirmative command form of *poner* is irregular and must be memorized: *pon*. In an affirmative command, the reflexive pronoun follows the verb and is attached to it.

13. **Answer: Acuérdate** Use the verb *acordarse* to express "to remember." To form an affirmative command with *tú*, drop the final *-s* from the second person singular present indicative form of *tú* (*acuerdas*). In the present, *acordar* undergoes an internal stem change from *o* to *ue* in all forms except *nosotros* and *vosotros*. In an affirmative command, the reflexive pronoun follows the verb and is attached to it. Count back three vowels and add an accent.

14. **Answer: Dúchate**   Use the verb *ducharse* to express "to take a shower." To form an affirmative command with *tú*, drop the final *-s* from the second person singular present indicative form of *tú (duchas)*. In an affirmative command, the reflexive pronoun follows the verb and is attached to it. Count back three vowels and add an accent.

15. **Answer: No te mojes**   Use the verb *mojarse* to express "to get wet." To form a negative command with *tú*, use the present subjunctive *tú* form. To form the present subjunctive for *mojar*, drop the final *-ar* infinitive ending and add the present subjunctive ending for *tú (-es)*. In a negative command, the reflexive pronoun precedes the verb.

16. **Answer: pusiste; te pusiste**   The reflexive verb is needed before the second verb because the subject, *tú*, is acting upon itself: "You" put on an apron. The reflexive pronoun for *tú* is *te*. The first verb is not used reflexively because the subject is not acting upon itself: "You" set the table. In the preterit stem, *poner* changes the *o* from the infinitive stem to *u*. The *n* from the infinitive stem changes to *s* in the preterit. The second person singular preterit ending for an *-er* verb is *-iste*.

17. **Answer: preparamos; nos preparamos**   The reflexive verb is needed before the second verb because the subject, *nosotros*, is acting upon itself: "We" prepared ourselves to leave. The reflexive pronoun for *nosotros* is *nos*. The first verb is not used reflexively because the subject is acting upon something else: "We" prepared dinner. To conjugate *preparar* in the preterit, drop the *-ar* ending and add *-amos* as the ending for *nosotros*.

18. **Answer: se sintieron; sintieron**   The reflexive verb is needed before the first verb because the subject, *Uds.*, is acting upon itself: "You" feel bad. The reflexive pronoun for *Uds.* is *se*. The second verb is not used reflexively because the subject is not acting upon itself: "You" had back pains. Present tense stem-changing verbs ending in *-ir* also undergo a stem change in the preterit. In the third person singular form, *e* changes to *i*. Drop the *-ir* ending and add the preterit ending for *Uds. (-ieron)*.

19. **Answer: me coloqué; coloqué**   The reflexive verb is needed before the first verb because the subject, *yo*, is acting upon itself: "I" stood up. The reflexive pronoun for *yo* is *me*. The second verb is not used reflexively because the subject is not acting upon itself: "I" hung a poster on the wall. To conjugate spelling-change *-car* verbs in the preterit, drop the *-ar* ending. For *yo*, change *c* to *qu* and add *-é* as the ending.

20. **Answer: escondió; se escondió**   The reflexive verb is needed before the second verb because the subject, *ella*, is acting upon itself: "She" hides. The reflexive pronoun for *ella* is *se*. The first verb is not used reflexively because the subject is acting upon something else: "She" hid the jewels. To conjugate *esconder* in the preterit, drop the *-er* ending and add *-ió* as the ending.

Supplemental Chapter Problems

Problems

Express what people would have been doing last night had guests not arrived.

1. (desvestirse) Tú_____.

2. (afeitarse) Ellos _____.

3. (ducharse) Yo_____.

4. (relajarse) Ud._____.

5. (acostarse) nosotros_____.

Express how people react to an argument. Follow the example in the "Problems" section.

6. yo/pretender/quedarse en mi cuarto

7. ella/querer/marcharse

8. tú/preferir/quejarse de todo

9. nosotros/ir/enojarse

10. ellos/pensar/pelearse

Express what a mother says to her child who is going on to camp.

11. (Don't catch a cold) _____.

12. (Go to bed)_____ temprano.

13. (Don't worry) _____ de los insectos.

14. (Brush your teeth) _____ todos los días.

15. (Take off) _____ tu abrigo cuando haga calor.

Complete the sentences by filling in the reflexive verb where needed to express what different people did yesterday.

16. (dormir/dormirse)Ella _____ a las diez de la tarde y _____ hasta las ocho de la mañana.

17. (ir/irse)Yo _____ de la escuela y _____ al parque.

18. (quitar/quitarse) Uds. _____ la mesa y después _____ la ropa.

19. (enfadar/enfadarse)Tú _____ cuando _____ a unas amigas.

20. (engañar/engañarse) Nosotros_____ a nuestros amigos y en eso _____.

Solutions

1. te hubieras estado desvistiendo/hubieras estado desvistiéndote (other uses of reflexive verbs, p. 388.)

2. se hubieran estado afeitando/hubieran estado afeitàndose (other uses of reflexive verbs, p. 388.)

3. me hubiera estado duchando/hubiera estado duchándome (other uses of reflexive verbs, p. 388.)

4. se hubiera estado relajando/hubiera estado relajándose (other uses of reflexive verbs, p. 388.)

5. nos hubieramos estado acostando/hubieramos estado acostándonos (other uses of reflexive verbs, p. 388.)

6. Yo pretendo quedarme en mi cuarto. (other uses of reflexive verbs, p. 388.)

7. Ella quiere marcharse. (other uses of reflexive verbs, p. 388.)

8. Tú prefieres quejarte de todo. (other uses of reflexive verbs, p. 388.)

9. Nosotros vamos a enojarnos. (other uses of reflexive verbs, p. 388.)

10. Ellos piensan pelearse. (other uses of reflexive verbs, p. 388.)

11. No te resfríes (other uses of reflexive verbs, p. 388.)

12. Acuéstate (other uses of reflexive verbs, p. 388.)

13. No te preocupes (other uses of reflexive verbs, p. 388.)

14. Cepíllate los dientes (other uses of reflexive verbs, p. 388.)

15. Quítate (other uses of reflexive verbs, p. 388.)

16. se durmió, durmió (verbs used reflexively in Spanish but not in English, p. 377; verbs with special reflexive meanings, p. 379.)

17. me fui, fui (verbs used reflexively in Spanish but not in English, p. 377; verbs with special reflexive meanings, p. 379.)

18. quitaron, se quitaron (verbs used reflexively in Spanish but not in English, p. 377; verbs with special reflexive meanings, p. 379.)

19. te enfadaste, enfadaste (verbs used reflexively in Spanish but not in English, p. 377; verbs with special reflexive meanings, p. 379.)

20. engañamos, nos engañamos (verbs used reflexively in Spanish but not in English, p. 377; verbs with special reflexive meanings, p. 379.)

Chapter 18
The Passive Voice

The Active Voice and the Passive Voice

The active voice is what you normally use when speaking or writing. In the active voice, the subject noun or pronoun performs the action. In the passive voice, however, someone or something else acts upon the subject. In general, it is considered preferable to avoid the passive voice, if possible.

> *Active:* Los fuegos destruyen muchos árboles.
>
> Fires destroy many trees.
>
> *Passive:* Muchos árboles son destruidos por los fuegos.
>
> Many trees are destroyed by fires.

The Passive Voice with *Ser*

The Spanish passive voice construction mirrors the English construction and is formed by using the following formula:

SUBJECT (noun or pronoun)	+ *SER* (conjugated)	+ PAST PARTICIPLE (agrees with subject)	+ *POR*	+ AGENT
Sus coches	son	reparados	por	ese mecánico.
Their cars	are	repaired	by	that mechanic.

In this passive construction, the past participle is used as an adjective and must, therefore, agree in number and gender with the subject. For example:

> Las mujeres fueron recompensadas por sus esfuerzos.
>
> The women were rewarded for their efforts.

If you are going to use a pronoun after por, it should be a prepositional pronoun (mí, ti, él, ella, Ud, nosotros, vosotros, ellos, ellas).

Todo el trabajo fue hecho por mí.	All the work was done by me.
¿Este libro fue escrito por tí?	Was this book written by you?

The Passive Voice in Simple Tenses

The passive voice can be used in simple tenses by using simple forms of *ser* as follows:

Tense	Example	Meaning
Present	Las comidas **son** preparadas por el padre.	The meals are prepared by the father.
Preterit	Los poemas **fueron** escritos por los alumnos.	The poems were written by the students.
Imperfect	Los ejercicios **eran** repetidos por los atletas.	The exercises were repeated by the athletes.
Future	El actor **será** admirado por todos.	The actor will be admired by all.
Pluperfect	El doctor no **sería** olvidado por sus pacientes.	The doctor wouldn't be forgotten by his patients.

Example Problems

Use the correct form of the passive voice to discuss the development of a city.

1. (was constucted) Ese rascacielos _____ por mi abuelo.

   Answer: fue construido

   Use the preterit tense to express what happened and was completed. The preterit of *ser* is irregular and must be memorized. Use the third person singular form of *ser (fue)*, which agrees with the subject: *rascacielos*. Use the verb *construir* to express " to construct." To form the past participle, drop the *-ir* ending and add *-ido*. When an *-ir* verb stem ends in a vowel, it is necessary to add an accent to the vowel before the *-do* ending. Because the past participle is used as an adjective, it agrees with the masculine singular noun *rascacielos*.

2. (are admired) Esos edificios _____ por todos.

   Answer: son admirados

   Use the present tense to express what takes place in the present. The present of *ser* is irregular and must be memorized. Use the third person plural form *ser (son)*, which agrees with the subject: *edificios*. Use the verb *admirar* to express " to admire." To form the past participle, drop the *-ar* ending and add *-ado*. Because the past participle is used as an adjective, an *-s* must be added so that it agrees with the masculine plural noun *edificios*.

3. (will be dedicated) Esta estatua _____ por el alcalde.

   Answer: será dedicada

   Use the future tense to express what will take place. The future of *ser* is irregular and must be memorized. Use the third person singular form *ser(será)*, which agrees with the subject: *estatua*. Use the verb *admirar* to express " to admire." To form the past participle, drop the *-ar* ending and add *-ado*. Because the past participle is used as an adjective, an *-a* must be added so that it agrees with the feminine singular noun *estatua*.

Work Problems

Use these problems to give yourself additional practice.

Continue using the correct form of the passive voice to discuss the development of a city.

1. (was urbanized) Esa ciudad _____ poco a poco por esos negociantes.

2. (will be paid) Esas fuentes _____ por los ciudadanos.

3. (were offered) Esos jardines _____ por la familia del alcalde.

4. (will be utilized) Esa autopista _____ por los habitantes.

5. (is appreciated) Ese centro comercial _____ por todos.

6. (would be donated) Esa exposición _____ por ese artista.

Worked Solutions

1. **era urbanizada**   Use the imperfect tense what was happening over a period of time. The imperfect of *ser* is irregular and must be memorized. Use the third person singular form of *ser* (*era*), which agrees with the subject: *ciudad*. Use the verb *urbanizar* to express " to urbanize." To form the past participle, drop the *-ar* ending and add *-ado*. Because the past participle is used as an adjective, the *-o* becomes an *-a* to agree with the feminine singular noun *ciudad*.

2. **serán pagadas**   Use the future tense to express what will take place. The future of *ser* is irregular and must be memorized. Use the third person plural form *ser* (*serán*), which agrees with the subject: *fuentes*. Use the verb *pagar* to express " to pay." To form the past participle, drop the *-ar* ending and add *-ado*. Because the past participle is used as an adjective, the *-o* becomes an *-a* and an *-s* must be added to agree with the feminine plural noun *fuentes*.

3. **fueron ofrecidos**   Use the preterit tense to express what happened and was completed. The preterit of *ser* is irregular and must be memorized. Use the third person plural form of *ser* (*fueron*), which agrees with the subject: *jardines*. Use the verb *ofrecer* to express " to offer." To form the past participle, drop the *-er* ending and add *-ido*. Because the past participle is used as an adjective, an *-s* must be added to agree with the masculine plural: *jardines*.

4. **será utilizada**   Use the future tense to express what will take place. The future of *ser* is irregular and must be memorized. Use the third person singular form *ser* (*será*), which agrees with the subject: *autopista*. Use the verb *utilizar* to express " to use." To form the past participle, drop the *-ar* ending and add *-ado*. Because the past participle is used as an adjective, an *-a* must be added to agree with the feminine plural noun *autopista*.

5. **es apreciado**   Use the present tense to express what takes place in the present. The present of *ser* is irregular and must be memorized. Use the third person singular form *ser* (*es*), which agrees with the subject: *centro comercial*. Use the verb *apreciar* to express " to appreciate (value, esteem)." To form the past participle, drop the *-ar* ending and add *-ado*.

6. **sería donada**   Use the conditional to express what would take place. The conditional of *ser* is irregular and must be memorized. Use the third person singular form *ser* (*sería*), which agrees with the subject: *exposición*. Use the verb *donar* to express " to donate." To form the past participle, drop the *-ar* ending and add *-ado*. Because the past participle is used as an adjective, the *-o* becomes an *-a* to agree with the feminine singular noun: *exposición*.

The Passive Voice in Compound Tenses

The passive voice can be used in compound tenses by linking compound forms of *ser* and the past participle of the action. Note that the past participle of *ser* remains invariable and is followed by the past participle of the action word, which agrees in number and gender with the subject:

Tense	Example	Meaning
Present Perfect	Esas películas han sido dirigidas por esa mujer.	Those films have been directed by that woman.
Pluperfect	El césped había sido cortado por el muchacho.	The grass had been cut by the boy.
Future Perfect	La factura habrá sido enviada por la compañía.	The bill will have been sent by the company.
Conditional Perfect	Los gastos habrían sido pagados por el señor Rivera.	The costs would have been paid by Mr. Rivera.

Example Problems

Express how chores get done using compound tenses.

1. El almuerzo _____ Elsa.
   (would have been served by)

   Answer: habría sido servido por

   Use the conditional perfect of *ser* to express what "would have" happened. To form the conditional perfect of *ser*, take the third person singular form of the conditional tense of the verb *haber (habría)*, which agrees with the subject: *el almuerzo*. Add the irregular past participle for *ser (sido)*, which is invariable. Use the verb *servir* to express "to serve." Form the past participle of the verb *servir* by dropping the *-ir* ending and adding *-ido*. Use *por* to express "by."

2. La ropa _____ Alberto.
   (has been ironed by)

   Answer: ha sido planchada por

   Use the present perfect of *ser* to express what "has" happened. To form the present perfect of *ser*, take the third person singular form of the present tense of the verb *haber (ha)*, which agrees with the subject: *la ropa*. Add the irregular past participle for *ser (sido)*, which is invariable. Use the verb *planchar* to express "to iron." Form the past participle of the verb *planchar* by dropping the *-ar* ending and adding *-ado*. Because the past participle is used as an adjective, the *-o* becomes an *-a* to agree with the feminine singular noun *ropa*. Use *por* to express "by."

3. Los muebles _____ Amalia.

(had been dusted by)

Answer: habían sido sacudidos por

Use the pluperfect of *ser* to express what "had" happened. To form the pluperfect of *ser*, take the third person plural form of the imperfect tense of the verb *haber (habían)*, which agrees with the subject *los muebles*. Add the irregular past participle for *ser (sido)*, which is invariable. Use the verb *sacudir* to express "to dust." Form the past participle of the verb *sacudir* by dropping the *-ir* ending and adding *-ido*. Because the past participle is used as an adjective, an *-s* must be added to agree with the masculine plural noun *muebles*. Use *por* to express "by."

Work Problems

Use these problems to give yourself additional practice.

Continue expressing how chores get done using compound tenses.

1. La mesa _____ Victoria.

(has been set by)

2. El césped _____ Rafael.

(had been cut by)

3. Los coches _____ Santiago y Soledad.

(would have been washed by)

4. Los cuartos _____ dos veces _____ Elena.

(will have been swept)   (by)

5. La basura _____ Jaime.

(has been taken out by)

6. Las comidas _____ Luz.

(had been prepared by)

Worked Solutions

1. **ha sido puesta por**   Use the present perfect of *ser* to express what "has" happened. To form the present perfect of *ser*, take the third person singular form of the present tense of the verb *haber (ha)*, which agrees with the subject: *la mesa*. Add the irregular past participle for *ser (sido)*, which is invariable. Use the verb *poner* to express "to set." The past participle of *poner* is irregular and must be memorized: *puesto*. Because the past participle is used as an adjective, the *-o* becomes an *-a* to agree with the feminine singular noun *mesa*. Use *por* to express "by."

2. **había sido cortado por**   Use the pluperfect of *ser* to express what "had" happened. To form the pluperfect of *ser*, take the third person singular form of the imperfect tense of the verb *haber (había)*, which agrees with the subject: *el césped*. Add the irregular past participle for *ser (sido)*, which is invariable. Use the verb *cortar* to express "to cut." Form the past participle of the verb *cortar* by dropping the *-ar* ending and adding *-ado*. Use *por* to express "by."

3. **habrían sido lavados por**   Use the conditional perfect of *ser* to express what "would have" happened. To form the conditional perfect of *ser*, take the third person plural form of the conditional tense of the verb *haber (habrían)*, which agrees with the subject: *los coches*. Add the irregular past participle for *ser (sido)*, which is invariable. Use the verb *lavar* to express "to wash." Form the past participle of the verb *lavar* by dropping the *-ar* ending and adding *-ado*. Because the past participle is used as an adjective, an *-s* must be added to agree with the masculine plural noun *coches*. Use *por* to express "by."

4. **habrán sido barridos/por**   Use the future perfect of *ser* to express what "will have" happened. To form the future perfect of *ser*, take the third person plural form of the future tense of the verb *haber (habrán)*, which agrees with the subject: *los cuartos*. Add the irregular past participle for *ser (sido)*, which is invariable. Use the verb *barrer* to express "to sweep." Form the past participle of the verb *barrer* by dropping the *-er* ending and adding *-ido*. Because the past participle is used as an adjective, an *-s* must be added to agree with the masculine plural noun *coches*. Use *por* to express "by."

5. **ha sido sacada por**   Use the present perfect of *ser* to express what "has" happened. To form the present perfect of *ser*, take the third person singular form of the present tense of the verb *haber (ha)*, which agrees with the subject: *la basura*. Add the irregular past participle for *ser (sido)*, which is invariable. Use the verb *sacar* to express "to take out." Form the past participle of the verb *sacar* by dropping the *-ar* ending and adding *-ado*. Because the past participle is used as an adjective, the *-o* becomes an *-a* to agree with the feminine singular noun *basura*. Use *por* to express "by."

6. **habían sido preparadas por**   Use the pluperfect of *ser* to express what "had" happened. To form the pluperfect of *ser*, take the third person plural form of the imperfect tense of the verb *haber (habían)*, which agrees with the subject: *las comidas*. Add the irregular past participle for *ser (sido)*, which is invariable. Use the verb *preparar* to express "to prepare." Form the past participle of the verb *preparar* by dropping the *-ar* ending and adding *-ado*. Because the past participle is used as an adjective, the *-o* becomes an *-a* and an *-s* must be added to agree with the feminine plural noun *comidas*. Use *por* to express "by."

Alternate Constructions for the Passive

The following constructions may be used to substitute for the passive voice:

❑ A reflexive construction with *se* is used to form the passive voice when the subject is a thing (not a person) and when the agent is not determined or is of no importance. When *se* is used, the verb agrees with the noun subject, which follows the verb:

Se vendió la casa.   The house was sold.

Se abren las tiendas a las nueve.   The stores are open at nine o'clock.

❑ The pronoun *se* may be used as an indefinite subject (not as a reflexive pronoun) to refer to "one," "people," "they," and "you." *Se* is only used with the third person singular form of the verb:

Se sabe que el ejercicio es importante para la buena salud.

It is known (one knows/people know/they know/you know) that exercise is important for good health.

❏ The indefinite *se* (followed by the third person singular *[él]* form of the verb) is also used to replace the passive when the agent is not mentioned or implied and a person is acted upon:

Se recompensará al niño.

The child will be rewarded. (Someone will reward the child.)

Se rescató a las víctimas.

The victims were saved. (Someone saved the victims.)

In the above examples, the person acted upon is a direct object. The direct object pronouns *le* or *les* (rather than *lo* or *los*) are used to replace these direct object nouns.

Se recompensará al niño (a los niños).	The child(ren) will be rewarded.
Se le (les) recompensará.	He (They) will be rewarded.
Se rescató a la(s) víctima(s).	The victim(s) was (were) saved.
Se la(s) rescató.	He/She (They) were saved.

The active third person plural (*ellos* form) is often used to avoid the indefinite *se* construction:

Recompensarán al niño.	They will reward the child.
Rescataron a las víctimas.	They saved the victims.

Example Problems

Use an alternative to the passive voice to speak about shopping. Express the following phrases in Spanish.

1. The stores close at 9 p.m.

   Answer: Se cierran las tiendas a las nueve de la noche.

   A reflexive construction with *se* is used as alternative to the passive voice when the subject is a thing and when the agent is not determined. When *se* is used, the verb agrees with the noun subject, which follows the verb. Use *las tiendas* to express "the stores." Use *cerrar* to express "to close." Use the reflexive pronoun *se* before the verb. *Cerrar* is a stem-changing verb whose internal *e* changes to *ie* in all forms except *nosotros* and *vosotros*. Drop the *-ar* ending and add *-an* for the third person plural form of *cerrar*. Use *a las nueve* to express "at nine o'clock." Use *de la noche* to express "in the evening" (p.m.).

2. They say that mall is the best.

   Answer: Se dice que ese centro comercial es el mejor.

   The pronoun *se* may be used as an indefinite subject to refer to "one," "people," "they," and "you." *Se* is used only with the third person singular of the verb. Use *decir* to express "to say." *Decir* is an irregular verb and must be memorized. Use the third person singular form: *dice*. Use *que* to express "that." Use *centro comercial* to express "mall." Use *ese* to express "that" before the masculine singular noun *centro comercial*. Use *es* to express "is." Use *el mejor* to express "the best" when referring to the masculine singular noun.

3. The clients will all be helped.

> **Answer: Se ayudará a todos los clientes.**

The indefinite *se* (followed by the third person singular *[él]* form of the verb) is also used to replace the passive when the agent is not mentioned or implied and a person is acted upon. Use *ayudar* to express "to help." Use the future to express that the action will take place. To form the future of *ayudar*, add the third person singular future ending *-á* to the infinitive. Use the personal *a* before the reference to people. Use the masculine plural adjective *todos* to express "all" before the masculine plural noun *los clientes* (clients).

Work Problems

Use these problems to give yourself additional practice.

Use an alternative to the passive voice to speak about a restaurant. Express the following phrases in Spanish.

1. The meals? They require (need) a meticulous preparation.

2. They prepare the soups with meat.

3. They fry the fish with olive oil.

4. They say it is the best restaurant in the city.

5. They serve the clients well.

6. One can say that the cook is famous.

Worked Solutions

1. **¿Las comidas? se necesita una preparación meticulosa.**   A reflexive construction with *se* is used as alternative to the passive voice when the subject is a thing and when the agent is not determined. When *se* is used, the verb agrees with the noun subject, which follows the verb. Use *las comidas* to express "the meals." Use *necesitar* to express "to require." *Necesitar* must agree with the subject *una preparación*. To conjugate *necesitar*, drop the *-ar* ending and add the third person singular ending: *-a*. Place the reflexive pronoun *se* before the conjugated verb. Use *una preparación* to express "a preparation." Use the feminine singular adjective *meticulosa* to express "meticulous" and to describe the feminine singular noun *una preparación*.

2. **Las sopas se preparan con carne.**   A reflexive construction with *se* is used as alternative to the passive voice when the subject is a thing and when the agent is not determined. When *se* is used, the verb agrees with the noun subject, which follows the verb. Use *preparar* to express "to prepare." *Preparar* must agree with the subject "las sopas." To conjugate *preparar*, drop the *-ar* ending and add the third person plural ending: *-an*. Put the reflexive pronoun *se* before the conjugated verb. Use *las sopas* to express "the soups." Use *con* to express "with." Use *carne* to express "meat."

3. **El pescado se fríe con aceite de oliva.**   A reflexive construction with *se* is used as alternative to the passive voice when the subject is a thing and when the agent is not determined. When *se* is used, the verb agrees with the noun subject, which follows the verb. Use *freír* to express "to fry." *Freír* is conjugated like the irregular verb *reír* and must be memorized. *Freír* must agree with the subject "el pescado." The third person singular form of *freír* is *fríe*. Use *el pecado* to express "the fish." Use *con* to express "with." Use *aceite de oliva* to express "olive oil."

4. **Se dice que es el mejor restaurante de la ciudad.**   The pronoun *se* may be used as an indefinite subject to refer to "one," "people," "they," and "you." *Se* is used only with the third person singular form of the verb. Use *decir* to express "to say." *Decir* is an irregular verb and must be memorized. Use the third person singular form: *dice*. Use *que* to express "that." Use *decir* to express "to say." Use *que* to express "that." Use *es* to express "it is." Use *el restaurante* to express "the restaurant." Use *mejor* to express "best" and place it before the noun it describes.

5. **Se sirve bien a los clientes.**   The indefinite *se* is used to replace the passive when the agent is not mentioned or implied and a person is acted upon. *Se* is followed by the third person singular form of the verb. Use *servir* to express "to serve." *Servir* undergoes an internal stem change of *e* to *i* in all forms except *nosotros* and *vosotros*. To conjugate *servir*, drop the *-ir* ending and add *-e* as the third person singular ending. Use *bien* to express "well." Use the personal *a* before the reference to people. Use *los clientes* to express "the clients."

6. **Se puede decir que el cocinero es famoso.**   The pronoun *se* may be used as an indefinite subject to refer to "one," "people," "they," and "you." *Se* is only used with the third person singular form of the verb. Use *poder* to express "to be able to." *Poder* undergoes an internal stem change of *o* to *u* in all forms except *nosotros* and *vosotros*. Drop the *-er* infinitive ending and add *-e* as the third person singular ending. A conjugated verb is immediately followed by an infinitive. Use *decir* to express "to say." Use *que* to express "that." Use *el cocinero* to express "the cook." Use the third person singular of the irregular verb *ser* to express "is." Use *famoso* to express "famous."

Chapter Problems

Problems

Express the preparations that were made for a party by changing the sentences from the active voice to the passive voice.

> Example: Yo escogí la música.
> La música fue escogida por mí.

1. Julio preparó los postres.

2. Tomás y yo arreglamos los cuartos.

3. Marta y Susana enviaron las invitaciones.

4. Tú quitaste los muebles del salón.

5. Ud. tocó la guitarra.

6.   Las muchachas adornaron el salón.

7.   Jaime colgó las luces.

8.   Vosotros comprasteis los comestibles.

9.   Uds. pagaron las bebidas.

10. La señora Cruz hizo los preparativos.

Use an alternate construction to avoid the passive voice and to speak about stores and places:

11. Los zapatos son reparados en una zapatería.

12. Las llaves son hechas en una ferretería.

13. Las pinturas son exhibidas en un museo.

14. Los vestidos son remendados en una sastrería.

15. Los carretes son revelados en el estudio del fotógrafo.

Use an alternative to the passive voice to express the following phrases about the weather.

16. (It is said that) _____ no nieva mucho en el sur.

17. (One needs) _____ un paraguas cuando llueve.

18. (People use) _____ un abrigo cuando hace frío.

19. (It is known that) _____ hay que protegerse contra el sol.

20. (You take off) _____ un suéter cuando hace calor.

Answers and Solutions

1.   **Answer: Los postres fueron preparados por Julio.**   *Preparó* is in the preterit tense. In the passive, *los postres* becomes the subject of the sentence and is followed by the verb. The preterit of *ser* is irregular and must be memorized. Use the third person plural form of *ser (fueron)*, which agrees with the subject: *postres*. To form the past participle, drop the *-ar* ending from the verb *preparar* and add *-ado*. Because the past participle is used as an adjective, an *-s* must be added to agree with the masculine singular plural form: *postres*. Use *por* to express "by." The agent is *Julio*.

2.   **Answer: Los cuartos fueron arreglados por Tomás y yo.**   *Arreglamos* is in the preterit tense. In the passive, *los cuartos* becomes the subject of the sentence and is followed by the verb. The preterit of *ser* is irregular and must be memorized. Use the third person plural form of *ser (fueron)*, which agrees with the subject: *cuartos*. To form the past participle, drop the *-ar* ending from the verb *arreglar* and add *-ado*. Because the past participle is used as an adjective, an *-s* must be added to agree with the masculine singular plural form: *cuartos*. Use *por* to express "by." The agents are *Tomás y yo*.

3. **Answer: Las invitaciones fueron enviadas por Marta y Susana.** *Enviaron* is in the preterit tense. In the passive, *las invitaciones* becomes the subject of the sentence and is followed by the verb. The preterit of *ser* is irregular and must be memorized. Use the third person plural form of *ser (fueron)*, which agrees with the subject: *invitaciones*. To form the past participle, drop the *-ar* ending and add *-ado*. Because the past participle is used as an adjective, the *-o* becomes an *-a* and an *-s* must be added to agree with the feminine plural noun: *invitaciones*. Use *por* to express "by." The agents are *Marta y Susana*.

4. **Answer: Los muebles fueron quitados del salón por ti.** *Quitaste* is in the preterit tense. In the passive, *los muebles* becomes the subject of the sentence and is followed by the verb. The preterit of *ser* is irregular and must be memorized. Use the third person plural form of *ser (fueron)*, which agrees with the subject: *muebles*. To form the past participle, drop the *-ar* ending and add *-ado*. Because the past participle is used as an adjective, an *-s* must be added to agrees with the feminine plural noun: *muebles*. Use *por* to express "by." The agent is expressed by the pronoun *ti*, which is used after the preposition *por*.

5. **Answer: La guitarra fue tocada por Ud.** *Tocó* is in the preterit tense. In the passive, *la guitarra* becomes the subject of the sentence and is followed by the verb. The preterit of *ser* is irregular and must be memorized. Use the third person singular form of *ser (fue)*, which agrees with the subject: *guitarra*. To form the past participle, drop the *-ar* ending and add *-ado*. Because the past participle is used as an adjective, the *-o* becomes an *-a* to agree with the feminine plural noun: *guitarra*. Use *por* to express "by." The agent is expressed by the pronoun *Ud.*, which is used after the preposition *por*.

6. **Answer: El salón fue adornado por las muchachas.** *Adornaron* is in the preterit tense. In the passive, *el salón* becomes the subject of the sentence and is followed by the verb. The preterit of *ser* is irregular and must be memorized. Use the third person singular form of *ser (fue)*, which agrees with the subject: *salón*. To form the past participle, drop the *-ar* ending and add *-ado*. Use *por* to express "by." The agents are *las muchachas*.

7. **Answer: Las luces fueron colgadas por Jaime.** *Colgó* is in the preterit tense. In the passive, *las luces* becomes the subject of the sentence and is followed by the verb. The preterit of *ser* is irregular and must be memorized. Use the third person plural form of *ser (fueron)*, which agrees with the subject: *luces*. To form the past participle, drop the *-ar* ending and add *-ado*. Because the past participle is used as an adjective, the *-o* becomes an *-a* and an *-s* must be added to agree with the feminine plural noun *luces*. Use *por* to express "by." The agent is *Jaime*.

8. **Answer: Los comestibles fueron comprados por vosotros.** *Comprasteis* is in the preterit tense. In the passive, *los comestibles* becomes the subject of the sentence and is followed by the verb. The preterit of *ser* is irregular and must be memorized. Use the third person plural form of *ser (fueron)*, which agrees with the subject: *comestibles*. To form the past participle, drop the *-ar* ending and add *-ado*. Because the past participle is used as an adjective, an *-s* must be added to agree with the masculine plural noun: *comestibles*. Use *por* to express "by." The agents are expressed by the pronoun *vosotros*, which is used after the preposition *por*.

9. **Answer: Las bebidas fueron pagadas por Uds.** *Pagaron* is in the preterit tense. In the passive, *las bebidas* becomes the subject of the sentence and is followed by the verb. The preterit of *ser* is irregular and must be memorized. Use the third person plural form of *ser (fueron)*, which agrees with the subject: *bebidas*. To form the past participle, drop the *-ar* ending and add *-ado*. Because the past participle is used as an adjective, the *-o* becomes an *-a* and an *-s* must be added to agree with the feminine plural noun: *bebidas*. Use *por* to express "by." The agents are expressed by the pronoun *Uds.*, which is used after the preposition *por*.

10. **Answer: Los preparativos fueron hechos por la señora Cruz.** *Hizo* is in the preterit tense. In the passive, *los preparativos* becomes the subject of the sentence and is followed by the verb. The preterit of *ser* is irregular and must be memorized. Use the third person plural form of *ser (fueron)*, which agrees with the subject: *preparativos*. The past participle of *hacer* is irregular and must be memorized: *hecho*. Because the past participle is used as an adjective, an *-s* must be added to agree with the masculine plural noun: *preparativos*. Use *por* to express "by." The agent is *la señora Cruz*.

11. **Answer: Se reparan zapatos en una zapatería.** A reflexive construction with *se* is used as alternative to the passive voice when the subject is a thing and when the agent is not determined. When *se* is used, the verb agrees with the noun subject, which follows the verb. To avoid the passive, remove the conjugated form of the verb *ser*. Change the past participle of the verb *reparar* to the third person plural form to agree with the subject: *zapatos*. Drop the *-ar* ending and add *-an*. Place *se* before the verb. The verb is followed by the noun without its definite article. The definite article is unnecessary if the noun is used in a nonspecific sense.

12. **Answer: Se hacen llaves en una ferretería.** A reflexive construction with *se* is used as alternative to the passive voice when the subject is a thing and when the agent is not determined. When *se* is used, the verb agrees with the noun subject, which follows the verb. To avoid the passive, remove the conjugated form of the verb *ser*. Change the past participle of the verb *hecho* to the third person plural form to agree with the subject: *llaves*. *Hacer* is regular in all present tense forms except *yo*. Drop the *-er* infinitive ending and add the *-en*. Place *se* before the verb. The verb is followed by the noun without its definite article. The definite article is unnecessary if the noun is used in a nonspecific sense.

13. **Answer: Se exhiben pinturas en un museo.** A reflexive construction with *se* is used as alternative to the passive voice when the subject is a thing and when the agent is not determined. When *se* is used, the verb agrees with the noun subject, which follows the verb. To avoid the passive, remove the conjugated form of the verb *ser*. Change the past participle of the verb *exhibir* to the third person plural form to agree with the subject: *pinturas*. Drop the *-ir* ending and add *-e*. Place *se* before the verb. The verb is followed by the noun with or without its definite article. The definite article is unnecessary if the noun is used in a nonspecific sense.

14. **Answer: Se remiendan vestidos en una sastrería.** A reflexive construction with *se* is used as alternative to the passive voice when the subject is a thing and when the agent is not determined. When *se* is used, the verb agrees with the noun subject, which follows the verb. To avoid the passive, remove the conjugated form of the verb *ser*. Change the past participle of the verb *remendar* to the third person plural form to agree with the subject: *vestidos*. Drop the *-ar* ending and add *-an*. Put *se* before the verb. The verb is followed by the noun without its definite article. The definite article is unnecessary if the noun is used in a nonspecific sense.

15. **Answer: Se revelan carretes en el estudio del fotógrafo.** A reflexive construction with *se* is used as alternative to the passive voice when the subject is a thing and when the agent is not determined. When *se* is used, the verb agrees with the noun subject, which follows the verb. To avoid the passive, remove the conjugated form of the verb *ser*. Change the past participle of the verb *revelar* to the third person plural form to agree with the subject: *carretes*. Drop the *-ar* ending and add *-an*. Place *se* before the verb. The verb is followed by the noun without its definite article. The definite article is unnecessary if the noun is used in a nonspecific sense.

16. **Answer: Se dice que**   The pronoun *se* may be used as an indefinite subject to refer to "one," "people," "they," "it is," and "you." *Se* is used only with the third person singular form of the verb. Use *decir* to express "to say." *Decir* is an irregular verb and must be memorized. Use the third person singular form: *dice*. Use *que* to express "that."

17. **Answer: Se necesita**   The pronoun *se* may be used as an indefinite subject to refer to "one," "people," "they," "it is," and "you." *Se* is used only with the third person singular form of the verb. Use *necesitar* to express "to need." To conjugate *necesitar,* drop the *-ar* ending and add *-a* as the third person singular ending.

18. **Answer: Se usa**   The pronoun *se* may be used as an indefinite subject to refer to "one," "people," "they," "it is," and "you." *Se* is used only with the third person singular form of the verb. Use *usar* to express "use" *Usar* is regular in all present tense forms. To conjugate *usar,* drop the *-ar* ending and add *-a* as the third person singular ending.

19. **Answer: Se sabe que**   The pronoun *se* may be used as an indefinite subject to refer to "one," "people," "they," "it is," and "you." *Se* is used only with the third person singular form of the verb. Use *saber* to express "to know." *Saber* is regular in all present tense forms except *yo.* To conjugate *saber,* drop the *-er* ending and add *-e* as the third person singular ending. Use *que* to express "that."

20. **Answer: Se quita**   The pronoun *se* may be used as an indefinite subject to refer to "one," "people," "they," "it is," and "you." *Se* is used only with the third person singular form of the verb. Use *quitar* to express "to take off." To conjugate *quitar,* drop the *-ar* ending and add *-a* as the third person singular ending.

Supplemental Chapter Problems

Problems
Express what people will do by changing the sentences from the active voice to the passive voice.

Example: Yo enseñaré el arte.
El arte será enseñado por mí.

1. Tú tocarás el piano.

2. Ellos juzgarán a los acusados.

3. Nosotros escribiremos los poemas.

4. Ella pilotará los aviones.

5. Uds. venderán las mercancías.

6. Yo defenderé a los clientes.

7. Ellas construirán los edificios importantes.

8. Ud. curará a los enfermos.

9. Vosotros haréis experimentos.

10. Él dirigirá la orquesta sinfónica.

Use an alternate construction to avoid the passive and to speak about stores and places:

11. Las flores son vendidas en una florería.

12. Las comidas son cocinadas en un restaurante.

13. Los libros son prestados en una biblioteca.

14. Las recetas son preparadas en una farmacia.

15. Los pasteles son hechos en una pastelería

Use an alternative to the passive to express the following daily chores:

16. (You go out) _____ para cortar el césped cada semana.

17. (One pays) _____ las cuentas cada mes.

18. (People prepare) _____ las comidas tres veces al día.

19. (It can be said) _____ que necesita ayuda para limpiar la casa.

20. (They pass) _____ por el mercado para comprar verduras y frutas frescas.

Solutions

1. El piano será tocado por ti. (the passive voice in simple tenses, p. 400)

2. Los acusados serán juzgados por ellos. (the passive voice in simple tenses, p. 400)

3. Los poemas serán escritos por nosotros. (the passive voice in simple tenses, p. 400)

4. Los aviones serán pilotados por ella. (the passive voice in simple tenses, p. 400)

5. Las mercancías serán vendidas por Uds. (the passive voice in simple tenses, p. 400)

6. Los clientes serán defendidos por mí. (the passive voice in simple tenses, p. 400)

7. Los edificios importantes serán construidos por ellas. (the passive voice in simple tenses, p. 400)

8. Los enfermos serán curados por Ud. (the passive voice in simple tenses, p. 400)

9. Los experimentos serán hechos por vosotros. (the passive voice in simple tenses, p. 400)

10. La orquesta sinfónica será dirigida por él. (the passive voice in simple tenses, p. 400)

11. Se venden flores en una florería. (alternate constructions for the passive, p. 404)

12. Se cocinan comidas en un restaurante. (alternate constructions for the passive, p. 404)

13. Se prestan libros en una biblioteca. (alternate constructions for the passive, p. 404)

14. Se preparan recetas en una farmacia. (alternate constructions for the passive, p. 404)

15. Se hacen pasteles en una pastelería. (alternate constructions for the passive, p. 404)

16. Se sale (alternate constructions for the passive, p. 404)

17. Se paga (alternate constructions for the passive, p. 404)

18. Se prepara (alternate constructions for the passive, p. 404)

19. Se puede decir (alternate constructions for the passive, p. 404)

20. Se pasa (alternate constructions for the passive, p. 404)

Customized Full-Length Exam

Problems 1–5

You are taking a bus trip. Read the following ticket and give the numbers, conventional time, and date indicated in Spanish.

N° 847.063 **(3)** 0274	BILLETE + RESERVA					000000
RENFRE		30/05/02 **(5)**				8:45 **(4)**
DE → A TREN	CLASE	FECHA	HORA	TIPO DE TREN	N°	
Mchamartin	Palencia 2	30/05	9.00	Talgo 00091 **(1)**		
	Hora de llegada → 11:58					
Tarifa Euros **(2)**	010 TARIFA GENERAL					

Answers 1–5

1. noventa y uno

If you answered problem 1 **correctly,** go to problem 2.
If you answered problem 1 **incorrectly,** go to problem 6.

2. cincuenta y cuatro

If you answered problem 2 **correctly,** go to problem 3.
If you answered problem 2 **incorrectly,** go to problem 7.

3. ochocientos cuarenta y siete mil sesenta y tres

If you answered problem 3 **correctly,** go to problem 4.
If you answered problem 3 **incorrectly,** go to problem 8.

4. las nueve menos cuarto

If you answered problem 4 **correctly,** go to problem 5.
If you answered problem 4 **incorrectly,** go to problem 9.

5.   el treinta de mayo del dos mil dos

If you answered problem 5 **correctly,** go to problem 11.
If you answered problem 5 **incorrectly,** go to problem 10.

Problems 6–10

You are taking a train trip. Read the following ticket and give the numbers, conventional time, and date indicated in Spanish.

IBERIA	TARJETA DE EMBARQUE			
	INFORMACIÓN DEL PASAJERO			
Vuelo	Destino	Hora	Puerta Acceso a Bordo	Su asiento
951	JFK	15:35 **(9)**	536 **(7)**	45A **(6)**
Rueda/Angel Mr.				
13ag./01 **(10)** 951/22/13	M148.739 **(8)**			

Answers 6–10

6.   cuarenta y cinco

If you answered problem 6 **correctly,** go to problem 7.
If you answered problem 6 **incorrectly,** review ordinal numbers, p. 19.

7.   quinientos treinta y seis

If you answered problem 7 **correctly,** go to problem 8.
If you answered problem 7 **incorrectly,** review ordinal numbers, p. 19.

8.   ciento cuarenta y ocho mil setecientos treinta y nueve

If you answered problem 8 **correctly,** go to problem 9.
If you answered problem 8 **incorrectly,** review ordinal numbers, p. 19.

9.   las cuatro menos veinticinco

If you answered problem 9 **correctly,** go to problem 10.
If you answered problem 9 **incorrectly,** review time, p. 31.

10.   el trece de agosto del dos mil uno

If you answered problem 10 **correctly,** go to problem 11.
If you answered problem 10 **incorrectly,** review dates, p. 27.

Problems 11–15

Express this person's opinions by selecting the correct missing word.

11. _____ esencial es ganarse la vida honradamente.

 a. El

 b. La

 c. Lo

 d. Ello

12. _____ opiniones importan mucho.

 a. Nuestro

 b. Nuestra

 c. Nuestros

 d. Nuestras

13. _____ capital de este país es muy famosa.

 a. El

 b. La

 c. Su

 d. Suyo

14. Ver_____ águila en su alféizar trae buena suerte.

 a. una

 b. un

 c. la

 d. lo

15. _____ poema es muy interesante.

 a. Ese

 b. Esa

 c. Suyo

 d. Una

Answers 11–15

11. c

If you answered problem 11 **correctly,** go to problem 12.
If you answered problem 11 **incorrectly,** go to problem 20.

12. d

If you answered problem 12 **correctly,** go to problem 13.
If you answered problem 12 **incorrectly,** go to problem 16.

13. b

If you answered problem 13 **correctly,** go to problem 14.
If you answered problem 13 **incorrectly,** go to problems 17 and 19.

14. b

If you answered problem 14 **correctly,** go to problem 15.
If you answered problem 14 **incorrectly,** go to problem 18.

15. a

If you answered problem 15 **correctly,** go to problem 21.
If you answered problem 15 **incorrectly,** go to problems 17 and 19.

Problems 16–20

Express another person's opinions by selecting the correct missing word.

16. La casa de tus padres es grande y la _____ es más grande.

   a. a las mías

   b. a los míos

   c. de las mías

   d. de los míos

17. _____ planeta está lejos de la Tierra.

   a. Aquel

   b. Aquella

   c. Aquellos

   d. Aquellas

18. Él tiene _____ hambre de lobo.

   a. uno

   b. una

   c. lo

   d. un

19. _____ problema no es tan grave.

   a. Nuestra

   b. Esa

   c. Lo

   d. El

20. Ellos viven a _____ grande.

   a. una

   b. lo

   c. e

   d. la

Answers 16–20

16. d

If you answered problem 16 **correctly,** go to problem 17.
If you answered problem 16 **incorrectly,** review demonstrative adjectives and pronouns, p. 47.

17. a

If you answered problem 17 **correctly,** go to problem 18.
If you answered problem 17 **incorrectly,** review demonstrative adjectives, p. 47, and gender of nouns, p. 50.

18. d

If you answered problem 18 **correctly,** go to problem 19.
If you answered problem 18 **incorrectly,** review gender of nouns, p. 50, and indefinite articles, p. 45.

19. d

If you answered problem 19 **correctly,** go to problem 20.
If you answered problem 19 **incorrectly,** review gender of nouns, p. 50, and definite articles, p. 41.

20. b

If you answered problem 20 **correctly,** go to problem 21.
If you answered problem 20 **incorrectly,** review the neuter *lo,* p. 42.

Problems 21–25

Express what the student does in class by giving the correct present tense form of the verb in the parentheses.

21. (corregir) Yo _____ mis errores.

22. (traducir) Yo _____ mis pensamientos en español.

23. (tener) Yo _____ que trabajar mucho.

24. (intuir) Yo _____ que habrá un examen mañana.

25. (pensar) Yo _____ estudiar mucho.

Answers 21–25

21. corrijo

If you answered problem 21 **correctly,** go to problem 22.
If you answered problem 21 **incorrectly,** go to problem 28.

22. traduzco

If you answered problem 22 **correctly,** go to problem 23.
If you answered problem 22 **incorrectly,** go to problem 30.

23. tengo

If you answered problem 23 **correctly,** go to problem 24.
If you answered problem 23 **incorrectly,** go to problem 27.

24. intuyo

If you answered problem 24 **correctly,** go to problem 25.
If you answered problem 24 **incorrectly,** go to problem 26.

25. pienso

If you answered problem 25 **correctly,** go to problem 31.
If you answered problem 25 **incorrectly,** go to problem 29.

Problems 26–30

Describe this person's experience buying a party gift by giving the correct present tense form of the verb in the parentheses.

26. (enviar) Mi amigo me _____ una invitación a su fiesta.

27. (ir) Yo _____ a la fiesta.

28. (pedir) Yo _____ dinero a mis padres para comprarle un regalo.

29. (mostrar) Yo _____ el regalo a mis padres.

30. (ofrecer) Yo _____ un reloj a mi amigo.

Answers 26–30

26. envía

If you answered problem 26 **correctly,** go to problem 22.
If you answered problem 26 **incorrectly,** review spelling-change verbs, p. 67.

27. voy

If you answered problem 27 **correctly,** go to problem 23.
If you answered problem 27 **incorrectly,** review irregular verbs, p. 71.

28.   pido

If you answered problem 28 **correctly,** go to problem 24.
If you answered problem 28 **incorrectly,** review stem-changing verbs, p. 69.

29.   muestro

If you answered problem 29 **correctly,** go to problem 25.
If you answered problem 29 **incorrectly,** review stem-changing verbs, p. 69.

30.   ofrezco

If you answered problem 30 **correctly,** go to problem 31.
If you answered problem 30 **incorrectly,** review stem-changing verbs, p. 69.

Problems 31–35

Write questions about the workplace that would give you the italicized answers.

31.   Jaime trabaja *en una gran empresa*.

32.   *Sus obreros* lo respetan.

33.   Jaime tiene *ideas innovadoras*.

34.   Él telefonea a su jefe hoy *porque necesita ayuda*.

35.   Necesita cierta información *para mañana*.

Answers 31–35

31.   ¿Dónde trabaja Jaime?

If you answered problem 31 **correctly,** go to problem 32.
If you answered problem 31 **incorrectly,** go to problem 39.

32.   ¿Quiénes lo respetan?

If you answered problem 32 **correctly,** go to problem 33.
If you answered problem 32 **incorrectly,** go to problem 36.

33.   ¿Qué tiene Jaime?

If you answered problem 33 **correctly,** go to problem 34.
If you answered problem 33 **incorrectly,** go to problem 40.

34.   ¿Por qué telefonea a su jefe hoy?

If you answered problem 34 **correctly,** go to problem 35.
If you answered problem 34 **incorrectly,** go to problem 37.

35.   ¿Para cuándo necesita cierta información?

If you answered problem 35 **correctly,** go to problem 41.
If you answered problem 35 **incorrectly,** go to problem 38.

Problems 36–40

Write questions about a person's shopping workplace that would give you the italicized answers.

36. Habla *al dependiente*.

37. Necesita *dos camisas*.

38. Prefiere *el rojo y el negro*.

39. Saca su carta de crédito *de su bolsillo*.

40. Firma *con un bolígrafo*.

Answers 36–40

36. ¿A quién habla?

If you answered problem 36 **correctly,** go to problem 41.
If you answered problem 36 **incorrectly,** review interrogative pronouns, p. 100.

37. ¿Qué necesita?

If you answered problem 37 **correctly,** go to problem 32.
If you answered problem 37 **incorrectly,** review interrogative adjectives, p. 95.

38. ¿Cuáles prefiere?

If you answered problem 38 **correctly,** go to problem 41.
If you answered problem 38 **incorrectly,** review interrogative pronouns, p. 100.

39. ¿De dónde saca su carta de crédito?

If you answered problem 39 **correctly,** go to problem 33.
If you answered problem 39 **incorrectly,** review interrogative adverbs, p. 97.

40. ¿Con qué firma?

If you answered problem 40 **correctly,** go to problem 41.
If you answered problem 40 **incorrectly,** review interrogative adjectives, p. 95.

Questions 41–45

Answer each question with an appropriate negative.

41. ¿Juegas bien al tenis?—Juego mejor que _____.

42. No sé nadar. ¿Y tú?—_____ sé nadar.

43. ¿Algunos van al estadio?—_____ van al estadio.

44. ¿Siempre mira los partidos deportivos en la televisión?—_____ los miro.

45. ¿Ya te has entrenado?—_____ me he entrenado.

Answers 41–45

41. nadie

If you answered problem 41 **correctly,** go to problem 42.
If you answered problem 41 **incorrectly,** go to problem 50.

42. Ni yo tampoco

If you answered problem 42 **correctly,** go to problem 43.
If you answered problem 42 **incorrectly,** go to problem 48.

43. Ningunos

If you answered problem 43 **correctly,** go to problem 44.
If you answered problem 43 **incorrectly,** go to problem 47.

44. Nunca

If you answered problem 44 **correctly,** go to problem 45.
If you answered problem 44 **incorrectly,** go to problem 49.

45. Todavía no

If you answered problem 45 **correctly,** go to problem 51.
If you answered problem 45 **incorrectly,** go to problem 46.

Problems 46–50

Answer each question with an appropriate negative.

46. ¿Todavía fumas? —Fumaba cuando era joven pero _____ fumo.

47. ¿Algunos muchachos te ayudan?—_____ muchacho me ayuda.

48. ¿Tomas té y también café?—No tomo té _____ café.

49. ¿Siempre haces ejercicios?—_____ hago ejercicios.

50. ¿Alguien te telefoneará más tarde?—_____ me telefoneará.

Answers 46–50

46. ya no

If you answered problem 46 **correctly,** go to problem 41.
If you answered problem 46 **incorrectly,** review negatives, p. 109, and indefinites, p. 114.

47. Ningún

If you answered problem 47 **correctly,** go to problem 32.
If you answered problem 47 **incorrectly,** review negatives, p. 109, and indefinites, p. 114.

48. ni

If you answered problem 48 **correctly,** go to problem 41.
If you answered problem 48 **incorrectly,** review negatives, p. 109, and indefinites, p. 114.

49. Nunca

If you answered problem 49 **correctly,** go to problem 33.
If you answered problem 49 **incorrectly,** review negatives, p. 109, and indefinites, p. 114.

50. Nadie

If you answered problem 50 **correctly,** go to problem 51.
If you answered problem 50 **incorrectly,** review negatives, p. 109, and indefinites, p. 114.

Problems 51–55

Express what the people at work do by substituting direct and indirect object pronouns for the nouns provided.

51. La secretaria está escribiendo (una carta/a un cliente).

52. El empleado ha llevado (documentos/a su jefe).

53. El señor Rivera dice: "Dé (este papel/a mí)."

54. Jorge puede cancelar (la entrega/a los señores González).

55. Las señoras Gómez dicen: "No entregue (estas facturas/a nosotros)."

Answers 51–55

51. La secretaria se la está escribiendo./La secretaria está escribiéndosela.

If you answered problem 51 **correctly,** go to problem 52.
If you answered problem 51 **incorrectly,** go to problem 56.

52. El empleado se los ha llevado.

If you answered problem 52 **correctly,** go to problem 53.
If you answered problem 52 **incorrectly,** go to problem 58.

53. Démelo.

If you answered problem 53 **correctly,** go to problem 54.
If you answered problem 53 **incorrectly,** go to problem 57.

54. Jorge se la puede cancelar./Jorge puede cancelársela.

If you answered problem 54 **correctly,** go to problem 55.
If you answered problem 54 **incorrectly,** go to problem 59.

55. No nos las entregue.

If you answered problem 55 **correctly,** go to problem 61.
If you answered problem 55 **incorrectly,** go to problem 60.

Questions 56–60

Express what the artists do by substituting direct and indirect object pronouns for the nouns provided.

56. Un poeta está leyendo (poemas/a las turistas).

57. Una artista dice: "Muestre (un paisaje extraordinario/a mí)."

58. Un músico había tocado (una sinfonía/al público).

59. Un actor quiere explicar (las obras/a ti).

60. Un escultor dice: "No diga (mis precios/a esos hombres)."

Answers 56–60

56. Un poeta se los está leyendo./Un poeta está leyéndoselos.

If you answered problem 56 **correctly,** go to problem 57.
If you answered problem 56 **incorrectly,** review double-object pronouns, p. 139.

57. Muéstremelo.

If you answered problem 57 **correctly,** go to problem 58.
If you answered problem 57 **incorrectly,** review double-object pronouns, p. 139.

58. Un músico se la había tocado.

If you answered problem 58 **correctly,** go to problem 59.
If you answered problem 58 **incorrectly,** review double-object pronouns, p. 139.

59. Un actor te las quiere explicar./Un actor quiere explicártelas.

If you answered problem 59 **correctly,** go to problem 60.
If you answered problem 59 **incorrectly,** review double-object pronouns, p. 139.

60. No se los diga.

If you answered problem 60 **correctly,** go to problem 61.
If you answered problem 60 **incorrectly,** review double-object pronouns, p. 139.

Problems 61–65

Express what each person dislikes in Spanish.

61. (It bores us) _____ mirar la televisión.

62. (They lack) _____ una buena imaginación.

63. (You [informal singular] don't like) _____ los documentales.

64. (I am bothered by) _____ el ruido.

65. (Hurt her) _____ los pies.

Answers 61–65

61. Nos aburre

If you answered problem 61 **correctly,** go to problem 62.
If you answered problem 61 **incorrectly,** go to problem 66.

62. Les falta

If you answered problem 62 **correctly,** go to problem 63.
If you answered problem 62 **incorrectly,** go to problem 67.

63. Te disgustan

If you answered problem 63 **correctly,** go to problem 64.
If you answered problem 63 **incorrectly,** go to problem 68.

64. Me molesta

If you answered problem 64 **correctly,** go to problem 65.
If you answered problem 64 **incorrectly,** go to problem 69.

65. Le duelen

If you answered problem 65 **correctly,** go to problem 71.
If you answered problem 65 **incorrectly,** go to problem 70.

Questions 66–70

Express each person's thoughts while shopping in Spanish.

66. (It is agreeable to us) _____ acompañarte a las tiendas.

67. (They surprise them) _____ los precios.

68. (It seems to me) _____ muy de moda estos abrigos.

69. (It enthuses you [informal singular]) _____ ir de compras.

70. (They are suitable to him) _____ esos trajes.

Answers 66–70

66. Nos agrada

If you answered problem 66 **correctly,** go to problem 62.
If you answered problem 66 **incorrectly,** review *gustar* and other similar verbs, p. 135.

67. Les sorprenden

If you answered problem 67 **correctly,** go to problem 63.
If you answered problem 67 **incorrectly,** review *gustar* and other similar verbs, p. 135.

68. Me parecen

If you answered problem 68 **correctly,** go to problem 64.
If you answered problem 68 **incorrectly,** review *gustar* and other similar verbs, p. 135.

69. Te entusiasma

If you answered problem 69 **correctly,** go to problem 65.
If you answered problem 69 **incorrectly,** review *gustar* and other similar verbs, p.135.

70. Le convienen

If you answered problem 70 **correctly,** go to problem 71.
If you answered problem 70 **incorrectly,** review *gustar* and other similar verbs, p. 135.

Problems 71–75

Two friends are speaking about politics. Complete their thoughts with the correct relative pronoun or adjective.

a quienes	cuyos	las cuales
con quien	de qué	lo que
cuya	de quien	los cuales
cuyas	el cual	que
cuyo	la cual	quien

71. No me acuerdo de _____ fue nuestro senador en 1998.

72. ¿Sabes _____ problemas el gobernador va a hablar?

73. _____ dicen nunca es la verdad.

74. El padre de Inés, _____ viaja mucho, tiene opiniones interesantes.

75. Ese hombre, _____ nietas trabajan conmigo, quiere ser alcalde de nuestra ciudad.

Answers 71–75

71.   quien

If you answered problem 71 **correctly,** go to problem 72.
If you answered problem 71 **incorrectly,** go to problems 76 and 79.

72.   de qué

If you answered problem 72 **correctly,** go to problem 73.
If you answered problem 72 **incorrectly,** go to problem 79.

73.   Lo que

If you answered problem 73 **correctly,** go to problem 74.
If you answered problem 73 **incorrectly,** go to problem 78.

74.   el cual

If you answered problem 74 **correctly,** go to problem 75.
If you answered problem 74 **incorrectly,** go to problem 80.

75.   cuyas

If you answered problem 75 **correctly,** go to problem 81.
If you answered problem 75 **incorrectly,** go to problem 77.

Problems 76–80

Two friends are speaking about acquaintances. Complete their thoughts with the correct relative pronoun or adjective from the preceding box.

76.   Esos son los muchachos _____ yo vi en el parque ayer.

77.   Miguel, _____ madre es mi profesora, es muy guapo.

78.   _____ busco en este momento es una amistad sincera.

79.   El muchacho, _____ lleva la gorra azul, es mi amigo.

80.   La hermana de José, _____ es abogada, me telefoneó anoche.

Answers 76–80

76.   a quienes/que

If you answered problem 76 **correctly,** go to problem 72.
If you answered problem 76 **incorrectly,** review relative pronouns, p. 143.

77.   cuya

If you answered problem 77 **correctly,** go to problem 73.
If you answered problem 77 **incorrectly,** review relative pronouns, p. 143.

78. Lo que

If you answered problem 78 **correctly,** go to problem 74.
If you answered problem 78 **incorrectly,** review relative pronouns, p. 143.

79. que/quien

If you answered problem 79 **correctly,** go to problem 75.
If you answered problem 79 **incorrectly,** review relative pronouns, p. 143.

80. la cual

If you answered problem 80 **correctly,** go to problem 81.
If you answered problem 80 **incorrectly,** review relative pronouns, p. 143.

Problems 81–85

Compare the following people using adjectives, adverbs, and nouns as necessary.

For example:

1. Enrique es deportivo. (–/Martín)
   Enrique es menos deportivo que Martín.

2. Julia habla con paciencia. (+/su amiga)
   Julia habla más pacientemente que su amiga.

3. Yo tengo hermanas. (=/Rogelio)
   Yo tengo tantas hermanas como Rogelio.

81. Tú sonríes con alegría. (+/yo)

82. Nosotros somos generosos. (=/ellos)

83. Él se expresa bien. (+/tú)

84. Ella es seria. (+/él)

85. Uds. dan cumplidos. (=/nosotros)

Answers 81–85

81. Tú sonríes más alegremente que yo.

If you answered problem 81 **correctly,** go to problem 82.
If you answered problem 81 **incorrectly,** go to problems 86 and 90.

82. Nosotros somos tan generosos como ellos.

If you answered problem 82 **correctly,** go to problem 83.
If you answered problem 82 **incorrectly,** go to problem 89.

83. Él se expresa mejor que tú.

If you answered problem 83 **correctly,** go to problem 84.
If you answered problem 83 **incorrectly,** go to problem 89.

84. Ella es más seria que él.

If you answered problem 84 **correctly,** go to problem 85.
If you answered problem 84 **incorrectly,** go to problems 88–89.

85. Uds. dan tantos cumplidos como nosotros.

If you answered problem 85 **correctly,** go to problem 91.
If you answered problem 85 **incorrectly,** go to problem 87.

Problems 86–90

Compare the follow people using adjectives, adverbs, and nouns as necessary.

86. Tú aceptas las críticas con facilidad. (–/él)

87. Yo tomo chocolate. (=/tú)

88. Ellos son buenos atletas. (-/sus amigos)

89. Ella es discreta. (=/su amiga)

90. Él piensa con objetividad. (+/Ud.)

Answers 86–90

86. Tú aceptas las críticas menos fácilmente que él.

If you answered problem 86 **correctly,** go to problem 83.
If you answered problem 86 **incorrectly,** review agreement of adjectives, p. 157.

87. Yo tomo tanto chocolate como tú.

If you answered problem 87 **correctly,** go to problem 84.
If you answered problem 87 **incorrectly,** review agreement of adjectives, p. 157.

88. Ellos son peores atletas que sus amigos.

If you answered problem 88 **correctly,** go to problem 85.
If you answered problem 88 **incorrectly,** review agreement of adjectives, p. 157.

89. Ella es tan discreta como su amiga.

If you answered problem 89 **correctly,** go to problem 86.
If you answered problem 89 **incorrectly,** review agreement of adjectives, p. 157.

90. Él piensa más objetivamente que Ud.

If you answered problem 90 **correctly,** go to problem 91.
If you answered problem 90 **incorrectly,** review agreement of adjectives, p. 157.

Problems 91–95

Choose the preposition, prepositional pronoun, or conjunction that best completes each thought.

91. Él no tiene paciencia para _____.

    a. lo
    b. la
    c. ello
    d. sí

92. Ellas la hicieron por _____ mismas.

    a. sí
    b. ellas
    c. ello
    d. las

93. Me gusta mucho esa pulsera _____ es muy cara.

    a. o
    b. e
    c. sino
    d. pero

94. Hay siete _____ ocho faltas en la composición.

    a. y
    b. e
    c. u
    d. o

95. Me queda un problema _____ terminar.

    a. para
    b. por
    c. que
    d. sin

Answers 91–95

91. c

If you answered problem 91 **correctly,** go to problem 92.
If you answered problem 91 **incorrectly,** go to problem 98.

92. a

If you answered problem 92 **correctly,** go to problem 93.
If you answered problem 92 **incorrectly,** go to problem 100.

93. d

If you answered problem 93 **correctly,** go to problem 94.
If you answered problem 93 **incorrectly,** go to problem 96.

94. c

If you answered problem 94 **correctly,** go to problem 95.
If you answered problem 94 **incorrectly,** go to problem 97.

95. b

If you answered problem 95 **correctly,** go to problem 101.
If you answered problem 95 **incorrectly,** go to problem 99.

Problems 96–100

Chose the preposition, prepositional pronoun, or conjunction that best completes each thought.

96. No son veinte _____ treinta.

   a. u

   b. y

   c. pero

   d. sino

97. Susana _____ Hilda van de compras.

   a. sino

   b. e

   c. y

   d. u

98. Ellas no tienen fuerzas para _____.

   a. ello

   b. ellas

   c. las

   d. los

99. Trabajo _____ ganar dinero.

   a. por

   b. para

   c. a

   d. de

100. Uds. siempre piensan por _____ mismos.

  a. los

  b. Uds.

  c. sus

  d. sí

Answers 96–100

96. d

If you answered problem 96 **correctly,** go to problem 92.
If you answered problem 96 **incorrectly,** review conjunctions, p. 191.

97. b

If you answered problem 97 **correctly,** go to problem 93.
If you answered problem 97 **incorrectly,** review conjunctions, p. 191.

98. a

If you answered problem 98 **correctly,** go to problem 94.
If you answered problem 98 **incorrectly,** review prepositional pronouns, p. 189.

99. b

If you answered problem 99 **correctly,** go to problem 95.
If you answered problem 99 **incorrectly,** review prepositions, p. 183.

100. d

If you answered problem 100 **correctly,** go to problem 101.
If you answered problem 100 **incorrectly,** review prepositional pronouns, p. 189.

Problems 101–105

Complete the story by using a preposition, if necessary.

101. Ella oyó _____ decir que sus jefes iban a darle nuevas responsabilidades.

102. Ella no cesó _____ hablar de sus planes.

103. Ella amenazó _____ renunciar a su puesto.

104. Ella se empeñó _____ irse a trabajar al extranjero.

105. Ella corrió _____ comprar un billete de avión.

Answers 101–105

101. none needed

If you answered problem 101 **correctly,** go to problem 102.
If you answered problem 101 **incorrectly,** go to problem 110.

102. de

If you answered problem 102 **correctly,** go to problem 103.
If you answered problem 102 **incorrectly,** go to problem 106.

103. con

If you answered problem 103 **correctly,** go to problem 104.
If you answered problem 103 **incorrectly,** go to problem 108.

104. en

If you answered problem 104 **correctly,** go to problem 105.
If you answered problem 104 **incorrectly,** go to problem 107.

105. a

If you answered problem 105 **correctly,** go to problem 111.
If you answered problem 105 **incorrectly,** go to problem 109.

Problems 106–110

Complete the story by using a preposition, if necessary.

106. Ellos se encargan _____ los negocios.

107. Ellos consienten _____ hacer todo el trabajo.

108. Ellos se tropiezan _____ muchos errores.

109. Ellos siempre se apresuran _____ resolver los problemas.

110. Ellos prefieren _____ quedarse en la oficina hasta muy tarde.

Answers 106–110

106. de

If you answered problem 106 **correctly,** go to problem 102.
If you answered problem 106 **incorrectly,** review verbs followed by *de*, p. 207.

107. en

If you answered problem 107 **correctly,** go to problem 103.
If you answered problem 107 **incorrectly,** review verbs followed by *en*, p. 208.

108. con

If you answered problem 108 **correctly,** go to problem 104.
If you answered problem 108 **incorrectly,** review verbs followed by *con*, p. 208.

109. a

If you answered problem 109 **correctly,** go to problem 105.
If you answered problem 109 **incorrectly,** review verbs followed by *a*, p. 206.

110. none needed

If you answered problem 110 **correctly,** go to problem 111.
If you answered problem 110 **incorrectly,** review infinitives requiring no preposition, p. 208.

Problems 111–115

Complete the story using the correct form of the preterit or the imperfect for the verbs in parentheses.

Esta mañana, yo (despertarse) _____ temprano. (Ser) _____ las seis. Yo (ir) _____
111   112   113

a la ventana. En ese momento, yo (poder) _____ ver que ya (haber) _____ gente
114   115

en la calle.

Answers 111–115

111. me desperté

If you answered problem 111 **correctly,** go to problem 112.
If you answered problem 111 **incorrectly,** go to problem 116.

112. Eran

If you answered problem 112 **correctly,** go to problem 113.
If you answered problem 112 **incorrectly,** go to problem 117.

113. fui

If you answered problem 113 **correctly,** go to problem 114.
If you answered problem 113 **incorrectly,** go to problem 118.

114. pude

If you answered problem 114 **correctly,** go to problem 115.
If you answered problem 114 **incorrectly,** go to problem 119.

115. había

If you answered problem 115 **correctly,** go to problem 121.
If you answered problem 115 **incorrectly,** go to problem 120.

Problems 116–120

Complete the paragraph using the correct form of the imperfect or preterit of the verbs in parentheses.

(Nevar) _____ . Yo no (querer) _____ salir afuera. Yo (almorzar) _____ en casa y yo
₁₁₆　　　　　　　　　　　　　　　₁₁₇　　　　　　　　　　　₁₁₈

(jugar) _____ a los naipes con mi hermana. Nosotros (estar) _____ muy contentas.
₁₁₉　　　　　　　　　　　　　　　　　　　　　　　　₁₂₀

Answers 116–120

116. Nevaba

If you answered problem 116 **correctly,** go to problem 112.
If you answered problem 116 **incorrectly,** review the formation of the imperfect, p. 225, and uses of the imperfect, p.225.)

117. quería

If you answered problem 117 **correctly,** go to problem 113.
If you answered problem 117 **incorrectly,** review the formation of the imperfect, p. 225, and uses of the imperfect, p. 225.

118. almorcé

If you answered problem 118 **correctly,** go to problem 114.
If you answered problem 118 **incorrectly,** review the formation of the preterit of spelling-change verbs, p. 219, and uses of the preterit, p. 222.

119. jugué

If you answered problem 119 **correctly,** go to problem 115.
If you answered problem 119 **incorrectly,** review the formation of the preterit of spelling-change verbs, p. 219, and uses of the preterit, p. 222.

120. estábamos

If you answered problem 120 **correctly,** go to problem 121.
If you answered problem 120 **incorrectly,** review the formation of the imperfect, p. 225, and uses of the imperfect, p. 225.

Problems 121–125

Complete the conversation about taking a trip. Use the correct tense (either the future or the conditional) of each verb.

121. Nosotros _____ una excursión.
　　　　　　　　　(will take)

122. Nosotros _____ todos en mi camioneta.
　　　　　　　　　(will fit)

123. Nosotros _____ a las ocho de la mañana.
　　　　　　　　　(will leave)

124. ¿_____ salir más temprano?

   (Would you want)

125. ¿_____ llevarnos con Uds.?

  (Would you be able to)

Answers 121–125

121. haremos

If you answered problem 121 **correctly,** go to problem 122.
If you answered problem 121 **incorrectly,** go to problems 126–128.

122. cabremos

If you answered problem 122 **correctly,** go to problem 123.
If you answered problem 122 **incorrectly,** go to problems 126–128.

123. saldremos

If you answered problem 123 **correctly,** go to problem 124.
If you answered problem 123 **incorrectly,** go to problems 126–128.

124. Querrían

If you answered problem 124 **correctly,** go to problem 125.
If you answered problem 124 **incorrectly,** go to problems 129–130.

125. Podrían

If you answered problem 125 **correctly,** go to problem 131.
If you answered problem 125 **incorrectly,** go to problems 129–130.

Problems 126–130

Complete the conversation about the weather. Use the correct tense (either the future or the conditional) of each verb.

126. El meteorólogo _____ su pronóstico.

    (will say)

127. ¿Qué piensas? ¿_____ buen tiempo?

    (Will it be)

128. Yo_____ una chaqueta ligerita.

   (will put on)

129. ¿_____ la pena ir al campo?

  (Would it be worth)

130. ¿_____ conmigo?

  (Would you come)

Answers 126–130

126. dirá

If you answered problem 126 **correctly,** go to problem 122.
If you answered problem 126 **incorrectly,** review the future of irregular verbs, p. 240.

127. Hará

If you answered problem 127 **correctly,** go to problem 123.
If you answered problem 127 **incorrectly,** review the future of irregular verbs, p. 240.

128. me pondré

If you answered problem 128 **correctly,** go to problem 125.
If you answered problem 128 **incorrectly,** review the future of irregular verbs, p. 240.

129. Valdría

If you answered problem 129 **correctly,** go to problem 124.
If you answered problem 129 **incorrectly,** review the conditional of irregular verbs, p. 243.

130. Vendrías

If you answered problem 130 **correctly,** go to problem 131.
If you answered problem 130 **incorrectly,** review the conditional of irregular verbs, p. 243.

Problems 131–140

Talk about the classroom events by using the correct progressive tense.

131. (were asking) Los alumnos _____ ayuda con sus ejercicios toda la tarde.

132. (are laughing) Ellos_____ en clase.

133. (was collecting) A las dos, el profesor _____ los libros.

134. (will be repeating) Esta noche los alumnos _____ las palabras del vocabulario.

135. (would be having fun) Si pudieran, ellos _____.

Answers 131–135

131. estuvieron pidiendo

If you answered problem 131 **correctly,** go to problem 132.
If you answered problem 131 **incorrectly,** go to problem 138.

132. están riendo

If you answered problem 132 **correctly,** go to problem 133.
If you answered problem 132 **incorrectly,** go to problem 136.

133. estaba coligiendo

If you answered problem 133 **correctly,** go to problem 134.
If you answered problem 133 **incorrectly,** go to problem 137.

134. estarán repitiendo

If you answered problem 134 **correctly,** go to problem 135.
If you answered problem 134 **incorrectly,** go to problem 139.

135. se estarían divirtiendo

If you answered problem 135 **correctly,** go to problem 136.
If you answered problem 135 **incorrectly,** go to problem 140.

Problems 136–140

Talk about a visit from friends by using the correct progressive tense.

136. (are coming) Mis amigos _____ a mi casa.

137. (was getting dressed) A las ocho de la mañana, yo_____.

138. (was suggesting) Todo el día, yo _____ a mi hermana que preparara/preparase algo especial.

139. (will be telling) Antes de muy poco mis amigos me _____ sus buenas noticias.

140. (would be continuing) Si pudiéramos, nosotros _____ con nuestros cuentos toda la noche.

Answers 136–140

136. están viniendo

If you answered problem 141 **correctly,** go to problem 142.
If you answered problem 141 **incorrectly,** review the present progressive, p. 255, and irregular gerunds, p. 254.

137. me estaba vistiendo/estaba vistiéndome

If you answered problem 142 **correctly,** go to problem 143.
If you answered problem 142 **incorrectly,** review the past progressive, p. 258, and irregular gerunds, p. 254.

138. estuve sugiriendo

If you answered problem 143 **correctly,** go to problem 144.
If you answered problem 143 **incorrectly,** review the past progressive, p. 258, and irregular gerunds, p. 254.

139. estarán diciendo

If you answered problem 144 **correctly,** go to problem 145.
If you answered problem 144 **incorrectly,** review the future progressive, p. 260, and irregular gerunds, p. 254.

140. estaríamos prosiguiendo

If you answered problem 145 **correctly,** go to problem 146.
If you answered problem 145 **incorrectly,** review the conditional progressive, p. 262, and irregular gerunds, p. 254.

Problems 141–145

Express what happened during the accident by choosing the correct compound tense.

141. (will have) Él se _____ caído tres veces hoy.

   a. había

   b. habrá

   c. habría

   d. haya

142. (had) Él no _____ visto el obstáculo.

   a. habrá

   b. haya

   c. había

   d. hube

143. (would have) Si hubiera podido, él _____ reído.

   a. haya

   b. habrá

   c. habría

   d. hube

144. (had) Él _____ impuesto a sus amigos que lo ayudaran.

   a. ha

   b. haya

   c. hará

   d. había

145. (has) Él se _____ roto la pierna.

    a. ha

    b. hará

    c. había

    d. habría

Answers 141-145

141. b

If you answered problem 141 **correctly,** go to problem 142.
If you answered problem 141 **incorrectly,** go to problem 148.

142. c

If you answered problem 142 **correctly,** go to problem 143.
If you answered problem 142 **incorrectly,** go to problems 146 and 149.

143. c

If you answered problem 143 **correctly,** go to problem 144.
If you answered problem 143 **incorrectly,** go to problem 150.

144. d

If you answered problem 144 **correctly,** go to problem 145.
If you answered problem 144 **incorrectly,** go to problems 146 and 149.

145. a

If you answered problem 145 **correctly,** go to problem 151.
If you answered problem 145 **incorrectly,** go to problem 147.

Problems 146–150

Express what happened when you returned from a trip by choosing the correct compound tense.

146. (had) Yo _____ vuelto de un viaje a Europa

    a. había

    b. habrá

    c. habría

    d. haya

147. (have) Yo _____ oído las noticias.

    a. habrá

    b. he

    c. había

    d. hube

148. (will have) Tú me _____ dicho todo antes del fin del día.

    a. hayas

    b. habrás

    c. habrías

    d. hubes

149. (had) Uds. no _____ escrito una carta.

    a. han

    b. hayan

    c. harán

    d. habían

150. (wouldn't have) Si tuvieran paciencia, nuestros amigos no _____ tenido problemas.

    a. han

    b. harán

    c. habían

    d. habrían

Answers 146–150

146. a

If you answered problem 146 **correctly,** go to problem 147.
If you answered problem 146 **incorrectly,** review the pluperfect, p. 276.

147. b

If you answered problem 147 **correctly,** go to problem 148.
If you answered problem 147 **incorrectly,** review the present perfect, p. 274.

148. b

If you answered problem 148 **correctly,** go to problem 149.
If you answered problem 148 **incorrectly,** review the future perfect, p. 279.

149. d

If you answered problem 149 **correctly,** go to problem 150.
If you answered problem 149 **incorrectly,** review the pluperfect, p. 276.

150. d

If you answered problem 150 **correctly,** go to problem 151.
If you answered problem 150 **incorrectly,** review the conditional perfect, p. 281.

Problems 151–155

Write this person's thoughts about buying a new house by completing each sentence with the correct form of the subjunctive or the present tense.

151. Busco a una casa que (valer) _____ mucho.

152. Es necesario que yo (ir) _____ a buscarla inmediatamente.

153. Yo compraré una casa con tal que el banco me (garantizar)_____ una hipoteca.

154. Es claro que no (haber) _____ muchas casas disponibles.

155. Cualquiera que (ser) _____ el precio, yo lo pagaré.

Answers 151–155

151. valga

If you answered problem 151 **correctly,** go to problem 152.
If you answered problem 151 **incorrectly,** go to problem 156.

152. vaya

If you answered problem 152 **correctly,** go to problem 153.
If you answered problem 152 **incorrectly,** go to problem 159.

153. garantice

If you answered problem 153 **correctly,** go to problem 154.
If you answered problem 153 **incorrectly,** go to problem 158.

154. hay

If you answered problem 154 **correctly,** go to problem 155.
If you answered problem 154 **incorrectly,** go to problem 160.

155. sea

If you answered problem 155 **correctly,** go to problem 161.
If you answered problem 155 **incorrectly,** go to problem 157.

Problems 156–160

Write this person's thoughts about his or her car by completing each sentence with the correct form of the subjunctive or the present tense.

156. Tengo un coche que (ser) _____ muy caro.

157. ¡Ojalá que tú lo (conducir) _____ con cuidado!

158. Te la prestaré para que tú (ir) _____ al centro.

159. Es imperativo que tú (seguir) _____ mis instrucciones.

160. Creo que tú (comprender) _____ lo que tienes que hacer.

Answers 156–160

156. es

If you answered problem 156 **correctly,** go to problem 152.
If you answered problem 156 **incorrectly,** review the subjunctive and the indicative in relative clauses, p. 314.

157. conduzcas

If you answered problem 157 **correctly**, go to problem 153.
If you answered problem 157 **incorrectly**, review the subjunctive in third person commands, p. 314, and the subjunctive of spelling-change verbs, p. 299.

158. vayas

If you answered problem 158 **correctly,** go to problem 154.
If you answered problem 158 **incorrectly,** review the subjunctive after certain conjunctions, p. 311, and the subjunctive of irregular verbs, p. 302.

159. sigas

If you answered problem 159 **correctly,** go to problem 155.
If you answered problem 159 **incorrectly,** review the subjunctive after impersonal expressions, p. 304; the subjunctive of stem-changing verbs, p. 299.; and the subjunctive of spelling-change verbs, p. 299.

160. comprendes

If you answered problem 160 **correctly,** go to problem 161.
If you answered problem 160 **incorrectly,** review using the subjunctive after certain adjectives showing emotion, p. 309.

Problems 161–165

Complete each thought about a day at home with the correct form of the verb in the subjunctive.

161. No creo que ella _____ temprano anoche.
        (volver)

162. Dudaba que ellos _____ la mesa.

(romper)

163. Si él _____, sus padres lo castigarían.

(mentir)

164. Si ellas _____ los juguetes, tendrían que comprar otros.

(destruir)

165. Si Ud. _____ esas mentiras, sus amigos se habrían puesto furiosos.

(decir)

Answers 161–165

161. haya vuelto

If you answered problem 161 **correctly,** go to problem 162.
If you answered problem 161 **incorrectly,** go to problem 166.

162. hubieran roto

If you answered problem 162 **correctly,** go to problem 163.
If you answered problem 162 **incorrectly,** go to problem 167.

163. mintiera

If you answered problem 163 **correctly,** go to problem 164.
If you answered problem 163 **incorrectly,** go to problem 168.

164. destruyeran

If you answered problem 164 **correctly,** go to problem 165.
If you answered problem 164 **incorrectly,** go to problem 169.

165. hubiera dicho

If you answered problem 165 **correctly,** go to problem 171.
If you answered problem 165 **incorrectly,** go to problem 170.

Problems 166–170

Complete each thought about preparing a meal with the correct form of the verb in the subjunctive.

166. No pienso que tú _____ las papas antes.

(freír)

167. No creía que tú _____ la cacerola.

(cubrir)

168. Si tú me _____ ayuda, yo te ayudaría.
         (pedir)

169. Si tú _____ la mantequilla por margarina, tu plato tendría un mejor sabor.
         (sustituir)

170. Si tú no _____ el azúcar, tu habrías cometido un error.
         (disolver)

Answers 166–170

166. hayas frito

If you answered problem 166 **correctly,** go to problem 162.
If you answered problem 166 **incorrectly,** review the present perfect subjunctive, p. 317, and irregular past participles.

167. hubieras cubierto

If you answered problem 167 **correctly,** go to problem 163.
If you answered problem 167 **incorrectly,** review the pluperfect subjunctive, p. 335, and irregular past participles.

168. pidieras

If you answered problem 168 **correctly,** go to problem 164.
If you answered problem 168 **incorrectly,** review the imperfect subjunctive, p. 325, and conditional sentences, p. 243.

169. sustituyeras

If you answered problem 169 **correctly,** go to problem 165.
If you answered problem 169 **incorrectly,** review the imperfect subjunctive, p. 325, and conditional sentences, p. 243.

170. hubieras disuelto

If you answered problem 170 **correctly,** go to problem 171.
If you answered problem 170 **incorrectly,** review the pluperfect subjunctive, p. 335, and conditional sentences, p. 243.

Problems 171–175

Express the rules of the house by giving the correct command form.

171. (nosotros/hacer) _____ las camas.

172. (vosotros/desobedecer) No _____ las reglas de la casa.

173. (tú/poner) _____ la mesa

174. (Uds./traer) _____ flores.

175. (tú/dormir) No _____ hasta muy tarde.

Answers 171–175

171. Hagamos

If you answered problem 171 **correctly,** go to problem 172.
If you answered problem 171 **incorrectly,** go to problem 177.

172. desobedezcáis

If you answered problem 172 **correctly,** go to problem 173.
If you answered problem 172 **incorrectly,** go to problem 180.

173. Pon

If you answered problem 173 **correctly,** go to problem 174.
If you answered problem 173 **incorrectly,** go to problem 176.

174. Traigan

If you answered problem 174 **correctly,** go to problem 175.
If you answered problem 174 **incorrectly,** go to problem 178.

175. duermas

If you answered problem 175 **correctly,** go to problem 181.
If you answered problem 175 **incorrectly,** go to problem 179.

Problems 176–180

Express what the teacher says to the students by giving the correct command form.

176. (tú/tener)_____ paciencia.

177. (nosotros/escoger) _____ un libro para leer.

178. (Uds./devolver) _____ estos papeles mañana.

179. (tú/cerrar) No_____ tu libro.

180. (vosotros/perder) No _____ vuestros libros.

Answers 176–180

176. Ten

If you answered problem 176 **correctly,** go to problem 172.
If you answered problem 176 **incorrectly,** review affirmative singular informal commands of irregular verbs, p. 357.

177. Escojamos

If you answered problem 177 **correctly,** go to problem 173.
If you answered problem 177 **incorrectly,** review indirect commands, p. 363, and the subjunctive of spelling-change verbs, p. 299.

178. Devuelvan

If you answered problem 178 **correctly,** go to problem 174.
If you answered problem 178 **incorrectly,** review formal commands, p. 351, and the subjunctive of stem-changing verbs, p. 299.

179. cierres

If you answered problem 179 **correctly,** go to problem 175.
If you answered problem 179 **incorrectly,** review negative singular informal commands, p. 335, and the subjunctive of stem-changing verbs, p. 299.

180. perdáis

If you answered problem 180 **correctly,** go to problem 181.
If you answered problem 180 **incorrectly,** review the negative plural informal, p. 359.

Problems 181–185

It is important to be on time. Express what different people say by giving the correct form of a reflexive verb.

181. (Don't go to bed) ¡_____ tarde!

182. (are hurrying up) Nosotros _____.

183. (will not wash) Yo _____ el pelo por la mañana.

184. (Get dressed) _____ Uds. rápidamente.

185. (eat breakfast) No es imperativo que tú _____ en casa.

Answers 181–185

181. No te acuestes

If you answered problem 181 **correctly,** go to problem 182.
If you answered problem 181 **incorrectly,** go to problem 190.

182. nos estamos apresurando/estamos apresurándonos

If you answered problem 182 **correctly,** go to problem 183.
If you answered problem 182 **incorrectly,** go to problem 189.

183. no me lavaré

If you answered problem 183 **correctly,** go to problem 184.
If you answered problem 183 **incorrectly,** go to problem 188.

184. Vístanse

If you answered problem 184 **correctly,** go to problem 185.
If you answered problem 184 **incorrectly,** go to problem 190.

185. te desayunes

If you answered problem 185 **correctly,** go to problem 191.
If you answered problem 185 **incorrectly,** go to problems 186–187.

Problems 186–190

Vacation time is important. Express what different people say by giving the correct form of a reflexive verb.

186. (to go away) Es bueno que yo _____ al extranjero.

187. (to become bored) Ella no quiere _____.

188. (will not remain) Tú _____ en casa.

189. (are relaxing) Ellos _____.

190. (Make yourself) _____ un suéter, mi amigo.

Answers 186–190

186. me vaya

If you answered problem 186 **correctly,** go to problem 187.
If you answered problem 186 **incorrectly,** review the uses of the subjunctive; p. 302; reflexive verbs in simple tenses, p. 383; and the formation of the present-tense subjunctive of irregular verbs, p. 302.

187. aburrirse

If you answered problem 187 **correctly,** go to problem 183.
If you answered problem 187 **incorrectly,** review reflexive verbs with infinitives, p. 389.

188. no te quedarás

If you answered problem 188 **correctly,** go to problem 184.
If you answered problem 188 **incorrectly,** review reflexive verbs in simple tenses, p. 383, and the formation of the future, p. 384.

189. se están relajando/están relajándose

If you answered problem 189 **correctly,** go to problem 185.
If you answered problem 189 **incorrectly,** review reflexive verbs in progressive tenses, p. 388.

190. Hazte

If you answered problem 190 **correctly,** go to problem 191.
If you answered problem 190 **incorrectly,** review reflexive verbs in commands, p. 389, and affirmative singular informal commands of irregular verbs, p. 357.

Problems 191–195

Use the passive voice of the verb in the sentence to express what is said about crime.

For example: La gente mira un programa.
Un programa fue mirado por la gente.

191. El señor Cruz identifica un problema.

192. La policía descubrió muchos crímenes.

193. Las autoridades pospondrán muchas actividades.

194. El alcalde suspendería un desfile.

195. Los propietarios cerraban poco a poco sus tiendas.

Answers 191–195

191. Un problema es identificado por el señor Cruz.

If you answered problem 191 **correctly,** go to problem 192.
If you answered problem 191 **incorrectly,** go to problem 196.

192. Muchos crímenes fueron descubiertos por la policía.

If you answered problem 192 **correctly,** go to problem 193.
If you answered problem 192 **incorrectly,** go to problem 197.

193. Muchas actividades serán pospuestas por las autoridades.

If you answered problem 193 **correctly,** go to problem 194.
If you answered problem 193 **incorrectly,** go to problem 199.

194. Un desfile sería suspendido por el alcalde.

If you answered problem 194 **correctly,** go to problem 195.
If you answered problem 194 **incorrectly,** go to problem 200.

195. Las tiendas eran cerradas poco a poco por los propietarios.

If you answered problem 195 **correctly,** congratulations! You have successfully completed the test.
If you answered problem 195 **incorrectly,** go to problem 198.

Problems 196–200

Use the passive voice of the verb in the sentence to express the effects of a storm. (See the previous example.)

196. La tormenta destruye dos tiendas.

197. El viento volcó un coche.

198. Poco a poco los ciudadanos abrían las ventanas.

199. Algunas familias sufrirán muchas pérdidas.

200. El gobierno pagaría los daños.

Answers 196–200

196. Dos tiendas son destruidas por la tormenta.

If you answered problem 196 **correctly,** go to problem 192.
If you answered problem 196 **incorrectly,** review the passive in simple tenses, p. 400.

197. Un coche fue volcado por el viento.

If you answered problem 197 **correctly,** go to problem 193.
If you answered problem 197 **incorrectly,** review the passive in simple tenses, p. 400.

198. Poco a poco las ventanas eran abiertas por los ciudadanos.

If you answered problem 198 **correctly,** go to problem 194.
If you answered problem 198 **incorrectly,** review the passive in simple tenses, p. 400.

199. Muchas pérdidas serán sufridas por algunas familias.

If you answered problem 199 **correctly,** go to problem 195.
If you answered problem 199 **incorrectly,** review the passive in simple tenses, p. 400.

200. Los daños serían pagados por el gobierno.

If you answered problem 200 **correctly,** congratulations! You have successfully completed the test.
If you answered problem 200 **incorrectly,** review the passive in simple tenses, p. 400.

Are You Up to the Task?

A thorough, comprehensive knowledge of Spanish ensures that you will be able to communicate in a variety of situations in a Spanish-speaking environment. The most common tasks you will be required to perform include obtaining information, providing information, socializing, expressing feelings and emotions, and persuading someone to follow a course of action.

Now that you've completed your review of the structure of the language, it is time to review certain key phrases that will help you express yourself in everyday situations. Then check to see if you are up to the tasks that follow.

Obtaining Information

If all you want is a yes/no answer, use intonation (*¿no es verdad?*, *¿está bien?*) or inversion, as stated in Chapter 4.

If you require more extensive information, commit these interrogative words (see Chapter 4) to memory:

are (is) there?	¿hay?
for what purpose?	¿para qué?
how much, how many?	¿cuánto (-a, -os, -as)?
how?	¿cómo?
what?	¿qué?
when?	¿cuándo?
where?	¿dónde?
which one(s)?	¿cuál(es)?
who(m)?	¿quién(es)?
why?	¿por qué?

Task 1

You are traveling through Europe and stop at a travel agency in Madrid. You are trying to make some plans for a trip to Barcelona. You need some information. Write five questions that you might ask the travel agent.

Sample Responses

1. ¿Cuándo hay vuelos a Barcelona?

2. ¿Qué línea aérea va a Barcelona?

3. ¿Cuánto cuesta un billete de ida y vuelta?

4. ¿Cuántas horas dura el vuelo?

5. ¿Cómo puedo pagar el billete?

Task 2

You are interested in dining at a Mexican restaurant and have some questions you'd like to ask before making a reservation. Write five questions that you might ask the person who answers your call.

Sample Responses

1. ¿Cuál es la dirección de su restaurante?

2. ¿A qué hora abre Ud.?

3. ¿Acepta Ud. reservaciones?

4. ¿Cuáles son sus especialidades?

5. ¿Cuánto cuesta un plato típico?

Task 3

You are touring Madrid and would like to go to the Prado Museum. Unfortunately, you are lost and need some directions. Write five questions that you might ask a passerby.

Sample Responses

1. ¿Cómo se va al Prado, por favor?

2. ¿Está lejos de aquí?

3. ¿Hay un autobús que va al museo?

4. ¿Dónde está la parada de autobús?

5. ¿Cuánto cuesta un billete?

Task 4

You are shopping in a department store in Chile and you need some information. Write five questions that you might ask a salesperson.

Sample Responses

1. ¿Dónde está el departamento de vestidos para mujer?

2. ¿Aceptan Uds. cheques de viajero?

3. ¿Cuáles son las marcas de camisas más populares?

4. Me gusta mucho esta camisa. ¿Qué talla llevo?

5. ¿Hay gangas hoy?

Task 5

You are staying in a hotel in Argentina and would like some information about the surrounding area. Write five questions that you might ask the concierge.

Sample Responses

1. ¿Qué restaurante recomienda Ud.?

2. ¿Cuáles sitios turísticos son los más interesantes?

3. ¿Dónde está el museo de arte moderno?

4. ¿Hay un alquiler de coches razonable por aquí?

5. ¿Cuándo se abren los bancos?

Task 6

It's summer, and you arrive at an inn in the Dominican Republic after a long car trip with your family. Write five questions that you might ask the person at the front desk.

Sample Responses

1. ¿Tiene Ud. una habitación para cuatro personas?

2. ¿Cuánto cuesta?

3. ¿Hay aire acondicionado?

4. ¿Dónde está la piscina?

5. ¿A qué hora tenemos que pagar y marcharnos?

Task 7
You are not feeling well and have been to visit a doctor. Write five questions that you might want to ask him.

Sample Responses

1. ¿Es serio?

2. ¿Para cuántos días tengo que guardar cama?

3. ¿Necesito tomar medicamentos? ¿Cuáles?

4. ¿Cuándo voy a sentirme mejor?

5. ¿Qué tengo que hacer si no me siento mejor muy pronto?

Task 8
You want to go on a tour of El Yunque in Puerto Rico. Write five questions that you might ask in order to obtain futher details about the tour.

Sample Responses

1. ¿A qué hora sale el autobús del hotel?

2. ¿Cuántas personas van a hacer la visita?

3. ¿Hay un descuento para los niños?

4. ¿Cuánto tiempo dura la visita?

5. ¿A qué hora vamos a regresar al hotel?

Task 9
You would like to go to the movies with a friend this evening. Write five questions that you might ask about the film.

Sample Responses

1. ¿Qué tipo de película están pasando?

2. ¿Dónde hay un cine?

3. ¿A qué hora empieza la película?

4. ¿Es prohibida a menores de dieciocho años?

5. ¿Tiene subtítulos en inglés?

Task 10

You are at a club in Venezuela and you see someone you would like to get to know better. Write five questions that you might ask that person.

Sample Responses

1. ¿Cómo se llama Ud.?

2. ¿Habla Ud. inglés?

3. ¿De dónde es Ud.?

4. ¿Cuántos años tiene Ud.?

5. ¿Cuál es su número de teléfono?

Providing Information

To give an affirmative answer to a yes/no question, simply use *sí*, followed by any relevant information. To give a negative answer, use *no* and another negative, if necessary (see Chapter 5).

neither	tampoco
neither . . . nor	ni . . . ni
never	nunca, jamás
nobody	nadie
none	ninguno(-a)
not	no
nothing	nada

Answer questions requiring information as follows:

Question	Answer with
¿adónde? (to where?)	the preposition *a* + a place
¿cómo? (how?)	a noun, a pronoun, or an explanation
¿cuál(es)? (which)	a noun or an adjective used as a noun
¿cuándo? (when?)	a time or expression of time
¿cuánto(-a, -os, -as) (how much, how many?)	a number or a quantity
¿dónde? (where?)	a place
¿hay? (is, are there?)	*hay* (there is, there are)
¿por qué? (why?)	*porque* and a reason
¿qué? (what?)	the name of a thing
¿quién? (who, whom?)	the name of or reference to a person

Task 1

You have made plans to play tennis with a friend. Your friend calls to ask for information. Provide answers to the following questions:

¿Dónde vamos a jugar? ¿Quién va a acompañarnos? ¿Cuándo vamos a jugar? ¿Por qué vamos a jugar a esa hora? ¿Cómo vamos a la cancha (pista) de tenis?

Sample Responses

1. Vamos a jugar al tenis en el parque.

2. Julio y María van a acompañarnos.

3. Vamos a jugar a las diez de la mañana.

4. Vamos a jugar a esa hora porque va a llover más tarde.

5. Vamos a la cancha (pista) de tenis en autobús.

Task 2

You are on a guided tour of a museum, and a friendly person on the tour asks you questions. Provide answers to the following questions:

¿Dónde se hospeda Ud.? ¿Cuál es su nacionalidad? ¿Cuánto tiempo pasa Ud. en España? ¿Con quién viaja Ud? ¿Qué piensa Ud. de esta visita?

Sample Responses

1. Me hospedo en el hotel Sevilla.

2. Soy americano(a).

3. Paso dos semanas en España.

4. Viajo con mi familia.

5. La visita es magnífica.

Task 3

You have a raging toothache and go to the dentist in Chile. The dentist asks you some questions. Provide answers to the following questions:

¿Cuáles son sus síntomas? ¿Desde cuándo sufre Ud.? ¿De qué enfermedades sufre Ud.? ¿Toma Ud. algunos medicamentos? ¿Tiene Ud. alergias?

Sample Responses

1. Yo tengo un dolor de muelas muy grave y no puedo ni dormir ni comer.

2. Sufro desde ayer por la noche.

3. Sufro del asma.

4. En este momento tengo solamente vitaminas.

5. Tengo alergia a la hierba.

Task 4

You are in a restaurant, and the waiter asks you for your order. Provide answers to the following questions:

¿Qué toma Ud. para empezar? ¿Qué quiere Ud. beber? ¿Qué plato principal prefiere Ud.? ¿Cómo quiere Ud. su plato? ¿Qué necesita Ud.?

Sample Responses

1. Yo tomo gazpacho, por favor.

2. Quiero beber un vaso de vino blanco.

3. Prefiero el bistec.

4. Lo quiero término medio.

5. Necesito una cuchara, por favor.

Task 5

You are shopping for a souvenir for your sister. The salesperson asks you some questions. Provide answers to the following questions:

¿Para quién compra Ud. el regalo? ¿Cuántos años tiene ella? ¿Qué le gusta a ella? ¿Cuál es su color favorito? ¿Cuánto dinero quiere Ud. gastar?

Sample Responses

1. Compro un regalo para mi hermana.

2. Ella tiene quince años.

3. Le gustan los vestidos.

4. El rojo es su color favorito.

5. Quiero gastar más o menos veinticinco euros.

Task 6

You meet someone in the park, and this person would like to get to know you better. Provide answers to the following questions:

¿Cómo se llama Ud. ¿De dónde es·Ud.? ¿Cuántos años tiene Ud.? ¿Cuál es su profesión? ¿Dónde aprendió Ud. el español?

Sample Responses

1. Me llamo John Smith.

2. Soy de Pittsburgh.

3. Tengo veinte años.

4. Soy estudiante.

5. Aprendí el español en la escuela.

Task 7

You call to reserve two one-way tickets on a train going from Cádiz to Málaga. Provide answers to the following questions that the clerk asks you:

¿Para qué día quisiera Ud. hacer una reservación? ¿Cuántos billetes va Ud. a comprar? ¿Qué tipo de billete necesita Ud.? ¿A qué hora prefiere Ud. partir? ¿Cuánto quiere Ud. pagar por billete?

Sample Responses

1. Quiero hacer una reservación para el sábado, seis de junio.

2. Necesito dos billetes.

3. Necesito billetes sencillos de primera clase.

4. Prefiero partir entre las ocho y las diez de la mañana.

5. No quiero pagar más de ochenta euros por billete.

Task 8

You are planning a trip abroad and must discuss certain problems with your Spanish-speaking neighbor. Provide answers to the following questions:

¿Adónde va Ud.? ¿Por qué? ¿Para cuántos días no va a estar en casa? ¿Cuándo va Ud. a regresar? ¿Cómo puedo ayudarle a Ud.?

Sample Responses

1. Voy a Chicago.

2. Tengo que irme allá porque mi sobrino se gradua de la universidad.

3. No voy a estar en casa por cuatro días.

4. Voy a regresar el jueves, trece de mayo, a las once de la mañana.

5. Por favor, ¿puede Ud. dar de comer a mi gato?

Task 9

You are at a reunion and meet a friend whom you haven't seen in a long time. Your friend wants to catch up and asks you many questions. Provide answers to the following questions:

¿Cómo estás? ¿Dónde trabajas ahora? ¿Cuánto tiempo hace que trabajas allá? ¿Todavía estudias el español? ¿Con quién sales en este momento?

Sample Responses

1. Estoy bien, gracias, ¿Y tú?

2. Ahora trabajo en un hospital.

3. Hace dos años que trabajo allá.

4. Ya no estudio el español.

5. En este momento no salgo con nadie.

Task 10

You are planning a party, and your friend has questions for you. Provide answers to the following questions:

¿Cuál es la fecha de la fiesta? ¿A qué hora va a tener lugar? ¿Quiénes vienen? ¿Qué vas a servir? ¿En qué puedo ayudarte?

Sample Responses

1. La fecha es sábado, el doce de septiembre.

2. Va a tener lugar desde las siete hasta la medianoche.

3. Todos mis amigos vienen.

4. Voy a servir sándwiches, bebidas y postres.

5. Puedes ayudarme a enviar las invitaciones.

Socializing

Socializing involves having a conversation with someone else in which each person involved obtains and provides information. Using the questioning and answering skills you have developed, write dialogues in which each person says five things relating to the task at hand.

Task 1

You are my friend, and you want to invite me to dinner at your house. Write a 10-line dialogue in which you begin by extending the invitation and then we discuss the details of the dinner.

Sample Dialogue

1. YOU: Quiero invitarte a cenar en mi casa. ¿Estás libre el domingo a las seis?

   ME: ¡Por supuesto! ¿Qué vas a preparar?

2. YOU: Voy a preparar una ensalada, el pollo, las papas, y las habichuelas. ¿Qué piensas?

   ME: ¡Qué bueno! ¿Cómo puedo ayudarte?

3. YOU: Puedes preparar o comprar un postre. ¿Está bien?

   ME: ¡Cómo no! Tengo una receta magnífica para el flan. ¿Te gustaría?

4. YOU: Sí, me gustaría muchísimo. ¿Puedes llegar a mi casa a eso de las cuatro?

   ME: Lo siento, pero estoy ocupada hasta las cinco. ¿Puedo venir a las cinco y media?

5. YOU: ¿Por qué no? ¿Qué vamos a hacer después de cenar?

   ME: Podemos ir al cine. Pasan una buena película.

Task 2

You want me to meet and go out with a cousin of yours. Write a 10-line dialogue in which you tell me that you'd like to introduce me to him and then we discuss what he is like.

Sample Dialogue

1. YOU: Quiero presentarte a mi primo.

   ME: ¿Cómo se llama?

2. YOU: Se llama Julio.

   ME: ¿Cómo es?

3. YOU: Es muy grande. Tiene el pelo negro y los ojos azules. Es bastante flaco, pero es muy deportivo y muy fuerte.

   ME: ¿Cuáles son sus pasatiempos favoritos?

4. YOU: A él le gusta mucho jugar a todos los deportes, especialmente al fútbol. También es muy aficionado al arte y le gusta ir al museo.

   ME: ¿Cuándo puedo conocerlo a él?

5. YOU: Él viene a mi casa este fin de semana. ¿Quieres venir el sábado por la tarde?

   ME: ¿Por qué no? Tengo ganas de hablarle. Me parece muy interesante.

Task 3

You and I are at the mall separately shopping for our winter wardrobe when we bump into each other. Write a 10-line dialogue in which you greet me and we talk about the things we are looking for.

Sample Dialogue

1. YOU: Hola, Graciela. ¿Cómo estás?

   ME: Estoy bien, gracias. ¿Y tú?

2. YOU: Estoy muy bien. ¿Qué estás buscando?

   ME: Estoy buscando un abrigo nuevo. Se dice que va a hacer mucho frío este invierno. ¿Y tú?

3. YOU: Necesito suéteres, guantes y botas. ¿Dónde prefieres hacer tus compras?

   ME: Me gusta mucho la tienda de ropa "Carisma."

4. YOU: Nunca he oído de ella. ¿Dónde está situada?

   ME: Está en la planta baja en frente del Banco Nacional.

5. YOU: ¿Por qué te gusta tanto esta tienda?

   ME: Los precios son bajos, los vestidos están muy de moda y siempre hay gangas.

Task 4

You and I are friends, and we had plans to spend the day together doing work. The weather is beautiful, and now we prefer not to stay indoors. Write a 10-line dialogue in which you express that we should change our plans and then we discuss what else we can do.

Sample Dialogue

1. YOU: Hace muy bien tiempo y no tengo ganas de trabajar.

    ME: Ni yo tampoco. ¿Qué sugieres?

2. YOU: ¿Quieres ir a la playa?

    ME: No. Fui a la playa la semana pasada. Podemos ir al campo.

3. YOU: ¿Qué vamos a hacer allá?

    ME: ¿Por qué no comemos al aire libre?

4. YOU: ¡Qué buena idea! Podemos invitar también a Gloria y a Jaime.

    ME: Sí. Jaime tiene un coche nuevo y puede conducirnos a un lugar especial.

5. YOU: ¿Cuándo puedes estar lista?

    ME: En media hora. Voy a telefonear a Gloria y a Jaime en seguida. Estoy segura que van a acompañarnos.

Task 5

You and I are friends, and you were supposed to come to my house this afternoon to work on a project with me. Unfortunately, you can't come. Write a 10-line dialogue in which you express that you can't work with me, give reasons why, and make other plans.

Sample Dialogue

1. YOU: Lo siento mucho pero no puedo ir a tu casa esta tarde.

    ME: ¿Por qué no?

2. YOU: Estoy muy cansado(a) y prefiero quedarme en casa.

    ME: ¿Por qué estás cansado(a)?

3. YOU: No dormí mucho anoche y hoy me siento enfermo(a).

    ME: ¿Cuándo quieres hacer el trabajo conmigo?

4. YOU: Tal vez en dos o tres días. ¿Está bien?

    ME: No, porque tengo que ir a Miami. ¿Qué vamos a hacer? Tenemos que terminar el trabajo antes de la semana próxima.

5. YOU: Tengo una buena idea. ¿Puedes venir a mi casa mañana? De esta manera puedo descansar un rato hoy y prepararme un poco.

    ME: ¡Claro que sí! Te veré a las cinco de la tarde.

Expressing Feelings and Emotions

When presented with a situation, we can express positive or negative feelings or feelings of indifference. Use the phrases given below to complete the tasks.

Expressing Positive Attitudes, Feelings, and Reactions

Use the adjectives that follow with the verb *estar* (conjugated) to express positive feelings and emotions:

astonished	asombrado(a)
content	contento(a)
delighted	encantado(a)
flattered	lisonjeado(a)
happy	alegre, feliz
proud	orgulloso(a)
surprised	sorprendido(a)

Use the positive expressions that follow when you agree to do something:

And how!	¡Cómo no!
Gladly!	¡Con mucho gusto!
Great!	¡Magnífico!
I adore . . .	Me encanta(n) . . .
I like . . .	Me gusta(n) . . .
It's a good idea.	Es una buena idea.
It's extraordinary.	Es extraordinario(a).
It's great.	Es excelente.
It's interesting.	Es interesante.
It's marvelous.	Es maravilloso(a).
It's sensational.	Es sensacional.
It's super.	Es estupendo(a).
It's superb.	Es fenomenal.
OK.	De acuerdo.
That interests me.	Me interesa.
That would please me.	Me gustaría.
What a good idea.	¡Qué buena idea!
Why not?	¿Por qué no?
With pleasure.	Con placer.

Expressing Negative Attitudes, Feelings, and Reactions

Use the adjectives that follow with the verb *estar* (conjugated) to express negative feelings and emotions:

afraid	asustado(a)
angry	enojado(a)

bothered	fastidiado(a)
displeased	enfadado(a)
embarrassed	avergonzado(a)
furious	furioso(a)
irritated	irritado(a)
sad	triste
unhappy	infeliz

Use the adjectives that follow with the verb *tener* (conjugated) to express negative feelings:

fear (of)	miedo de
shame (of)	vergüenza de

Use the negative expressions that follow when you disagree about something:

I don't like . . .	No me gusta . . .
I hate . . .	Odio . . .
I'm not a fan of . . .	No soy aficionado(a) a . . .
I'm sorry, but . . .	Lo siento pero . . .
It's annoying.	Es fastidioso(a).
It's boring.	Es aburrido(a).
It's difficult.	Es difícil.
It's the same old thing.	Siempre es la misma cosa.
It's tiresome.	Es pesado(a).
That doesn't interest me.	No me interesa.
That wouldn't please me.	No me gustaría.
What a bad idea!	¡Qué mala idea!
You've got to be kidding!	¡Qué va!

Use the expressions that follow when you are indifferent:

I don't care.	No me importa.
I doubt it.	Lo dudo.
I really don't know.	No sé.
It depends.	Depende.
It depends on you.	Depende de Ud. (de ti).
It doesn't matter.	Me da igual.
It's the same to me.	Me da lo mismo.
Perhaps. Maybe.	Quizás. Tal vez.
Whatever you want.	Como quiera(s).

For each of the following situations, express your feelings:

1. Ud. quiere ir a un concierto pero no hay más billetes. Ud. responde:

2. Su amigo le dice que prefiere películas de ciencia ficción. Ud. responde:

3. Yo digo que mi materia favorita es el español. Ud. responde:

4. Su vecino le dice que quiere ir a un partido de fútbol con Ud. Ud. responde:

5. Yo le pregunto si quiere hacer una caminata conmigo. Ud. responde:

6. Ud. y yo vamos al centro juntos. Yo quiero invitar otro amigo a acompañarnos. Ud. responde:

7. Yo quiero comer en un restaurante italiano. Ud. responde:

8. Un amigo suyo le regaló una camisa negra. Su madre le pregunta si le gusta. Ud. responde:

9. Su amigo acaba de decirle que no puede acompañarle a una fiesta. Ud. responde:

10. El director de su escuela anunció que tal vez haya clases durante todo el año. Ud. responde:

11. Su vuelo a Puerto Rico fue anulado. Ud. responde:

12. Ud. quiere tomar un bistec en su restaurante favorito pero no hay más. Ud. responde:

13. Su amigo le dice que va a mudarse. Ud. responde:

14. Ud. recibió A en su clase de español. Ud. responde:

15. Sus padres le dijeron que no podía salir durante el fin de semana. Ud. responde:

16. Yo le sugiero que vayamos al museo. Ud. responde:

17. Su amigo le pregunta si quiere ir al parque esta tarde. Ud. responde:

18. Ud. no puede ir a una fiesta porque está enfermo. Ud. responde:

19. Su amigo olvidó su aniversario. Ud. responde:

20. Yo quiero saber si Ud. tiene ganas de ir de compras hoy. Ud. responde:

Sample Responses

1. No me importa.

2. No soy aficionado(a) a la ciencia ficción.

3. ¡Qué va!

4. Lo siento pero estoy ocupado(a).

5. Me da igual.

6. ¡Qué buena idea!

7. Me gustaría.

8. Me gusta mucho.

9. Estoy enojado(a).

10. ¡Qué mala idea!

11. Estoy furioso(a).

12. Estoy enfadado(a).

13. Estoy triste.

14. ¡Magnífico!

15. Estoy irritado(a).

16. Es pesado.

17. No me interesa.

18. Estoy infeliz.

19. Estoy fastidiado(a).

20. No sé.

Persuasion

Use the conjugated form of the verb *deber* (to have to); the expression *tener que* (to have to), where *tener* is conjugated; or an impersonal expression followed by the subjunctive (Chapter 14) or the indicative to convince someone to follow a course of action. Use the imperative (Chapter 16) and use the positive and negative expressions above to persuade someone to do something.

These expressions take the subjunctive:

it is absurd that	es absurdo que
it is advisable that	conviene que
it is amazing that	es asombroso que
it is amusing that	es divertido que
it is bad that	es malo que
it is better that	es mejor que, más vale que
it is curious that	es curioso que
it is difficult that	es difícil que
it is doubtful that	es dudoso que
it is easy that	es fácil que
it is enough that	es suficiente que, basta que
it is essential that	es esencial que

it is fair that	es justo que
it is fitting that	es conveniente que
it is good that	es bueno que
it is imperative that	es imperativo que
it is important that	es importante que, importa que
it is impossible that	es imposible que
it is improbable that	es improbable que
it is incredible that	es increíble que
it is indispensable that	es indispensable que
it is interesting that	es interesante que
it is ironic that	es irónico que
it is natural that	es natural que
it is necessary that	es necesario que, es preciso que, es menester que
it is nice that	es bueno que
it is a pity that	es lástima que
it is possible that	es posible que
it is preferable that	es preferible que
it is probable that	es probable que
it is rare that	es raro que
it is regrettable that	es lamentable que
it seems untrue that	parece mentira que
it is strange that	es extraño que
it is surprising that	es sorprendiente que
it is unfair that	es injusto que
it is urgent that	es urgente que
it is useful that	es útil que

Use these expressions with the indicative:

it is certain, it is sure	es cierto
it is clear	es claro
it is evident	es evidente
it is exact	es exacto
it is obvious	es obvio
it is sure	es seguro
it is true	es verdad
it seems	parece

For each situation provided, express what you might say to get someone to persuade that person to follow a different or a particular course of action.

1. Yo no quiero ir a la escuela hoy y no estoy enfermo. Ud. dice:

2. Yo no quiero estudiar para mi examen en la clase de matemáticas. Ud. dice:

3. Yo quiero ir a un concierto de música clásica y Ud. no quiere acompañarme. Ud dice:

4. Yo quiero ver una película policíaca y Ud. quiere ver una comedia. Ud. dice:

5. Nosotros tenemos hambre. Yo quiere comer un postre y Ud. quiere comer una fruta. Ud. dice:

6. Yo quiero jugar en el parque pero Ud. prefiere hacer las tareas. Ud. dice:

7. Yo escucho un CD que a Ud. no le gusta. Ud. dice:

8. Yo quiero ir al centro comercial pero Ud. no lo prefiere. Ud. dice:

9. Yo estoy enfermo pero pienso ir al club esta noche. Ud. dice:

10. Sus padres quieren pasar las vacaciones en España pero Ud. quiere ir a México. Ud. dice:

Sample Responses

1. Es importante asistir a la escuela todos los días.

2. No es cierto que tú recibas una buena nota.

3. Es preferible que vayamos a un concierto de música rock.

4. No es justo que tú siempre escojas las películas.

5. Es seguro que vamos a engordar.

6. Es preferible que hagamos primero nuestro trabajo escolar.

7. Es extraño que tú prefieras ese CD.

8. Es indispensable que yo ayude a mi madre.

9. Es importante que tú te quedes en casa.

10. Es esencial que nosotros veamos las ruinas de los aztecas.

Thematic Vocabulary

The Family

Males		Females	
boyfriend	novio	girlfriend	novia
brother	hermano	sister	hermana
brother-in-law	cuñado	sister-in-law	cuñada
child	niño	child	niña
cousin	primo	cousin	prima
father	padre	mother	madre
father-in-law	suegro	mother-in-law	suegra
godfather	padrino	godmother	madrina
grandfather	abuelo	grandmother	abuela
grandson	nieto	granddaughter	nieta
husband	esposo	wife	esposa
nephew	sobrino	niece	sobrina
son	hijo	daughter	hija
son-in-law	yerno	daughter-in-law	nuera
stepbrother	hermanastro	stepsister	hermanastra
stepfather	padrastro	stepmother	madrastra
stepson	hijastro	stepdaughter	hijastra
uncle	tío	aunt	tía

The House

Places			
apartment	el apartamento	ground floor	la planta baja
apartment building	el edificio de apartamentos	hall	el pasillo
attic	el desván, el ático, el entretecho	house	la casa
backyard	el jardín	kitchen	la cocina

(continued)

The House (continued)

Places

balcony	el balcón	laundry room	la lavandería
basement	el sótano	lawn	el césped
bathroom	el (cuarto de) baño	living room	la sala
bathtub	la bañera	owner	el dueño
bedroom	el dormitorio, la habitación	patio	el patio
ceiling	el techo	roof	el techo
closet	el armario	room	el cuarto, la habitación
courtyard	el patio	shower	la ducha
den	el estudio	sink (bathroom)	el lavabo
dining room	el comedor	sink (kitchen)	el fregadero
door	la puerta	stairs	la(s) escalera(s)
elevator	el ascensor	story (floor)	el piso
fireplace	la chimenea	study	el estudio
floor	el suelo	terrace	la terraza
floor (story)	el piso	wall	la pared
garage	el garaje	window	la ventana
garden	el jardín		

Furniture

armchair	el sillón	nightstand	el buró
bed	la cama	painting	el cuadro
bookcase	el librero	picture	la pintura
carpet	la moqueta	rug	la alfombra
chair	la silla	sofa	el sofá
clock	el reloj	stereo	el estéreo
curtain	la cortina	table	la mesa
dresser	el tocador, la cómoda	television set	el televisor
lamp	la lámpara	wardrobe	el guardarropa, el armario
mirror	el espejo		

Appliances			
clothes dryer	la secadora	oven	el horno
computer	el ordenador, la computadora	refrigerator	el refrigerador
dishwasher	el lavaplatos	stove	la estufa
freezer	el congelador	washing machine	la lavadora
microwave oven	el horno de microondas	VCR	el video

Household Chores			
to babysit	cuidar/guardar a los niños	to make the bed	hacer la cama
to clean the house	limpiar la casa	to mow the lawn	cortar el césped
to clear the table	quitar la mesa	to prepare the meals	preparar las comidas
to cook	cocinar	to repair	reparar
to do housework	hacer los quehaceres domésticos	to set the table	poner la mesa
to do the laundry	lavar la ropa	to straighten	ordenar
to dust	sacudir los muebles	to take out the garbage	sacar la basura
to go downtown	ir al centro	to vacuum	pasar la aspiradora
to go shopping	ir de compras	to wash the dishes	lavar los platos
to iron	planchar la ropa	to wash the car	lavar el coche

Animals and Insects			
bear	el oso	leopard	el leopardo
bee	la abeja	lion	el león
bird	el pájaro, el ave	monkey	el mono
bull	el toro	panther	la pantera
cat	el gato	pig	el cochino, el cerdo
chicken	el pollo	rabbit	el conejo
cow	la vaca	rooster	el gallo
crocodile	el cocodrilo	shark	el tiburón
dog	el perro	sheep	la oveja
dolphin	el delfín	snake	la serpiente
donkey	el burro	spider	la araña

(continued)

Animals and Insects (continued)

elephant	el elefante	squirrel	la ardilla
fish	el pez	swan	el cisne
fox	el zorro	tiger	el tigre
giraffe	la jirafa	tortoise	la tortuga
goat	la cabra	turkey	el pavo
gorilla	el gorila	turtle	la tortuga
hen	la gallina	whale	la ballena
horse	el caballo	wolf	el lobo
kangaroo	el canguro	zebra	la cebra

Foods

Meats

bacon	el tocino	mutton	el carnero
beef	la carne de vaca	oxtail	el rabo de buey
blood pudding	la morcilla	pork	el puerco, el cerdo
brains	los sesos	roast beef	el rosbif
chop	la chuleta	sausages	las salchichas
filet mignon	el lomo fino	sirloin	el solomillo
goat	el cabrito	steak	el bistec
ham	el jamón	steak (chargrilled)	el churrasco
hamburger	la hamburguesa	stew	el estofado, el guisado
kidneys	los riñones	sweetbreads	las criadillas
lamb	el cordero	veal	la ternera
liver	el hígado	venison	el venado
meat	la carne		

Fowl

chicken	el pollo	goose	el ganso
duck	el pato	turkey	el pavo
fowl	la carne de ave		

Fish and Seafood

anchovy	la anchoa	octopus	el pulpo
bass	la merluza	oyster	la ostra
clams	las almejas	red snapper	el pargo colorado
codfish	el bacalao	salmon	el salmón
crab	el cangrejo	sardines	las sardinas
eel	la anguila	scallops	las vieiras
fish	el pescado	seafood	los mariscos
flounder	la platija	shrimp	los camarones, las gambas
grouper	el mero	snails	los caracoles
herring	el arenque	sole	el lenguado
lobster	la langosta	squid	el calamar
mackerel	la caballa	swordfish	el pez espada
monkfish	el rape	trout	la trucha
mussel	el mejillón	tuna	el atún

Vegetables

artichoke	la alcachofa	mushroom	el champiñón
asparagus	los espárragos	onion	la cebolla
beet	la remolacha	peas	las arvejas, los guisantes
broccoli	el brócoli (el brécol)	pepper	el pimiento
Brussels sprouts	los bretones, las coles pequeñas	potato	la papa, la patata
cabbage	la col, el repollo	rice	el arroz
carrot	la zanahoria	salad	la ensalada
cauliflower	la coliflor	sauerkraut	la chucruta
celery	el apio	spinach	la espinaca
corn	el maíz	squash	la cucurbitácea, el calabacín
cucumber	el pepino	sweet potato	la batata, el boniato, el camote
eggplant	la berenjena	tomato	el tomate

(continued)

Foods (continued)

Vegetables

green beans	los ejotes, las judías	turnip	el nabo
leeks	los puerros	vegetable	la verdura
lettuce	le lechuga	zucchini	el calabacín

Fruits and Nuts

almond	la almendra	melon	el melón
apple	la manzana	olive	la oliva
apricot	el albaricoque	orange	la naranja
avocado	el aguacate	peach	el melocotón
banana	la banana	pear	la pera
blueberry	el mirtilo, el arándano azul	pineapple	la piña
cherry	la cereza	plantain	el plátano
chestnut	la castaña	plum	la ciruela
coconut	el coco	prune	la ciruela pasa
fruit	la fruta	raisin	la pasa, la uva seca
grape	la uva	raspberry	la frambuesa, la mora
grapefruit	la toronja, el pomelo	strawberry	la fresa
hazelnut	la avellana	tangerine	la mandarina
lemon	el limón	walnut	la nuez
lime	la lima	watermelon	la sandía

Dairy Products and Condiments

basil	la albahaca	mint	la menta
butter	la mantequilla	mustard	la mostaza
capers	los alcaparrones	nutmeg	la nuez moscada
cheese	el queso	oil	el aceite
chives	el cebollino	oregano	el orégano
cream	la crema	paprika	el pimentón dulce
dill	el eneldo	parsley	el perejil
eggs	los huevos	pepper (black)	la pimienta
garlic	el ajo	pepper (red)	el pimiento, el ají

Dairy Products and Condiments

ginger	el jenjibre	saffron	el azafrán
honey	la miel	salt	la sal
horseradish	el rábano picante	sesame	el ajonjolí
jam, jelly	la mermelada	sugar	el azúcar
ketchup	la salsa de tomate	thyme	el tomillo
lemon	el limón	vinegar	el vinagre
maple syrup	el jarabe de arce	Worchestershire sauce	la salsa inglesa
mayonnaise	la mayonesa	yogurt	el yogur
rosemary	el romero		

Eggs

fried	huevos fritos	scrambled	huevos revueltos
hard-boiled	huevos duros	soft-boiled	huevos pasados por agua
omelette	una tortilla	with spicy sausage	huevos con chorizo
poached	huevos escalfados	with spicy tomato sauce (fried)	huevos rancheros

Breads and Desserts

bread	el pan	meringue	el merengue
cake	el pastel, la torta	pie	el pastel
caramel custard	el flan	pudding	la natilla, el pudín
cookie	la galletita	rice pudding	el arroz con leche
cracker	la galleta	rolls	los panecillos
dessert	el postre	sandwich	el sándwich
gelatin	la gelatina	sponge cake	el bizcocho
ice cream	el helado	tart	la tarta
marzipan	el mazapán		

Drinks

beer	la cerveza	milk	la leche
champagne	el champán	milkshake	la batida, la licuada
(hot) chocolate	el chocolate	soda	la gaseosa
cider	la sidra	soup	la sopa

(continued)

Foods *(continued)*			
Drinks			
coffee (decaffeinated)	el café (descafeinado)	tea (herbal)	el té (herbario)
juice	el jugo	(mineral) water (carbonated) (non-carbonated)	el agua (mineral) (con gas) (sin gas)
lemonade	la limonada	wine	el vino
Meals			
breakfast	el desayuno	dinner	la cena
lunch	el almuerzo	snack	la merienda
Table Setting			
bowl	el tazón	pepper shaker	el pimentero
carafe	la garrafa	place setting	el cubierto
cup	la taza	salt shaker	el salero
dinner plate	el plato	saucer	el platillo
fork	el tenedor	soup dish	la sopera
glass	el vaso	soup spoon	la cuchara
knife	el cuchillo	tablecloth	el mantel
menu	el menú	teaspoon	la cucharita
napkin	la servilleta	wine glass	la copa

Quantities			
a bag of	un saco de	a half pound of	doscientos gramos de, una media libra de
a bar of	una tableta de, una barra de	a jar of	un pomo de, un frasco de
a bottle of	una botella de	a package of	un paquete de
a box of	una caja de	a pound of	quinientos gramos de, una libra de
a can of	una lata de	a quart of	un litro de
a dozen of	una docena de	a slice of	un trozo de

Parts of the Body

ankle	el tobillo	hand	la mano
arm	el brazo	head	la cabeza
back	la espalda	heart	el corazón
beard	la barba	hip	la cadera
blood	la sangre	knee	la rodilla
body	el cuerpo	leg	la pierna
brain	el cerebro	lip	el labio
calf	la pantorrilla	liver	el hígado
cheek	la mejilla	lung	el pulmón
chest	el pecho	mouth	la boca
chin	la barbilla	nail	la uña
ear	la oreja	neck	el cuello
elbow	el codo	nose	la nariz
eye	el ojo	shoulder	el hombro
eyebrows	las cejas	skin	la piel
eyelashes	las pestañas	stomach	el estómago
eyelid	el párpado	throat	la garganta
face	la cara	toe	el dedo del pie
finger	el dedo	tongue	la lengua
foot	el pie	tooth	el diente
forehead	la frente	wrist	la muñeca
hair	el cabello, el pelo		

Places in Town

airport	el aeropuerto	museum	el museo
avenue	la avenida	neighborhood	el barrio
bakery	la panadería	newsstand	el quiosco de periódicos
bank	el banco	park	el parque
bookstore	la librería	pastry shop	la pastelería
building	el edificio	police station	la comisaría
butcher shop	la carnicería	post office	el correo

(continued)

Places in Town (continued)

cafe	el café	record store	la tienda de discos
camera shop	la tienda del fotógrafo	restaurant	el restaurante
cathedral	la catedral	school	la escuela
church	la iglesia	sidewalk	la acera
clothing store	la tienda de ropa	skyscraper	el rascacielos
department store	los almacenes	souvenir shop	la tienda de recuerdos
drugstore	la farmacia	square	la plaza
dry cleaner	la tintorería	stadium	el estadio
factory	la fábrica	station	la estación
florist	la florería	store	la tienda
gas station	la gasolinera	street	la calle
grocery store	la bodega	suburbs	el suburbio
hospital	el hospital	supermarket	el supermercado
hotel	el hotel	swimming pool	la piscina
jewelry store	la joyería	theater	el teatro
laundromat	la lavandería	tobacco store	la tabaquería
leather goods store	la marroquinería	town	el pueblo
library	la biblioteca	town hall	el ayuntamiento
mall	el centro comercial	toy store	la juguetería
market	el mercado	university	la universidad
monument	el monumento	youth center	el centro junvenil
movies	el cine		

The Classroom

academy	el colegio	notebook	el cuaderno
answer	la respuesta	page	la página
ballpoint pen	el bolígrafo	paper	el papel
bell	el timbre	pen	la pluma
bench	el banco	pencil	el lápiz
book	el libro	poetry	la poesía
		principal	el director

backpack	la mochila	pupil	el alumno, el estudiante
calculator	la calculadora	question	la pregunta
calendar	el calendario	quiz	la prueba
chalk	la tiza	reading	la lectura
chalkboard	la pizarra	rule	la regla
class	la clase	ruler	la regla
classroom	la sala de clase	schedule	el horario
counselor	el consejero	school	la escuela
(student) desk	el pupitre	school supplies	los útiles
dictionary	el diccionario	scissors	las tijeras
eraser	la goma	sentence	la frase, la oración
error	la falta	student	el (la) alumno(a), el (la) estudiante
exercise	el ejercicio	subject	la materia
explanation	la explicación	summary	el resumen
grade	la nota	teacher	el (la) profesor(a)
grammar	la gramática	test	el examen
homework	la tarea	vocabulary	el vocabulario
lesson	la lección	word	la palabra
map	el mapa	work	el trabajo

Subjects and Activities

		geography	la geografía
algebra	el álgebra	gym	la educación física
art	el arte	history	la historia
arts and crafts	la artesanía	Latin	el latín
band	la banda	math	las matemáticas
biology	la biología	music	la música
chemistry	la química	orchestra	la orquesta
chorus	el coro	physics	la física
club	el círculo	science	la ciencia
computer science	la informática	shop	las artes industriales

(continued)

Subjects and Activities *(continued)*			
drawing	el diseño	Spanish	el español
English	el inglés	team	el equipo
French	el francés	technology	la tecnología

Professions		
Meaning	*Male*	*Female*
accountant	el contable (el contador)	la contable (la contadora)
actor/actress	el actor	la actriz
artist	el artista	la artista
athlete	el atleta	la atleta
baker	el panadero	la panadera
barber	el peluquero	la peluquera
business person	el hombre de negocios	la mujer de negocios
butcher	el carnicero	la carnicera
cashier	el cajero	la cajera
cook	el cocinero	la cocinera
dentist	el dentista	la dentista
designer	el diseñador	la diseñadora
doctor	el médico	la médica
electrician	el electricista	la electricista
engineer	el ingeniero	la ingeniera
farmer	el campesino	la campesina
firefighter	el bombero	la bombera
flight attendant	el aeromozo	la aeromoza, la azafata
government employee	el empleado del gobierno	la empleada del gobierno
hairstylist	el peluquero	la peluquera
jeweler	el joyero	la joyera
judge	el juez	la juez
laborer	el obrero	la obrera
lawyer	el abogado	la abogada
mail carrier	el cartero	la cartera

Meaning	Male	Female
manager	el director, el gerente	la directora, la gerente
mechanic	el mecánico	la mecánica
merchant	el comerciante	la comerciante
musician	el músico	la música
nurse	el enfermero	la enfermera
painter	el pintor	la pintora
pharmacist	el farmacéutico	la farmacéutica
pilot	el piloto	la pilota
poet	el poeta	la poetisa
police officer	el policía	la policía
president	el presidente	la presidenta
programmer	el programador	la programadora
researcher	el investigador	la investigadora
salesperson	el dependiente	la dependiente
scientist	el científico	la científica
secretary	el secretario	la secretaria
server	el mesero, el mozo	la mesera, la moza
soldier	el soldado	la soldada
teacher	el profesor	la profesora
waiter	el camarero, el mesero, el mozo	la camarera, la mesera, la moza
writer	el escritor	la escritora

Leisure Time

Hobbies and Leisure Activities

ballet	el ballet	mountain	la montaña
beach	la playa	movies	el cine
cards	los naipes	opera	la ópera
concert	el concierto	picnic	el picnic
country	el campo	play	la obra teatral

(continued)

Leisure Time (continued)

Hobbies and Leisure Activities

dance	el baile	show	la exposición
fair	la feria	theater	el teatro
hike	la caminata	walk	el paseo
holiday	la fiesta	zoo	el parque zoológico

Musical Instruments

accordion	el acordeón	horn	el cuerno
cello	el violoncelo	oboe	el oboe
clarinet	el clarinete	piano	el piano
drum	el tambor	piccolo	el piccolo
drum set	la batería	saxophone	el saxofón
flute	la flauta	trombone	el trombón
guitar	la guitarra	trumpet	la trompeta
harp	el arpa	violin	el violín

Sports

aerobics	los aeróbicos	jai alai	el jai alai
athletics	el atletismo	jogging	el trotar (el footing)
baseball	el béisbol	mountain climbing	el alpinismo
body-building	el fisi culturismo	ping-pong	el ping-pong
bowling	los bolos	roller skating	el patinaje sobre ruedas
canoeing	el piragüismo	sailing	la navegación
cycling	el ciclismo	scuba diving	el buceo
deep-sea fishing	la pesca de altura	skate boarding	el patinaje sobre plancha, el monopatín
diving	el buceo	skiing	el esquí
fishing	la pesca	soccer	el fútbol
football	el fútbol americano	surfing	el surf
golf	el golf	swimming	la natación
hockey	el hockey	tennis	el tenis
hunting	la cazala	track	la carrera
horseback riding	equitación	volleyball	el vóleibol

Sports			
hunting	la caza	waterskiing	el esquí acuático
ice skating	el patinaje sobre hielo	windsurfing	el windsurf
Playing Fields			
beach	la playa	park	el parque
(golf) course	el campo	pool	la piscina
court	la cancha	rink	la pista
field	el campo	sea	el mar
gymnasium	el gimnasio	slope	la pista
mountain	la montaña	stadium	el estadio
ocean	el océano	track	la pista
Equipment			
ball (basketball)	el balón	jogging shoes	los tenis
ball (football, soccer)	la bola	jogging suit	el traje de trotar
ball (baseball, jai alai, tennis)	la pelota	knee pads	las rodilleras
bat	el bate	mitt	el guante
bathing suit	el traje de baño	net	la red
bicycle	la bicicleta	poles (ski)	los palos
boat	el barco	puck	el puck, el disco
boots (ski)	las botas	racket	la raqueta
canoe	la canoa	rifle	el fusil, el rifle
diving suit	la escafandra	sailboard	la plancha de vela
fishing rod	la caña de pesca	skateboard	la plancha de ruedas, el monopatín
flippers	las aletas	skates	los patines
goggles (ski)	las gafas de esquí	ski bindings	las ataduras
goggles (swimming)	las gafas submarinas	skis	los esquís
golf clubs	los palos de golf	surfboard	el acuaplano
helmet (diving)	el casco el yelmo	waterskis	los esquís acuáticos
		wet suit	la escafandra

(continued)

Leisure Time *(continued)*

Nature

beach	la playa	mountain	la montaña
cloud	la nube	planet	el planeta
coast	la costa	plant	la planta
country, field	el campo	rain	la lluvia
desert	el desierto	river	el río
earth	la tierra	sand	la arena
flower	la flor	sea	el/la mar
fog	la niebla	sky	el cielo
forest	la selva	snow	la nieve
grass	la hierba	star	la estrella
island	la isla	stream	el arroyo
hill	la colina	sun	el sol
lagoon	la laguna	tree	el árbol
lake	el lago	waterfall	la cascada
landscape	el paisaje	wind	el viento
leaf	la hoja	woods	el bosque
moon	la luna	world	el mundo

Clothing and Accessories

bathing suit	el traje de baño	robe	la bata
belt	el cinturón	sandals	las sandalias
blouse	la blusa	scarf	la bufanda
boots	las botas	shirt	la camisa
clothing	la ropa	shoe	el zapato
coat	el abrigo	shorts	los pantalones cortos
dress	el vestido	skirt	la falda
evening gown	el traje de noche	slip (half)	el faldellín
gloves	los guantes	slip (full)	la combinación
handkerchief	el pañuelo	sneakers	los tenis

hat	el sombrero	socks	los calcetines
jacket	la chaqueta	sports coat	la chaqueta de esport
jeans	los vaqueros (los jeans)	stockings	las medias
lingerie	la ropa interior feminina	suit	el traje
night shirt	la camisa de dormir	sweater	el suéter
overcoat	el abrigo	tie	la corbata
pajamas	los pijamas	T-shirt	la camiseta
pants	el pantalón	umbrella	el paraguas
pantsuit	el traje de pantalones	underwear	la ropa interior
pantyhose	las pantimedias	vest	el chaleco
pocketbook	la bolsa	wallet	la cartera
pullover	el jersey	windbreaker	el abrigo contra el viento

Materials

cashmere	la cachemira	linen	el lino
corduroy	la pana	nylon	el nilón
cotton	el algodón	polyester	el sintético
denim	la tela tejana	satin	el raso
flannel	la franela	silk	la seda
fur	la piel	suede	la gamusa
gabardine	la gabardina	taffeta	el tafetán
knit	el tejido de punto	velvet	el terciopelo
lace	el encaje	wool	la lana
leather	el cuero		

Parts of Clothing

back	el atrás, la espalda	lining	el forro
back pocket	el bolsillo anterior	pleat	el pliegue, la pinza
button	el botón	pocket	el bolsillo
cuff (shirt)	el puño	shoelaces	los cordones
cuff (pants)	la vuelta, el doblez	side pocket	el bolsillo de lado
fly	la bragueta	sleeve	la manga

(continued)

Materials *(continued)*

Parts of Clothing			
front	el frente	waist	la cintura
heel	el tacón	zipper	el cierre
hem	el bajo, el ruedo		

Clothing Descriptions			
baggy	holgado(a)	short	corto(a)
long	largo(a)	small	pequeño(a)
loose	hogado(a), suelto(a)	sporty	deportivo(a)
loud	chillón(ona)	tight (clothing)	apretado(a)
low-cut	escotado(a)	tight (shoes)	estrecho(a)
narrow	estrecho(a)	wide	ancho(a)

Colors

beige	beige	pink	rosado
black	negro	purple	morado
blue (navy)	azul (azul marino)	red	rojo
brown	café, marrón, pardo	salmon	color salmón
chestnut	marrón	tan	marrón claro
coffee	color café	violet	violeta
gray	gris	white	blanco
green (olive)	verde (verde oliva)	yellow	amarillo
orange	anaranjado(a)		

Jewelry

bracelet	la pulsera	pin	el broche
chain	la cadena	ring (jeweled)	la sortija
earring	el arete	ring (plain)	el anillo
necklace	el collar	watch	el reloj

Jewels			
amethyst	la amatista	onyx	el ónix
aquamarine	el aguamarina	pearl	la perla
diamond	el diamante	ruby	el rubí
emerald	la esmeralda	sapphire	el zafiro
ivory	el marfil	topaz	el topacio
jade	el jade	turquoise	la turquesa

Travel and Transportation

airplane	el avión	railroad	el ferrocarril
airport	el aeropuerto	road	el camino
bicycle	la bicicleta	route	la ruta
boat	el barco	subway	el metro
bus terminal	la terminal de autobuses	taxi	el taxi
bus	el autobús	ticket	el boleto, el billete
car	el automóvil, el coche, el carro	ticket window	la ventanilla
flight	el vuelo	toll	el peaje
freeway	la autopista	train	el tren
gate	la puerta	train station	la estación
highway	la carretera	traveler	el viajero
motorcycle	la motocicleta, la moto	trip	el viaje
passenger	el pasajero	truck	el camión
pier	el muelle	van	la camioneta

Car Parts

accelerator	el acelerador	glove compartment	la guantera
air bag	la bolsa de aire	hand brake	el freno de mano
anti-lock brakes	los frenos anti-bloqueantes	headlight	el faro delantero
battery	la batería	hood	la capota

(continued)

Car Parts

brakes	los frenos	license plate	la placa de matrícula
bumper	el parachoques	motor	el motor
carburetor	el carburador	radiator	el radiador
clutch pedal	el embrague	tail light	el faro trasero
door handle	el tirador de puerta	tire	la goma, la llanta
fan	el ventilador	transmission	la transmisión
fender	el guardafango	trunk	el baúl
gas tank	el tanque	turn signal	el direccional
gear shift	el cambio de velocidades	windshield	el parabrisas
horn	la bocina	windshield wiper	el limpia parabrisas
ignition	el contacto		

Countries

Algeria	Argelia
Argentina	la Argentina
Austria	Austria
Belgium	Bélgica
Belize	Belice
Bolivia	Bolivia
Brazil	el Brasil
Canada	el Canadá
Chile	Chile
China	China
Colombia	Colombia
Costa Rica	Costa Rica
Cuba	Cuba
Denmark	Dinamarca
Dominican Republic	la República Dominicana
Ecuador	el Ecuador
Egypt	Egipto
El Salvador	El Salvador
England	Inglaterra

Finland	Finlandia
France	Francia
Germany	Alemania
Greece	Grecia
Guatemala	Guatemala
Haiti	Haití
Honduras	Honduras
Hungary	Hungría
India	India
Ireland	Irlanda
Israel	Israel
Italy	Italia
Japan	el Japón
Lebanon	Líbano
Mexico	México (Méjico)
Morocco	el Marruecos
Netherlands	los Países Bajos, Holanda
Nicaragua	Nicaragua
Norway	Noruega
Panama	Panamá
Paraguay	Paraguay
Peru	el Perú
Poland	Polonia
Portugal	Portugal
Puerto Rico	Puerto Rico
Romania	Rumania
Russia	Rusia
Scotland	Escocia
Spain	España
Sweden	Suecia
Switzerland	Suiza
Tunisia	Túnez

(continued)

Countries *(continued)*	
Turkey	Turquía
United States	los Estados Unidos
Uruguay	el Uruguay
Venezuela	Venezuela

The Continents	
Africa	África
Antarctica	la Antártida
Asia	Asia
Australia	Australia
Europe	Europa
North America	Norte América, la América del Norte
South America	Sudamérica, la América del Sur

The Weather	
It's bad weather.	Hace mal tiempo.
It's beautiful weather.	Hace buen tiempo.
It's cloudy.	Está cubierto. Está nubloso.
It's cold.	Hace frío.
It's cool.	Hace fresco.
It's hailing.	Hay granizo.
It's hot.	Hace calor.
It's humid.	Hay humedad.
It's lightning.	Hay relámpagos.
It's overcast.	Está cubierto.
It's pouring.	Hay lluvias torrenciales.
It's raining.	Llueve. Está lloviendo.
It's showery.	Está lluvioso.
It's snowing.	Nieva. Está nevando.
It's sunny.	Hace sol.
It's thundering.	Truena.
It's windy.	Hace viento.

Glossary

active voice   The subject performs an action.

adjective   A word that modifies a noun or a pronoun.

adverb   A word that modifies a verb, an adjective, or another adverb.

antecedent   A word or group of words to which a relative pronoun refers.

articles   Small words that are generally classified as adjectives. An article indicates that a noun or noun substitute will follow.

auxiliary verb   One of two elements needed to form a compound tense. Also called a *helping verb*.

cardinal numbers   The numbers used in counting.

cognates   Words that are the same or similar in Spanish and English.

compound tense   A past, present, or future tense that requires a helping verb plus a past participle.

conditional   A mood that expresses what a subject *would do* under certain circumstances.

conditional perfect   A mood that expresses what a subject *would have* done under certain circumstances.

conjugation   The action of changing the ending of the verb so that it agrees with the subject noun or pronoun performing the task.

conjunction   A part of speech used to connect words, phrases, or clauses.

definite article (the)   An article that indicates a specific person or thing (for example, "the house").

demonstrative adjective (this, that, these, those)   An adjective that precedes a noun to indicate the person, place, or thing that is being referred to.

demonstrative pronoun   A pronoun that stands alone to indicate the person or thing that is being referred to.

direct object   Answers the question "Upon *whom* or *what* is the subject acting?" and may refer to a person, place, thing, or idea. May be a noun or pronoun.

future   A tense that expresses what the subject *will do* or *is going to do* or what action *will* or *is going to take place* in a future time.

future perfect   A tense that expresses what the subject *will have done* by a future time.

gender   Indicates whether a word is masculine or feminine.

gerund   A verb form (ending in *-ing* in English) that expresses an action that is taking place.

idiom   A particular word or expression whose meaning cannot be readily understood by either its grammar or the words used.

imperative   A verb form used to give commands or make requests.

imperfect   A past tense that expresses a continuous, repeated, habitual, or incomplete action, situation, or event in the past that *was* going on at an indefinite time or that *used to* happen in the past.

indefinite adjective   An indefinite adjective is used before a noun to express an indefinite quantity (any, no, other, certain, some, each, the same, several, all and so on)

indefinite article (a)   An article that refers to a person or object that is not specifically identified.

indefinite pronoun An indefinite pronoun is used in place of a noun to express an indefinite quantity (any, no one, none, other[s], other one[s], certain one[s], some, each one, everyone, the same one[s], one, several, someone, anyone, a few, something, anything, nothing, all, everything, anything, and so on)

independent (stress) pronoun   A pronoun that is used to emphasize a fact and to highlight or replace a noun or pronoun.

indicative   A verb tense that states a fact.

indirect object   Answers the question "*To whom* or *for whom* is the subject doing something?" and refers only to people. May be a noun or pronoun.

infinitive   The basic *to* form of the verb.

interrogative   A word that asks a question.

intonation   The act of asking a question by inserting a rising inflection at the end of a statement.

inversion   The reversal of the word order of the subject pronoun and the conjugated verb in order to form a question.

number   Indicates whether a word is singular or plural.

ordinal numbers   The numbers that are used to express rank order.

passive voice   The subject is acted upon.

past conditional   A tense that expresses what the subject *would have done* under certain conditions.

pluperfect   A tense that expresses what the subject *had* done.

preposition   A word that is used to relate elements in a sentence, such as noun to noun, verb to verb, or verb to noun/pronoun.

present tense   A tense that expresses what is happening now.

preterit   A tense that expresses an action or event that was completed in the past.

progressive tense   A past, present, or future form of the verb that shows what the subject is in the act of doing at the time mentioned.

reflexive verb   A verb that shows that the subject is performing the action upon itself.

relative pronoun (who, which, that)   A pronoun that joins a main clause (a clause that can stand alone) to a dependent clause (a subordinate clause that cannot stand alone).

subjunctive   A mood expressing wishing, emotion, doubt, or denial.

Index